Epicureanism at the Origins of Modernity

This landmark study examines the role played by the rediscovery of the writings of the ancient atomists, Epicurus and Lucretius, in the articulation of the major philosophical systems of the seventeenth century, and, more broadly, their influence on the evolution of natural science and moral and political philosophy. The target of sustained and trenchant philosophical criticism by Cicero, and of opprobrium by the Christian Fathers of the early Church, for its unflinching commitment to the absence of divine supervision and the finitude of life, the Epicurean philosophy surfaced again in the period of the Scientific Revolution, when it displaced scholastic Aristotelianism. Both modern social contract theory and utilitarianism in ethics were grounded in its tenets. Catherine Wilson shows how the distinctive Epicurean image of the natural and social worlds took hold in philosophy, and how it is an acknowledged, and often unacknowledged presence in the writings of Descartes, Gassendi, Hobbes, Boyle, Locke, Leibniz, and Berkeley. With chapters devoted to Epicurean physics and cosmology, the corpuscularian or 'mechanical' philosophy, the question of the mortality of the soul, the grounds of political authority, the contested nature of the experimental philosophy, sensuality, curiosity, and the role of pleasure and utility in ethics, the author makes a persuasive case for the significance of materialism in seventeenth-century philosophy, and for its continued importance in the contemporary world, without underestimating the depth and significance of the opposition to it. Lucretius's great poem, *On the Nature of Things*, supplies the frame of reference for this deeply-researched inquiry into the origins of modern philosophy.

Catherine Wilson is Regius Professor of Moral Philosophy at the University of Aberdeen.

Epicureanism at the Origins of Modernity

Catherine Wilson

CLARENDON PRESS · OXFORD

OXFORD
UNIVERSITY PRESS

Great Clarendon Street, Oxford OX2 6DP

Oxford University Press is a department of the University of Oxford.
It furthers the University's objective of excellence in research, scholarship,
and education by publishing worldwide in

Oxford New York

Auckland Cape Town Dar es Salaam Hong Kong Karachi
Kuala Lumpur Madrid Melbourne Mexico City Nairobi
New Delhi Shanghai Taipei Toronto

With offices in

Argentina Austria Brazil Chile Czech Republic France Greece
Guatemala Hungary Italy Japan Poland Portugal Singapore
South Korea Switzerland Thailand Turkey Ukraine Vietnam

Oxford is a registered trade mark of Oxford University Press
in the UK and in certain other countries

Published in the United States
by Oxford University Press Inc., New York

British Library Cataloguing in Publication Data

Data available

Library of Congress Cataloging in Publication Data

Data available

Typeset by SPI Publisher Services, Pondicherry, India
Printed in the United Kingdom by
Lightning Source UK Ltd., Milton Keynes

ISBN 978-0-19-923881-1 (Hbk.)
ISBN 978-0-19-959555-6 (Pbk.)

Preface

A systematic survey of Epicurean philosophy in the seventeenth century would be an accomplishment requiring many volumes, many more years, and the efforts of many investigators. The aim of the present study is a more limited one: it is to argue for the contribution of Epicurean natural, moral, and political philosophy to early modern theory and practice. I wanted to show how the theory of atoms, and the political contractualism and ethical hedonism that were conceptually bound to it, were addressed, adopted, and battled against by the canonical philosophers of the period. And I wanted to establish that an intellectually compelling and robust tradition took materialism as the only valid frame of reference, not only for scientific inquiry but for the solution of the deepest problems of ethics and politics.

Literary excursions to and fro over the millennia are apt to raise some eyebrows. The methodological perils of studies of reception are well known to historians; the preference in intellectual history has been for studies of the decade or the generation, not of the century, and the positive influences of immediate predecessors and contemporaries are easier to document than philosophical anxieties over what a philosopher wrote in the third century BCE. Was it really the same atom in the texts of the ancients and the texts of the early moderns? I make no a priori assumptions about identity of reference. Rather, that the ancient atom and the early modern atom were linked by a continuous and documentable history of reading and responding is a hypothesis to be demonstrated. The descriptive parallels in ancient and early modern texts have to be evaluated against the background of the different contexts in which Epicurean doctrines were discussed and debated. The force of Christian doctrine and institutions in the modern era, and the technological ambitions of the moderns, stand in contrast to the relative disorganization of ancient religion, and to ancient patrician attitudes towards novelty and improvement. Much of my story concerns the import of those differences. Nevertheless, the moderns read the old texts and interpreted their own contemporaries in light of them. In a philosophical sense as well, the ancients and the early moderns thought about the same atom, whereas we now think about a different entity, one whose existence is confirmed by experiments and observations inconceivable in the seventeenth century.

The literary history of atomism frayed and fragmented, as experimental science came to define itself in opposition to metaphysics and natural philosophy. Paradoxically, our contemporary insistence on the physicality of nearly everything that really exists, and on the primacy of experience and experiment over faith and intuition, has tended to mask the role of the Epicurean tradition. The quantifiable, the experimentally testable, have been extracted from the discipline of natural philosophy and handed over to science. Metaphysics, epistemology, philosophy of mind, and metaethics proudly distinguish themselves from the natural and social sciences, and from empirical approaches to normativity, for philosophy has historically derived its prestige from its promise to reveal the mysteries of the incorporeal, the divine, and the posthumous by supersensory means. To skirt them or scorn them is to find one's practice dismissed, in good or bad humour, as not philosophy. I hope nevertheless to have shown that whatever position the reader might take on the question of the ubiquity and exclusivity of the physical, or on the persistence of metaphysical illusion, the identification of Epicurean topics and themes and the analysis of their reception offers a useful framework for understanding and interpreting the history of early modern thought. I hope as well to have shown that the phrase 'soulless materialism' is scarcely applicable to a philosophy in which color, friendship, flowers, curiosity, and complexity play leading roles.

Many institutions and people have assisted these researches. For essential financial support, I would like to thank the Social Sciences and Research Council of Canada; for generous institutional support and access to collections, Trinity College, Cambridge, and its Wren Library, the Max-Planck Institut für Wissenschaftsgeschichte in Berlin, the Department of the History and Philosophy of Science, Cambridge, and the Warburg Institute, London. For discussion, critical comment, inspiration, and assistance, I am especially indebted to Gábor Boros, Lorraine Daston, Saul Fisher, Daniel Garber, Stephen Gaukroger, David Glidden, Michael Hunter, Brad Inwood, Susan James, Monte Johnson, Jill Kraye, Neven Leddy, Tom Lennon, Jon Miller, Margaret Osler, Malcolm Oster, David Rueger, Richard Serjeantson, Quentin Skinner, James Snyder, and Richard Sorabji. They are not responsible for errors, and do not necessarily share the author's views.

Portions of this work have been previously published under the following titles:

'Leibniz and Atomism', *Studies in the History and Philosophy of Science*, 15 (1982), 175–99, repr. in Roger Woolhouse (ed.), *Leibniz: Critical Assessments* (London: Routledge, 1995), iii. 342–68; 'Berkeley and the Microworld', *Archiv für Geschichte der Philosophie*, 76 (1994), 37–64; 'Atoms, Minds and Vortices in *De Summa Rerum*', in Stuart Brown (ed.), *The Young Leibniz* (Dordrecht: Kluwer, 1999), 223–43; 'Corpuscular Effluvia: Between Imagination and Experiment', in Claus Zittel and Wolfgang Detel (eds.), *Ideals and Cultures of Knowledge in Early Modern Europe: Concepts, Methods, Historical Conditions and Social Impact*, 2 vols. (Berlin: Akademie-Verlag, 2002), i. 161–84; 'Epicureanism in Early Modern Philosophy: Leibniz and his Contemporaries', in Brad Inwood and Jon Miller (eds.), *Hellenistic and Early Modern Philosophy* (Cambridge: Cambridge University Press, 2003), 90–115; 'Some Responses to Lucretian Mortalism', in Gábor Boros (ed.), *Der Einfluss des Hellenismus auf der Philosophie der Fruehen Neuzeit* (Wiesbaden: Harrassowitz, 2005) 137–59; 'The Theory and Regulation of Love in Seventeenth-century Philosophy', in Gábor Boros, Martin Moors, and Herbert De Dijn (eds.) *The Concept of Love in Modern Philosophy: Descartes to Kant* (Budapest/Leuven: Eötvös/Leuven University Presses, 2008), 142–161; 'The Problem of Materialism in the *New Essays*', in *Leibniz selon les* Nouveaux Essais sur l'entendement humain, ed. F. Duchesneau and S. Auroux, (Paris/Montreal: Vrin/Bellarmin-Fides, 2006), 249–64; 'What is the Importance of Descartes's Sixth Meditation?' *Philosophica*, 74 (2006), 67–90; (with Monte Ransome Johnson), 'Lucretius and the History of Science', in Philip Hardie and Stuart Gillespie (eds.), *The Cambridge Companion to Lucretius* (Cambridge: Cambridge University Press, 2007); 'From Limits to Laws: Origins of the Seventeenth Century Conception of Nature as *Legalité*,' in Lorraine Daston and Michael Stolleis (eds.), *The Laws of Nature* (Aldershot: Ashgate, 2007); 'Two Opponents of Epicurean Atomism: Leibniz and Cavendish', in Stuart Brown and Pauline Phemister (eds.), *Leibniz and the English Speaking World* (Aldershot: Ashgate, 2007); 'Motives and Incentives for the Study of Natural Philosophy: The Case of Robert Boyle', in Charles Ramond and Myriam Dennehy (eds.), (eds.), *La philosophie naturelle de Robert Boyle* (Paris: Vrin, 2007).

Quotations at the start of each chapter are taken from Lucy Hutchinson's translation of Lucretius' *De rerum natura* from the early 1650s, edited and published by Hugh de Quehen (London: Duckworth, 1996), from a British Library manuscript. Line numbers in this edition are slightly different from those in the Loeb edition cited in the footnotes.

The cover illustration, *The Forest Fire* is from Piero di Cosimo's cycle, *Storie dell' umanita primitiva*, painted about 1500. (See p. 189.)

Contents

Il a celebré dans ses Vers la Volupté, les Amours & les Graces; je consacre les miens à l'austere Vérité: les cords de ma lyre ne rendent q'un son grave & serieux. Les fleurs niassent sous les pas de Lucrece: la nature lui prodigue tous ses tresors.... Si vous jetez vos regards sur la Terre, elle vous offre des forêts qui la couvrent de leur ombre, des ruisseaux qui serpentent en murmurant, des vastes plaines ou l'abondance coule avec les fleuves qui les arrosent. Les oiseaux charment à la fois les oreilles & les yeux.... L'Univers est l'empire de Vénus, Vénus rend la terre féconde; elle peuple les régnes de l'air & les abymes de l'océan.... C'est ainsi que les plus brilliants fleurs couronnent les bords de cette coupe enchanteresse dans laquelle il nous offre un poison préparé par les mains des Grecs.

Cardinal Melchior Polignac, *L'Anti-Lucrece: Poëme sur la Religion Naturelle* (Bruxelles, 1765).

Introduction:
The Revival of Ancient
Materialism

When humane life on earth was much distrest,
With burth'nsome superstition sore opprest,
Who from the starry regions shewd her head,
And with fierce lookes poore mortalls menaced,
A Greeke it was that first durst lift his eies
Against her, and oppose her tirannies;
Whose courage neither heav'ns loud threatenings quell'd,
Nor tales of Gods, nor thunder bolts repelld,
But rather did his valour animate,
To force his way through natures closebard gate.

(*De rerum natura*, i. 62–71)

Natural philosophers of the seventeenth century rediscovered ancient mechanics and the experimental medical practice of the Alexandrian school. They absorbed and improved upon the classical optics, astronomy, mathematics, and physiology that had circulated, first in manuscripts, and then, from the end of the fifteenth century, in printed texts. Their humanist predecessors had attacked scholastic logic and metaphysics as sterile and rebarbative and had pleaded for attention to a broad range of Greek and Roman authors. Homer, Horace, Ovid, Vergil, Thucydides, Tacitus, and Plato were edited, translated into the vernacular, and widely studied. However much philosophers might proclaim themselves mistrustful of ancient sects and schools, weary of the books of men, and attentive exclusively to the book of nature, they found their current predicaments illuminated and their horizons enlarged by the old texts.

Until the early fifteenth century the doctrines of the ancient atomists, Democritus, Epicurus, and Lucretius, were known chiefly through the disparaging presentations of their critics. The discovery of perhaps the last surviving manuscript of Titus Carus Lucretius' *De rerum natura*, written and circulated shortly before the poet's suicide in 49 BCE, was a chance event of considerable consequence. Edited, printed, and eventually translated into living languages, Lucretius' didactic poem was widely known and cited by the middle of the seventeenth century. Apparently based on Epicurus' long-lost treatise 'On Nature', it added to the cosmological, physical, and ethical doctrines associated with his school a number of characteristically Lucretian elements: the author's fondness for landscape and his tenderness towards animals; a view of love that is both reverential and pessimistic; a sense of the relentless abrasions of living; and an interest in the prehistoric state of nature and the evolution of law and civilization. The Epicurean system that it expounded with the help of vivid imagery knitted together a theory of the physical and living world with a system of ethics. Its reappearance, in a period of civil unrest and religious controversy, coincided with the emergence of ambitions to transform the material world to suit human interests. The philosophical skepticism that is sometimes said to have generated a crisis in the early modern period was not so much an expression of genuine bewilderment as a rhetorical tactic facilitating the reworking and assimilation of the Epicureans' remarkable philosophy of nature and society in the early modern context.

It is far from being the case that Epicureanism was a minority position, represented in early modern philosophy by no one of significance besides the enigmatic Pierre Gassendi, the largely forgotten opponent of Descartes whom no one bothered to take to task because his Christianized version of Epicureanism was so innocuous. Gassendi's philosophy, it is true, did not mobilize partisans and opponents under a banner in the same way that Cartesianism did; and his antiquarianism, his empiricism, and his wearying discursiveness have not contributed to his habilitation as one of the most important of seventeenth-century philosophers. However, as recent scholarship is establishing, his influence was significant.[1] As Thomas Lennon has demonstrated, the contest between proponents of Augustinian

---

[1] See Saul Fisher, *Pierre Gassendi's Philosophy and Science* (Leiden: Brill, 2005); Antonia LoLordo, *Pierre Gassendi and the Birth of Modern Philosophy* (Cambridge: Cambridge University Press, 2006).

metaphysics and proponents of Epicurean materialism was actual in the second half of the seventeenth century, evoking the ancient quarrel between the gods and the giants described by Plato in his *Sophist*.[2] Gassendi's contributions to experimental physics and his philosophy of science were admired by his contemporaries, especially members of the English Royal Society, including Walter Charleton, Robert Boyle, and Isaac Newton. His vehement attacks on the Cartesian soul and on the very notion of immaterial substance were echoed by Thomas Hobbes and by John Locke. His efforts to reconcile Epicurean natural and moral philosophy with Christian doctrine by expurgating Epicurus' most characteristic doctrines, his anti-providentialism, his doctrine of the mortality of the human soul, and his many-worlds theory, were ambitious and largely successful. With his theory of an inferential science of appearances and his rejection of a priori knowledge, Gassendi can be considered the foreign parent of British empiricism.[3]

The doctrinal overlap between Cartesianism and Gassendism, was, at the same time, considerable. The revival of atomism and mechanism gave a grounding to experimental science and altered the assumptions of political and moral theory in ways we now take for granted. The ancient atomists' epistemology, based on appearances, was careless about logical relations, and their ontology, based on the material corpuscle, could be wedded to mechanical accounts. Some early modern texts were essentially reformulations of Epicurean natural philosophy, fabricated within the moral and theological constraints and aspirations of, as well as within the institutional constraints posed by, a dominant Christian culture. Other texts presented systems that contested the Epicurean image from the ground up, making few or no concessions. If the incorporeal *res cogitans* of Descartes, the unextended immortal monads of Leibniz, the world in the mind of Berkeley are salient concepts in the history of modern philosophy, this is chiefly because we are all, in a sense, Epicureans now. We regard the metaphysical systems of the past with aesthetic interest, and with appreciation for the ingenuity with which, applying logic and analysis,

---

[2] Thomas M. Lennon, *The Battle of the Gods and Giants* (Princeton, NJ: Princeton University Press, 1993), 35 ff., citing Plato, *Sophist*, 246a–c. Lennon places Descartes on the side of the gods, but observes that Descartes's piety and spirituality were not universally acknowledged.

[3] As proposed by David Fate Norton, 'The Myth of British Empiricism', *History of European Ideas*, 1 (1981), 331–44. For some disputed aspects of Norton's thesis see below p. 151.

their authors reasoned out and invented alternatives to and barriers against the philosophy they thought of as atheistic corporealism. To problematize and contest the image of the world offered by natural science is still a feature of the philosopher's role.

That attention to ancient atomism should have had a substantial effect on philosophy in the seventeenth and early eighteenth century might seem an implausible thesis. The incompatibility—and indeed the incommensurability—between the atomists' system and the jumbled mixture of patristic, scholastic, and scriptural doctrine, with its mysteries, contradictions, and quarrels, with which western European intellectuals found themselves saddled did not suggest the possibility of synthesis, at least not of any synthesis more substantial than the anti-monastic and mildly hedonistic version of Christianity floated by Erasmus. Theology had adopted many useful concepts from Aristotle and Plato, notably the long-lived scheme of matter and form, efficient and final causes, and the participation of earthly things in a supramundane reality, but Epicureanism was not capable of assimilation in the same way.

Where Aristotle taught that the world was eternal and unique, Plato and the Church Fathers maintained that it was unique and specially created. Christian doctrine posited an omnipotent creator and judge, whose wrath against individuals was to be feared as much as this God was to be loved for sending us his only son for our possible salvation. The immortal soul of man was destined for postmortem bliss or eternal torment. Christ's suffering on the cross, and the imitative martyrdom of the saints, indicated that torment was nevertheless a holy condition, and Augustinian doctrine represented the desire for pleasure as a prompting of the devil.

Epicurean cosmology and philosophy contradicted the Christian theses of the uniqueness of the world, the special status of men vis-à-vis other animals, and the doctrine of original sin. It implied that prayer and sacrifice were useless and made the notion of a providential plan in history unthinkable. The Epicureans maintained that there was an infinite number of *cosmoi*. Worlds, they declared, come into being from the chance combination of atoms, and animals and men are generated from the same atomic primordia or 'seeds'. Death, they said, is inevitable and irreversible, for every atomic composite is subject to dissolution and the dispersal of its constituents. Yet it is not to be feared. Because experience depends on the integrity of the human body and its sensory organs, death and its aftermath will not be experienced. The atoms composing the soul will drift away, and we will no longer sense, or feel, or be anything at all.

There is no ambivalence about pain in Epicurean morals; it is an unqualified evil. Because death is the end for each sentient being, we should enjoy ourselves to the extent that our enjoyment of present pleasures does not diminish the quantity of pleasure we can enjoy in the future, to the extent that our present enjoyments do not destroy health, bring down the wrath or contempt of others upon us, or subject us to the torments of guilt and regret. Moral wisdom consists not in ascetic practice, but in prudence and foresight, for the age-old experience of mankind assures us that moderation and avoidance of dissipation tend to make for a less painful life. Endurance of our mundane sufferings has, at the same time, its own dignity, although it is not a foretaste of hell or morally glorious. The recognition that human life is temporary and fragile follows from physics, as does the recognition that all suffering comes to an end. '[A]ll the punishments that tradition locates in the abysm of Acheron', said Lucretius, 'actually exist in our life.' An emblematic figure for the poet is the mythical giant Tityos, whose type, he thinks, exists among us. 'He is the person lying in bonds of love, and consumed by agonizing anxiety or rent by the anguish of some other passion.'[4] Lucretius' pacifism, his sense of closeness to the animal world, and his sympathetic portrayal of the effects of romantic uncertainty and jealousy, but also the reawakening, renewing effects of the goddess Venus, are still moving to his readers.

Limits and boundaries, said the atomists, set a term to the existence of each composite individual. Yet nature herself is eternal and renews herself perpetually through new combinations of atoms. Though our earth, like a middle-aged woman, has lost most of her capacity to bear and no longer brings forth large animals spontaneously, she can still produce insects and smaller creatures, and the growth of plants and the birth of animals testifies to her eternal powers. For Lucretius, desire was the reigning motive of the animate portion of the world, although its fulfillment was episodic in human life. He describes the soothing and fructifying touch of the goddess who, in springtime, instills 'seductive love into the heart of every creature that lives in the seas and mountains and river torrents and

---

[4] T. C. Lucretius, *On the Nature of Things* (*ONT*), III. 978 ff., trans. Martin Ferguson Smith (Indianapolis, Ind.: Hackett, 2001), 94–5.

bird-haunted thickets and verdant plains, implanting in it the passionate urge to reproduce its kind'.[5]

The reference to Venus at the start of *On the Nature of Things* is, to be sure, paratheology, not theology. Epicurus' own theory of religion was not straightforward, but it was often read as offering a kind of conventionalist account of religious truth. Cicero explained that Epicurus 'alone perceived ... that the gods exist, because nature herself has imprinted a conception of them on the minds of all mankind ... [T]heir existence is therefore a necessary inference, since we possess an instinctive or rather an innate conception of them'.[6] The Epicurean gods were, however, remote, corporeal, and unconcerned with human welfare, and in their perfection they were deemed to feel neither anger with men, nor affection for them. Lucretius was more explicit in supposing that the gods are only images, 'visions of divine figures of matchless beauty and stupendous stature',[7] that appear to men in their dreams and reveries. Perhaps these images correspond to happy material beings existing in the intercosmic spaces, he allowed, but if so they take no account of us and have no power over us.

The threats of priests, the cruelties exacted by superstition, and the obsessive observances of ritual religion are nugatory. No demonic forces lower over individuals or promote war, famine, and plague. No one is destined for the fiery pits of hell, Lucretius assured his readers. The ceremonies of religion were far worse than empty superstition in the eyes of the Epicureans. They were indoctrination into a fiction, as one of Cicero's Epicurean characters remarks, 'invented by wise men in the interest of the state, to the end that those whom reason was powerless to control might be led in the path of duty by religion',[8] or indeed indoctrination into a fiction invented by crafty men to secure priestly privileges. Lucretius was the first philosopher to articulate a theory of ideology, the means by which a powerful elite promulgates a deceptive image of reality for the purpose of maintaining a submissive population and serving its own interests. Prayer and sacrifice are not only useless, but dangerous, as men are led by religion to perpetrate appalling acts of cruelty, such as the sacrifice of Iphigenia. The

---

[5] Lucretius, *ONT* I. 19–20; trans. Smith, 2–3; cf. I. 225–38; trans. Smith, 9.

[6] Marcus Tullius Cicero, *On the Nature of the Gods*, bk. I, chs. 16–17; trans. H. Rackham (Cambridge, Mass.: Harvard University Press, 1951), 45.

[7] Lucretius, *ONT* V. 1170 ff.; trans. Smith, 169.

[8] Cicero, *Nature of the Gods*, bk. I, ch. 42; trans. Rackham, 113.

aim of philosophy is to free humans from 'the fears of the mind'. These fears are aroused by celestial and atmospheric phenomena such as eclipses, storms, and earthquakes that are taken as manifestations of divine wrath, as intentional attempts on the part of the gods to injure men and destroy their possessions. Philosophy enables us to explain their occurrence, and even if we cannot know that our explanations are correct in all details, we do well, they insisted, to credit them.

The moderns valued the atomical philosophy less for its ability to calm fears and quell anxiety than for what they saw as its practical implications, prizing it for its promise of works—medical, chemical, metallurgical. The system of the atomists was easily visualized and easy to understand. In contrast to Aristotle, whose ontology embraced matter and form, substance, qualities, four elements, four types of cause, celestial and terrestrial motion, and processes of generation and corruption, the Epicureans formally acknowledged only two principles, the full and the empty, *corpus et inane*, along with motion. They reverted to explanatory schema not entirely foreign to Aristotelian natural philosophy, but of whose limited applicability Aristotle was firmly convinced, those citing material conditions, and efficient causes. The latent reality of tiny colorless particles, drifting, colliding, and aggregating, projected into the manifest image of the visible world.

For Aristotle, scientific research began with attentive perception and was aimed at understanding and appreciation; it was a form of contemplative activity, unconnected with the human desire to predict and control. Aristotelian hylomorphs, with their own indwelling principles of intentionality and development, had to be ascribed their own nonhuman agendas. By rejecting the Aristotelian premise that the true physicist studies both form and matter, along with the premise that the study of the soul falls within the science of nature, the experimental philosophers of the seventeenth century pointed to a boundary—however dotted and wavering it appeared in their individual writings—between empirical inquiry and metaphysics. Their subject was, to employ Boyle's term, 'mere corporeal nature', and their aim was to work useful changes in it that presupposed its passivity. They were successful, as their humanist predecessors had not been, in displacing scholastic philosophy from the universities. Instead of a reversion to a multitude of classic texts, they promoted an engagement with things, founded upon the classical framework of the ancient materialists alone. They laid the groundwork for modern science in the experimental academies and by means of the friendships established and maintained through them.

The rehabilitation of Epicurean atomism and many-worlds theory was not a smooth process. In the early seventeenth century the name of Epicurus was associated with anti-authoritarianism and with a libertinism that no respectable or self-interested philosopher could wish to endorse. The very possibility that 'God' named only an instinctual, 'proleptic' idea spontaneously arising in the human mind, rather than a being who had impressed an idea of himself on the human mind, a being whose existence was proved by testimony, or logically necessary, or made certain by physics, was incompatible with the existence of that elaborate, wealthy, and powerful social institution, the Church, which defined and controlled education in Protestant and Catholic countries and shaped moral expectations even if it failed to control behavior. The mythological status of the Christian religion was a theoretical possibility that tore into the categories in which men and women conceptualized their personal experience and their own agency in terms of sin, placation, and preparation for the hereafter. Epicureanism refused to accommodate the hope on the part of human beings that there is a life after death, and the delusion that in this life too they interact with agents in a spirit world, hopes and delusions that are recognized by anthropologists as ubiquitous, and by psychologists as springing from innate dispositions reinforced by cultural elaboration and transmission. The doctrine of the materiality and mortality of the soul seemed harsh and hopeless to some philosophers, and even those who were not personally repelled recognized that opinions that might be entertained, discussed, and debated as matters of intellectual interest could not be presented to the masses. In the absence of effective secular policing they understandably wondered what could thwart the criminal impulses of their untutored and malicious fellows, except the fear of God. With the possible exception of Thomas Hobbes, no seventeenth-century philosopher of note could reconcile his or her mind to the Epicurean system and its consequences for morals, politics, and religion.

The systems of the moderns required more by way of invention than the simple insertion into the Epicurean philosophy of a transcendent invisible ruler and a heaven whose attainment was conditional on divine favor and the avoidance of sin. The old articles of faith and hope had to be rethought and reinterpreted, not only the doctrine of transubstantiation, threatened by atomism, but the uniqueness of the world and the revelatory events supposed to have occurred within it, the difference between men and animals, the power of the human will, and the possibility of interaction between the soul and body, or God and the world. Hence the complexity of these systems and their differing types and degrees of accommodation with Christian doctrine. Even the iconoclastic Hobbes chose to present his political scheme under the rubric of a design for a Christian commonwealth.

At the same time, the points of Epicurean doctrine that conflicted with Stoic and patristic teaching made it emotionally attractive, even to morally correct and devout readers. Lactantius had explained the appeal of Epicureanism by reference to the problem of evil. 'Epicurus saw that adversities were always befalling the good: poverty, labors, exiles, loss of dear ones; that the evil on the contrary were happy, were gaining in wealth, were given honors. He saw that innocence was not safe, that crimes were committed with impunity; he saw that death raged without concern for mortals.'[9] Epicureanism's promise to take away the fear of death and the dread of hell was appealing in the face of the ferocity of the clerics and the horrifying Calvinist doctrine of arbitrary election that had infiltrated the Protestant churches. The moral message that pleasure and self-sufficiency were good was simple and congenial, provided it could be purified of the *libertinage* with which it had been branded. Lucy Hutchinson, the first English translator of Lucretius, professed her disapproval of the wickedness of men who denied providence, and she accused the Epicureans of a 'silly, foolish, and false account of nature'. She later represented her reason for engaging with the text, as a 'youthful curiositie to understand things I heard so much discourse of at second hand', and she expressed her sorrow and horror that 'men should be found so presumptuously wicked to studie and adhere to his and his masters ridiculous, impious, execrable doctrines, reviving the foppish, causall dance of attoms, and deniing the Soveraigne Wisdom of God in the great Designe of the whole Universe'.[10] Nevertheless, despite her sturdy rejection of atheism and atomism, Hutchinson commended the Epicureans' moral and religious

---

[9] Lactantius, *The Divine Institutes*, bk. III, ch. 17; trans. Sister Mary Francis McDonald OP (Washington, DC: Catholic University of America Press, 1965), 208.

[10] Lucy Hutchinson, dedication to the Earl of Anglesey, repr. in Lucy Hutchinson, *Lucy Hutchinson's Translation of Lucretius* De rerum natura, ed. Hugh de Quehen (London: Duckworth, 1996), 23–5.

sensibility, referring with approval to their revulsion at those who, like the Presbyterian clerics of her time, 'set up their vaine imagination in the roome of God, and devize superstitions foolish services to avert his wrath, suitable to their devized God'. The Epicureans, she ventured pointedly,

thinke they treated more reverently of Gods, when they placed them above the cares and disturbances of humane affaires, and set them in an unperturbed rest and felicity, leaving all things here, to Accident and Chance…and deriding Heaven and Hell, Eternall Rewards and Punishments, as fictions in the whole…as…rather stories invented to fright children, then to perswade reasonable men; therefore they fancied another kind of heaven and hell, in the internall peace or horror of the conscience, upon which account they urgd the persuite of vertue and the avoyding of vice, as the spring of joy or sorrow, and defind vertue to be all those things that are just equall and profitable to humane Society, wherein this Poet makes true religion to consist.[11]

Increasingly appealing as well was Epicurus' approach to political theory. Epicurus had naturalized the notion of justice, detaching it from metaphysics and theology, and he explained the evolution of civil society from the state of nature. Justice consisted, in his view, in the invention of a set of norms whose function was to provide protection for the weak and to promote human ends. Its basis was consensus, and its particular standards, which assuredly had not been given by the gods but only found out by trial and error, were subject to revision and improvement, as human circumstances changed. Uniquely among Greek philosophical cults, the Epicureans insisted on withdrawal from the wider society and seclusion in a garden, a suburban grove—the ancients cultivated trees, but not flowers—where enlightened followers lived together in a condition of relative sexual equality, separated and protected from the majority. They were bound together by a shared commitment to the simple life, and Epicurus maintained that friendship was the chief source of happiness in life.[12] His concept of friendship was not hedged round, as was Aristotle's, with moralistic qualifications and criteria to

See Reid Barbour, 'Lucy Hutchinson, Atomism, and the Atheist Dog', in Lynette Hunter and Sarah Hutton (eds.), *Women, Science and Medicine 1500–1700* (Stroud: Sutton, 1997).

[11] Hutchinson, *De rerum natura*, p. 25.
[12] Epicurus, saying no. 27, in Diogenes Laertius, *Lives of the Eminent Philosophers*, X. 148; trans. R. D. Hicks (Cambridge, Mass.: Harvard University Press, 1925), ii. 673.

be met by appropriate friends, nor, however, was friendship capable of generalization, like Stoic benevolence, to an entire city or to the whole human race.

'With Epicurus', says Bernard Frischer, 'a new spirit enters Greek philosophy, one that is light, warm, and humane'.[13] Epicurus had asserted forthrightly, 'I know not how to conceive the good, apart from the pleasures of taste, sexual pleasures, the pleasures of sound and the pleasures of beautiful form'.[14] However, he insisted on selectivity and moderation; for greedy licentiousness brought pain and sorrow in its wake.

When we say that pleasure is the goal we do not mean the pleasures of the profligate or the pleasures of consumption, as some believe, either from ignorance and disagreement or from deliberate misinterpretation, but rather the lack of pain in the body and disturbance in the soul. For it is not drinking bouts and continuous partying and enjoying boys and women, or consuming fish and the other dainties of an extravagant table, which produce the pleasant life, but sober calculation.... [P]rudence is the source of all the other virtues, teaching that that it is impossible to live pleasantly without living prudently, honourably and justly.[15]

Pleasure was, however, a contested notion in both ancient and early modern philosophy, and its incorporation into the in metaphysics and ethics was cautious, qualified, and occasionally tortured, insofar as mundane suffering and the ascetic life appeared to be valued by Christian prophets, saints, and authors, and so by God himself.

Cicero's critique of Epicureanism, which later critics drew on extensively, was motivated both morally and politically. In ancient Rome, as later in Renaissance Italy, the sect was associated with underground republican and even populist sentiments that were repugnant to him.[16] His refusal to address his contemporary Lucretius directly has aroused scholarly comment, with explanations ranging from Cicero's reluctance to give recognition to a popular movement committed to undermining 'an aspect of religion

---

[13] Bernard Frischer, *The Sculpted Word: Epicureanism and Philosophical Recruitment in Ancient Greece* (Berkeley/Los Angeles, Calif.: University of California Press, 1982), 61.

[14] Epicurus, in Diogenes Laertius, *Lives* X. 6; trans. Hicks, ii. 535.

[15] Epicurus, letter to Menoeceus, in Diogenes Laertius, *Lives* X. 131–2; trans. Brad Inwood and L. P. Gerson, in *The Epicurus Reader* (Indianapolis, Ind.: Hackett, 1994), 30–1.

[16] Benjamin Farrington, 'The Gods of Epicurus and the Roman State', in *Head and Hand in Ancient Greece* (London: Watts, 1947), 88–113.

which the state thought wise to encourage' as[17] to personal rivalry.[18] There is no question, however, that Cicero's philosophical thinking was reactive, and organized around his opposition to Lucretian atheism, hedonism, and conventionalism.

Cicero took issue with the image of the anti-providential universe of Epicurus, insisting that the world's beauty and order bespoke a divine origin, and he attacked the doctrine of pleasure as one unworthy of the dignity of man and countered the Epicurean theory of justice with one based on objective laws of nature and an innate social instinct. Epicurus had never proved, Cicero pointed out, that pleasure was desirable; he had merely noted that animals appeared from birth to seek pleasure and to shun pain, and he had denied that right conduct and moral worth were intrinsically pleasurable. Cicero posited as well a thirst for knowledge that markedly distinguished him from the Epicureans, who saw no value in science except as it removed fear. We derive no utility, he insisted, from studying 'the motions of the stars and in contemplating the heavenly bodies and studying all the obscure and secret realms of nature'.[19] Even Ulysses' sirens fascinated and transfixed men by promising wisdom and knowledge, not by the mere sweetness or novelty of their singing. 'Homer was aware that his story would not sound plausible if the magic that held his hero immeshed was merely an idle song!'[20] It was evident, Cicero thought, that men acted for reasons other than the pursuit of pleasure and the avoidance of pain, renouncing comfort and convenience for the sake of duty, loyalty, and country, and that they found satisfaction in doing so. Epicurus' claim that men are just because justice ensures peace of mind and injustice brings disquietude was antithetical to his conviction that goodness, like knowledge, ought to be and could be pursued for its own sake. His belief that men could and ought to act for purely moral reasons, anticipating no benefit even in terms of reputation or social regard from compliance

---

[17] Farrington, 'Gods of Epicurus', p. 110. At the same time, the apolitical stance of the Epicureans was condemned by Cicero and, according to Howard Jones, was partly responsible for the sect's decline (*The Epicurean Tradition* (London: Routledge, 1992), 78).

[18] 'Cicero was anxious to present himself as the sole representative of philosophy in Latin even if this meant leaving out of account the one writer whose contribution to the Roman philosophical tradition was arguably as decisive as his own' (Jones, *Epicurean Tradition*, p. 73).

[19] Marcus Tullius Cicero, *On Ends*, bk. V, ch. 19; trans. H. Rackham, 2nd edn. (Cambridge, Mass.: Harvard University Press, 1931), 453.

[20] Ibid., bk. V, ch. 8; trans. Rackham, p. 449.

with moral rules, was at the time, and has remained ever since, the most intellectually compelling alternative to utilitarian and contractualist positions in moral philosophy.

Epicurus had died in 270 BCE. The main discussions of atomism and its associated doctrines in antiquity were to be found in Diogenes Laertius' accounts of Democritus and Epicurus in books IX and X of his *Lives of the Philosophers*, in Plutarch's *Moralia*, and in Cicero's discussions in *On the Nature of the Gods*, the *Tusculan Disputations*, and *On Ends*. (The commentaries of the Epicurean Philodemus, buried at Herculaneum in the explosion of Vesuvius, have only recently been recovered, together with the text of Epicurus' *On Nature*.) Diogenes defended Epicurus against calumny, but not until he had repeated every scurrilous story told against him. His valuable chapter included reproductions of Epicurus' letters to Herodotus, Pythocles, and Menoeceus, references to his lost work, *On Nature*, and forty short maxims dealing with cosmological, anthropological, and ethical topics. This collection of sayings overlapped for the most part with a fourteenth-century compilation known as the 'Vatican Sayings', presumably consulted by a select group of clerics.

Epicurus' insistence on frugality and the rationing of pleasures did not correspond to the lesson internalized by many of his followers in the late Roman era,[21] and authors of the early Christian era transformed Epicureanism into a moral philosophy of decadence and self-interest. Seneca indulged in his usual purple passages:

Virtue is something elevated, exalted, and regal, unconquered and unvaried; pleasure is something lowly, servile, weak and unsteady, whose haunt and dwelling place are the brothel and tavern. You will meet virtue in the temple, the forum, the senate house; standing in defense of the city walls, dusty and sunburnt, with calloused hands. Pleasure will more often be found lurking away and hugging the darkness around the baths and sweating rooms and places that fear the magistrates, feeble, languid, soaked in wine and perfume,

---

[21] Stoicism alone, according to Lecky, retained ethical credibility in the Roman Empire: 'Epicureanism ... proved little more than a principle of disintegration, or an apology for vice, or at best the religion of tranquil and indifferent natures animated by no strong moral enthusiasm.... [T]he Epicureans' ... elevated conceptions of what constitutes the true happiness of men, were unintelligible to the Romans, who knew how to sacrifice enjoyment, but who, when pursuing it, gravitated naturally to the coarsest forms' (W. H. Lecky, *A History of European Morals* (New York: Braziller, 1955), 175–6).

and either pale or painted with cosmetics and smeared with unguents like a corpse.[22]

The condemnations of Epicurean doctrine in the tracts, sermons, and letters of Augustine, Lactantius, Arnobius, Ambrose, and Jerome that followed contrasted with the more balanced and analytical discussions by Plutarch and Cicero. Amongst the Fathers of the early Church it was Lactantius, a popular author and one much favored in the early modern era, who gave the most attention to the physical side of Epicureanism, which he ridiculed in passages such as the following:

Whence, therefore, are [the atoms] born, or how do all things which happen come to be? [Epicurus] says that it is not the work of providence. There are seeds flying about through the void, and when these have massed together at random among themselves, all things are born and grow. Why, then, do we not feel them or perceive them? Because they have neither color, nor heat, nor odor. They are free of taste also and moisture, and they are so minute that they cannot be cut and divided.[23]

Lactantius referred to the dreams of Leucippus, and the 'wild ravings' and 'inheritance of foolishness' left by Democritus to Epicurus. He found the doctrine of atomic concatenation absurd. '[B]y what pact, by what agreement do they come together among themselves that something may be formed of them? If they lack sense, they are not able to come together with such order, for it is not possible for anything but reason to bring about anything rational.'[24]

The Fathers could not conceive of a materialism that did not license hedonism, or a hedonism that did not spiral into depravity. Those who deny the existence of God, said Lactantius, are 'similar to the beasts, they seem to have consisted of body alone, discerning nothing with their minds and referring all things to a sense of the body, for they thought that there was nothing save that which was beheld by the eyes'.[25] In *The Wrath of God*, his jeremiad against Epicurean morals, the complement to his creationist tract, *The Workmanship of God*, he referred to 'vicious and nefarious men, who pollute all things with lusts, plague others with killings, defraud them,

---

[22] Seneca, *De vita beata* § 7, in *Seneca: Four Dialogues*, ed. C. D. N. da Costa (Warminster: Aris and Phillip 1994), 19.

[23] Lactantius, *Divine Institutes*, bk. III, ch. 17; trans. McDonald, 210.   [24] Ibid. 210–11.

[25] Ibid., bk. VII, ch. 9; trans. McDonald, p. 495.

steal and perjure; they spare neither their relatives nor their parents, and they ignore laws and even God himself'.[26] Ambrose, the Bishop of Milan, though he distinguished between Epicurus and his followers, had nothing good to say of either: 'How reprobate is that which prompts wantonness, bribery, and lewdness, namely the incitement to lust, the enticement to sinful pleasure, the fuel of incontinency, the fire of greed'.[27] The Epicureans 'show that they are living only carnally, not spiritually, and they do not discharge the duty of the soul, but only that of the flesh, thinking that all life's duty is ended with the separation of soul and body'.[28] St Jerome introduced the memorable fiction that Lucretius had been driven mad by a love potion and that he had killed himself at the age of forty-four after composing his poem 'in his lucid intervals'.

By the mid-fifteenth century Epicureanism, or 'Epicurism', was a convenient target for moralists, who portrayed it as a corrupting force, dragging men into a condition of degradation and promoting malice and social unrest. Luther disparaged the Pope as an 'Epicurean Sow' and claimed that the spread of Epicureanism indicated that the end of world was at hand.[29] Lucretius' poem was banned by the Florentine synod in 1517 as 'a lascivious and wicked work, in which every effort is used to demonstrate the mortality of the soul'.[30] Calvin was moved to denounce Epicureanism in a work of 1545.[31] The young Marsilio Ficino wrote a commentary on Lucretius, which, after his turn to Platonic theology, he repudiated and burned. The explosion of printed books in the early seventeenth century furthered the dissemination of careless and obscene works, and unbelievers seemed to the godly to be multiplying without limit. Atheists, said Philippe de Mornay in 1587, bemire reason 'in the filthie and beastlie pleasures of the world'. They 'match their pleasures with malice, and to make short weaie to the atteinement of goods or honour doo overreach and betraie other men, selling their freends, their kinsfolke, yea and their owne soules,

[26] Lactantius, *Wrath of God*, in *The Minor Works*, trans. Sister Mary Francis McDonald OP (Washington, DC: Catholic University of America Press, 1965), 97.

[27] St Ambrose, 'Letters to Priests, in *St Ambrose: Theological and Dogmatic Works*, trans. Roy J. Deferrari (Washington, DC: Catholic University Press of America, 1967), 321.

[28] Ambrose, 'Letters to Priests', in *Theological and Dogmatic Works*, p. 327.

[29] Jones, *Epicurean Tradition*, pp. 162–3.

[30] Alison, Brown, 'Lucretius and the Epicureans in the Social and Political Context of Renaissance Florence', *I Tatti Studies: Essays in the Renaissance*, 9 (2001), 12.

[31] Jean Calvin, *Contre la secte fantastique et furieuse des libertins qui se nomment spirituels* (Geneva: 1545).

& not sticking to do anie evill, that may serve their turn'. They hold
to their views for, out of self-deception, 'bicause they feele their minds
guiltie of so many crimes, [they] do thinke themselves to have escaped
the Justice and providence of GOD by denying it'.[32] In *Natures Embassie,
or, The Wilde-mans Measures* of 1621 Richard Braithwaite portrayed his
contemporaries as 'drawne and allured by the vaine baits and deceits of
worldly suggestions ... Every one ... a hogge wallowing in the mire of their
vaine conceits, [roving] from the marke of pietie and sobrietie'.[33] The
cause, he said, was Epicurism, the 'private and peculiar Sect', which 'like
a noisome and spreading Canker, eats into the bodie and soule of the
professor, making them both prostitute to pleasure and a very sink of
sinne'.[34] These interpretations and verdicts were replaced over the course
of the century by more accurate and measured ones.

Some more objective knowledge of ancient atomism, sustained by a few
manuscripts, had persisted in the medieval era. The text circulated in the
Low Countries, in France, and in St Gall, near Lake Constance.[35] The
author was quoted approvingly by Isidore of Seville and the Venerable
Bede, and the twelfth-century philosopher William of Conches suggested in
a dialogue that the Epicureans were correct in saying that the earth consists
of atoms, and only mistaken in supposing that 'those atoms were without
beginning and "flew to and fro separately through the great void", then
massed themselves into four great bodies'. Nothing, William maintained,
'can be without beginning and place except God'.[36] John Wycliff (1320–84)
professed admiration for Democritus and for his atomism.[37] His doctrines
were posthumously condemned by the Council of Constance in 1415.
Diogenes' *Lives* were brought to Italy from Constantinople in 1416 and
translated into Latin in the 1420s and 1430s.[38] By then, however, Lucretius
had nearly disappeared from view. A single copy of *De rerum natura* was
located by the apostolic secretary and dedicated manuscript-hunter Poggio

---

[32] Philippe de Mornay, preface to A *Woorke Concerning the Trewnesse of the Christian Religion*, trans.
Sir Philip Sydney and Arthur Golding (London: 1587).

[33] Richard Braithwaite, *Natures Embassie, or The Wilde-mans Measures Danced Naked by Twelve Satyres*,
(London: 1621), 129.

[34] Ibid.   [35] See L. D. Reynolds (ed.), *Texts and Transmissions* (Oxford: Clarendon, 1983), 220.

[36] William of Conches, *Dragmaticon philosophiae*, trans. and ed. Italo Ronca and Matthew Carr (Notre
Dame, Ind.: Notre Dame University Press, 1998), bk. I, ch. 6, pp. 8–9.

[37] Emily Michael, 'John Wyclif on Body and Mind', *Journal of the History of Ideas*, 64, (2003), 343–60.

[38] Brown, 'Lucretius and the Epicureans', p. 12.

Bracciolini, in Germany in 1417, but it took twelve years to copy, and Lucretius was hardly read or cited before 1450. The first printed edition appeared in Brescia (1473), the second in Verona (1486), and the third in Venice (1495). Though the poem enjoyed twenty-eight further printings before 1600, Lucretius still lagged considerably behind other ancient poets in popularity.[39]

Scholarly commentary on the poem throughout the fifteenth and sixteenth centuries was chiefly philological, with little attention given to its philosophical, scientific, or political dimensions. Yet Epicurean ideas began to arouse interest and to find new defenders, first in Italy, later in the north. Pietro Pomponazzi wrote sceptically against the possibility of thought without a bodily substrate in 1516 and suggested that the human soul was a 'material form', a form arising from the powers of matter, and accordingly mortal. Bernardo Telesio and Tommaso Campanella read and adapted elements of Epicurean natural philosophy, and Giordano Bruno, a visitor to England in 1583–5, defended, against Aristotelian objections, an immaterial atomism in his *De triplici minimo et mesura* published in Frankfurt in 1591. He asserted the multiplicity of worlds and was executed for heresy in 1600. Michel de Montaigne writing in the last quarter of the sixteenth century was favorably disposed to Lucretius, citing numerous verses of his poem, though he had no use for Epicurean atomism or cosmology. A much-improved third Latin edition of *De rerum natura* with commentary was brought out by Denys Lambin in 1570, and his and other Continental editions of Lucretius were early on available to English readers. Lucy Hutchinson, the wife of the Puritan colonel and regicide John Hutchinson, began to translate Lucretius into English in the 1640s, but she did not publish her version, though she sent it as a present to the Earl of Anglesey in 1675. John Evelyn completed a translation of the poem, prefaced by a passionately partisan introduction, but published only the first book, in 1656.[40] The first full Latin edition appeared in England in 1675, antedated by Thomas Sprat's translation of the Plague of Athens that takes up its sixth book, and the first complete translation of Lucretius was published

---

[39] Jones, *Epicurean Tradition*, p. 154.

[40] Books 3–6 are in the British Library under the designation Evelyn MSS 33–4. On Evelyn's context, motives, and changes of heart see Michael Hunter, 'John Evelyn in the 1650s', in his *Science and the Shape of Orthodoxy: Intellectual Change in Late Seventeenth-century Britain* (Woodbridge: Boydell, 1995).

in 1682, by Thomas Creech, with an appendix of sixty pages of 'scathing commentary'.[41] Creech's translation was avidly consumed, with four reprints before 1714. The poet John Dryden translated five selections in his *Sylvae* that are still praised for their elegance and accuracy.

The rehabilitation of Epicurean ethical hedonism began in Italy as well, spreading northward into France and England. Cosma Raimondi, in what has been described as 'the only thoroughgoing espousal of Epicurean ethical doctrine in the Quattrocento',[42] was an early admirer. If we were merely minds, he said, the Stoics would be right. 'But since we are composed of a mind *and* a body, why do they leave out of the account of human happiness something that is part of mankind and properly pertains to it?' Nature, said Cosma, fashioned man for pleasure, and for the appreciation of beauty, and even scholarship is undertaken in the hope of finding enjoyment. 'I do not see what sort of pleasure can be found without the aid of the senses, unless perhaps it lies in study of the deep mysteries of the universe, which I do not deny can be a source of great mental delight.'[43] Lorenzo Valla's remarkable dialogue *De voluptate* (1431), later retitled *De vero bono*,[44] was followed by Marsilio Ficino's *De voluptate* of 1492.[45]

In Thomas More's *Utopia* (1516) the pursuit of knowledge and social equality are instantiated in a context of minimal theology and extravagant sensuality. Though their temples contain no images of god, the Utopians use candles and incense. Sweet savors and lights elevate their thoughts, and their priests wear costumes made of the multicolored plumes of birds. They are receptive to the 'secret unseen Virtue' of music. The Utopian philosophers spend no time on metaphysical disputations; instead they discuss what is good for human beings, concluding that 'all our Actions,

[41] Jones, *Epicurean Tradition*, 212.

[42] Martin Davies, introduction to Cosma Raimondi, 'Letter to Ambrogio Tignosi in Defense of Epicurus against the Stoics, Academics, and Peripatetics', trans. Davies in *Cambridge Translations of Renaissance Texts*, ed. J. Kraye (Cambridge: Cambridge University Press, 1992), i. 238.

[43] Ibid. i. 240.

[44] It is described by Lynn Joy as containing 'one of the most ambitious projects for reform in the history of ethics' ('Epicureanism in Renaissance Moral and Natural Philosophy', *Journal of the History of Ideas*, 53 (1992), 573). Despite some debate over Valla's intentions, it is difficult to read his text as anything except a hymn of praise to love and beauty, with the Epicurean Vegio representing the author's favored perspective.

[45] Cited in turn by Don Cameron Allen as 'the fairest discussion of Epicurus and his ethics prior to that of Gassendi' ('The Rehabilitation of Epicurus and His Theory of Pleasure in the Early Renaissance', *Studies in Philology*, 41 (1944), 10). Allen argues persuasively for an Italian, rather than a French, origin for moral Epicureanism in English philosophy.

and even all our Virtues terminate in Pleasure, as in our chief End and greatest Happiness'.[46] And, what may seem stranger, More reports, 'they make use of Arguments even from Religion, notwithstanding its Severity and Roughness, for the Support of that Opinion, so indulgent to Pleasure'.[47] Carefully observing the Epicurean maxim that pleasures that draw pains after them should be avoided, the Utopians devote themselves to pleasures of the mind and also of the body. The latter arise, according to More, when we 'feed the internal Heat of Life by eating and drinking', or when we are relieved of surcharge or pain in 'satisfying the Appetite which Nature has wisely given to lead us to the Propagation of the Species'. The feeling of vitality and health is 'the greatest of all Pleasures, and almost all the *Utopians* reckon it the Foundation and Basis of all the other Joys of Life; since this alone makes the State of Life easy and desirable'.[48]

The Utopians 'freely confess' that if the soul were not immortal and susceptible of reward and punishment 'no Man would be so insensible, as not to seek after Pleasure by all possible Means, lawful or unlawful'.[49] However, most of the community believes in the immortality of the soul and divine reward and punishment, and they despise as 'men of base and sordid minds' and bar from public office and high honours those who 'so far degenerate from the Dignity of human Nature, as to think that our Souls died with our Bodies, or that the World was governed by Chance, without a wise overruling Providence'.[50] While these heretics are not permitted to preach their opinions before the common people, they are allowed to dispute in private with priests 'for the Cure of their mad Opinions'. It is a maxim amongst the Utopians that belief cannot be compelled.[51]

By the beginning of the seventeenth century, Epicurean circles flourished in France, with the self-proclaimed *beaux esprits* distinguishing themselves from *les superstitieux*. Marin Mersenne remarked despairingly in 1623 that there were over 50,000 atheists in Paris alone, and while his tally presumably included his attempted headcount of heretics and infidels of all sorts, including astrologers and 'magicians', he doubtless had Epicurean libertine circles in mind.[52] Epicurean poetry instructed readers that life

---

[46] Thomas More, *Utopia*, trans. Gilbert Burnet (London: 1751), 96.   [47] Ibid. 92.
[48] Ibid. 101–2.   [49] Ibid. 92.   [50] Ibid. 144–5.
[51] An interesting proposition in light of More's vigorous persecution of Protestant heretics.
[52] He retracted this overstated claim later. See Lynn Thorndyke, 'Censorship by the Sorbonne of Science and Superstition in the First Half of the Seventeenth Century', *Journal of the History of Ideas*, 16

was brief and followed by an endless sleep, that men and animals were no different and experienced the same pleasures and desires, and that one ought to enjoy life to the full as long as possible.[53] Members of one cult, according to their critic François Garasse, subscribed to the following two extravagant theses: first, 'There is no other divinity or supreme power in the world except NATURE, who requires to be pleased in everything, refusing nothing to our bodies and our senses of what they desire from us in the exercise of their powers and natural faculties'; and second, 'Assuming there is a God, as it is well to maintain to avoid constant conflict with superstitious people, it does not follow that there are purely intellectual creatures separated from matter. Everything in nature is a composite. There are neither angels nor devils in the world and it is not assured that the soul of man is immortal'.[54] While the Bible was a fine book, the libertines maintained, no one was required to believe all that it said on pain of damnation. In 1624 the medical faculty of the Sorbonne condemned three chemical philosophers, Jean Bitaud, Antoine de Villon, and Étienne de Clave, for defending atomism against Aristotle and forbade such teachings on pain of death.

England as well sheltered the heterodox.[55] In his *Anatomy of Melancholy* Richard Burton crisply addressed the topic of the rational soul as 'a pleasant but doubtfull subject ... and to be discussed with like brevity'.[56] Several atheistic circles existed at least from the late 1500s, amongst them Sir Walter Raleigh's band of freethinkers, which included the mathematically and philosophically talented Thomas Hariot, whose manuscripts later made their way to the enlightened Cavendish family, and a related group assembled by Henry Percy.[57] The Civil War of mid-century and

(1955), pp. 119–20. Parisian Epicureans of the early seventeenth century included Gabriel Naudé, Elio Diodatai, François de la Mothe de Vayer, and, on the periphery, the story writer Cyrano de Bergerac and the playwright Molière.

[53] 'A quoy bon tant craindre | Les horreurs du tombeau | Quand on voit éteindre | De nos jours le flambeau? | L'ame est une étincelle | Et tout ce qu'on dit de l'esprit | Est bagatelle' (Charles Blot, in Antoine Adam (ed.), *Les libertins au XVIIe siècle* (Paris: Buchet-Chastel, 1964), 84). See also Françoise Charles-Daubert, *Les Libertins erudits en France au XVIIe siècle* (Paris: Presses Universitaires, 1998), 74 ff.

[54] Adam (ed.), *Libertins*, p. 42.

[55] Christopher Hill, *The World Turned Upside Down* (London: Temple Smith, 1972), 173–4. See also his *Milton and the English Revolution* (London: Faber & Faber, 1977), 317 ff.

[56] Robert Burton, *The Anatomy of Melancholy*, ed. Thomas C. Faulkner, Nicholas Kiessling, and Rhonda L. Blair (Oxford: Clarendon 1989), i. 156.

[57] R. H. Kargon, *Atomism in England from Hariot to Newton* (Oxford: Clarendon, 1966), 7–8.

the suspension of censorship were accompanied by the spread of rebellious sects who rejected Puritan morality as well as Anglican theology, and mortalist tracts and treatises circulated in an increasingly literate working-class population, as the expression of grievances against the clergy, the magistrates, the monarch, and other authorities reached new heights. In 1643 or 1644 the English Leveller Richard Overton, 'the pamphleteer of Amsterdam', published a tract, *Mans Mortalitie*, that was expanded and reprinted several times, later retitled *Man Wholly Mortal*. Overton offered a battery of arguments and scriptural citations against the 'Fancie of the Soul'. Apart from the citation of many ancient authorities, including Pliny, on human mortality, the general line of argument was that the soul is nothing over and above the faculties of man, including reason, consideration, and science. These faculties, Overton said, are 'temperatures' in beasts, depending on 'corpulent matter', so they must be so as well in man. In man they achieve a higher degree of perfection, as a result of learning and education. But they are subject to extinction, and so 'the invention of the Soule upon that ground [the immortality of the higher human faculties] vanisheth'.[58] Finding various difficulties in the notion of a divinely infused incorporeal soul, Overton maintained that

Fish, Birds, and Beasts each in their kinde procreate their kinde without any transcendency of nature: So man in his kinde begets man, corruptable man begets nothing but what is corruptable, not halfe mortal, half immortal, halfe Angel, halfe man, but compleat man totally mortal: for through mortal organs immortality cannot be conveyed, or therein possibly reside.[59]

Overton insisted that he was not questioning the resurrection. Indeed, he said, an advantage of not taking the soul to be naturally immortal was that the preferential salvation of the virtuous made sense. Thus the Epicurean blasphemy 'Let us eate, and drinke, for tomorrow we die' is, he said, avoided.[60] Other writers, including John Milton,[61] took the same care to allow in principle for an afterlife in heaven or hell, pointing out that even if the human soul was corporeal, or an epiphenomenon of material organization, and not intrinsically immortal, God could revive or reassemble persons by fiat.

---

[58] Richard Overton, *Man Wholly Mortal*, 2nd edn. (London: 1655), 5.   [59] Ibid. 103.
[60] Ibid. 106–7.   [61] On Milton and mortalism see Hill, *Milton*, esp. ch. 25.

The first well-known English philosopher to defend the atomic philo-sophy, to declare its conformity with religion, and to link it to the old alchemical ambition of controlling natural processes and transforming base and useless material into valuable metals and medicines was Francis Bacon. Bacon was a friend of Percy and Hariot, and his *Thoughts on the Nature of Things* (1605) and his *On Principles and Origins* (1612), although they were not published until 1653, cited the effects of mechanical processes on qualities. In the *New Organon* of 1620 he announced a jettisoning of past Greek-inspired systems, and a turn to a practical philosophy. He criticized the atomists for being as one-sided as the Aristotelians. '[T]hat school is so busied with the particles that it hardly attends to the struc-ture, while the others are so lost in admiration of the structure that they do not penetrate to the simplicity of nature.'[62] He nevertheless favoured the atomists, for he praised Leucippus and Democritus, whose doctrines, by contrast with Aristotle's, he said, 'have ... some taste of the natural philosopher (some savor of the nature of things, and experience, and bodies)'.[63]

Matter, rather than forms, said Bacon, 'should be the object of our attention, its configurations and changes of configuration, and simple action, and law of action or motion; for forms are figments of the human mind, unless you will call those laws of action forms'.[64] He went on to introduce the concepts of 'latent process' and 'latent configuration' into philosophical discourse. These notions were the key to the transformation of substances, the superinduction of new natures that was 'the work and aim of human power'. Every natural action, he declared, 'depends on things infinitely small, or at least too small to strike the sense, [and] no one can hope to govern or change nature until he has duly comprehended and observed them'.[65] The sparse ontology of *corpus et inane* was inhospitable to the spirits he believed pervaded material bodies, accounting for many of their properties and effects, and Democritus' insistence on the diversity of atoms offered no hope after all of achieving the radical transmutations and transformations he envisioned. He nevertheless admitted subvisible 'real particles, such as really exist', which he believed experiment and induction

---

[62] Francis Bacon, *New Organon*, pt. I, aphorism 57, in *Works*, ed. J. Spedding, R. Ellis, D. Heath, and W. Rawley (Boston: Mass.: Brown and Taggard, 1860–4), viii. 86.

[63] Ibid. pt. I, aphorism 63, in *Works*, viii. 92.   [64] Ibid. pt. I, aphorism 51, in *Works*, viii. 83.

[65] Ibid. pt. II, aphorism 6, in *Works*, viii. 174.

would reveal,[66] and he accepted that color and other forms depended on the 'texture' of composite bodies.

Daniel Sennert, the German chemist, who died in 1637, recommended atoms in his *Hyponemata physica*, a text admired and translated in England, and Amos Comenius, the Utopian projector close to Samuel Hartlib, the founder of the Invisible College (the London group of pansophists), defended atoms as crucial items in Christian ontology in his *Natural Philosophy Reformed by a Divine Light* (1651). In Florence, meanwhile, Galileo Galilei, according to a complaint brought by one Brother Ximenes, was promulgating amongst his students a doctrine 'taught by some ancient philosophers, but effectively refuted by Aristotle'; namely, that 'there is no such thing as the substance of things, nor is there continuous quantity, but everything is a discrete quantity and contains empty space'.[67] Galileo went on formally to introduce a particle theory of heat, light, and color in *The Assayer*, and he presented a theory of infinitely minute atoms in the *Two New Sciences* (1638).[68] He revived the study of animals as mechanical devices, showing how they supported their own weight.

The construction of zoomorphic automata, resembling the moving statues described and constructed by the ancients, further reduced the conceptual distance between machines and animals, even when a soul was deemed necessary to initiate movement in animals. The lifelike figures in the gardens of St-Germain-en-Laye made a remarkable impression on René Descartes. Stipulating that nonhuman animals did not really initiate movement but only reacted physically to changes in their environments, he drew up a sketch for a mechanical system of nature incorporating a corpuscularian theory and a Galilean analysis of qualities he had probably learned through Isaac Beeckman. This system, sketched in his *The World*, completed but not published in the late 1620s and alluded to in his *Discourse on Method*, was joined to a Platonic theory of the human soul in his *Meditations* (1640) and his *Principles of Philosophy* (1644). Opinions varied as to how seriously to take this fusion philosophy. John Webster thought

[66] Ibid. pt. II, aphorism 8, in *Works*, viii. 177.

[67] Maurice A. Finocchiaro, *The Galileo Affair* (Berkeley/Los Angeles, Calif.: University of California Press, 1989), 141.

[68] According to Pietro Redondi, Galileo's troubles with the Church owed more to the incompatibility of his matter theory with Aristotelianism and with the metaphysics of transubstantiation than to his comparatively inoffensive Copernicanism (*Galileo: Heretic* (Princeton, NJ: Princeton University Press, 1987), 333–5); some relevant texts are reprinted in Finocchiaro, *The Galileo Affair*, pp. 202–4.

that Descartes had merely 'brought in, revived and refreshed the old Doctrine of Atoms ascribed to Democritus',[69] and in Cyrano de Bergerac's Epicurean fable *Other Worlds*, written in 1650 and published posthumously in 1657, Descartes was portrayed as having rejected the existence of the void in order to, as the author put it, have the honor of upholding the principles of Epicurus.[70] Joseph Glanvill concluded that Descartes had left readers 'deluded, effascinated and befooled with his jocular Subtilty and prestigious Abstractions'.[71] Henry More first perceived Descartes's philosophy as complementary to his own, 'the one travelling the lower Rode of Democritisme, amidst the thick dust of Atoms and flying particles of Matter, the other tracing it over the high and airey Hills of Platonism, in that thin and subtil Region of Immateriality'.[72] Soon, however, he found cause to complain of Descartes's 'making Brutes mere Machine's, the making every Extension really the same with Matter, [and] his averring all the Phaenomena of the World to arise from mere Mechanicall causes'.[73] These 'gross Extravagancies', he thought, 'will be more stared upon and hooted at by impartial Posterity' than Descartes's other innovations would be 'admired or applauded'. More insisted that 'the curious frame of Mans Body, and Apparitions' were the most telling arguments against the atheistic adherent of mechanism.[74] His coreligionist Ralph Cudworth, though well aware of the 'Feigning Power' of the human soul to represent imaginary objects, devoted almost a third of his nearly 900-page *True Intellectual System* of 1678 to the refutation of the 'Atheistic Corporealism' of Hobbes and Descartes.

Epicureanism was decisively recast by the anti-Aristotelian humanist scholar Pierre Gassendi, who maintained friendly relations with members of Parisian libertine circles whilst managing to remain above suspicion. His rejection of Aristotle and his embrace of Epicurus were two facets of his reformulation of seventeenth-century philosophy of science. Echoing

[69] John Webster, *The Displaying of Supposed Witchcraft* (London: 1677), 5; see also Lennon, *Battle of the Gods and Giants*, 9–17.

[70] Cyrano de Bergerac, *Other Worlds*, trans. Geoffrey Strachan (London: Oxford University Press, 1965), 213.

[71] Joseph Glanvill and Henry More, *Saducismus triumphatus*, trans. A. Horneck (London: 1681), § 6, p. 111.

[72] Henry More, preface to *An Antidote Against Atheism* (London: 1653), p. xii.

[73] Ibid., *Divine Dialogues* (London: 1668), 360.

[74] More, *Antidote Against Atheism*, p. 151.

Michel de Montaigne and Francisco Sanchez, who maintained that nothing could be known, Gassendi proceeded, in his unfinished *Exercitationes adversus Aristotelicos* of 1624, to attack the entire edifice of Aristotelian physics, metaphysics, his theory of the soul, and of generation and corruption. The notions of matter, form, and privation were, he declared, terms of an 'unnourishing and indigestible philosophy'; and, thanks to Aristotle, '[i]t is manifestly clear that so far we know nothing about natural things through the efforts of all philosophy'. Gassendi planned, according to his preface to the work, to defend the existence of the void; to explain the nature of time and of corporeal substance; to justify the posits of the moving earth, the stabile sun, and the multiplicity of worlds, or at least the immensity of the world.[75]

Only the skeptical portions of the announced work were published. Even they did not reflect humanistic intellectual melancholy, but only Baconian indignation with the state of the sciences and with Aristotelianism. Probably stimulated, like Descartes, by his conversations with Beeckman, whom he met at Dordrecht in 1628 or 1629,[76] as well as by Galileo, Gassendi was convinced of the value of the mathematical and experimental sciences on the basis of his involvement with astronomy, physics, and optics, and he considered conjectural or inferential knowledge well within reach. Like Galileo, who had declared that he knew and could know no more about the essences of the earth and fire than of the sun and the moon,[77] Gassendi maintained that human beings could acquire knowledge only 'within the limitations of appearances'. Knowledge of inner natures and necessary causes 'belongs to angelic natures, or even to the divinity, and is not proper for paltry men'.[78]

Having rejected the conception of scientific knowledge as demonstrative knowledge of essences and natures, Gassendi tackled the traditional objections against atoms, insisting that 'there is nothing to prevent us from defending the opinion which decides that the matter of the world and all

---

[75] Pierre Gassendi, preface to *Exercitationes paradoxicae adversus Aristotelicos* (1624), in *The Selected Works of Pierre Gassendi*, trans. and ed. Craig Brush (New York/London: Johnson, 1972), 24–5.

[76] Jones, *Epicurean Tradition*, p. 169.

[77] Galileo Galilei, letter on sunspots to Marcus Walser, 1 December 1612, in *Opere* (Milan: Riccardo Ricciardi 1953), 949; *Discoveries and Opinions of Galileo* (Garden City, New York: Doubleday, 1957), 123–4.

[78] Gassendi, *Exercitationes*, bk. II, ex. VI, in *Selected Works*, art. 8; trans. Brush, 103–4. On the uses of skepticism see further Jose R. Maia Neto, 'Boyle's Carneades', *Ambix*, 49/2 (2002), 97–111.

the things contained in it is made up of atoms, provided that we repudiate whatever falsehood is mixed in with it'.[79] He devoted much of his career to studying and elaborating on Epicurus' philosophy and to attacking Cartesian metaphysics and philosophy of mind as another manifestation of ungrounded apriorism. At the same time, the empiricist who professed to be concerned only with the appearances asserted certain experience-transcending propositions that signaled his acceptance of naturalism, his conviction that human and animal life, generation, and mentality could be described and analyzed in common terms. 'I give a soul to semen; I restore reason to animals; I find no distinction between the understanding and the imagination.'[80]

In a lengthy and widely read epistolary treatise on the apparent magnitude of the sun published in 1642, Gassendi expounded a corpuscularian theory of color that Boyle described as perfectly original and cited as the inspiration for his own work on colors twenty or so years later.[81] De vita et moribus Epicuri, libri octo, published in 1647, was Gassendi's initial apology for Epicurus, devoted to an account of the life and reputation of his author. A very popular book, it mostly ignored Epicurus' teachings. The publication of his Animadversiones in decimum librum Diogenis Laertii and his Syntagma philosophi Epicuri (1649), appearing in English editions of 1660 and 1668, remedied this deficiency. Though the Syntagma philosophi Epicuri began with a discussion of experience as the basis of knowledge, the book went on to lay out the theory of atoms in a world regulated by God doxastically. Gassendi made no serious attempt to reconcile his doctrine that men are denied knowledge of inner essences and are restricted to knowledge of appearances with his endorsement of the atom. The atom, he admitted, is neither immediately revealed to perception, nor divinely revealed; it is not signaled, as smoke signals fire, nor seen with a microscope. His argumentation on behalf of the atom was dialectical. In rejecting Aristotle, he accepted the philosophy Aristotle had conspicuously rejected, and he addressed the old objections to the atomic hypothesis propagated by Lactantius. The atoms, he explained, are created by God; and they

[79] Gassendi, Syntagma philosophicum (Lyon, 1658), sect. I, bk. III, ch. 8; Selected Works, trans. Brush, p. 398.

[80] Gassendi, preface to Exercitationes; Selected Works, trans. Brush, 25.

[81] Gassendi, letter 3 in De apparente magnitudine solis (Paris: 1642), 469; Robert Boyle, Experiments and Considerations Touching Colours, in Works, ed. Michael Hunter and Edward B. Davis (London: Pickering and Chatto, 2000), iv. 193.

concatenate by means of hooks. Sensate things can arise from insensate atoms. The generation of kinds requires eggs or soil because seeds—which are composite atomic *moleculae*—need a medium in which to develop.

In his sprawling *Syntagma philosophicum*, which formed a major part of his *Opera omnia*, collected and published posthumously in 1658, Gassendi presented a theo-mechanical system that posited the entanglement, motion, and interaction of invisible corpuscles as the basis of all phenomena. The atom—a 'material principle', 'the primary and universal material of all things'—was the source of all variety in objects, rarity and density, softness and hardness. It was the ground of sensation in animals, and the cause of generation.[82] Gassendi added to Epicurus' system a transcendent God, divine creation *ex nihilo*, and an incorporeal, immortal human soul supplementary to the corporeal soul men shared with animals that made sensation and perhaps even some forms of rationality—Gassendi wavered on this point—possible. Nothing, Gassendi assured his readers, 'was created without the deliberation and providence of God, and if atoms were the instrument used, they coalesced into the magnificent work of the universe, not by a chance occurrence, but according to divine disposition'.[83] His declared commitments to a providential world order and an immortal, incorporeal soul have struck some interpreters as insincere, but the persistence of controversy testifies to the great care Gassendi took in his presentations, and to the likelihood that his stance amounted, in Bloch's phrase, to an agnostic *refus de choisir*.[84]

English philosophers influenced by Cartesian and Gassendist corpuscularianism included Kenelm Digby, whose *Two Treatises* appeared in 1644, Margaret Cavendish, and Thomas Hobbes. The Cavendish salon in Paris in the mid-1640s, overseen by Margaret, her husband William, and his brother, the mathematician Charles Cavendish, was the center of a revival of Epicureanism led by Hobbes and Gassendi, who were 'joined in a great friendship'.[85] Descartes, whom they did not like, who spoke no English,

[82] Gassendi, *Syntagma*, sect. I, bk. III, ch. 8; *Selected Works*, trans. Brush, pp. 399 ff.

[83] Ibid.; *Selected Works*, trans. Brush, p. 408.

[84] See Olivier Bloch, *La philosophie de Gassendi* (The Hague: Nijhoff, 1971), ch. 3, esp. pp. 108–9; LoLordo, *Pierre Gassendi*, ch. 10; Monte Ransome Johnson, 'Was Gassendi an Epicurean?', *History of Philosophy Quarterly*, 20 (2003), 339–59.

[85] Letter of Sir Charles Cavendish to John Pell, December 1644, quoted in Richard W. F. Kroll, *The Material Word: Literate Culture in the Restoration and Early Eighteenth Century* (Baltimore, Md.: Johns Hopkins University Press, 1991), 135 n. 154.

and who seems to have been difficult to engage conversationally in any case, came twice to dinner, according to Margaret, and other celebrities of natural philosophy including Marin Mersenne were in occasional attendance. Cavendish's *Poems and Fancies* and her *Philosophicall Fancies*, both appearing after the family's return to England in 1653, furnished some of the earliest print references to the reviving doctrine that, as Lucy Hutchinson later remarked, was so much discoursed of. Cavendish, unlike Hutchinson, could not read Latin, or indeed any language except English, and she derived her knowledge of natural philosophy from conversation and through a few translations she had made for herself.[86] It is conceivable that Hutchinson herself showed Cavendish some passages from her secret Lucretius translation, or that Cavendish encouraged Hutchinson's interests, for the two women knew each other. Echoing Lucretius' unforgettable opening passage on the murder of Iphigenia by Agamemnon, Cavendish went on to say in *The World's Olio* of 1655 that it was better to be an atheist than superstitious; atheism fostered humanity and civility, whereas superstition only bred cruelty. Unlike More and Descartes, Cavendish recognized no spirits or incorporeal substances in her metaphysical system. Consciousness depended in her view on a material substrate: Nature makes a brain out of matter so that there can be perception and appreciation of the material world.

Cavendish's religious skepticism and her initial attraction to the atomic philosophy reflected the somewhat rebellious and resentful attitudes of one excluded from participation in the learned world and essentially powerless. Accustomed to being ruled and ordered about by fathers, husbands, and even sons, early modern women might have been drawn to a philosophy in which nature was depicted as accomplishing everything by herself without taking direction from an autocratic and psychologically impenetrable divinity. Lucretius insisted that 'nature is her own mistress and is exempt from the oppression of arrogant despots, accomplishing everything by herself spontaneously and independently and free from the jurisdiction of the gods',[87] and Cavendish proposed that:

[86] Sarah Hutton argues that Hobbes was her source, in 'In Dialogue with Thomas Hobbes: Margaret Cavendish's Natural Philosophy', *Women's Writing*, 4 (1997), 421–32.

[87] Lucretius, *ONT* II. 1090; trans. Smith, p. 63.

> Small *Atomes* of themselves a *World* may make,
> For being subtile, every shape they take;
> And as they dance about, they places find,
> Of *Forms*, that best agree, make every Kind.[88]

Cavendish was enchanted by tiny things generally, and so by the notion of worlds within worlds. 'Just like unto a *Nest* of *Boxes* round | *Degrees* of *Sizes* in each *Box* are found; | *So* in this *World* may others be, | Thinner and less, and less still by degree; | Although they are not subject to our *Sense* | A *World* may be no bigger than *Two-pence.*' The tiny worlds in a lady's earring, she enthused, may have their own houses, cattle, sun, moon and stars, and wars.

Fantasies involving multiple worlds and the discovery of new worlds in the sun and moon began to appear by the middle of the seventeenth century. Pierre Borel published a *Discours nouveau prouvant la pluralité des mondes*, arguing that the moon and stars were inhabited, and Cyrano de Bergerac wrote in 1649 and published in 1657 an *Histoire comique ou etats et empires de la lune*. In the story, the author visits the Utopian projector Tomasso Campanella, who is living in the sun, where they discuss Descartes's Epicureanism. Bernard de Fontenelle's *Conversations sur la pluralité des mondes* appeared in 1686. These imaginative exercises reflected the close association between Epicurean many-worlds theory and Copernicanism, but the interest in tiny, embedded worlds shown by Cavendish implied a rejection of the classical atom. Within a few years Cavendish had decided that atomism was philosophically unacceptable. She expressed her doubts that 'Chance should produce all things in such Order and Method'. The foppish, casual dance of atoms, she maintained, might describe the political world in its worst moments, but not the natural world. On the one hand, she doubted that 'such Curious Compositions, such Subtil Contrivances, such Distinctions of Several Kinds, Sorts, Times, Seasons, such Exact Rules, Fixt Decrees, Perfect Figures, Constant Succession and the Like', could manifest themselves 'unless every Single Atome were Animated'.[89] On the other hand, 'if Every and Each Atome were of a Living Substance, and had Equal Power, Life and Knowledge ... they

---

[88] Margaret Cavendish, *Poems and Fancies* (London: 1664), 6.
[89] Ibid., 'Another Epistle to the Reader', *Philosophical and Physical Opinions* (London: 1655), c2ʳ.

would hardly Agree in one Government'; and even their 'Consent and Agreement' would not prevent 'Alterations and Confusions'.[90] In her *Observations upon Experimental Philosophy* of 1666, Cavendish alleged that the corpuscularian philosophy showed a want of depth. The atomical writers 'reduce the parts of nature to one certain and proportioned atom, beyond which they imagine nature cannot go, because their brain or particular finite reason cannot reach further... and commit a fallacy in concluding the finiteness and limitation of nature from the narrowness of their rational conceptions'.[91] Cavendish nevertheless remained a materialist and never showed much interest in the Christian God.

The third volume of Thomas Stanley's *History of Philosophy* (1660) devoted over a hundred pages to Epicurus, and was probably one of Cavendish's sources for physics and metaphysics. In the meantime, her friend Walter Charleton, the main vector for Gassendism in England, had edited and published J. B. van Helmont's *A Ternary of Paradoxes*, which discussed corpuscular effluvia, in 1650. He followed it with the *Darknes of Atheism* in 1652, with its cautious reference to the 'pure and rich Metall' hidden amongst detestable doctrines in Epicureanism, and with his *magnum opus*—in fact an elaborate paraphrase of Gassendi—the *Physiologia Epicuro-Gassendo-Charletoniana* in 1654. Within a few years Charleton's *Epicurus's Morals* (1656) and his dialogue on Lucretian mortalism, *The Immortality of the Soul* (1657), had given an airing to Epicurean moral philosophy and anti-theology.

Robert Boyle in turn wrote down his thoughts in 'Of the Atomicall Philosophy' in 1652–4, a text which he later instructed was 'without fayle to be burnt' after his death. Nevertheless, he began to publish corpuscularian treatises, beginning in the late 1650s. In the *Sceptical Chymist* of 1661, and in *The Origin of Forms and Qualities* of 1666, he laid out his own version of corpuscularian theory, later emphasizing, in numerous tracts and essays, its insufficiency to explain many observed phenomena and its subordination to theology. Having eliminated forms from his ontology and having explained how qualities originated in the interaction between corpuscular aggregates and perceivers, he struggled with the question of the human soul—an incorporeal form, as far as the scholastics were concerned—admitting the

---

[90] Cavendish, 'Another Epistle', c2^r.

[91] Margaret Cavendish, *Observations upon Experimental Philosophy*, ed. Eileen O'Neill (Cambridge: Cambridge University Press, 2003), 199.

radical inadequacy of the Cartesian arguments for its immortality. He hoped to find experimental evidence for the resurrection, and also for witchcraft and demonic activity,[92] and he endowed the Boyle Lectures to continue his struggle against atheism, materialism, and mortalism, as well as to combat Judaism, Islam, and other alleged heresies.

Hobbes's visit to Paris for three years beginning in 1634 had introduced him to the thought of Gassendi, Galileo, and Descartes, and his *Humane Nature*, *De corpore politico*, and *De cive* were all completed within a few years of his return to England, though the first two were not published until 1650, followed by *Leviathan* in 1651. Hobbes tended to recycle his main ideas from book to book. In a chapter of *Leviathan* entitled 'Of Darknesse from Vain Philosophy, and Fabulous Traditions' he condemned the 'Aristotelity' of the universities as a 'handmaid of the Romane religion' and as subversive of legitimate secular authority.[93] Like Gassendi, and later Locke, Hobbes always began the presentation of his views with human ideation and with epistemology, not with ontology. His view that all was body nevertheless emerged sooner or later. Though a plenist who took some states of matter to be irreducibly fluid, Hobbes went further than any of the other moderns in denying the reality of gods, ghosts, souls, angels, and other incorporeal entities, and in reinventing the Epicurean account of justice as a nonaggression pact forged amongst hostile parties.

Hobbes had some protectors and many opponents, amongst them Edward Stillingfleet, who took up arms against the 'the Atomical or Epicurean Hypothesis', as 'that which makes most noise in the world',[94] in his *Origines sacrae* of 1662, devoting over a hundred pages to its refutation and serving up phrases—'blind and fortuitous concourse', 'merely causal concourse of Atoms'—that reverberated in the polemical literature. Stillingfleet's arguments rested on what he took to be the sheer implausibility of supposing that atoms could join together to form an orderly world. These arguments had no originality whatsoever and lacked Cavendish's visionary expansiveness, but he presented them cleverly and urged them

[92] Hunter, 'Boyle et le surnaturel', forthcoming in *La philosophie naturelle de Robert Boyle*, eds. Charles Ramond and Myriam Dennehy (Paris: Vrin, 2008).

[93] Thomas Hobbes, *Leviathan*, pt. IV, ch. 46; ed. Richard Tuck (Cambridge: Cambridge University Press, 1996), 462 ff. See Steven Shapin and Simon Schaffer on 'Seeing Double', in *Leviathan and the Air Pump* (Princeton, NJ; Princeton University Press, 1985), 80–110.

[94] Edward Stillingfleet, *Origines sacrae: A Rational Account of the Grounds of Christian Faith* (London: 1662), bk. III, ch. 2, p. 447.

with considerable rhetorical force. 'We must wholly alter the present stage of the World, and crumble the Whole Universe into little Particles; we must grind the Sun to Powder, and by a new way of Interment turn the Earth into Dust and Ashes before we can so much as imagine how the World could be fram'd.'[95] He maintained that atoms could not explain thought, and he would, thirty years later, urge this equally trite objection against Locke. 'Can *Atomes* forme *Syllogisms* in *Mood* and *Figure?*', he asked in the *Origines*.[96]

[W]hen once I see a *thousand* blind men run the *point* of a *sword* in at a *key hole* without *one* missing; when I find them all *frisking* together in a *spacious* field, and exactly meeting all at last in the very *middle* of it; when I once find, as *Tully* speaks, the *Annals* of *Ennius* fairly written in a *heap* of *sand*, and as *Keplers wife* told him, a *room full* of *herbs* moving up and down, fall into the exact *order* of *sallets*, I may then think the *Atomical Hypothesis probable*, and not before.[97]

Stillingfleet allowed nevertheless that a particle theory might 'give us a tolerable account of many Appearances as to Bodies'.[98] He was far from dismissing corpuscularianism as the delusion of a madman, or a poetic fancy, or even as an element of a Cartesian fable. He deemed it the 'Atomical Hypothesis' and it was as a hypothesis that Boyle and Locke could defend it as highly probable.

Though Newton claimed that he did not frame hypotheses, he did not mean that he avoided speculation regarding the existence and behavior of subvisible entities. He meant only that he did not try to explain in awkward micromechanical terms—impact, pressure, and conspiring motion—effects that he thought neatly, precisely, and mathematically explained by attractive forces deduced or deducible from the phenomena. In book III of his *Principia mathematica philosophiae naturalis* (1687), and in the last query of the first Latin edition of his *Opticks* (1706), he gave his stamp of approval to corpuscularianism, declaring that it seemed probable 'that God in the beginning form'd Matter in solid, massy, hard, impenetrable, moveable Particles, of such Sizes and Figures, and with such other Properties, and in such Proportion to Space, as most conduced to the End for which he form'd them'.[99] These particles were, he said, 'incomparably harder than

---

[95] Edward Stillingfleet, *Origines sacrae*, bk. III, ch. 1 p. 238.   [96] Ibid. 262.
[97] Ibid., bk. III, ch. 1, p. 378.   [98] Ibid., bk. III, ch. 1, p. 239.
[99] Isaac Newton, query 31, in *Opticks*, 4th edn., ed. I. B. Cohen (New York: Dover, 1952), 400.

any porous Bodies compounded of them; even so very hard, as never to wear or break in pieces; no ordinary Power being able to divide what God himself made one in the first Creation'.[100]

The text of the *Principia* was prefaced by a Latin 'Ode', written by the suspected atheist Edmund Halley, that drew on Lucretius' poem to imply flattering parallels between Newton and Epicurus as liberators of humanity from the oppression of superstition.[101] Richard Bentley, a follower of Newton of a somewhat different stamp, rewrote sections of the Ode, emphasizing Newton's contributions to physico-theology, rather than his success in banishing men's fears of the heavens.[102] In the series of six sermons endowed by Robert Boyle and preached at the church of St Mary Le Bow in 1692 that provided a widely imitated model for future attempts to reconcile science and religion, Bentley raised the old doubts about the ability of senseless and randomly moving atoms to become a cosmos, to produce well-formed animals and men, and to coalesce into thinking beings. At the same time, he defended the corpuscularian philosophy as friendly to the doctrine of immortality, and he used the occasion to describe gravity as the cement which held the universe together and as the 'fiat and finger of God'. Bentley contended directly against the Epicurean thesis that religion is a human invention for the domination and control of credulous populations, but much of his argument in favor of the Christian religion and its account of things turned on its consoling powers; the uses of faith, rather than its epistemological validation.

The cessation of wars with Spain, and then the end of the Civil War in England and the Restoration of the monarch beginning in 1660, had brought leisure and new opportunities for consumption. Disarmament restored civil and mixed society, and the turn from Mars to Venus encouraged not only the dissipation associated with Lords Rochester and Buckingham, but more moderate enjoyments. Later in the century Locke, who enjoyed food, flirtation, and furniture, and whose chest hurt, was able to allow pleasure and pain a central role in his moral psychology.

---

[100] Ibid.

[101] See W. R. Albury, 'Halley's Ode on the *Principia* of Newton and the Epicurean Revival in England', *Journal of the History of Ideas*, 39 (1978), 24–43. Bentley, Albury notes, was one of the examiners who had rejected Halley's application for Savilian Chair of Astronomy on the grounds of his unorthodoxy.

[102] Ibid. 39–40.

The Cartesian Antoine Le Grand, along with Walter Charleton, and later the sentimental bon vivant Charles de Marguetel Saint-Évremond, promoted openly Epicurean systems of morals. Epicurus was portrayed as deliberately and unjustly maligned by his enemies and as poorly understood. The image of the Epicurean pig swilling in a filthy trough was replaced by a new image of the Epicurean as a man of taste, refinement, and delicate feeling. Charleton proposed to create in his reader 'a very great dearnesse towards [Epicurus] not a patron of Impiety, Gluttony, Drunkenness, Luxury, and all kinds of Intemperance'. Felicity, he decided was 'that good, to which all other Goods ought to be referred, and cannot itself be referred to any other thing'.[103] Saint-Évremond, a paragon of worldliness and tenderness admired by even the devout Mary Astell, said that 'Honours, Reputation, Riches, Amours, & well-manag'd Pleasures, are a mighty Relief, against the Rigours of Nature and the Miseries of Life'.[104] We live, he urged, 'in the midst of an infinite number of Goods and Evils, with senses capable of being affected with one, and tormented with the other; without very much Philosophy, a little Reason will make us relish good things as deliciously as possible, and instruct us to bear the bad with all the patience we can'.[105]

Epicureanism in its original form was not especially favourable to the open-ended investigation of nature. According to Epicurus, 'Happiness depends on [accurate knowledge of the causes of celestial and atmospheric phenomena] and upon knowing what the heavenly bodies really are, and any kindred facts contributing to exact knowledge in this respect'.[106] His good opinion of the merits of exact knowledge was qualified by his claim that 'special inquiry' was useless, that there was nothing in 'the knowledge of risings and settings and solstices and eclipses and all kindred subjects that contributes to our happiness'.[107] Further, '[i]f we had never been molested by alarms at celestial and atmospheric phenomena, nor by the misgiving that death somehow affects us, nor by neglect of the proper limits of pains and desires, we should have had no need to study natural science'.[108] Both

[103] Walter Charleton, *Epicurus's Morals* (London: 1670), 7.
[104] Charles de Marguetel Saint-Évremond, *Works*, ed. Pierre des Maizeaux (London: 1714), II. 43–4.
[105] Quoted in Thomas Mayo, *Epicurus in England 1650–1725* (Dallas, Tex.: Southwest Press, 1934), 89.
[106] Epicurus, letter to Herodotus, in Diogenes Laertius, *Lives* X. 78; trans. Hicks, ii. 607.
[107] Ibid. X 79; trans. Hicks, ii. 607.
[108] Epicurus, saying no. 11, in Diogenes Laertius, *Lives* X. 142; trans. Hicks, ii. 667.

ignorance of the causes of celestial phenomena and anxiety about arriving at the proper account of them in perfect detail destroyed tranquility. One should believe that all celestial phenomena, even the most alarming, have atomic explanations, as there are no coherent alternatives to that position, but it is counterproductive to try for more, for there are many ways in which such phenomena can come about, all of them consistent with sensory experience.[109] The boundaries to knowledge were set in his view by the invisibility of the atoms, and by the subordination of science to moral and psychological needs.

One strand of late seventeenth-century Epicureanism, represented by the antiquarian aesthete Sir William Temple, emphasized this theme. Solomon, Socrates, and Marcus Antoninus have all spoken, Temple reminded his readers, of 'the Vanity of all that mortal Man can ever attain to know of Nature, in its Originals or Operations'. Knowledge of such things, he declared, 'is not our Game; and (like the pursuit of a Stag by a little Spaniel) may serve to amuse and to weary us, but will never be hunted down'.[110] Quoting Alfonso the Wise to the effect that old wood, old wine, old friends, and old books are the best,[111] Temple repeated some familiar laments: 'We are born to grovel upon the Earth, and we would fain soar up to the Skies. We cannot comprehend the growth of a Kernel or Seed, the frame of an *Ant* or *Bee* ... Nay, we do not so much as know what Motion is, nor how a Stone moves from our Hand, when we throw it cross the Street'.[112]

Temple commended moral philosophy while decrying natural philosophy. 'What has been produced for the use, benefit or pleasure of mankind, by all the airy speculations of those who have passed for the great advancers of knowledge and learning these last fifty years?', he asked in 1685. 'Have the studies, the writings, the productions of Gresham College, or the late Academies of Paris, outshined or eclipsed the Lycaeum of Plato, the Academy of Aristotle, the Stoa of Zeno, the Garden of Epicurus?'[113] He cited the academicians' pointless search for the universal medicine, the philosopher's stone, 'the transfusion of young blood into old men's veins, which will make them as gamesome as the lambs from which it is to be

---

[109] Epicurus, letter to Herodotus, in Diogenes Laertius, *Lives* X. 85–6; trans. Hicks, p. 615.
[110] Sir William Temple, 'Upon the Gardens of Epicurus', *Miscellanea* (London: 1690), 83–4.
[111] Temple, 'Essay of Ancient and Modern Learning', *Miscellanea*, p. 75.   [112] Ibid. 54–5.
[113] Ibid. 57.

derived; an universal language, which may serve all men's turn, when they have forgotten their own ... the art of flying till a man happens to fall down and break his neck ... discoveries of new worlds in the planets, and voyages between this and that in the moon'.[114]

While Temple's predictions of the end of science were not fulfilled, his grounded pessimism was shared to some extent by John Locke, who considered morality as accessible to reason, even if corporeal substance was opaque to perception and so to understanding. Though we should accept it as overwhelmingly probable that particles can produce the appearances of colors and other secondary properties, and that they produce the physical and chemical effects of purging, bleaching, and softening, Locke maintained, we will never understand how they do so, and it is not worth trying. 'These insensible Corpuscles, being the active parts of Matter, and the great Instruments of Nature, on which depend not only all their secondary Qualities, but also most of their natural Operations, our want of precise distinct *Ideas* of [the] primary Qualities [of rhubarb, hemlock, etc.] keeps us in an uncurable Ignorance of what we desire to know about them.'[115]

It is in some respects unsurprising that Thomas Mayo came to the conclusion that Epicureanism was a fashionable aristocratic movement, stimulated by the collapse of Puritan rigour and repression in the Restoration, that had largely died out in English philosophy by the end of the century.[116] The aristocratic libertinage of the Stuart court was frowned upon in the regime of William and Mary, and the Royal Society filled up with bishops and archbishops. Creech, the translator of Lucretius, had nearly killed himself over a woman and then went on to hang himself in a fit of gloom brought on by money troubles; this was thought to be a fitting end for an atheist.[117] Of the radical egalitarianism, anticlericalism, free-love propaganda, and mortalism of interregnum populist philosophy, little remained. Direct references to Epicureanism in English letters became increasingly rare and increasingly uninteresting. Despite the author's materialistic and

[114] Sir William Temple, 'Some Thoughts Upon Reviewing the "Essay of Ancient and Modern Learning"', in *Five Miscellaneous Essays*, ed. Samuel H. Monk (Ann Arbor, Mich.: University of Michigan, 1963), 96. Cf. Wotton's defense of experimental science and modernity in his *Reflections upon Ancient and Modern Learning*.

[115] John Locke, *An Essay Concerning Human Understanding*, bk. IV, ch. 3, § 25; ed. P. H. Nidditch, (Oxford: Clarendon, 1975), 555–6.

[116] Mayo, *Epicurus in England*, p. 54.   [117] Ibid. 101 ff.

atheistic leanings, Hume's essay 'The Epicurean'[118] must be judged a virtually worthless piece of literary trivia. In chemistry and physiology, the impression is one of a sprawling scientific ontology of organic molecules, chemical affinities, electrical, attractive, repulsive, magnetic, and mesmeric forces, and imponderable fluids, seemingly more closely related to the eclectic systems of the Renaissance than to classical atomism.

Epicureanism was nevertheless not merely a movement tied to a particular social context in post-Puritan England, a frothy philosophy for gentlemen, and a mistaken basis for physical science. The central premises of the Epicurean system were its denial that any supernatural agents engage in the design, generation, maintenance, or moral regulation of the world; its assertion that self-moving, subvisible material particles acting blindly, without intention or purpose, bring about all growth, change, and decline; and its insistence that the point of ethical discipline and self-denial could only be the minimization of mental and physical suffering. The philosophically and morally attractive features of Epicureanism were its integration of human beings into the natural world, the postulate of human equality that it implied, and the notion that pain and pleasure, both psychological and physical, mattered, regardless of who was experiencing them and what that person's status or merits might be. The Epicurean presentation of law and justice as needing legitimation in terms of the benefits to men of submitting to authority was a rejection of de facto hierarchies.

Between the acceptable—corpuscles, secondary qualities—and the unacceptable for all except a radical fringe—atheism, libertinage—there were Epicurean teachings that were available for rethinking that became elements of the many particular versions of the 'new philosophy'. Into this category fell such theses as the plurality of worlds, their self-formation, the spontaneous emergence of order and patterning from the initially chaotic motion of the atoms, the indifference of the gods and their inability to intervene in the affairs of men, and the centrality and validity of the hedonic motive in human life. Seventeenth- and eighteenth-century controversies over thinking matter and mortalism were stimulated by Epicurean reflection, and by the attempt to purify religion of its extraneous, superstitious,

---

[118] David Hume, 'The Epicurean', in *Essays: Moral, Political and Literary*, ed. Eugene F. Miller (Indianapolis, Ind.: Liberty, 1987), 138–45. Hume was more Epicurean than Stoic, but 'The Stoic' is by far the more substantial essay.

and persecutory elements, leaving only a minimal core of belief, only so much as was essential for the coherence of the political community and the control of individual passions. The early modern philosophers whom we continue to read because their concerns seem understandable to us and their argumentation sufficiently complex were those who had a certain feature in common. They were trying to assimilate what they could of Epicurus' challenges to the background assumptions of a guiding providence, a spirit-imbued nature, and the liability to retributive torture and eligibility for reward in paradise of the immortal human soul. The staunchest seventeenth-century critics of Epicureanism—More, Cavendish, Stillingfleet, Tenison, numberless preachers—by contrast, stand outside the main currents of early modern philosophy. The success of Epicureanism can be measured by the extent to which the universities abandoned, as they did to a remarkable extent, their role as centers for the study of incorporeal entities and eschatological and miraculous states of affairs. They became instead institutions devoted to the close and careful examination and remodelling of the material and social worlds and devoted as well to the cultivation of intellectual and sensory pleasures and the remediation of pain and deprivation.

1

Atomism and Mechanism

> were there noe individuall least,
> The smallest would of infinite parts consist
> And nothing could a certeine end attaine
> While halfe of the halfe part would still remaine.
> What difference then could there have bene betweene
> Little and great; for though the greate had bene
> Made up of infinite parts, the smallest yett
> Would equall multiplicitie admitt.
> Which since our reasons and our faith oppose
> Convinc'd, we must with this opinion close,
> That there are bodies with no parts indued
> Most small in nature; this if we conclude
> We them both solid and eternall yeild.
>
> (*De rerum natura*, i. 611–23)

The material corpuscle played a starring role in the scientific revolution of the mid-seventeenth century. The 'corpuscularian philosophy', was the 'new philosophy', the 'reformed philosophy', the philosophy of the 'innovators'. Yet, as the chemist Daniel Sennert wonderingly pointed out in 1618, the doctrine of subvisible particles was not new in his own time, and was indeed older than Aristotle. '[E]very where amongst Philosophers and Physicians both Ancient and Modern', he mused, 'mention is made of these little Bodies or Atomes, that I wonder the Doctrine of Atomes should be traduced as Novelty.' 'All the Learnedest Philosophers', he says, 'have acknowledged that there are such Atomes, not to speak of *Empedocles*, *Democritus*, *Epicurus*, whose Doctrine is suspected, perhaps because it is not understood.'[1]

---

[1] Daniel Sennert, *Epitome naturalis scientiae* (1600; rev. Wittenberg: 1618); trans. A. Cole and N. Culpeper as *Thirteen Books of Natural Philosophy* (London: 1660), bk. XI, ch. 1, p. 446.

Sennert's remarks raise a number of historiographical questions. How was the doctrine of atoms integrated into the culture of empiricism with its rejection of humanistic learning? Why were the new philosophers concerned sometimes to deny, at other times to affirm, the ancient lineage of their commitments? What qualifications and amendments to the pure Epicurean system did they introduce and why? How did they reconcile the unobservability of material corpuscles with their demand for direct ocular experience, and their insistence on multiple witnessing as a criterion of truth? To answer these questions, it is useful to look briefly at the original arguments for the exclusivity of matter and void as ontological principles advanced by the Epicureans, and at the philosophical criticism leveled against the teachings of their fifth-century BCE predecessors, Democritus and Empedocles, by Plato and Aristotle.

1.1   Ancient atomism

Diogenes Laertius cited Leucippus as the first defender of the view that infinite worlds arise from atoms and are dissolved into them and that moving atoms fall naturally into vortices.[2] Democritus expanded on his view, leaving behind his recorded claims, though few actual arguments. 'Beyond bodies and space', he declared, 'there is nothing which by mental apprehension or on its analogy we can conceive to exist.'[3] The atoms, he said, 'are unlimited in size and number; and they are borne along in the whole universe in a vortex, and thereby generate all composite things—fire, water, air, earth; for even these are conglomerations of given atoms'.[4] The Democritean atoms possessed only magnitude, figure, and motion. They were indivisible and surrounded by void, and they had no powers, except that they could strike and move one another, dislodge one another, filter through porous structures, abrade macroscopic structures by acting en masse, and, by coming into contact with sentient beings, produce experiences. The qualities of material objects, Democritus maintained, were dependent on

---

[2] Diogenes Laertius, *Lives of the Eminent Philosophers*, IX. 30 ff., trans. R. D. Hicks (Cambridge, Mass.: Harvard University Press, 1925), ii. 440–1.

[3] Epicurus, letter to Herodotus, in Diogenes Laertius, *Lives* X. 40; trans. Hicks, ii. 57.

[4] Democritus, in Diogenes Laertius, *Lives* IX. 44; trans. Hicks, ii. 455.

human perception; they were conventional, rather than being given by nature.[5]

Epicurus in turn defended the inference to atoms by appealing to the senses, 'upon [which] ... reason must rely when it attempts to infer the unknown from the known',[6] as the criterion of knowledge. Sensation attests to the existence of bodies, and reason then allows us to infer the existence of a void that provides a location for them and that makes their movement possible. He endorsed and amplified earlier arguments for the existence of indestructible simples, arguing that if all bodies were vulnerable to breakage or dissolution, nothing whatsoever could exist and appear to us.

Epicurus' argument was, it might be observed, metaphysical, rather than physical. The assumption upon which it rested was not simply that anything breakable will eventually be broken, though he posited a limited term of existence for any ordinary compound entity, for the recombination of the broken-off parts of broken-up entities might well sustain a material world. Rather, the complex bodies populating the visible world logically require the existence of simple, persisting 'thises'.[7] These eternal entities 'vary indefinitely in their shapes', he went on to say, though not infinitely. There is an infinite number of atoms of each particular shape, and they have different sizes and weights. They move constantly, either colliding and rebounding if their paths are free, or oscillating in place if they are entangled with other atoms. All atoms move at equal speed, regardless of their size and heaviness, provided they have somewhere to go and 'meet with no obstruction'.[8] Though Epicurus admitted that there could be no absolute upwards or downwards in infinite space, he conceived the atoms as moving both up and down relative to observers, and he saw their weight as enjoining a motion 'down'.[9] To that downward tendency Epicurus added the *clinamen* or swerve, which produced entanglements and combinations, as well as allowing, somehow,

[5] 'By convention sweet, by convention bitter, by convention hot, by convention cold, by convention colour: but in reality atoms and the void' (Democritus, quoted by Sextus Empiricus, *Adversus Mathematicos*, VII. 35; *The Presocratic Philosophers*, ed. and trans. G. S. Kirk and J. E. Raven (Cambridge: Cambridge University Press, 1983), 410).

[6] Epicurus, letter to Herodotus, in Diogenes Laertius, *Lives* X. 39–40; trans. Hicks, ii. 569.

[7] Ibid., in *Lives* X. 41; trans. Hicks, ii. 571.

[8] Ibid., in *Lives* X. 42–3, 61–2; trans. Hicks, ii. 573, 591.

[9] Ibid., in *Lives* X. 61; trans. Hicks, ii. 591.

for free will.[10] Atoms continually stream from bodies, but their substance is not thereby attenuated; all bodies are nourished by taking in atoms. The atoms, he maintained, following Democritus, must be devoid of all perishable qualities; they 'possess none of the qualities belonging to things which come under our observation, except shape, weight, and size, and the properties necessarily conjoined with shape'.[11] Because all qualities are observed to change over time, the vivid colors and tastes of nature would not persist unless these qualities were constantly regenerated by entities which did not possess the qualities they generated, but that could not lose the power to generate them.

Lucretius followed the reasoning of his predecessors closely, acknowledging indivisible particles, the void, and motion, permitting and necessitating collision, rebound, aggregation, entangling, and so on. His principal argument for atomism in book I of *On the Nature of Things* departed as well from the observation that every object of our acquaintance is perishable. Attrition is ongoing: '[N]ature resolves everything into its constituent particles'.[12] There must be a limit to division, for otherwise everything in the world would run down into nothingness, and renewal would be impossible. 'Something must survive insusceptible of change; otherwise everything would be utterly annihilated'.[13] This persisting entity had to be indivisible, for if there were no smallest elements, everything would be composed of an infinite number of parts, and in that case 'what will distinguish the whole universe from the smallest thing in it?'.[14] And, finally, the persisting indivisible thing had to be devoid of all perishable qualities. 'The particles of matter have absolutely no colour, either like or unlike that of compound bodies.... [B]eware of daubing the seeds of things with color, or you will find everything without exception returning to nothing.'[15] Nevertheless, they exhibited variety. Just as not all ears of corn and all seashells are alike, the atoms, 'since they are natural formations and are not modeled by hand after a single, fixed pattern ... are bound to be marked by differences of shape as they fly about'.[16]

---

[10] On the 'swerve' and free will, see A. A. Long and David Sedley, *The Hellenistic Philosophers* (Cambridge: Cambridge University Press, 1987), i. 104–7, 110–12.

[11] Epicurus, letter to Herodotus, in Diogenes Laertius, *Lives* X. 54; trans. Hicks, ii. 583–5.

[12] T. C. Lucretius, *On the Nature of Things* (ONT), I. 215–16; trans. Martin Ferguson Smith (Indianapolis, Ind.: Hackett, 2001), 9.

[13] Ibid. I. 790; trans. Smith, p. 24.   [14] Ibid. I. 619; trans. Smith, p. 19.

[15] Ibid. II. 737 ff.; trans. Smith, p. 54.   [16] Ibid. II. 371; trans. Smith, pp. 44–5.

Lucretius cited the phenomena of erosion, the gradual wearing away of rings, steps, cliffs, and tools, bit by imperceptible bit, as empirical evidence for the existence of atoms. He suggested that nutrition, the penetration of noise through walls and sweat through the skin, and the conduction of heat by metals indicated the porousness of seemingly solid bodies. The phenomena of contagion and diffusion were especially impressive in suggesting the smallness of these particles, once assumed. He offered several further arguments for the claim that atoms are colorless, one consisting of the phenomenological observation that it is difficult to discern the colors of very small objects, which 'exhale all their color before they are resolved into their constituent atoms'.[17] He proposed that sudden changes in perceived color, such as the transformation of the dark sea into 'white-flecked billows of gleaming marble',[18] are best explained by changes in the 'groupings and positions' of the elements whipped up by the wind. If the sea were composed of 'azure seeds', such transformations could not occur. And, finally, the relation between illumination and visible color implied, in his view, that color as such could not be ascribed to the atoms.[19]

The poet repeatedly made his metaphysical point about the colorless, soundless, odorless entities that really exist, by describing the quasi-illusory visible world in the most vivid possible terms, decorating his exposition with references to the changing tail of the peacock as it turns about in the light, and to the 'iridescence imparted by sunlight to the plumage that rings and garlands the neck of the dove', which is sometimes 'glossed with red garnet', at other times 'appears to blend green emeralds with blue lazuli'.[20] The difference between the manifest image of the world and its latent reality is easily grasped on analogy with a familiar experience. Our perceptual apparatus fails to register the tiny moving particles composing everything, just as 'on a hillside fleecy sheep crop the luxuriant pasture

---

[17] '[T]he more minute the pieces into which anything is broken up, the more you can perceive the color gradually fading away and being extinguished. This is what happens when purple stuff is picked into tiny pieces; when it is shredded thread by thread, all the purple or scarlet color, in spite of its unsurpassed brilliance, is shed' (ibid. II. 826 ff.; trans. Smith, p. 56).

[18] Ibid. II. 757 ff.; trans. Smith, pp. 54–5.

[19] '[S]ince colors depend upon light for their existence, and the primary elements of things do not emerge into the light, it is evident that they are not robed in any color. For what color can there be in blinding darkness? Why, even in the light color varies according as the incident ray that it reflects is perpendicular or oblique' (ibid. II. 795 ff.; trans. Smith, p. 55).

[20] Ibid. II. 801 ff.; trans. Smith, p. 55.

and inch forward wherever the tempting grass, pearled with fresh dew, summons them, while their lambs, replete with food, gambol and gently butt'. The distant observer sees only 'a motionless white blur on the green of the hill'.[21]

The beauty of the visible world is accidental, and the usefulness of plants, animals, and bodily limbs and organs is accidental as well. Nothing has been created for the sake of anything else. Lucretius left the reader in no doubt about this or about his opinion of those who read divine purpose behind beauty and utility:

To assert that ... the gods purposely prepared the world and its wonders for the sake of human beings; that we should therefore praise their admirable handiwork and regard it as eternal and immortal; that it is sinful to use any means at any time to displace what was established by the ancient design of the gods for the perpetual use of the human race ... to invent all these and all other such conceits ... is preposterous.[22]

No gods created the world following a pattern or employing a model. Rather, the atoms 'from time everlasting, impelled by blows and by their own weight, have never ceased to move in manifold ways, making all kinds of unions and experimenting with everything they could combine to create'. They have fallen into the arrangements we now observe, and 'acquired such movements, as those whereby this aggregate of things is maintained and constantly renewed'.[23]

The rejection of incorporeal entities was a feature Epicureanism shared with early versions of Stoicism.[24] The Stoics, however, considered the world to be an animal, with mind, sensation, and emotion, pervaded by a numinous aether, preserved and protected by a living God of 'supreme beauty of form', though not of human shape.[25] The restriction of reality to atoms and void—*corpus et inane*—and the rejection of holistic and anthropomorphic concepts such as care and governance, was characteristic of the exiguous Democritean philosophy.

---

[21] Lucretius, *ONT* II. 317 ff.; trans. Smith, p. 43.   [22] Ibid. V. 157 ff.; trans. Smith, p. 141.

[23] Ibid. V. 188 ff.; trans. Smith, p. 142.

[24] Zeno of Citium, the founder of the latter movement, maintained, according to the recitation of Cicero, that it was impossible that anything incorporeal could be an agent, or act on anything else; only body was a cause (Cicero, *On the Nature of the Gods*, bk. I, ch. 11, §§39–40; trans. H. Rackham (Cambridge, Mass.: Harvard University Press, 1951), 449).

[25] Cicero, *Nature of the Gods*, bk. II, ch. 22; trans. Rackham, 179.

1.2 Platonic and Aristotelian criticism

Powerful arguments were raised against the Democritean atom—the only version with which they were familiar—and against the absence of cosmic purposes and plans by Plato and Aristotle.

On the Platonic side, these arguments reflected the conviction that the world had been fashioned by a divinity who had created land, sea, plants, animals, and people; that the human soul was incorporeal and indestructible; and that matter was not fully real. The *Timaeus*, although it posited triangular fire atoms and other geometrical atoms, expounded the doctrine that the universe was the creation of a benevolent deity, free of jealousy and dedicated to producing 'a piece of work that would be as excellent and supreme as its nature would allow'. Platonic doctrine posited a good world, brought from a state of 'discordant and disorderly motion' into a state of order by a divinity who 'believed that order was in every way better than disorder'.[26]

While the Platonic world was, overall, beautiful and good, there was something wrong in Plato's eyes with matter, and something discreditable about those who attempted to 'define reality as body', and who tried to 'chase everything down to earth out of heaven and the unseen'.[27] Location in space and perceptibility were not, for Plato, the criterion of the real. Rather, we look at things as in a dream 'when we say that everything that exists must of necessity be somewhere, in some place and occupying some space, and that that which doesn't exist somewhere, whether on earth or in heaven, doesn't exist at all'.[28] The real is 'that which keeps its own form unchangingly, which has not been brought into being and is not destroyed, which neither receives into itself anything else from anywhere else, nor itself enters into anything else anywhere, is one thing. It is invisible—it cannot be perceived by the senses at all—and it is the role of understanding to study it'.[29] Matter, by contrast is 'this thing [that] can be perceived by the senses, and [that] has been begotten.... It is apprehended by opinion, which involves sense perception'.[30] Observing that the phenomena varied

---

[26] Plato, *Timaeus*, 29e–30c, in *Complete Works*, ed. John M. Cooper and D. S. Hutchinson (Princeton, NJ: Princeton University Press, 1997), 1236.

[27] Plato, *Sophist*, 246a–c, quoted in Thomas M. Lennon, *The Battle of the Gods and Giants* (Princeton, NJ: Princeton University Press, 1993), 41.

[28] Plato, *Timaeus*, 52a–b; ed. Cooper and Hutchinson, pp. 1254–5.

[29] Ibid.   [30] Ibid. 1255.

constantly, the atomists posited an unchanging material substrate. Plato claimed on the same basis that matter was something of an illusion. The fluctuating and fleeting character of material things prevented them from being grasped intellectually: Matter 'always makes opposites appear'.

Plato did not say that sensible objects were perceived dreamily. He did, however, say: 'Our dreaming state renders us incapable of waking up and stating the truth' about 'that unsleeping, truly existing reality'.[31] He said that sensible things were images, modeled after another reality, which somehow cling to being.[32] It was easy for readers to conclude that there was something dreamlike or phantasmagorical about the experience of ordinary objects. His follower Plotinus maintained explicitly that visible things were 'unreal, having at no point any similarity with [their] source and cause'.[33]

Matter is ... veritable Not-Being ... no more than the image and phantasm of Mass, a bare aspiration towards substantial existence ... invisible, eluding all our effort to observe it, present where no one can look, unseen for all our gazing, ceaselessly presenting contraries in the things based upon it; it is large and small, more and less, deficient and excessive, a phantasm unabiding and yet unable to withdraw.[34]

Plotinus further cited for lack of philosophical understanding 'those who ... on the evidence of thrust and resistance, identify body with real being and find assurance of truth in the phantasms that reach us through the senses, those, in a word, who, like dreamers, take for actualities the figments of their sleeping vision'.[35]

Where the Epicurean tradition was neutral about 'the world'—its existence as such had no value one way or the other—the later Platonic tradition was excitedly ambivalent. Plato's doctrine of the good and orderly cosmos was fused with the Christian theory of a benevolent creator by St Augustine, who, at the close of his *Confessions*, praised the beauty of nature as it issued from the hand of God, and this premise furnished the point of reference for later European physico-theology, whether the argument ran from the wisdom, goodness, and power of God to the

[31]   Plato, *Timaeus*, 52b–c; ed. Cooper and Hutchinson, p. 1255.
[32]   Ibid. 52c; ed. Cooper and Hutchinson, p. 1255.
[33]   Plotinus, *Enneads*, bk. III, ch. 6, §7; trans. Stephen MacKenna, 3rd edn. rev. B. S. Page (London: Faber & Faber, 1956), 209.
[34]   Ibid.   [35]   Ibid., bk. III, ch. 6, §6; trans. MacKenna, p. 208.

desirability of all that existed and happened, or from the desirability of what existed and happened to the existence of a wise, benevolent, powerful God. At the same time, the Platonic and Augustinian traditions dwelled on the moral and spiritual perils of the most natural forms of engagement with objects, events, and people: curiosity and concupiscence. It was not simply the case that the ambient world might be admired but not touched; it ought not even to be looked upon too admiringly.

Aristotle, who had no patience with Platonic metaphysics, rejected claims for the unreality of matter and the creation of the world by an intelligent deity. The world and its substances had always existed, in his view, and the theory of Democritus, amongst all the Ionian systems, was treated by him with the most respect, though Aristotle strenuously objected to atomism on mathematical grounds, to the associated theory of emergent qualities on logical grounds, and to the rejection of final causes on grounds of sheer implausibility. Every individual object is a hylomorph, a material thing inhabited by qualities and properties, or forms; 'prime matter' is only an abstraction. The theory of atoms, Aristotle maintained, is vague, contradicts the observation that any magnitude is divisible, and further invalidates 'many reputable opinions and phenomena of sense perception'.[36] These observations included the division of the elements of all things into earth, air, water, and fire.

The theory of the four terrestrial elements was, as is often noted, phe-nomenological in that it followed closely the observation that there are three states of matter, solid, liquid, and gaseous, and that fire seems to be different from all three, and so an element in its own right. The four elements exhaust the possible combinations of the hot and the cold, the moist and the dry, and these qualities give rise to other primary qualities of bodies, those that exhibit 'contrarieties' and are found in pairs, heavy–light, hard–soft, viscous–brittle, rough–smooth, coarse–fine. There are living creatures adapted to each element, and whether any animals naturally lived in fire, as logic seemed to demand, was much debated in the Renaissance, the salamander coming in for special consideration in this regard. The ele-ments are not fixed; they undergo quick or slow reciprocal transformation; for example, fire becomes air when its dryness is overcome by moistness;

---

[36] Aristotle, *On the Heavens*, bk. III, ch. 4, 303ª, in *Complete Works*, ed. Jonathan Barnes (Princeton, NJ: Princeton University Press, 1984), i. 496.

and air, water, if its heat is overcome by cold; brittleness is a kind of drying out. The 'forms' of bodies that are perceived by sight and that are multiple and do not have contraries (shape and color) are not elementary; they are not explained by the primary qualities either. The matter of the stars, Aristotle thought, must be of another sort altogether from that of the terrestrial elements; it is luminous like fire, but it neither consumes nor is quenched.

There could be, in Aristotle's opinion, 'no single type of matter from which all the elements originate' by, for example, condensation and rarefaction or heating and cooling. For either the analysis of elemental bodies continues forever, or else analysis results in, and synthesis begins with, atoms that are either logically or practically indivisible. If analysis and synthesis are unterminating, there are two opposing processes, the destruction and creation of visible bodies, one preceding the other, and both taking an infinite amount of time, which is impossible.[37] Alternatively, if the analysis stops somewhere, '[t]hen the body at which it stops will be either atomic or, as Empedocles seems to have intended, a divisible body which will yet never be divided'. However, such practically or theoretically indivisible entities cannot exist, for 'a destructive process which succeeds in destroying, that is, in resolving into smaller bodies, a body of some size, cannot reasonably be expected to fail with the smaller body'.[38] Consequently, there cannot be indivisible magnitudes.

There were many ambiguities and unclarities in Aristotle's discussion. He conceded that magnitudes cannot be composed of mathematical points, and he acknowledged that indivisible magnitudes appeared to be the only live option in ontology, despite the difficulty of seeing why they are indivisible.[39] He agreed with the atomists that, in at least some kinds of mixing, no true blending occurred; rather, the minute particles of one substance were combined with the other only 'relatively to perception' and could be distinguished by a lyncean eye.[40] Other mixtures, however, were true blendings that eliminated at least one of the old substances.[41] So, for example, a little water added to wine increased, on Aristotle's view, the volume of the wine—the mixture appeared to be wine and

[37] Aristotle, On the Heavens, bk. III, ch. 6, 304^b–305^a, in Complete Works, ed. Barnes, i. 498.
[38] Ibid.
[39] Aristotle, Generation and Corruption, bk. I, ch. 2, 316^a, in Complete Works, ed. Barnes, i. 516.
[40] Ibid. bk. I, ch. 10, 328^a, in Complete Works, ed. Barnes, i. 536.
[41] Aristotle, 'Sense and Sensibility', §3, 440^b, in Complete Works, ed. Barnes, i. 699.

acted like wine, and so, for Aristotle, was wine—though a lot of water added to it would turn the wine into water.[42] Some observations, in other words, seemed to support the supposition that qualitatively distinct *minima* persisted unchanged in mixtures, even when their qualities were no longer perceptible, while other observations suggested that forms came and went in the mixture. The problem of matter was, Aristotle admitted, exceedingly perplexing, and he allowed that Democritus, as one who had dwelt 'in intimate association with nature and its phenomena', had treated it more adequately than had Plato.

In the explanatory dimension, Aristotle's views rested on the distinction between natural and unnatural motions, and between intentional and blind forms of causality, and he regarded order as descending from higher forms to lower. He saw himself as a philosopher of nature, not a student of the crafts or a doctor. His interest was drawn by the normal and the healthy, not by the artificial or the pathological, and his hylomorphs, driven by internal principles of change, developed and declined gracefully, in accord with the principles of generation and corruption. In the ordinary course of nature qualities seem to change slowly and predictably—colors fade through the bleaching action of the sun, plants and animals grow, food items become tough or tender when heat is applied to them; well-nourished and poorly nourished men and animals thrive and fail respectively. Natural changes in form or quality can be sorted into common types of 'motion', such as nutrition and concoction, and Aristotle's natural philosophy categorized and analyzed them efficiently.

Human art, by contrast, brought about rapid and unexpected transformations in color, taste, and odor, and epidemical diseases extinguished life in the young and healthy almost as rapidly as did poisons. The Aristotelian vocabulary of change encompassed roasting and boiling, evaporating, and other processes effected by the sun and the culinary fire, but it was radically inadequate to the description and explanation of the physical and chemical properties of substances, as these were known to artisans—potters, dyers, jewelers, metalworkers, druggists, and alchemists. The color changes and transformations of high-temperature metallurgy and chemical mixing, the powers of chemicals to corrode and plate, of herbs to poison, to induce vomiting and sleep, the occult activity of matter, could not be explained

---

[42] Aristotle, *Generation and Corruption*, bk. I, ch. 5, 321^a–^{b}, in *Complete Works*, ed. Barnes, i. 525.

by reference to slow transformations of the elements, or by concoction, or ripening. These were violent changes, yet no motor for them was observable.

Aristotle's framework was rejected in the course of the seventeenth century in favor of a widespread commitment to the homogeneity of matter, and to the production of qualities and effects by the motion of subvisible particles. The accumulation of artisanal and pharmacological knowledge and the creation of a magisterial role for the student of nature in the fifteenth and sixteenth centuries might suggest that new observations and experiments led to the breakdown of Aristotelian physics and its replacement with the mechanical philosophy. However, the overall impression of what Kuhn called a paradigm shift should be regarded with some caution for two reasons. First, the Aristotelian posits were not the basis of a research programme that encountered obstacles in the form of recalcitrant observations and experimental outcomes, or at least it would be fanciful to see them as such. They were philosophical theses that faced the tribunal of experience and reason separately and that were argued against and defeated separately. Second, meaningful convergence on a scientific ontology for the material world did not begin to occur until the nineteenth century, with the systematization of chemistry. The schemes of natural philosophy available at the end of the seventeenth century were themselves too speculative and too idiosyncratic to form the basis of a Kuhnian research programme. The mechanico–corpuscularian philosophy of the seventeenth century did not, with the important exception of the study of respiration addressed in Chapter 2, suggest experiments or advance knowledge any more than the Aristotelian element theory and hylomorphism it replaced had. Nevertheless, Aristotelian matter theory was repudiated and the dethronement of its author is best explained by the rediscovery and reconsideration of the arguments of the ancient atomists, especially the arguments to be found in Lucretius, and by the conformity the moderns perceived between their aims and the atomic philosophy. The moderns hoped and believed that through philosophy they could improve on nature; in this respect they resembled the Alexandrian physicians and mechanics more than they did the Athenian philosophers.

Plato and Aristotle considered law, government, and morals, the remodeling of civic and personal life, as lofty enterprises falling within the province of the philosopher, whereas the production of useful and admirable objects from minerals, plants, and other earthy materials and the healing of the sick and injured with fire, tools, and drugs was mere craftsmanship. The ancient Epicureans were no different in this respect; they were practical philosophers only with respect to human institutions. Their philosophy was, however, for reasons to be explored below, perceived by early modern philosophers to be consistent with the aim of refashioning nature, and this perception was, as it turned out, largely justified.

1.3 The corpuscularian philosophy

The dominant philosophy of the early modern philosophers of the seventeenth century can be summarized as follows: Solid material things, and, for some philosophers, fluids, and also air and fire, are composed of discrete subvisible particles. These particles compose by aggregation all the bodies around us, as well as the sun, stars, and planets. There exist ultimate particles that can perhaps be further divided by God but never by human effort. The ultimate particles are composed of a universal common matter and possess only the characteristics of magnitude and figure. Their arrangement and motion produce the qualities and powers of substances. They may be joined together into complex corpuscles, composing, for example, silver and gold. Further, they can move under their own power, or by means of a force implanted in them, or by sympathy or attraction, or they may simply drift a great distance. Corpuscles, complex or not, may be endowed with powers such as the ability to replicate themselves, or to infiltrate and abrade living bodies. The action of minute particles depended, Boyle thought, on 'the *congruity* and *incongruity* of their Bulk and Shape to the Pores of the Bodies they are to act upon'; also on 'the *motions of one* part *upon another*, that they excite or occasion in the Body they work upon, according to its Structure'.[43] But their effects also depended on their huge number, their '*penetrating* and pervading nature', their '*celerity* and other Modifications of their Motion' and, more mysteriously, on the assistance of 'the *more Catholick Agents* of the Universe'.[44] These other agents included light, magnetism, the atmosphere, gravity, and others.[45]

---

[43] Robert Boyle, 'Of the great Efficacy of Effluviums', in *Works*, ed. Michael Hunter and Edward B. Davis (London: Pickering and Chatto, 2000), vii. 258.
[44] Ibid.   [45] Ibid. vii. 270.

Bacon, though a corpuscularian, had his 'spirits', as well, performing all manner of operations. Only one philosopher, Hobbes, the most thoroughgoing Democritean philosopher of the seventeenth century, despite his denial of the void and his belief in absolute fluidity, held to the view that there is nothing that is not material. Souls, colors, images, dreams, ghosts, virtue and vice, gods, thoughts and ideas, powers and propensities, numbers, society—all such seemingly incorporeal things were, he maintained, either real and material; or they had a merely 'conventional' or 'nominal' existence; or they were fictions and did not exist at all. For Descartes, animal souls, colors, and powers were not real, but rather imaginary or conventional, but God and incorporeal ideas existing in spiritual substances were assuredly real. For Leibniz, colors were not real, but animal souls, forces, and virtue and vice were real. While the dogmatic atheist Hobbes and the pious experimentalist Boyle differed in ways significant for many interpretive purposes, the similarity of their individual images of corporeal nature is better explained by their reference to a common literary tradition than by their experimental endeavors. Even the old Leibniz and the young Berkeley, who, like the Cambridge Platonists, contested that set of images in its fundamentals, preserved some of its features.

Underlying the collection of theses just cited was a claim for the homogeneity of material substance. While Aristotle had allowed that the four terrestrial elements were interconvertible, his theory ruled out the possibility that fire and water, stars and mud, vegetables and smoke, fish and gems, were all made of the same stuff, and that any substance could be transformed into any other.

The unification of the theory of material substance proceeded on two levels. First, the supralunary realm was declared to be stocked with ordinary material bodies, not bodies made of a celestial quintessence; and second, terrestrial substances of different phenomenological types were declared to share a common material substrate. Galileo was both sarcastic and eloquent in his insistence that the ordinary earth in which plants could grow was as noble and excellent a substance as the fictitious crystalline material of the celestial orbs, and he could adduce the imperfections and oddities of heavenly bodies—the pitted surface of the moon, sunspots, and the rings of Saturn—as evidence that the region above the moon was in no way ontologically exclusive. The Baconian cataloguing of many forms of natural luminescence—of marine creatures, rotting flesh, and phosphorus—indicated that shining was not the prerogative of the quintessential. Chemistry, meanwhile, offered tantalizing hints that radical transformation was possible. The alchemist's hope of making gold presupposed that base metals could be stripped of their defining qualities by human art and endowed with new ones, and the Baconian program for science, the superinduction of new, desirable forms by art, presupposed the homogeneity thesis.

A presupposition of alchemy is however very different from a perfectly general thesis about the entire visible world. Medieval chemists might conceptualize their transformative processes as requiring the reduction of substances to their 'prime matter'—for Aristotle, a purely conceptual entity with no empirical reality—but their achievements in making alloys, powders, distillations, and platings proved nothing definite. The hypothesis of a universal matter of which everything is made was not established by experimental means, by the collection of striking instances, or by observation with new instruments that discredited the theory of elements. Rather, the basic homogeneity of matter was asserted on philosophical grounds, and observations were recruited to support it. Bacon was one of the early champions of particle theory, describing the atoms in Democritean fashion as 'neither like sparks of fire, nor drops of water, nor bubbles of air, nor grains of dust, nor particles of spirit or ether'.[46] They are neither heavy nor light, hot nor cold, dense nor rare, hard nor soft, since those qualities appear in greater bodies. Heat, Bacon decided, after a lengthy process of the classification and tabulation of instances, could be nothing except the motion of these tiny particles.

Galileo, whose references to the *particelle minimi* of substances led him to be accused of atomism, appealed to thought-experiments reminiscent of book II of *On the Nature of Things*. In *The Assayer* of 1623 he argued for the Democritean conclusion that matter possesses only the properties of size, shape, motion, and situation as though he had arrived at it by sheer introspection:

[W]henever I conceive any material or corporeal substance, I immediately feel the need to think of it as bounded, and as having this or that shape; as being large or small in relation to other things, and in some specific place at any given time; as

---

[46] Francis Bacon, 'On Principles and Origins', in *Works*, ed. J. Spedding, R. Ellis, D. Heath, and W. Rawley (Boston, Mass.: Brown and Taggard, 1860–4), x. 347.

being in motion or at rest; as touching or not touching some other body; and as being one in number, or few, or many. From these conditions I cannot separate such a substance by any stretch of my imagination. But that it must be white or red, bitter or sweet, noisy or silent, and of sweet or foul odor, my mind does not feel compelled to bring in as necessary accompaniments.[47]

The exhibition of the characteristics of matter as such by thought-experiment was approached along similar lines and carried out with unprecedented elegance by Descartes in his *Meditations* of 1640. In this artful work, an ordinary person, without equipment or books, confused by the plethora of opinions about the material world he has encountered, decides to jettison all his previous beliefs. By applying reason systematically, with mathematical rigour, he discovers that matter exists and has only the properties of extension, flexibility, and changeableness.[48] Corporeal substance, the Meditator finds, by reflecting on the appearance of a piece of wax, does not intrinsically possess sweetness, fragrance, shape, and sound, but it does have 'all the properties which I clearly and distinctly understand, that is, all those which, viewed in general terms, are comprised within the subject matter of pure mathematics'.[49]

The conclusions established a priori by Galileo and Descartes were consistent with the presuppositions of chemical practice that could not by themselves establish the homogeneity thesis. They were evidently experienced as compelling by the new philosophers. Boyle was won over to the theory of 'universal, primary catholic matter' and propounded it tirelessly in his programmatic writings, beginning with the *Sceptical Chymist* of 1663. By the end of the century it was widely accepted in French and English natural philosophy that heaven and earth were ontologically and nomologically a single realm, even while traces of the notion of the heavenly origination of terrestrial things remained. Newton imaginatively suggested in the *Principia* of 1687 that the primary form of matter was a vaporous aether, born in the sun and stars and in the tails of comets, that condensed into water and was then transformed into

---

[47] Galileo Galilei, *Il Saggiatore*, in *Opere* (Milan: Riccardo Ricciardi, 1953), pp. 311–12; trans. Stillman Drake, *Discoveries and Opinions of Galileo* (Garden City, NY: Doubleday, 1957), 274.

[48] René Descartes, Meditation II, in *Oeuvres*, ed. C. Adam and P. Tannery (Paris: Vrin, 1964–76), vii. 30; trans. and ed. J. Cottingham et al., in *Philosophical Writings* (Cambridge: Cambridge University Press, 1985–9), ii. 20.

[49] Descartes, Meditation VI, in *Oeuvres*, vii. 80; *Writings*, ii. 55.

'salts, sulphurs, tinctures, slime, mud, clay, sand, stones, corals, and other earthy substances'.[50]

Galileo did not venture opinions on the atomic origins of the cosmos, but Descartes was shockingly bold in this respect. His suppressed treatise *The World* portrayed a God who, rather than creating species, substances, and celestial bodies, created only extended substance, cut it up into particles, and set it moving according to certain laws of motion. In the *Principles of Philosophy* he returned to the view that corporeal substance is divided into an indefinite number of particles, 'although it is beyond our power to grasp them all' or even 'exactly how it occurs',[51] showing how the entire visible world could have come into existence over time as a result of God's initial creative act and nothing more.

1.4 Particles and qualities

The thesis of the homogeneity of matter, once accepted, strongly indicated its division into minute corpuscles. The universe was not a single lump, and, for differentiation and movement to be possible, the parts of matter had to be mobile and capable of arrangement. It has been argued, however, that, apart from the results of their thought-experiments, seventeenth-century natural philosophers had little or no genuinely new evidence to hand in favor of the proposal that all seemingly continuous substances were composed of discrete particles, and that their arrangement and motion were productive of all observable effects.[52] This claim is correct in many respects but requires important qualifications.

Practical chemistry furnished a number of illustrative examples, instances of phenomena that lent themselves to interpretation in corpuscularian terms. A metal, for example, may be roasted until it becomes a fine powder; fire may separate a mixture, perhaps by forcing upward the lighter particles of which it is composed, leaving the heavier behind; the heaviness

---

[50] Newton, *Principia*, bk. III, prop. 42; trans. I. B. Cohen and Anne Whitman as *Mathematical Principles of Natural Philosophy* (Berkeley, Calif.: University of California Press, 2001), 938.

[51] Descartes, *Principles*, pt. II, in *Oeuvres*, viiiA. 59; *Writings*, i. 239.

[52] Christoph Meinel, 'Early Seventeenth Century Atomism', *Isis*, 79 (1988), 68–103; repr. in Peter Dear, *The Scientific Enterprise in Early Modern Europe* (Chicago, Ill.: University of Chicago Press, 1997), 193.

of a substance like gold suggests that its parts are tightly packed together, interspersed with very little void space.[53] Sennert cited the experiment of dissolving and then recovering silver particles as good evidence for the existence of indestructible atoms.[54] Many arguments for them were however simply updated versions of Lucretius'. Bacon pointed to the ability of a small amount of colorant to tinge a liquid as an argument for the existence of insensible corpuscles, and Boyle as well interpreted dilution and diffusion in corpuscularian terms. A few drops of scent could perfume a whole room, and a drop of dye could color a barrel of water. A single portion of matter, Boyle claimed, could impart a conspicuous color to above 256,806 times its bulk of water, and a faint but discernible tinge to a larger bulk above 513,620 times its size.[55] Seemingly solid bodies—especially glass, now much in use for experimental purposes—were subject to invasion and penetration, by fire, light, and magnetism, suggesting that small particles found their way into the void spaces unoccupied by atoms, or found their way through them, though large particles such as those of water might be too big to pass through the void spaces of some substances, but not others.

The existence of indivisible particles was a separate question from the existence of subvisible particles, which even Aristotle had admitted; and the existence of particles of particular substances, such as silver, a separate question again from the existence of particles of universal matter. For the classical atomists, indivisibility was a necessary tenet. Only indivisible atoms could furnish the permanent substrate required for a universe that had not run down into nothing and that never would. Sennert plumped for the possibility at least of indivisible particles, arguing that the comparison of the mathematical continuum with corporeal substance was inappropriate as an argument against the existence of indivisible particles and told against Aristotle. The philosopher, in his view, knew that he 'could not solidly refute this Opinion, and therefore he used not proper and Physical Reasons as he ought to have done, but Mathematical

[53] See W. R. Newman, 'The Alchemical Sources of Robert Boyle's Corpuscular Philosophy', *Annals of Science*, 53 (1996), 571–3. Newman argues that corpuscles entered Renaissance and early modern chemical texts through the qualitative atomism of 'Geber's' *Summa perfectionis*. See also Christoph Lüthy, 'Thoughts and Circumstances of Sebastien Basson', *Early Science and Medicine*, 2 (1997), esp. pp. 24–34.

[54] Sennert, *Epitome*, bk. XI, ch. 1; trans. Cole and Culpeper, pp. 453–4.

[55] Boyle, 'Of the Strange Subtlety of Effluviums', in *Works*, ed. Hunter and Davis, vii. 242.

and extravagant ones'.[56] For the most part, however, the moderns saw no need to insist on the absolutely indivisible nature of their particles or to reject the Aristotelian argument that anything extended was capable of division. Descartes denied the possibility of atoms—indivisible least particles—on the grounds that they conflicted with God's power to do anything, including dividing arbitrarily small particles into yet smaller ones.[57] Seventeenth-century corpuscularians either assumed without much argument that many things that were in principle divisible would never be divided by nature, or they invoked God, who had created the atoms, as the guarantor of their integrity; Leibniz was exceptional in making the problem of the material continuum central to his metaphysics.

Whether seventeenth-century natural philosophers had any new evidence to hand in favor of quality-denuded particles and a mechanical origin for forms and qualities is not a simple question either. Color, taste, odor, and sound exist 'by convention', according to Democritus and his followers; that is to say, these terms designate features of the experience of sentient observers but do not apply to the ultimately real things in themselves. Lucretius explained in turn how collections of particles stimulate the perception of qualities; that is, smooth atoms can give rise to a taste of sweetness, jagged, to bitterness. At the same time, he regarded perception as accomplished by means of eidetic films: 'membranes stripped from the surfaces of objects', which 'bear the appearance and form of the object from whose body [they] are shed and [wander] away'.[58] The description of these films as bearing the appearances of their sources suggests that they are composed of colored particles; if so, however, these colored particles cannot be atoms. Collectively, perhaps, atoms, once arranged into the thinnest of layers, are colored, but they stimulate perception mechanically, by exerting pressure, insofar as they 'pass through the interstices of the body, stir the subtle substance of the mind within and so provoke sensation'.[59]

---

[56] Sennert, *Epitome*, trans. Cole and Culpeper, p. 446. 'The Question is not here ... Whether a thing continued be perpetually divisible Mathematically? But Whether or no Nature in her Generation and resolution of Bodies does not stop at some smallest Bodies, than which there are not, nor can be any smaller' (ibid. 454).

[57] Descartes, *Principles*, pt. II § 20, in *Oeuvres*, viiiA. 51; *Writings*, trans. and ed. Cottingham et al., i. 231.

[58] Lucretius, *ONT* IV. 31 ff.; trans. Smith, p. 101.   [59] Ibid. IV. 730 ff.; trans. Smith, p. 120.

Neither Epicurus nor Lucretius distinguished between what Boyle and then Locke would term 'primary', and 'secondary' affections or properties of bodies, a distinction anticipated by Aristotle, who took the elemental quality-pairs to be primary and the tactile qualities of hardness, softness, and brittleness to be derivative. While the Epicurean-Lucretian account of perception left the ontological status of colors somewhat unclear, the position that color and other qualities exist by convention was available to seventeenth-century philosophers, and they repeated and varied Lucretius' arguments for the dependence of color on mechanical operations and perceptual contexts. Mashing a pear, Bacon noted, causes it to become sweet, and a jewel or amber reduced to a powder loses its color. Lucretius had given numerous examples of changes in color induced by motion or perspective,[60] and Boyle followed him, invoking iridescence and nap phenomena as evidence that colors depended upon the position and arrangement of singly invisible corpuscles. Galileo, employing the ingenious thought-experiment of an insentient statue that comes to life and begins to register mechanical stimulation, repeated that tastes, odors, colors, and other qualities were 'no more than mere names so far as the object in which we place them is concerned, and that they reside only in consciousness'. They are excited in us by 'shapes, numbers, and slow or rapid movements'.[61] Sweet and savory flavors are caused by differently shaped particles of different speeds that strike the tongue, scents by particles that strike small protuberances in the nostrils, and heat and light are corpuscular phenomena: when the *particelle minimi* of fire 'arrive at a final and deepest resolution into truly indivisible atoms', light is created.[62] Descartes, in turn, repeated, in his early *Treatise of Light*, the first part of *The World*, the Galilean argument that sensory qualities do not resemble their causes. The feather passed over the lips of a drowsy child contains nothing resembling the tickling he feels, and Descartes insisted on a distinction between the 'light in objects' and the 'light in our eyes', the former consisting in the motion of something material.[63]

Hobbes followed the Democritean trend. His *Humane Nature*, one of the components of his planned trilogy the *Elements of Philosophy*, pleaded, with respect to 'the opinion that some may have, that ... Colour, Heat,

---

[60] Lucretius, *ONT* IV. 730 ff.; trans. Smith, p. 120.   [61] Galileo, *Opere*, 314; trans. Drake, p. 275.
[62] Ibid. 316; trans. Drake, p. 278.
[63] Descartes, *Treatise of Light* (*The World*), in *Oeuvres*, xi. 5–6; *Writings*, trans. and ed. Cottingham et al., i. 82.

Odour, Vertue, Vice, and the like, are otherwise in bodies, and (as they say) *inherent*', that they 'would suspend their judgement for the present, and expect a little, till it be found out by Ratiocination, whether these very Accidents are not also certain Motions, either of the Mind of the perceiver; or of the Bodies themselves which are perceived'.[64] In his *Leviathan*, he described sensible qualities as 'motions' in the bodies that press upon our sensory organs, whose appearances as color, sound, and savor, are 'Fancy, the same waking, that dreaming'.[65] Boyle thought as much, arguing in *The Origin of Forms and Qualities*, of 1666, that the primary corpuscles of matter possessed only magnitude, figure, and motion, and that the corpuscular 'textures' of different substances explained their chemical powers as well as their appearances, tastes, and odors. Locke, borrowing his convictions from Boyle or Gassendi, and his argumentation from Galileo or Descartes, advanced a version of Lucretius' 'purple-thread' argument implying the absence of secondary qualities in individual particles of matter: 'Take a grain of Wheat, divide it into two parts, each part has still *Solidity*, *Extension*, *Figure*, and *Mobility*; divide it again, and it retains still the same qualities; and so divide it on, till the parts become insensible, they must retain still each of them all those qualities'.[66]

One argument in favor of the corpuscularian hypothesis was both a version of the Lucretian argument that the sheer variety of colors that a single object could exhibit under different conditions was evidence for the relational nature of color and its absence in the fundamental elements of things, and an important extension of it: Boyle suggested that the sheer number of new powers and qualities exhibited by chemical substances when they were subjected to mechanical operations argued for the ontological dependency of forms as opposed to their autonomy as distinct principles complementary to matter.

[N]ature her self doth, sometimes otherwise and sometimes by Chance, produce so many things that have new Relations unto others: And Art, especially assisted by Chymistry, may ... make such an Innumerable Company of new Productions, that will each of Them have new operations either immediately upon our Sensories

[64] Thomas Hobbes, *Elements of Philosophy* (London: 1656), pt. II, ch. 8, p. 76.
[65] Thomas Hobbes, *Leviathan*, pt. I, ch. 1; ed. Richard Tuck (Cambridge: Cambridge University Press, 1996), 14.
[66] John Locke, *An Essay Concerning Human Understanding*, bk. II, ch. 8, §9; ed. P. H. Nidditch (Oxford: Clarendon, 1975), 135.

or upon other Bodies whose Changes we are able to perceive, that no man can know, but that the most Familiar Bodies may have Multitudes of Qualities, that he dreams not of.[67]

The importation of the perceptual argument into a new arena, chemical operations, where bodies effect changes in other bodies that affect their powers, and not only their appearances, gave it additional force. The truth of the atomic hypothesis appeared more consequential when chemical properties, not only colors, were understood to be variable and dependent on texture and motion, and this consequentiality was an important factor in its uptake, as I argue more fully below.

1.5. Mechanism

Still, neither the essential homogeneity of matter, nor its division into particles possessing primary properties alone, nor the great variety of effects producible by mixing, heating, and other physical manipulations implied that all operations in nature were mechanical. For that radical thesis to be sustained, it would have had to be shown that there was nothing in the cosmos except matter—no minds, spirits, forms, *archaei*, operative principles, or superadded or occult powers of the sort beloved by Renaissance chemists. This might be asserted, but it could not be demonstrated. Even if, as Descartes maintained, extension was the only essential property of matter, and shape, figure, and motion or rest the only attributes that could not be separated from it in thought, other inessential powers might well inhere in it, and immaterial principles might work in it. Even Boyle thought that some 'Juicy and Spiritous parts of... living Creatures must be fit to be turn'd into Prolifick Seeds, whereby they may have a power, by generating their like, to propagate their *Species*'.[68] These possibilities stimulated much controversy later in the century.

Initially corpuscles and their workings were simply added to the hodge-podge of theoretical entities and processes that Descartes, for one, longed to simplify and bring into order. Jean d'Espagnet's *Physica restaurata* (1623) dealt with celestial virtues, salt, sulfur, and mercury, considered as secondary

---

[67] Boyle, *Origin of Forms and Qualities*, in *Works*, ed. Hunter and Davies, v. 311.
[68] Ibid. v. 354.

mixtures of the four Aristotelian elements, the world soul in the sun, rational forms in vegetation—and atoms.[69] Atoms were mixed up in the chemical doctrines condemned by the faculty of theology of Paris in 1624 that fell well short of the explanatory demands of the mechanical philosophy.[70] Rosetti of Pisa in 1667 placed a heart at the earth's center whose dilation and contraction explained the tides, and proposed that the universe consists of atoms that attract or repel one another.[71]

Inclusive ontologies that acknowledged atoms and much else, and open-mindedness about their effects, persisted though the entire seventeenth century. Sennert recognized souls, 'Specifick Forms', and 'Occult Qualities', along with atoms. Occult qualities, he thought, divided into six categories, including the marvellous ones, allergies and antipathies, properties of inanimate and formerly living things, 'hidden qualities naturally bred in things', and 'malignant humours and Poysons'.[72] Only some properties were material, in Sennert's view; the remainder were spiritual. While the actions of poisons and diseases, including leprosy, fever, plague, and venereal disease, depended upon corpuscular effluvia, the ability of a dog to recognize its master and to track a beast by smell were not atomic phenomena. Amos Comenius, another polemical anti-Aristotelian, praised Democritus and took atoms to be original elements of the creation, but his system also embraced 'spirit', which formed plants and animals, and light. Kenelm Digby admitted corpuscles and expressed scorn for philosophers who had recourse to a *vis formatrix*, or to secret instinct and sympathies, or who flew to 'occult and imaginary qualities, to shroud their ignorance under inconceivable termes'.[73] He denied that plants were, strictly speaking, alive, insofar as they lacked a principle of motion. But in his account of growth and resurrection in his *Discourse Concerning the Vegetation of Plants* he referred to a 'balsamick Saline juyce',[74] to 'aereall and sulphureous parts of...rectifyed spirit', to an 'aethereall or wild spirit', 'aereall bodies' that

[69] Lynn Thorndyke, *A History of Magic and Experimental Science* (New York: Columbia University Press, 1931), vii. 388–9.

[70] Lynn Thorndyke, 'Censorship by the Sorbonne of Science and Superstition in the First Half of the Seventeenth Century, *Journal of the History of Ideas*, 16 (1955), 120; Thorndyke, *History of Magic*, vii. 124. Nicholas Hill's *Philosophia epicurea, democritiana, theophrastica* (Paris: 1601) is an example.

[71] Thorndyke, *History of Magic*, vii. 583.

[72] Sennert, *Epitome*, bk. XI, ch. 1; trans. Cole and Culpeper, pp. 438 ff.

[73] Kenelm Digby, *A Discourse Concerning the Vegetation of Plants* (London: 1661), 48.

[74] Ibid. 58.

subsisted when a plant was destroyed, to matter and form, and to 'a tincture extracted out of the whole plant... dryed up into a kind of Magistery, full of Fire and of Salt'.[75] More and Cudworth admitted atoms, but insisted that a spirit of nature or plastic natures worked on corporeal substance, shaping it and maintaining observed regularities. Newton suggested that '[o]ne use of matter is to admit menstruums easily into its pores in order to [generate] new mixtures by fermentation, putrefaction, corruption, and generation'.[76] Comets, he suspected, had their uses in the cosmic economy; they might be the source of the 'spirit which is the smallest but most subtle and most excellent part of our air, and which is required for the life of all things'.[77]

The corpuscularian philosophy was accordingly an enabling doctrine, not a restrictive one, and its appeal to experimentalists is partly to be explained by the suitability of what Bacon called latent process and latent configuration to explain effects that the Aristotelian categories of the hot and the cold, the moist and the dry and their derivatives could not handle. That wine promotes cheerfulness and opium sleep, that the sun melts wax and bleaches linen, that humans and animals take immediate likings and dislikings to one another, approaching and avoiding, and that rottenness and contagion can spread themselves through a barrel of apples or a village were familiar observations that could readily be interpreted in terms of the action of minute particles with certain powers that could penetrate seemingly dense substances and act upon them. The further powers of gems, stones, poisons, and medicines, perhaps mediated by atoms and their effluvia, perhaps not, were open to discussion and debate.

By contrast, the mechanical philosophy implied a narrowing of permissible explanations, through the exclusion of all virtues, forms, and powers except those that corresponded to dispositions of material particles. Descartes was the first of the moderns to insist that there was nothing in external objects except particles with different shapes, sizes, and motions, and that 'the general nature of material things' could be explained exclusively by reference to 'the necessary results of their mutual interaction

---

[75] Digby, *Vegetation of Plants*, 44.

[76] Isaac Newton, Cambridge MS 3970, quoted in J. E. McGuire and P. Rattansi, 'Newton and the Pipes of Pan', *Notes and Records of the Royal Society*, 21 (1966), 108–43.

[77] Newton, *Principia Mathematica*, bk. III, prop. 41; trans. I. B. Cohen and Anne Whitman as *Mathematical Principles of Natural Philosophy* (Berkeley, Calif.: University of California Press, 2001), 936.

in accordance with the laws of mechanics'.[78] He dispensed thereby not only with the purposive natures of Aristotle and the direct creative action of God, but with the intentional formative agents of Renaissance philosophy, including the stars, considered by Thomas Aquinas to educe some forms from matter, the *archaei* of the chemists, and entities like Kepler's snowflake-forming ludic spirit. His faith seemed to rest on the following support. The generation and ordinary operation of the living, feeling, self-moving animal body was regarded by Aristotle, ridiculing Empedocles and Democritus, as inexplicable by reference to mechanical principles. To Descartes it seemed that if he could knock down the argument for vital and sensitive principles, he would have defeated the main objection to a rather comprehensive materialism, and, with his account of the mechanical animal, he believed himself to have done so. According to Boyle, who followed him in this, natural phenomena could generally be referred to the action of 'such Corporeall Agents, as do not appear, to Work otherwise, then by vertue of the Motion, Size, Figure, and Contrivance of their own Parts, or ... by changing the *Texture*, or *Motion*, or some other *Mechanical Affection*, of the Body wrought upon'.[79]

1.6 Corpuscularianism and the experimental philosophy

Thomas Sprat, in his *History of the Royal Society*, reported on the exhibition by Christopher Wren of an ingenious apparatus for showing what happened when two hard balls of different sizes and speeds were made to collide with each other. Wren had declared such collision effects 'the Principles of *all Demonstrations* in *Natural Philosophy*', and Sprat agreed: 'Nor can it seem strange, that these *Elements* should be of such Universal Use; if we consider that *Generation*, *Corruption*, *Alteration*, and all the Vicissitudes of *Nature*, are nothing else, but the effects arising from the meeting of little Bodies, of differing Figures, Magnitudes, and Velocities'.[80]

---

[78] Descartes, *Principles*, pt. IV, §§ 198–200, in *Oeuvres*, viiiA. 322–4; *Writings*, trans. and ed. Cottingham et al., i. 284–6.

[79] Boyle, *Origin of Forms and Qualities*, in *Works*, ed. Hunter and Davis, v. 302.

[80] Thomas Sprat, *A History of the Royal Society* (London: 1667), 312.

The 'new philosophy' of the seventeenth century was not, however, founded upon new observations and experiments that decisively altered the a priori probability that tiny corpuscles and their aggregates, engaged in exclusively mechanical interactions, brought about the phenomena of the visible world. Rather, natural philosophers increasingly interpreted their observations in corpuscularian terms, sometimes referencing Epicurus and Lucretius, but often denying that they had been influenced by their texts. Why they found it necessary or desirable to turn back to ancient philosophy, to a single ancient philosophy at that, and to reissue its ontological proclamations is a question deserving exploration. Bacon had characterized all the philosophies of the past, including Democritus', as dreams and stage-settings. Why overthrow Aristotle and enslave oneself to another system? Why not, like the ferociously anti-scholastic reformer John Webster, insist that the views of all the naturalists be taken under advisement, so as to have as many alternatives to Aristotle as possible, and to miss nothing that might be found 'agreeable to truth and demonstration'.[81]

According to Shapin and Schaffer, in the early Royal Society '[m]atters of fact were the outcome of the process of having an empirical experience, warranting it to oneself, and assuring others that grounds for their belief were adequate. In that process a multiplication of the witnessing experience was fundamental'.[82] Atoms and their interactions were not witnessable, and an empirically minded philosopher of the seventeenth century, one might think, had every reason to remain uncommitted to any ontological position involving invisible entities.[83] The microscope seemed a promising instrument, capable of further development, and it had already afforded extraordinary and unforgettable glimpses into the microworld, but it did not reveal atoms, and suggested rather the infinite divisibility and unfathomable complexity of material objects.

If a commitment to the existence of subvisible corpuscles possessing only the primary affections of matter, and to the unique fruitfulness

---

[81] Webster demanded a rebalancing of the university curriculum, incorporating the Paracelsian school, Plato, Patrizi, Ficino, Descartes, Regius, Phocylides, Epicurus, Gassendi, Philolaus, Empedocles, Telesio, Campanella, 'and some besides; and that excellent *Magnetical Philosophy* found out by Doctor Gilbert' (*Academiarum Examen* (London, 1654), p. 106).

[82] Steven Shapin and Simon Schaffer, *Leviathan and the Air Pump* (Princeton, NJ: Princeton University Press, 1985), 25.

[83] Webster, *Academiarum Examen*, p. 106.

of the mechanical approach to explanation, was out of keeping with the experimentalist's rejection of texts and authorities, it was politically inconvenient as well. In the struggle for legitimation of the study of corporeal nature, Epicurus and Lucretius were unlikely allies. The fledgling Royal Society chartered by Charles II in 1660 stood under his protection but faced opposition from clergymen who regarded its commitments and activities with suspicion. The background hostility between the universities, which were staffed by men with theological qualifications, and the Society was fueled by immoderate and provocative language employed by both sides. The Society tried to avoid discussion of all contentious subjects, including politics and religion. Could not basic ontological questions, one might wonder, have been shelved in favor of a concentration on experimental practice?

To be sure, the corpusculo-mechanical philosophy was not treated, at least by English experimentalists, as a matter of fact. Its epistemological status was typically referred to as probable, and philosophers grappled with the problems posed by atomic invisibility and the perils of inference to the best explanation.[84] Descartes's confidence that not only his corpuscularian theory but his particular explanations of vision, magnetism, and meteors would perhaps 'be allowed into the class of absolute certainties, if people consider how they have been deduced in an unbroken chain from the first and simplest principles of human knowledge'[85] was considered unacceptably dogmatic by many of his readers. Yet the Royal Society's postures of uncertainty and indifference have to be interpreted in light of the fact that, even if some particular explanations were regarded as contentious, and others as merely probable, probabilists assigned no degree of probability whatsoever to rival ontologies, including Aristotle's hylomorphism, Fludd's occult philosophy, or Paracelsian hermeticism. Evidently, the chief apologists for experimentalism found the attractions of the corpusculo-mechanical philosophy sufficient to outweigh the disadvantages of its experimental indemonstrability. Even John Locke, who complained of

---

[84] On Epicurus' epistemology of science see esp. Elizabeth Asmis, *Epicurus's Scientific Method* (Ithaca: Cornell University Press, 1984).

[85] Descartes, *Principles*, pt. IV, prop. 206, in *Oeuvres*, viiiA. 328; *Writings*, trans. and ed. Cottingham et al., i. 290. '[A]ll the ... phenomena, or at least the general features of the universe and the earth which I have described, can hardly be intelligibly explained except in the way I have suggested' (*Oeuvres*, viiiA. 329; *Writings*, i. 291).

the obscurity of theoretical chemistry by contrast with practical medicine
and moral philosophy, deemed the mechanical philosophy of Boyle 'that
which is thought to go farthest in an intelligible Explication of the Qualities of Bodies', and confessed his 'fear' that 'the Weakness of humane
Understanding is scarce able to substitute another, which will afford us a
fuller and clearer discovery of the necessary Connexion, and *Co-existence*
of the Powers, which are to be observed united in several sorts of them'.[86]
Evidently, a Baconian fidelity to experiment and observation that did not
sink philosophical roots and remained aloof from all sects and systems was
neither necessary nor desirable for seventeenth-century naturalists.

The appeal of atomism is sometimes said to lie in a compelling analogy:
the proposal that the variety and splendor of the visible world are produced
from the arrangement of a limited number of primary forms, as different
names, sentences, and verses are produced from a small alphabet of meaningless linguistic elements, an analogy introduced by Lucretius in book I.[87]
Boyle pointed out that the principles of the mechanical philosophy were
few, primary, and simple, that it was unparalleled in its 'intelligibleness
or clearness'. The atomic theory was reassuringly tidy, unlike the chaotic
and idiosyncratic versions of invisible reality presented in the literature of
practical chemistry, and the Epicurean texts furnished an interpretation of
observed phenomena that was highly pictorial, if not a proper object for
multiple witnessing. As Meinel points out, 'the persuasive idea that truth
should be visible or could be thought of in a pictorial way, infiltrated
scholarly discourse and the very language of science'.[88]

Nature, one might object, is anything but simple; it is complex and
mysterious, and the simplicity of the atomic theory was precisely the feature
that had been held against it for many centuries. The gap between the
latent image and the manifest image was vast, despite the vivid analogies

---

[86] Locke, *Essay*, bk. IV, ch. 3, § 16, ed. Nidditch, p. 547.

[87] '[T]he same atoms constitute sky, sea, lands, rivers, and sun; the same compose crops, trees, and
animals; only they differ in their combinations and movements. Similarly, throughout these verses of
mine you see many letters common to many words, even though you must concede that the verses
and the words differ both in sense and in resonant sound. Such is the power letters derive from mere
alteration of order' (Lucretius, *ONT* I. 820 ff.; trans. Smith, p. 25).

[88] 'There is little doubt ... that [physical and chemical] phenomena were not adequate for definitely
deciding the question of matter ... Yet the frequent occurrence and repetition of these observations,
the persuasive idea that truth should be visible or could be thought of in a pictorial way, infiltrated
scholarly discourse and the very language of science. Atomism was an enticingly pictorial image of
reality' (Meinel, 'Early Seventeenth-century Atomism', p. 193).

and explanations of Lucretius. However, Boyle and his contemporaries were not measuring the atomic philosophy directly against the world, but against available alternative theories of nature, as these were represented in philosophical texts. The establishment of print culture, and the expansion of the universities that drew on it, introduced new intellectual standards and pedagogical requirements; the idiosyncratic language of the chemists did not qualify and that of the metaphysicans did not either. What had been intelligible and clear enough—if not perhaps ideally clear—in Aristotle's own time had become confused and confounded through its enthusiastic adoption, and through generations of interpretation and commentary. The shunning of the Epicurean philosophy had preserved it from development, leaving it in its original, and so most intelligible, form, as a philosophy designed for the instruction of eager novices.

In appealing to an old philosophy the revivers of Epicurus signaled their respect for the ancients and their distance from the radical fringe of prophets and Utopian reformers. While especially keen to read the book of nature, they could show that they did not reject all the books of men, that they valued the contributions of the past and saw their own work in light of it, questioning only the exaggerated status of Aristotle vis-à-vis other great philosophers of antiquity. The experimentalists could further capitalize on the old complaint that Aristotelian philosophy was pagan through and through, by suggesting that Epicureanism was in fact easier to marry to Christianity than Aristotelianism. By repudiating Aristotle and the old philo- sophy of forms and virtues as heathen and idolatrous, the experimentalists established (barely and controversially) their Christian credentials and settled in their own minds the permissibility of their activities. God was given a new role as master and commander of the mindless atoms. Like Gassendi, Boyle considered God's action necessary to 'dispose that *Chaos*, or confus'd heap of numberless Atoms into the World, to establish the universal and conspiring Harmonie of things; and especially to connect those Atoms into those various seminal Contextures, upon which most of the more abstruse Operations and elaborate Productions of Nature appear to depend'.[89]

Tying the experimental philosophy to a classical system gave it a sense and a dignity that distinguished the methodical investigation of the academies

---

[89] Boyle, 'A Requisite Digression Concerning Those that would Exclude the Deity from Inter- meddling with Matter', Essay IV of *The Usefulness of Natural Philosophy against Epicureans*, in *Works*, ed. Hunter and Davis, iii. 259.

from the casual curiosity of the Renaissance virtuoso. For Henry Percy, the atomic theory 'unfoldeth to our understanding the method general of all atomical combinations possible of generating of the same substance, as by semination, vegetation … etc. with all the accidents and qualities arising from those generated substances, as hardness, softness, heaviness, lightness, tenacity, frangibility, fusibility, ductibility, sound, colour, taste, smell, etc., the application of which doctrine satisfieth the mind in the generation and corruption'. The practice of alchemy without theoretical foundations was in percy's eyes 'a mere mechanical broiling without this philosophical project'.[90] This supra-mechanical aspect of his work was equally important for the aristocratic Boyle, who, without denying that his aim was utility, had to distinguish his own activity from that of the greedy alchemist, working for profit amongst stinks and smells.[91] The triviality into which the Royal Society's activity often descended in its early years, the target of so many satires, was countered by the exalted and elevated philosophical rhetoric of Boyle's defense of his 'Anaxagorean' system of the world. Boyle complained that the 'Corpuscular Philosophers' looked on the chemists as 'a company of meer and irrational Operators … whose Experiments … are useless to a Philosopher that aims at curing no disease but that of Ignorance', while the chemists looked upon the Philosophers as 'empty and extravagant Speculators'.[92] He saw the importance of integrating theory and practice in his writings, as well as mixing gentlemen and mechanics in his laboratory.

Most important, however, was the ability of the atomic philosophy to show how experimental endeavors were related to the created world. 'I know not', said Bacon, 'whether this inquiry I speak of concerning the first condition of seeds or atoms be not the most useful of all; as being the supreme rule of act and power, and the true moderator of hope and works'.[93] Bacon, Descartes, and Boyle were aware of the increasing power and the greater potential power of human beings to effect technological changes

[90] Henry Percy, 'Advice to his Son', quoted in R. H. Kargon, *Atomism in England from Hariot to Newton* (Oxford: Clarendon, 1966), 14.

[91] Yung Sik Kim points out that corpuscularians were 'ingenious persons', 'found amongst [men of] nobility and genius', whilst chemists were seen as 'illiterate operators' and 'whimsical fanaticks' ('Another Look at Robert Boyle's Acceptance of the Mechanical Philosophy', *Ambix*, 38 (1991), 1).

[92] Boyle, 'Some Specimens of an Attempt to Make Chemical Experiments Useful to Illustrate the Notions of the Corpuscular Philosophy', in *Works*, ed. Hunter and Davis, ii. 90.

[93] Bacon, 'Thoughts on the Nature of Things', in *Works*, x. 292.

in the world, to improve and to heal. They often tried to justify their curiosity-driven endeavors in humanitarian terms; the production of new drugs was a recurrent theme. '[B]y insight into Chymistry', said Boyle, 'one may be enabl'd to make some Meliorations (I speak not of Transmutations) of Mineral and Metalline Bodies, and many excellent Medicines for the Health of Men, besides divers other Preparations of good use in particular Trades, and in several Occurrences of Humane life.'[94] Their stripping matter of qualities and powers constituted the presupposition of their own efforts and their effects: What must created nature be like if we are able to and permitted to destroy and reconstruct it according to our preferences? God can have made no initial investment in the integrity of the various species, and in the powers of natural substances available for exploitation by human beings. His appreciation for his creation as good must concern its potentials and hidden features, so that he does not object to our intermeddlings. Boyle's observation that the corpuscularian philosophy best explains how it is that no man can deny that 'the most Familiar Bodies may have Multitudes of Qualities that he dreams not of' was in the nature of a promise of new helps. It was reassuring to know that black magic and the assistance of demons were not required for curing or transforming, only structural changes induced by mechanical operations.

The moderns did not share the relatively passive attitude of their ancient forebears who saw the atoms as existing irremediably outside the range of human perception and manipulation. Because the atoms are invisible and beyond control, the ancients thought, men can only resign themselves to relying on sense perception—the standard of truth—and try to enjoy life for as long as they are able, avoiding the known triggers of pain that are relatively easy to avoid. For the moderns, by contrast, atomism awarded a permission and provided for a locus of control that hexameral creationism and Aristotelian hylomorphism did not. By experimentation and reason the natural philosopher might succeed in inferring his way to the original alphabet and its combinatorial principles, and human art could emulate nature's own productions by mastering her mechanical methods of transformation. Because the chemist can only heat, mix, and evaporate substances, Boyle argued implicitly, he could not effect so many changes in qualities if these changes depended on more than magnitude, figure,

---

[94] Ibid. ii. 86.

and motion. The Boylean chemist did not show the reader that the world had to be understood in corpuscularian terms, but he invited the reader to interpret his work in these terms, and promised him great things on that basis. Matter can be *our* victim, the corpuscularians urged, and *our* slave alone; matter is not controlled by forms, *archaei*, operative ideas, and other agents that must be presumed to have their own agendas.

Over the following two centuries the material corpuscle gained in epistemological stature, as the range of effects for which it could be held responsible was compressed as well as enlarged. The invisible, active particle that had first been only an element of a rejected and refuted body of ancient doctrine and then a poetic fancy became, in Descartes's hands, an element of a fable, then a hypothetical entity whose existence was considered to have been established by rigorous deduction, then an entity whose existence was said to be probable in light of experiment and observation. The process of conversion from poetic fiction or philosophical dogma to solid scientific theory was well under way but hardly complete by 1700. The discourse of atoms retained much of its imaginative character, and the process of subjecting the material corpuscle to experimental discipline had barely begun.

To become a scientific entity, that is to erase the history of its connection with its philosophical past, the material corpuscle had first to be detached from anti-theology and ethical prescriptivity, second, it had to become an element in sober, restrained, truth-seeking discourse devoid of poetic embellishment; and third, it had to be subjected to observational and experimental regimens. The theory of corporeal effluvia as it developed in the late seventeenth century illustrates some early aspects of this process.

2

Corpuscular Effluvia: Between Imagination and Experiment

> First you must grant, that from all things you see
> Constant effluxes of the bodies be,
> Some doe the sight provoke, striking the eies,
> From other things perpetuall odors rise,
>
> .   .   .   .
>
> I have shewd, that of the flowing seeds
> Which things emitt, some cherish life, by some
> Mortallity and pale diseases come
> When many of these seeds spring up by chance
> And, towards the troubled heaven, in throngs advance
> The ayre is made infectious, thus that power
> Of dire contagions which mens lives devoure,
> Either like clowds and mists, bred in the skies,
> Falls on us from above, or elce doth rise
> From th earthe it selfe.
>
> (*De rerum natura*, vi. 979–82, 1146–55)

Seventeenth-century corpuscularians acknowledged many instances of apparent action at a distance, and they turned to aerial particles to account for a number of effects, not all of which were real. The superficial, vision-based approach of the school philosophers, their distinction between 'manifest' and 'occult' qualities, the latter of which were, by definition, inexplicable by philosophy, had prevented them, the moderns maintained, from recognizing as fully natural a range of phenomena. These the corpuscularian philosophy made intelligible by positing invisible, mobile, active particles capable of agitating within corporeal objects and also capable of traveling great distances—perhaps even from celestial objects to the earth.[1] The clockwork universe and the animal automaton—macromachines—should not be taken as paradigmatic images of the corpuscularian philosophy of the early moderns. Invisible airborne particles—corpuscular effluvia—and their workings were a pre-occupation of the mechanical philosophers.

2.1 Morbific and salutary particles

'Ever since the treatise of Fracastoro on contagion and contagious diseases appeared in 1546', says Thorndyke, 'with its explanation of infection as produced by the exhalation of seeds of diseases in the form of minute insensible particles, there had been an increasing and spreading tendency to resort to such effluvia as a physical and natural, even mechanical solution of what had before seemed magical and occult.'[2] Daniel Sennert regarded fascination as proceeding from effluvia.[3] J. B. van Helmont explained the action of the 'weapon-salve' on the distant wound the weapon had caused in the same manner, and Walter Charleton, who issued an edition of Helmont's treatise on the magnetic cure of wounds, explained sympathies and antipathies in terms of a flow of atoms between the impassioned parties. Charleton maintained that a boy could infect his sister residing miles away with smallpox or plague because of the sympathy between the two, which attracted the pestilential atoms.[4]

The modern view of the body as a micromechanical apparatus depended on an understanding of its interactions with nourishing and destructive particles, and much of the groundwork for this understanding was laid in the study of their possible role in respiration and in epidemical disease. Lucretius' theory of contagious illness as a form of aerial poisoning, expounded in the book VI of *On the Nature of Things*, was not unique to him in ancient times, but its presentation in his poem revived interest in the ambient air and its invisible constituents. As John Henry has pointed

---

[1] See further Keith Hutchison, 'What Happened to Occult Qualities in the Scientific Revolution?', *Isis*, 73 (1982), 233–53; repr. in Peter Dean (ed.), *The Scientific Enterprise in Early Modern Europe* (Chicago, Ill.: University of Chicago Press, 1996).

[2] Lynn Thorndyke, *A History of Magic and Experimental Science* (New York: Columbia University Press, 1931), viii. 174.

[3] Ibid. vii. 210–11.

[4] Walter Charleton, prolegomena to *A Ternary of Paradoxes* (London: 1650), e1^v.

out, it is often hard to distinguish between the actions of a vital, incorporeal aether and those of subtle corporeal particles.[5] Digby said that the natural action of fire was to 'stream out from its Center on all hands in a continued floud of extreamly rarifyed atomes'.[6] Henry Power hoped to see magnetic effluvia as well as atoms of light with the microscope.[7] Twenty years later Thomas Willis described 'Spirits' as 'Substances highly subtil, and Aetherial particles of a more Divine Breathing, which our Parent Nature hath hid in this Sublunary World, as it were the instruments of Life and Soul, of Motion and Sense, of every thing'.[8] English texts of the seventeenth century abounded with references to the aerial nitre, fermentative spirits, aethers, airs, vital, animal, and seminal principles, chemical essences, and invisible fire.

Lucretius had explained dreams, ghosts, plagues, and poisoning in atomistic terms. He depicted men and animals as living in an atmosphere of minute corpuscles capable of entering their bodies without it being registered, and as taking in invisible and unknown substances with their food and water.

[T]he earth contains elements of all kinds of things—many that are nutritious and beneficial to life, and many that are capable of causing disease and hastening the approach of death....Many noxious elements pass through the ears; many that are offensive and rough in contact penetrate the nostrils; and there are more than a few that should be avoided by the touch or shunned by the sight or that are bitter to the taste.[9]

He referred in this connection to trees that emitted poisonous vapours, soporific perfumes, intoxication by the fumes of charcoal, Avernal regions that killed the birds flying over them, and to the perils of mining. '[W]hen men are exploiting veins of silver and gold, exploring with their picks the hidden depths of the earth, what fumes Scaptensula exhales underground! What noxious exhalations issue from gold mines! What

---

[5] John Henry, 'Occult Qualities and the Experimental Philosophy', *History of Science*, 24 (1986), 335–81.

[6] Kenelm Digby, *A Discourse Concerning the Vegetation of Plants* (London: 1661), 12.

[7] Henry Power, preface to *Experimental Philosophy, in Three Books* (London: 1664).

[8] Thomas Willis, *The Remaining Medical Works* (London: 1681), 3, quoted in Antonio Clericuzio, 'Carneades and the Chemists', in Michael Hunter (ed.), *Robert Boyle Reconsidered* (Cambridge: Cambridge University Press, 1994), 90.

[9] T. C. Lucretius, *On the Nature of Things* (*ONT*), VI 770 ff; trans. Martin Ferguson Smith (Indianapolis, Ind.: Hackett, 2001), 198–9.

faces, what complexions they give the workers!...All these vapours...are emitted by the earth, which exhales them into the open air, into the clear spaces of the sky'.[10]

Boyle was much concerned with these corpuscular vapours. Though he insisted that all the phenomena of corporeal nature were explicable by reference to corpuscles possessing only magnitude, figure, and motion, he had little idea how to construct such explanatory accounts, and contented himself with conjectures. His defense of the mechanical philosophy consisted of historical observations and accounts of experiments which referred surprising or interesting effects to the agency of different types of corpuscles that he credited with highly specific modes of action.[11] He surmised that seeds, including mineral seeds and seeds of epidemic diseases, were widely dispersed over and under the surface of the earth,[12] and he believed that minute bodies of terrestrial and celestial origin had profound toxic and beneficial effects on human and animal physiology.

While he never relinquished his philosophical commitment to the existence of a common matter underlying all substances, Boyle showed more concern in his experimental papers with composite, speciated particles.[13] What Boyle referred to as a 'sulphureous particle' or an 'arsenical particle' was, following Gassendi, not an indivisible unit, but a secondary 'molecule', composed of some arrangement of genuinely primary particles. Substances like earth, water, and salt were made up of coalitions or clusters of primitive particles that adhered to one another closely.[14] These composites could in principle be decomposed into true atoms, so that by 'an orderly series of alterations...almost of any thing may at length be made any thing', but Boyle realized that it would be very difficult in practice, if not impossible, to break down or dissolve some chemical substances.[15] Solid bodies could, however, vaporize, and Boyle adduced the results of experiments to show

[10] Lucretius, *ONT* VI. 806 ff.; trans. Smith, p. 199–200.

[11] See Antonio Clericuzio, 'A Redefinition of Boyle's Chemistry and Corpuscular Philosophy', *Annals of Science*, 47 (1990), 584–5.

[12] Boyle's two treatises on 'Seminal principles' and 'Seeds of Plants, Animals, &c.' were unfortunately missing when his manuscripts were collected.

[13] Clericuzio, 'A Redefinition', pp. 580 ff.

[14] Robert Boyle, *Origin of Forms and Qualities*, in *Works*, ed. Michael Hunter and Edward B. Davis (London: Pickering and Chatto, 2000), v. 32

[15] Clericuzio, 'A Redefinition', p. 582.

that even 'Fix't and solid Bodies, such as metals are, may by art be reduc'd into such minute Corpuscles, that, without loosing their nature and all their Properties, they may become parts of Fumes, or perhaps of invisible Vapours, or even of Flame itself'.[16]

Effluviums, Boyle said, 'at their first parting from the Bodies, whence they take wing... may retain as much of the nature of those Bodies, as we have ascribed to them'.[17] Effluvia thus corresponded to natural kinds, and Boyle emphasized their determinate and specific nature, criticizing Aristotle for having crudely distinguished only between vapours and exhalations. It is as though, he said, one were to divide all animals into the horned and the two-footed, ignoring the fact that there are also four-footed beasts and fishes, and many divisions and subdivisions even within those two: sea monsters, rhinoceroses, deer, elk, unicorns, eagles, nightingales, and so on. Were our sensories 'sufficiently subtile and tender', he observed, they might perceive differences in the shape, motion, and colour of effluvia as marked as between 'differing sorts of Birds... as Hawks, and Partridges, and Sparrows, and Swallows'.[18] He explained how butter could take on a rank taste when cows fed on certain weeds, noting how 'vegetable corpuscles may by association, pass through divers disguises, without loosing their Nature; especially considering, that the essential Attributes of such Corpuscles may remain undestroyed'.[19]

In the early 1670s Boyle began to write tracts on subterranean, aerial, and celestial effluvia, beginning with 'Cosmicall Suspicions' (1671), followed by 'Essays of the Strange Subtilty, Great Efficacy, and Determinate Nature of Effluviums' (1673), and 'Some additional Suspicions especially relevant to the Hidden Qualities of the Air' (1674). Plants and animals, as well as minerals and gems, Boyle thought, emit streams of invisible particles, and curative stones and amulets held next to the skin work by the insinuation of minute corpuscles.[20] He gave many examples of their powerful effects on life and health. Mercury can be absorbed into the bones of venereal patients.[21] It is lethal to worms in water not because of some irradiation, but by some kind of corporeal action.[22] People can be killed in their sleep by

---

[16] Boyle, 'Insalubrity and Salubrity of the Air', in *Works*, ed. Hunter and Davis, x. 346.
[17] Boyle, 'Of the Determinate Nature of Effluviums', in *Works*, vii. 285.   [18] Ibid. 281.
[19] Boyle, 'Possibility of the Resurrection', in *Works*, viii. 306.
[20] Boyle, 'Of the Great Efficacy of Effluviums', in *Works*, vii. 271.   [21] Ibid. 260.
[22] Boyle, 'Of the Strange Subtilty of Effluviums', in *Works*, vii. 247.

the fumes of a charcoal fire in a newly plastered room,[23] and Boyle repeated Lucretius' story of the lakes that poison birds as they fly overhead.[24] When a partridge or a hare walks on the ground, 'effluxions' transpire from its feet that the hounds can detect.[25] Around and above us the atmosphere 'abounds with vapours and exhalations', some, as Newton supposed, from extraterrestrial sources.

It seems not absurd to me to suspect, that the Subtil, but Corporeal, Emanations [of the sun, planets, and stars] may ... reach to our Air, and mingle with those of our globe in that great receptacle or rendezvous of Celestial and Terrestrial Effluviums, the *Atmosphere*.[26]

Boyle surmised that these emanations might have a nature 'quite different from those we take notice of here about us', and might operate 'after a very different and peculiar manner'.[27] The earth emits from its bowels both ordinary and extraordinary exhalations, and these had a profound effect, he thought, on human health. Saline, sulphureous, arsenical, and antimonial particles may 'impregnate the Air ... in the way requisite to produce this or that determinate Disease'.[28] Alternatively, 'fossiles' might be 'enriched with medicinal and fugitive salts and spirits' that were beneficial. Friendly particles might work 'either by promoting *transpiration* ... or by hindering the production, or checking the Activity, of Morbifick ferments; or by mortifying and disabling some noxious Particles, that would otherwise infest the Air'.[29] Health, as well as disease, might be the result of corpuscles 'sent up from the soil', with the power to multiply as well as to disseminate themselves. Tin miners, who apparently do not suffer the ghastly diseases of other miners, appeared to benefit from the activity of salubrious particles.[30]

2.2 The experimental capture of the aerial corpuscle

Air, Boyle surmised, was not a 'Simple and Elementary Body, but a confus'd Aggregate of Effluviums from such differing Bodies, that ... perhaps there is scarce a more heterogeneous Body in the world'.[31] It had, he thought,

23 Boyle, 'Of the Strange Subtilty of Effluviums', in *Works*, vii 259.
24 Boyle, 'Insalubrity and Salubrity of the Air', in *Works*, x. 311.
25 Boyle, 'Of the Strange Subtilty of Effluviums', in *Works*, vii. 250.
26 Boyle, 'Suspicions about some Hidden Qualities of the Air', in *Works*, viii. 122.   27 Ibid.
28 Boyle, 'Insalubrity and Salubrity of the Air', in *Works*, x. 313.   29 Ibid. 308.   30 Ibid.
31 Boyle, 'Suspicions about some Hidden Qualities of the Air', in *Works*, viii. 121.

'known uses in Respiration, Sayling, Pneumatical Engines &c.' that might well deserve the reader's curiosity.[32] His *New Experiments Physico-Mechanicall Touching the Spring of the Air, and its Effects* published in 1660 summarized a series of experiments with the newly invented air pump intended to clear up a long-standing question: What was the function of breathing in animals? Was it to force the blood around the body? Or to cool it through the expulsion of heat particles, or to purify it by expelling some form of excrement? Or was the function of breathing nutritional?[33] It was debated whether the death of animals and the extinction of flames in closed vessels was caused by the loss of mechanical spring in the exhausted air, by their suffocation in exhaust vapours, or by starvation from a lack of a necessary nutrient.

One possibility that initially occurred to Boyle was that the fall in air pressure in the exhausted receiver of the air pump enabled ethereal matter to penetrate the pores of the glass to take its place, leading to an expansion in its blood that killed the animal within. But Boyle was less drawn to mechanical theories of breathing than to poisoning and nourishment theories, and he tended to the view that the air supplied a *pablum vitae*. 'There is some use of the Air', he mused, 'which we do not yet so well understand, that makes it so continually needful to the Life of Animals. *Paracelsus* indeed tells us, *That as the Stomack concocts Meat, and makes part of it useful to the Body, rejecting the other part; so the Lungs consume part of the Air and proscribe the rest....* [I]t seems we may suppose, that there is in the Air a little vital Quintessence ... which serves to the refreshment and restauration of our vital Spirits.'[34]

While pondering this mystery, Boyle grew interested in saltpeter or niter. The awarding of commercial patents for novel methods of manufacturing saltpeter had fostered investigation into this curious and potentially lucrative substance from the mid-1640s.[35] Niter was fascinating because of its relationship to growth, preservation, and heat. Dung, sprinkled with

---

[32] Boyle, 'A Physico-chemical Essay ... touching the Differing Parts and Redintegration of Salt-petre', in *Works*, ii. 107.

[33] See McKie's survey 'Fire and the Flamma Vitalis: Boyle, Hooke, and Mayow', in E. A. Underwood (ed.), *Science, Medicine, and History* (Oxford: Oxford University Press, 1953), and Robert Frank, *Harvey and the Oxford Physiologists* (Berkeley/Los Angeles, Calif.: University of California Press, 1980), 100 ff.

[34] Boyle, *New Experiments*, in *Works*, i. 287. Paracelsus had referred to 'an astral balsam, an invisible fire, an included air, and a tingeing spirit of salt' as the principle of life.

[35] Henry Guerlac, 'The Poets' Nitre, Studies in the Chemistry of John Mayow', *Isis*, 45 (1954), 248.

urine and left in the fields irradiated by the sun, turns to niter, which is a powerful fertilizer able to promote rapid growth in plants. Niter preserves meat, turning it bright red. As a component of gunpowder it seems to confer flammability. In his *Discourse on the Vegetation of Plants* read to the Royal Society in 1661, Kenelm Digby described a nitrous salt that 'Foecundateth the Aire and… gave cause to the Cosmopolite to say, there is in the Aire a hidden food of life'. This salt was 'the food of the Lungs, and the nourishment of the Spirits'. It was a 'Universal Spirit' that was of the same nature, Digby surmised, as gold.

Boyle posited that saltpeter was composed of two types of corpuscle, one of which was acidic and volatile, the other of which was alkaline and fixed,[36] and he guessed, like Digby, that there was some connection between the formation of niter crystals and the life- and flame-supporting properties of air. But the relationship between niter, air, life, and flame was anything but clear. Air did not seem to be absolutely necessary for the production and conservation of flame, for Boyle found that a mixture of gunpowder, charcoal, sulfur and saltpeter would burn underwater. He was also puzzled by the observation that a bird continued to live for a time in a closed vessel in which a candle had gone out. Was this because the candle and the bird needed different nourishment, or because the 'more temperate flame' of the bird needed less? Boyle had, understandably, no idea.

By 1668 Boyle's sometime assistant John Mayow had amassed good evidence that the function of breathing was not macromechanical but micromechanical, that breathing extracted something from the air that was taken up by the 'pores' of the lungs, as these had been recently revealed by the microscope, and, further, that the source of the warmth of the body was the blood, not the heart. Animal warmth was, he argued, the result of mechanical interaction between blood particles and particles of what he called 'nitro-aerial spirit'.

The opening of Mayow's treatise on saltpeter, the first essay of his *Tractatus quinque* published in 1674, stated that 'the surrounding air, which escapes our eyes through its fineness, which appears to be like empty space, contains a substance with a connection to saltpetre. It is a spirit which is connected with the phenomenon of life, with burning, and with

---

[36] Frank, *Oxford Physiologists*, p. 124. See also Clericuzio, 'A Redefinition', p. 576.

fermentation'.[37] Contrary to Boyle's negative results, Mayow found that something in the air is used up by respiration and burning alike: water rises in a closed vessel in which a candle or animal is allowed to extinguish itself.[38] He noted that exhausted air that has lost some of its elasticity still has a mechanical effect on the lungs, though it will not support life. He observed that the fetus in the womb does not need to breathe, but that once it has drawn breath it can no longer survive on maternal blood. Impressed by the comparable redness of spirit-saturated blood and the redness of flame, Mayow drew on Richard Lower's finding that artificially insufflated blood turns from dark to bright and that fresh arterial blood froths in a vacuum while darker venous blood does not. These observations indicated to him that breathing served to introduce air, a combination of 'nitro-aerial' particles, which he described as 'very subtle, movable, ethereal particles of a fiery nature', with the stiff, interlaced twiglike particles with which it was normally bound, into the blood, causing a disposition to froth and brightening its colour. In the blood, he thought, nitro-aerial particles were dislodged by friction against the blood particles, and rubbed up against particles of the body's sulfur, producing warmth and a vital fermentation. In a candle flame, nitro-aerial particles were dislodged by heated sulfur and given off as heat or light.[39]

These were remarkable speculations, and Mayow's experimental designs won the admiration of later commentators, but Boyle and Henry Oldenburg, the secretary of the Royal Society, refused to support them. The 1668 review of the first edition of Mayow's De respiratione and the 1674 review of his Tractatus quinque published in Philosophical Transactions were not unfavorable. Mayow's assertion that the sun was a 'vast Chaos of nitro-aerial corpuscles, wheeled about by a perpetual and very swift rotation' did not arouse negative comment.[40] Nor did his notion that the macrocosm takes in nitro-aerial spirit, and exercises a kind of respiration, and that air is its blood.[41] Even his proposal that the sensitive soul is 'a more divine aura, endow'd with sense from its first creation, and co-extended to the whole world; a small portion of which being contain'd

---

[37] John Mayow, Untersuchungen über den Salpeter und den salpetrigen Luftgeist, das Brennen und das Athmen, trans. and ed. F. G. Donnan (Leipzig: Engelmann, 1901).

[38] John Mayow, Tractatus quinque, in Medico-Physico Works (Oxford: Ashmolean Museum, 1926), 36.

[39] Hall, History of General Physiology, i. 329–30.

[40] Anon., 'An Accompt of Two Books', Philosophical Transactions, 9 (1674), 106.   [41] Ibid.

in a duly disposed subject exerts such functions, as we see and admire in the bodies of Animals' was reported without any tinge of skepticism.[42] The second review noted, however, a conflict between Mayow's theory of fire and that of the 'Noble R. Boyle's' as outlined in his *Excellency and Grounds of the Mechanical Hypothesis* of 1674. Mayow was, according to the reviewer,

rejecting the opinion of those, that will have Fire producible by the subtile and briskly mov'd parts of *any* matter, and declaring on this occasion his dissent from those Philosophers, that deduce all Effects of Nature from the same Uniform Matter, and the various Modifications thereof, which he thinks inconsistent with the *Phaenomena* of Fire, not at all, *in his opinion*, producible but by a certain determinat kind of particles, such as he calls Nitro-aerial. This he endeavors to prove by divers Experiments.[43]

Where Boyle maintained that the diversity of substances could arise only from complex structure, common matter 'being in its own nature but one' and separated into corpuscles, and that the unitary nature of matter made general transmutation possible, Mayow argued for diversity and fixity on the most basic level: 'I believe that the particles of matter are distinguished from one another in their form and thickness in such a way that no force of nature can transform one into another'.[44] He sought what he called a 'middle way' between that of the peripatetics, who, he said, called in a new being to explain every type of phenomenon, and the neoterics, who referred all phenomena to the 'form, movement and rest of one type of matter'.[45] Although Boyle was sympathetic to the nutritive account of respiration, Mayow's insistence that fire was composed of or produced by a special kind of particle evidently discredited him in the eyes of Boyle and Oldenburg, and his skepticism over the possibility of transmutation offended them.[46] While Boyle recognized that the 'primary and minute Concretions' have particles 'so minute and strongly coherent,

---

[42] Anon., 'An Accompt of Two Books', 112.   [43] Ibid. 103.   [44] Mayow, *Salpeter*, p. 13.
[45] Ibid.

[46] Oldenburg wrote to Boyle, 'I heare some very Learn'd and knowing men speake very slightly of yᶜ Quinque Tractatus of J.M.; and a particular friend of yrs and mine told me yesterday, yᵗ, as farr as he had read him, he would shew to any impartiall and considering man more errors than one in every page' (Henry Oldenburg, letter of 10 July 1674, in *The Correspondence of Henry Oldenburg*, trans. and ed. A. Rupert Hall and Marie Boas Hall (Madison, Wisc.: University of Wisconsin Press, 1965–83), xi. 50 (no. 2514)).

that Nature of her self does scarce ever tear them asunder',[47] faith in the possibility of transmutation was still central to the experimental program, which rationalized its successes and excused its shortcomings in terms of the ambition to effect unlimited changes in corporeal nature.

Thomas Kuhn properly remarks that 'a retrospective glance at the history of seventeenth and early eighteenth century chemistry suggests that the true progenitors of Lavoisier's chemical revolution were necessarily among Boyle's opponents'.[48] The fate of Mayow's experimental program bears out this judgement admirably. His premature death put an end to what might have been an enlightening program of pure research, and further investigation into the puzzling relationship between breathing, the circulation of the blood, and animal heat stalled until the late eighteenth century.[49] The *pablum vitae* was, of course, oxygen, responsible for a seemingly unrelated range of effects from rusting and putrefaction to ruddiness and vitality.

Oliver Ellis, in his *History of Fire and Flame*, describes how the atmosphere appeared to our ancestors. It was 'the great receptacle of things that disappeared from sight'. The air retained the species of everything—it was a 'sea of things invisible',[50] replete with vapours, dews, powders, dusts, rays, tinctures, and influences, and forms.[51] For the corpuscularian Digby, the aerial niter furnished the essence of gold; it induced wonderful transformations; it was a gift of heaven, belonging to the realm of wonders; and for Mayow as well, niter was bound up with exotic speculations concerning the sun and cosmic principles of vitality. Until the seventeenth century these invisible inhabitants of the air could only be imagined. Subsequently some of them—but only some—would make the transition into scientific ontology, entering the space of practice with the help of new observational and experimental apparatus. The aerial effluvia posited by Lucretius bound together the mechanical philosophy of the second half of the seventeenth century with emerging experimental practice.

[47] Boyle, *Excellency and Grounds of the Corpuscular or Mechanical Philosophy*, in *Works*, ed. Hunter and Davies, viii. 13.
[48] Thomas Kuhn, 'Robert Boyle and Structural Chemistry', *Isis*, 43 (1952); repr. in Peter Dear (ed.), *The Scientific Enterprise*, 236.
[49] Frank, *Oxford Physiologists*, p. 282.
[50] Oliver Ellis, *The History of Fire and Flame* (London: Simpkin Marshall, 1932), p. 191.
[51] Ibid. 228.

3

Order and Disorder

This universe had its originall
From free encounters of the seeds, who met
Oft with vaine stroakes, did at the length begett,
By casuall occursions, this great frame,
And from one right conjunction came
Both heaven, earth, sea and every animall;
We must confesse, the matter then may fall
Elce where into the like conjunctures, and frame there
Such worlds as this, enclosd with ambient ayre

.   .   .   .

Nature, if this you rightly understand,
Will thus appeare free from the proud command
Of soveraigne power, who of her owne accord
Doth all things act, subjected to no lord.

(*De rerum natura*, ii. 1083−91, 1118−21)

For Aristotle, the world had always existed, and the task of the scientist was not to explain its origins, as his myth-minded predecessors had tried to do, but to inventory its contents and explain the modes of operation characterizing different kinds of entity. To that end, he distinguished carefully between formal, final, efficient, and material causes, and between phenomena that came about merely by chance, phenomena brought about by the craft and intelligence-simulating agency of nature, and phenomena caused by intelligent movers, such as the revolutions of the heavens and purposive human actions.

While the god of Aristotle was impersonal, it was not without agency. Something animate and divine, by bringing about the movement of the celestial spheres, was responsible for a cascade of further events. The regular motion of the heavenly bodies caused, he thought, the regular, but still slightly unpredictable, succession of the seasons; the seasons brought about the still more unpredictable weather; and the weather influenced the even less predictable growth of crops and increase of flocks. Some events occurred by chance, like rain in summer, and others were necessary, like rain in winter, but chance and necessity were the exceptions in the living realm; that is, in most of nature. Some biological processes, notably the assembly of the embryonic body, which Aristotle compared to the motion of a puppet, were mechanically inevitable.[1] But he dismissed as absurd Empedocles' account of the original formation of animal bodies through some accidental 'right conjunction', his proposal that those 'organized spontaneously in a fitting way' survived while their unfit counterparts, including ox-faced men, perished. 'It is impossible', said Aristotle, 'that this should be the true view. For teeth and all other natural things either invariably or for the most part come about in a given way; but of not one of the results of chance or spontaneity is this true.'[2]

Despite the plausibility of Epicurus' arguments for the existence of atoms and their lack of perceptual qualities, the system of nature the atomists propounded appeared in many respects deeply implausible in comparison with Aristotle's. It was ontologically as parsimonious as a theory could be; it recognized only body and void as principles, and atomic motion and 'chance' as causes and reasons. Atomism appeared especially inadequate where Aristotle's hylomorphic theory looked strong; that is to say, with respect to the issues of cohesion, integrity, individuation, growth, development, and regularity.

If the atomic theory is true, why isn't the universe simply a confused, structureless chaos of tiny particles, macroscopically analogous to the minute particles in '*solis radiis turbare videntur*' which, Lucretius said, present an image of the 'perpetual restless movement... in the vast void?'.[3] Why do the atoms of ordinary material objects stick together? 'By what pact, by

---

[1] 'As, then, in these automatic puppets, the external force moves the parts in a certain sense (not by touching any part at the moment, but by having touched one previously), in like manner also that from which the semen comes, or in other words that which made the semen, sets up the movement in the embryo and makes the parts of it by having first touched something though not continuing to touch it' (Aristotle, *Generation of Animals*, bk. II, ch. 1, 734[b]; in *Complete Works*, ed. Jonathan Barnes (Princeton, NJ: Princeton University Press, 1984), i. 1140).

[2] Aristotle, *Physics*, bk. II, ch. 8, 198[b]; in *Complete Works*, ed. Barnes, i. 339.

[3] T. C. Lucretius, *On the Nature of Things* (*ONT*), II. 121–2; trans. Martin Ferguson Smith (Indianapolis, Ind.: Hackett, 2001), 38.

what agreement do they come together among themselves that something may be formed of them?', Lactantius had asked. 'If they lack sense, they are not able to come together with such order, for it is not possible for anything but reason to bring about anything rational.'[4] How can a collection of similar particles that vary as ears of corn or seashells do project into distinct species and substances like lemons, gold, or ink, and why do the various species of animal breed true? What accounts for the orderly motions of the stars and planets, and the recurrence of the seasons? To these questions, which he had anticipated, Lucretius had some answers, but they were not good ones.

The early modern corpuscularians were faced with an explanatory challenge and with an opportunity as well. The challenge was to show that the mechanical philosophy could perform as well as Aristotelianism when it came to explaining the phenomena of the world, and the opportunity involved the reintroduction of deontological principles. As the mind and soul govern the whole body, Lactantius had asserted, 'so does God govern the world. Nor is it likely, indeed, that lesser and lowly things have power of control and that greater and supreme things do not'.[5] The thesis that order descends from the superior to the inferior could be happily married, they discovered, to the Epicurean thesis that order is a feature of the manifest image grounded in the incessant yet planless activities of tiny unintelligent particles. With the help of the concept of a law of nature, it was possible to embrace the corpuscularian philosophy and yet deny Lucretius' claim that the universe is maintained without the aid of gods.

The representation of nature as a system of bodies governed by divinely instituted laws of nature was facilitated by seventeenth-century discoveries in the mathematical sciences, astronomy, optics, mechanics, and dynamics. Within only a hundred or so years, Kepler's three rules of planetary motion, Galileo's law of falling bodies, Descartes's laws of motion and his rules of collision, emended by Huygens and Wallis, Snell's law of optics, Boyle's law of gases, and Newton's inverse-square law made their debuts. These discoveries did not, however, generate what might be called the nomological image of nature. Rather, they were fitted into a much older

---

[4] Lactantius, *The Divine Institutes*, bk. III, ch. 17, trans. Sister Mary Francis McDonald OP (Washington, DC: Catholic University of America Press, 1965), 211.

[5] Lactantius, *Wrath of God*, in *Minor Works*, trans. Sister Mary Francis McDonald OP (Washington, DC: Catholic University of America Press, 1965), 83–4.

qualitative discourse, ubiquitous in philosophy and theology, of divine regulation.

3.1 Order and regularity in the Epicurean cosmos

Later Epicureanism is deterministic and form-preserving in its overall intention. Lucretius frequently referred to nature under the description '*certa*', best interpreted as 'definite'—e.g. *certa ratio, certa semina, certa genetrix, certum tempus*, etc.[6] The atomists indicated that there were pathways their primordial particles would follow, were they unimpeded, but they recognized that they usually met with obstructions and barriers that deflected them. Lucretius followed his predecessor in maintaining that the atoms move, when unobstructed, with equal speed, regardless of weight and size. He pointed out against Aristotle that heavier objects do not fall faster than lighter objects in a void—'The heavier will therefore never be able to fall on the lighter from above'[7]—though he allowed that the resistance of air and water slows down the lighter ones. Yet, while the manifest order supervenes on the motions of the atoms, there is no latent order of the sort posited later by Descartes and his followers, only 'secret and unseen motions'.

Comparing the universe to a collection of storm-tossed debris, Lucretius acknowledged that if there were only a limited number of atoms, nothing would be able to be created or grow, and the world would be a chaos:

[B]y what force and in what way will [the right atoms] meet and combine in this mighty ocean of matter? ... It is my opinion that they have no means of achieving union. Compare what happens when many mighty vessels have been wrecked: transoms, ribs, yardarms, prows, masts, and buoyant oars are tossed this way and that by the vast sea ... Similarly you may be sure that, once you lay down that the elements of a certain class are limited in number, they will be scattered and tossed this way and that by contrary tides of matter throughout all time.[8]

Pointing out that 'everyday experience plainly teaches us' that objects come into being and grow, he concluded simply that 'there is an abundant supply of material for everything', an infinite number of atoms of every type, so that the requisites are always nearby.

---

[6] A. A. Long, 'Chance and Natural Law in Epicureanism', *Phronesis*, 22 (1977), 63–88.
[7] Lucretius, *ONT* II. 240–1 f; trans. Smith, p. 41.   [8] Ibid. II. 540 ff., trans. Smith, p. 49.

The atomists avoided the topic of celestial motions, the best and most mysterious example of natural order. Epicurus' astronomy was less impressive than his meteorology. He insisted that 'in the sky revolutions, solstices, eclipses, risings and settings and the like, take place without the ministration or command, either now or in the future, of any being who at the same time enjoys perfect bliss along with immortality',[9] but he had little to say about the pathways of celestial objects in the night sky, and, as noted earlier, he justified his neglect by saying that so long as one believed celestial occurrences to be natural rather than supernatural, achieving a precise understanding of them was unimportant. He was on more comfortable ground with thunder, lightning, rain, hail, and snow, conjuring up ingenious mechanisms involving friction, pressure, tearing, compression, collision, and congelation to explain them. Lucretius in turn provided explanations for physical, psychological, and even historical phenomena, encompassing color vision, the weather, epidemics, the formation of government and the social contract, dreams, love, and death, as well as describing the origins of our world and of all the other worlds in the cosmos. But he too showed no interest in mathematical astronomy.

At the same time, Lucretius acknowledged the problems of stability and cohesion that greatly preoccupied his seventeenth-century successors. Some of his solutions to them were crudely mechanical. Combinations of a few atoms provide a framework on which other atoms can hang, like objects caught in a net, or trapped in a filter, or swept up in a whirlpool, or stuck on like snow to a snowball. Entities so formed cohere, at least for a while. Often, though, Lucretius did little more than assure his readers that the universe is a fairly dependable place. 'Things that have always been produced will continue to be produced under the same conditions, and each will exist, grow, and prosper in its strength, insofar as it is permitted by the ordinances of nature [per foedera naturae]'.[10] Animals grow from seeds that are initially differentiated and that can give rise only to particular types of beings that conform to the nature, habits, mode of life, and movements of their parents, and Lucretius assured his readers that 'so far from any species being susceptible of variation, each is so constant that from generation to

---

[9] Epicurus, letter to Herodotus, in Diogenes Laertius, *Lives of the Eminent Philosophers*, X. 76–7; trans. R. D. Hicks (Cambridge, Mass.: Harvard University Press, 1925), ii. 607.

[10] Lucretius, *ONT* II. 300 ff; trans. Smith, p. 43.

generation all the variegated birds display on their bodies the markings of their kind'.[11] In this context he referred several times to 'laws':

[E]verything is created from definite seeds and a definite parent and is able to preserve its specific character as it grows. It is evident that this must happen according to a fixed law [*certa ratione*].... Do not imagine that animals alone are governed by these laws [*legibus*]; all things are subject to the same restriction.[12]

A general feature of the Lucretian universe is that all atomic composites are limited, not only in the duration of their existence, but also in their qualities and powers. Lucretius ascribed this insight to Epicurus, who taught that 'each thing has its scope restricted and its deep-implanted boundary stone'.[13] We can assume that 'in the case of each species, a fixed limit of growth and tenure of life has been established, and... the powers of each have been defined by solemn decree in accordance with the ordinances of nature'.[14] The notion of the *foedera naturae* reappears in other contexts where stabilization is discussed. '[T]he things that even now shoot in profusion from the earth—the various kinds of grasses and crops and exuberant trees—cannot, despite their abundance, be created intermixed... all preserve their distinguishing characteristics in conformity with an immutable law of nature [*foedere naturae certo*].'[15]

Lucretius' poetic imagination was captured, however, by variety and the transitory; every object that comes into existence is temporary, and, from the perspective of eternity, short-lived, and Epicurus had seen little need to insist on the uniformity of nature. Other worlds may be dissimilar to ours, he thought, with different plants and animals.[16] The ancient atomists touched only lightly on the theme of natural order, both because they rejected claims for a creative intelligence, and because they wanted to allow for natural and human spontaneity and variety. They had reason to be somewhat vague about the motion of individual atoms, and both Epicurus and Lucretius ascribed a swerve to the atoms, not only to 'initiate movement that can annul the decrees of destiny and prevent the existence of an endless chain of causation' and to explain the 'free will possessed by creatures all over the earth',[17] but also lest the atoms' overall

---

[11] Ibid. I. 586 ff.; trans. Smith, p. 18.   [12] Ibid. II. 707 ff.; trans. Smith, p. 53.
[13] Ibid. I. 76–7; trans. Smith, p. 5.   [14] Ibid. I. 584 ff.; trans. Smith, p. 18.
[15] Ibid. V. 916 ff; trans. Smith, p. 161.
[16] Epicurus, letter to Herodotus, in Diogenes Laertius, *Lives* X. 74; trans. Hicks, ii. 605.
[17] Lucretius, *ONT* II. 251 ff.; trans. Smith, p. 41.

tendency to fall downwards like rain eventually bring the universe to a condition of stasis.[18] Insofar as Epicurean morals were based on prediction and calculation, rather than requiring obedience to a fixed moral law posited as inherent in nature or commanded by a divinity, the Epicureans were generally insensitive to deontological considerations.

3.2 Theology and deontology

Lucretius' contemporary and rival Cicero was meanwhile articulating a vision of order descending *de supra* in his anti-Epicurean *De natura deorum*, employing the language of administration, rule, subjection, and obedience that later Christian opponents of atomism found so congenial. He remained wedded to the notion that perfect order pertains to the celestial regions only, where 'there is nothing of chance or hazard, no error, no frustration, but absolute order, accuracy, calculation and regularity', not to the realm below the moon.[19] It is not *nature*, Cicero emphasized, that 'rules the sky, sea and land'. On the contrary: 'Nothing exists that is superior to god; it follows therefore that the world is ruled by him; therefore god is not obedient or subject to any form of nature, and therefore he himself rules all nature'.[20] On Cicero's conception, sky, sea, and land are all 'obedient and subject'. The elements of which they are composed do not however perform stereotyped actions, any more than the builders of a beautiful edifice do; they are commanded to do whatever is necessary to ensure that objects and relations remain stable and good. 'Thus the parts of the world are held in union by the constant passage up and down, to and fro, of these four elements of which all things are composed. And this world structure must either be everlasting in the same form in which we see it, or at all events extremely durable.'[21]

---

[18] Lucretius, *ONT* II. 221 ff.; trans. Smith, p. 41.

[19] Marcus Tullius Cicero, *On the Nature of the Gods*, bk. II, ch. 21; trans. H. Rackham (Cambridge, Mass.: Harvard University Press, 1931), 177.

[20] Ibid. bk. II, ch. 30; trans. Rackham, p. 197. Cicero does, however, refer to nature as 'ruling'; hence the suspicion of Christian commentators that Stoicism was pantheistic nature-philosophy. (Cf. bk. II, chs. 33–4; trans. Rackham, p. 205.)

[21] Ibid.

Cicero's model of *de supra* regulation was a compelling alternative to the atomists' vague and poorly articulated hypothesis of emergent order *ab infra*; and the Judaeo-Christian notion that God bound human beings by moral laws which they mostly observed could be conveniently though imperfectly fitted together with the notion that God imposed laws dictating their behavior to inanimate substances as well. Fleeting references in St Augustine to the laws of nature were followed by a well-developed law concept in St Thomas, one in which the human subjection to divine moral law is considered as one aspect of law-obeying tendencies in created things generally.[22] While human beings, it was noted, are incapable of imposing laws on inanimate objects that have neither reason nor understanding, this is not true of God, who 'commands the whole of nature', through the 'imprint of inner sources of activity'.[23]

Such formulations were commonplace in the sixteenth and seventeenth centuries. Richard Hooker in the *Laws of Ecclesiastical Polity* (1593) distinguished three kinds of law 'laid up in the bosom of God and eternal'; to wit, celestial law, governing the angels; reason, which 'bindeth creatures reasonable in this world'; and nature's law, which 'ordereth natural agents'.[24] Natural agents 'keep the law of their kind unwittingly, as the heavens and elements of the world... can do no other than they do'. John Wilkins in *Mathematicall Magick* (1648) cited Eusebius as 'speaking with what necessity every thing is confined by the laws of nature and the decrees of providence, so that nothing can goe out of the way, unto which naturally it is designed; as a fish cannot reside on the land, nor a man in the water'.[25] According to Nathaniel Culverwel in 1652, 'God has set a Law to the waves, and a

[22] David C. Lindberg and Ronald L. Numbers, *God and Nature* (Berkeley, Calif.: University of California Press, 1986), 19–48. Cf. Thomas Aquinas, *Treatise on Law*, trans. Richard J. Regan (Indianapolis, Ind.: Hackett, 2000), 9: '[T]he eternal law rules and measures everything subject to God's providence ... But the rational creature is subject to God's providence in a more excellent way than other things ... [T]he natural law is simply rational creatures' participation in the eternal law'. Francis Oakley argued that Descartes transferred the law concept from morality to physics ('Christian Theology and the Newtonian Science', *Church History*, 30 (1961), 441).

[23] Aquinas, *Treatise on Law*, trans. Regan, p. 29.

[24] Richard Hooker, *The Laws of Ecclesiastical Polity*, bk. I, ch. 3; ed. A. S. McGrade (Cambridge: Cambridge University Press, 1981) 58 ff. In a much-quoted passage Hooker describes what would happen if nature departed from her course and ceased to obey her own laws, concluding that 'obedience of creatures unto the law of nature is the stay of the whole world'.

[25] Wilkins, *Mathematicall Magick*, bk. II, ch. 6, p. 197.

Law to the windes; nay, thus clocks have their lawes, and Lutes have their Lawes, and whatsoever has the least appearance of motion, has some rule proportionable to it'.[26] And the young Locke imitated his much-admired Cicero in his *Essays on the Law of Nature* composed in 1664, asserting that '[I]t is by his order that the heaven revolves in unbroken rotation, the earth stands fast [*sic*] and the stars shine'.[27]

Inevitably, it occurred to philosophers that God might be considered not as the ruler of wind, waves, lutes, stars, and living beings, but rather as master and commander of the corpuscles composing everything, and that such a reconciliation of Christianity and atomism could be easy and effective. In an essay on atheism of 1607, Bacon propounded a paradox: 'Most of all that schoole which is most accused of Atheisme doth demonstrate Religion. That is, the school of *Leusippus* and *Democritus* and *Epicurus*'. It is more credible, he claimed, that the theory of four elements and an immutable fifth essence, 'duely and eternally placed, neede no God, then that an Army of infinite small portions, or seeds unplaced, should have produced this order and beauty, without a divine Marshall'.[28] The notion that the Epicurean mechanical philosophy was more compatible with Christianity than scholastic metaphysics was amplified by Descartes, Gassendi, Boyle, and the young Leibniz, each of whom tried to paint scholastic Aristotelianism as a kind of pagan naturalism that lodged autonomous powers and virtues in substances. The twin posits of mindless particles and a single divine intelligence and will were potent, Leibniz declared, against the 'heathen polytheism' of philosophers who 'speak of incorporeal substances of bodies and who cannot explain what they mean without a translation into terms of mind'.[29]

The discovery of rules and laws governing the motion of bodies in optical and mechanical contexts was fortuitous for metaphysics. Rules and

---

[26] Nathaniel Culverwel, *Discourse of the Light of Nature* (1652; repr. New York/London: Garland, 1978), 20.

[27] 'It is He who has set bounds even to the wild sea and prescribed to every kind of plants the manner and periods of germination and growth; it is in obedience to His will that all living beings have their own laws of birth and life; and there is nothing so unstable, so uncertain in this whole constitution of things as not to admit of valid and fixed laws of operation appropriate to its nature' (Locke, *Law of Nature*, p. 109).

[28] Francis Bacon, 'On Atheisme', in *Works*, ed. J. Spedding, R. Ellis, D. Heath, and W. Rawley (Boston, Mass.: Brown and Taggard, 1860–4), xii. 338.

[29] G. W. Leibniz, letter to Thomasius, 20/30 April 1669, in *Die Philosophische Schriften von Leibniz*, ed. C. I. Gerhardt (Berlin 1875–90; repr. Hildesheim: Olms, 1965), i. 25; trans. and ed. L. E. Loemker as *Philosophical Papers and Letters* (2nd edn., Dordrecht: Reidel, 1969), 101.

laws, it seemed, necessarily implied the existence of a ruler or lawgiver, even if it was acknowledged that mindless atoms could not understand and intentionally obey them. Insofar as they could not resist them either, God's omnipotence could at least ensure formal compliance.[30] Descartes was the first philosopher to be explicit about what the laws of nature actually say, as opposed to what types of natural entities are subordinated to God, and the first to introduce systematic quantification into his account of the interactions of corporeal things. 'The motion which I posit', he declared in his suppressed *Treatise of Light*, 'follows the same laws of nature as do generally all the dispositions and qualities found in matter'.[31] The laws of nature included the principle of inertia, the rectilinearity of unconstrained motion, the generation of a centrifugal force as a result of constrained circular motion, and the tendency of a body to rebound when it encounters a 'stronger' body. To these principles he added the precise 'rules' of mechanics, governing the collision of two bodies of the same and different sizes and speeds.[32] These rules were held to govern microscopic as well as macroscopic bodies; a visible object is an ensemble of particles of matter that happen to be moving together or resting together. No federation or mutual recognition amongst corpuscles was necessary, he maintained, to explain the stability of ordinary material things.

Availing himself of the Thomistic distinction between primary and secondary causes, Descartes was careful to insist that the self-sufficiency of the world was only physical and relative. On the metaphysical level God was the cause of all motion. He preserved a constant quantity of it in the universe, and his concourse was required to maintain the world in existence from moment to moment, lest it slip into nothingness.[33] 'By Nature', he declared, 'I do not understand some Goddess, or some other

[30] Cudworth claimed that the revival of Epicurean and Democritean atomism was linked with voluntarist theology. The claim is repeated by modern commentators, including Francis Oakley, 'Christian Theology and the Newtonian Science: The Rise of the Concept of the Laws of Nature', *Church History*, 30 (1961), 438 ff.; Gary Deason, 'Reformation Theology and the Mechanistic Conception of Nature', in Lindberg and Numbers, *God and Nature*; and Margaret Osler, *Divine Will and the Mechanical Philosophy* (Cambridge: Cambridge University Press, 1994), *passim*. See also Michael Foster, 'The Christian Doctrine of Creation and the Rise of Modern Natural Science', *Mind*, 43 (1934), 446–58.

[31] René Descartes, *Treatise of the World*, ch. 7, in *Oeuvres*, ed. C. Adam and P. Tannery (Paris: Vrin, 1964–74), xi. 40; *Writings*, trans. and ed. J. Cottingham et al. (Cambridge: Cambridge University Press, 1985–9), i. 94.

[32] Descartes, *Principles*, pt. II, §§ 36 ff; *Oeuvres* viiiA. 63 ff.; *Writings*, i. 240 ff.

[33] Ibid. viiiA. 61; i. 240.

imaginary power; I make use of this word to signify matter itself... under the condition that God continues to preserve it in the same way he created it'.[34] His insistence that creation and conservation were metaphysically equivalent and required the same effort on the part of God has been interpreted as expressing a commitment to the impotence of nature and to God's unique responsibility for all change and motion: occasionalism. Even if Descartes wished to be interpreted in this manner, he appears to have been equally committed to the reverse point as well; namely, that the laws of motion that maintain the universe in the reasonably steady but still somewhat variable state that it is in were sufficient to bring its contents into existence in the first place. There are not two sorts of actions required of God, a kind of sculptural activity in fashioning various celestial and terrestrial objects to plan, and then a very different kind of maintenance activity in keeping their actions and interactions current, but only one form of legislation that can accomplish both ends.[35]

God, to be sure, 'lays his hand' upon the initial chaos or perfect homogeneity of the creation in Descartes's system. The chance of the atomists, he agreed, was insufficient to bring stable structures and animal forms into existence. The divinely imposed laws of motion were, however, sufficient, Descartes insisted, even if one preferred to believe that the world had not actually come to be in this way. He waved away all questions of divine purpose and intention in his replies to the objections posed to the *Meditations*, where he had first declared that he considered 'the customary search for final causes to be totally useless in physics; there is considerable rashness in thinking myself capable of investigating the impenetrable purposes of God'.[36]

Boyle, who had encountered Epicurean ideas through Walter Charleton's transcriptions of Gassendi in his *Physiologia*, as well as in classical and patristic sources, worried exceedingly about being taken for an Epicurean.[37] He might well have worried, insofar as he rejected Aristotelian substantial

---

[34] Descartes, *Treatise of Light*, ch. 7; *Oeuvres*, xi. 37, *Writings*, i. 92.

[35] This unifying intention was brought out in Malebranche's explication of Descartes's creation theory in his own *Search After Truth*, bk. VI, pt. II, ch. 4; trans. Lennon and Olscamp p. 464.

[36] Descartes, *Meditations*, in *Oeuvres*, vii. 55; *Writings*, trans. and ed. Cottingham et al., ii. 39.

[37] Yang Sik Kim, 'Another Look at Robert Boyle's Acceptance of the Mechanical Philosophy', *Ambix*, 38 (1991), 1–10. See also J. J. MacIntosh, 'Robert Boyle on Epicurean Atheism and Atomism', in Margaret J. Oslter (ed.), *Atoms, Pneuma, and Tranquillity: Epicurean and Stoic Themes in European Thought* (Cambridge: Cambridge University Press, 1991).

forms, real qualities, the *archaeus*, astral beings, gas, and *blas*,[38] as well as the Platonic soul of the world and the universal spirit.[39] He insisted that the mechanical philosophy applied comprehensively to chemical and pharmacological phenomena, and he criticized Platonists who 'think the Mechanical principles may serve indeed to give an account of this or that particular part of natural philosophy, as statics, hydrostatics, the theory of planetary motions & c., but can never be applied to all the phenomena of things corporeal'. He accused them of resembling those persons who think that alphabetic principles can account for English books, but not books in general.[40] Following Descartes, he declared that nature could be considered simply as 'the Systeme of the Corporeal works of God',[41] or as 'the Aggregate of the Bodies, that make up the World',[42] and in his *Free Inquiry into the Vulgarly Received Notion of Nature* (1686) he proposed that God

settled such Laws or Rules of local Motion, among the Parts of the Universal Matter, that by his ordinary and preserving *Concourse*, the several Parts of the Universe, thus once completed, should be able to maintain the great Construction, or *System* and Oeconomy, of the Mundane Bodies, and propagate the *Species* of *Living Creatures*.[43]

Boyle denied that 'either these *Cartesian laws of motion*, or the *Epicurean casual Concourse* of Atoms, could bring meer Matter into so orderly and well contriv'd a Fabrick as This World'.[44] His 'Anaxagorean mechanism', as he called it, emphasized the role played by a single guiding intelligence. The precise boundary between settling and maintaining, between creation and conservation, was not, however perfectly sharp in Boyle's philosophy, and he agreed that some effects were not produced mechanically and that others, though produced mechanically, could never be understood in mechanical terms by human beings.[45] Like the majority of

---

[38] Robert Boyle, *Excellency and Grounds*, in *Works*, ed. Michael Hunter and Edward B. Davis (London: Pickering and Chatto, 2000), viii. 104.

[39] Ibid. viii. 109.   [40] Ibid.   [41] Boyle, *Free Inquiry*, in *Works*, x. 456.   [42] Ibid. x. 467.

[43] Ibid. x. 469.   [44] Boyle, *Origin of Forms and Qualities*, in *Works*, v. 354.

[45] A passage discovered by John Henry amongst Boyle's unpublished manuscripts reads as follows: '[It would] be backward to reject or despise all explications that are not immediately deduced from the shape, bigness, and motion of atoms or other insensible particles of matter ... [for those who] pretend to explicate every phenomenon by deducing it from the mechanical affections of atoms undertake a harder task than they imagine' (quoted in John Henry, 'Boyle and Cosmical Qualities', in Michael Hunter (ed.), *Robert Boyle Reconsidered* (Cambridge: Cambridge University Press, 1994), 123.

his contemporaries, Boyle recognized the possibility of direct interventions in human affairs by God, and by good and evil spirits. On a more impersonal level, he thought that the maximum height to which water could be raised in 'sucking tubes' was the result of divine decree, along with the age of onset of menstruation in young females.[46] The 'General Fabrick of the World' influenced the behavior of individual things; and the phenomena we observe, he thought, depend on the confluence of the actions of a number of agents, 'the admirable conspiring of the several parts of the Universe to the production of particular Effects'.[47]

[A]n Individual Body, being but a Part of the World...needs the Assistance, or Concourse, of other Bodies...to perform divers of its Operations, and exhibit several *Phenomena's*, that belong to it. This would quickly and manifestly appear, if, for Instance, an Animal or an Herb could be remov'd into those Imaginary Spaces, the School-men tell us of, beyond the World; or into such a place, as the Epicureans fancy their *Intermundia*.... For, whatever the Structures of these Living Engines be, they would as little, without the Co-operations of external Agents; such as the *Sun, Aether, Air* &c., be able to exercise their Functions, as the great Mills, commonly us'd with us would be to Grind Corn, without the assistance of Wind or running Water.[48]

Their programmatic statements of the commitment to corpuscles and the laws of motion as sufficient for the production of all effects on the part of Descartes and Boyle were not, in the end, consistent with their knowledge and experience. The discovery of *some* quantitative laws of nature did not imply that all of nature was a mechanical system, simple in its principles and complex in its effects. While Descartes struck many of his contemporaries as wildly overconfident, both in his conviction on this score and in his belief that he, personally, could explain everything, Boyle at times appeared radically unsure whether all of nature really is such a system, and whether the human mind can master it if it is.[49]

Gassendi, as Margaret Osler points out, did not project the nomological image of nature as governed by immutable laws in his own writings, though he regarded God as the creator and ruler of his atoms, and although he acknowledged natural regularities—that fire is hot, that the

---

[46] Boyle, 'A Requisite Digression', in *Works*, ed. Hunter and Davis, iii. 247.
[47] Ibid. iii. 245–6; cf. *Free Inquiry*, in *Works*, x. 457.   [48] Ibid. x. 469.
[49] Rose-Mary Sargent, in *The Diffident Naturalist: Robert Boyle and the Philosophy of Experiment* (Chicago, Ill.: University of Chicago Press, 1995), emphasizes this aspect of his character.

sun rises in the east, that water flows downhill, and so on. According to Osler, Gassendi's relative lack of interest in the laws of nature reflected his belief that God's absolute power is inconsistent with any kind of natural necessity.[50] Yet his de-emphasis is perhaps better explained by Gassendi's rather negative attitude towards theology and scholastic philosophy than by his positive commitment to the theological doctrine of voluntarism. His text is closer to that of the ancient atomists in having recourse to mechanistic explanations without explicit references to the laws of nature.

For Descartes and Boyle the image of nature as a divinely designed system of obedient creatures, these creatures being not the birds of the air and the animals of the forest envisioned by St Thomas, but only material corpuscles, enabled them to distance themselves conceptually from the ancient atomists. It was no more extrapolated from their own cogitations and researches than their commitment to quality-denuded particles; it was drawn from texts. In articulating it in the new context of experimental science, they excised a problematic feature of classical atomism—its inability to account for order and regularity—and replaced it with a version of the ancient notion of a supervisory providence and the medieval notion of nature as the kingdom of God. And where Descartes's appeals to the concept of the laws of nature surrounded his unprovable speculations with an air of certainty, Boyle's helped to confer dignity on experimental practice that was only sporadically successful and that was vulnerable to criticism as frivolous entertainment.[51]

3.3 Cosmogenesis: ancient and modern

For Plato and Aristotle there was only one world, the ensemble of phenomena, terrestrial and celestial, that we can perceive. According to subsequent Christian doctrine, this world was the scene of important happenings. It was created *ex nihilo*, then came the Fall of Man and the Flood, followed by the coming of Christ, and His Crucifixion and Resurrection, and soon the world will be the scene of the second coming

---

[50] Osler, *Divine Will*, pp. 51 ff.

[51] Friedrich Steinle, 'From Principles to Regularities', in Lorraine Daston and Michael Stolleis (eds.), *Natural Laws and the Laws of Nature in Early Modern Europe* (Aldershot: Ashgate, 2007).

and the general resurrection. The uniqueness of the world was accordingly tied by association to other singularities: the one Christian God, the one authoritative book, the one Redeemer of mankind.

Copernicanism, with its vast empty spaces and huge interstellar distances, implied that the sun is a star and that every star may be a sun. The doctrine of the plurality of widely separated worlds threatened the Christian drama with absurdity. Why should events of such fatal significance have occurred exclusively on this planet and not elsewhere? How could the history of our world be consequential if there are rational beings like us but whom we will never encounter in other worlds? The moral aspirations required by Christianity, as well as the doctrine of God's special care for humanity, seem to make sense only in a unique and bounded world. Alexandre Koyré, who rightly pointed to the significance of the Epicurean revival for the acceptance of heliocentrism,[52] suggested that the Copernican explosion of the size of the known universe produced anxiety and disorientation, but many philosophers and poets were enchanted with the new, open universe.[53] Our world was not, as the theologians had claimed, the sinkhole of the universe, sodden and groaning with original sin, but another floating, shining planet. Giordano Bruno, known to carry Lucretius in his pocket, claimed that an infinity of beings and of worlds glorified God. 'Why', he asked, 'should the infinite capacity be frustrated, the possibility of the existence of infinite worlds be cheated, the perfection of the divine image be impaired—that image which ought rather to be reflected back in a mirror as immeasurable as itself?'[54]

It was one thing however to agree with Copernicus and the Epicureans, against Aristotle, Plato, and the Fathers of the Church, that there were many worlds, and another thing entirely to assert with the Epicureans that these worlds had come into existence on their own rather than through the omnipotence of the creator. 'A cosmos', according to Epicurus, is 'a circumscribed portion of the heavens which contains stars and an earth and all the phenomena, whose dissolution will involve the destruction of

---

[52] Alexandre Koyré, *From the Closed World to the Infinite Universe* (Baltimore, Md.: Johns Hopkins University Press, 1953), 29.

[53] According to Arthur O. Lovejoy, 'The geocentric cosmography served rather for man's humiliation than for his exaltation, and … Copernicanism was opposed partly on the ground that it assigned too dignified and lofty a position to this dwelling place' (*The Great Chain of Being* (Cambridge, Mass.: Harvard University Press, 1964), 102).

[54] Giordano Bruno, *De l'infinito universo e mondi*, trans. Lovejoy, *Great Chain of Being*, p. 118.

everything within it'.[55] The number of *cosmoi* was 'unlimited', he said; they were separated by void and were inaccessible to one another. In his letter to Pythocles he explained that a cosmos can come into existence

when certain seeds of the right sort rush in from one cosmos or intercosmos ...gradually causing conjunctions and articulations and...influxes from [atoms] which are in the right condition, until the cosmos is completed and achieves stability, [i.e.] for as long as the foundations laid can accept additional material.... The sun and the moon and the other heavenly bodies did not come into being on their own and then get included by the cosmos, but they immediately begin to take shape and grow (and similarly for the earth and sea) by means of infusions and rotations of certain natures with fine parts; either breath-like or fire or both.[56]

The archaic poet Hesiod had posited the emergence of the world from an initial chaos in his *Theogony*, but many divinities, including night, earth, and love, were involved in its development. Epicurus, by contrast, not only began with a material chaos as the primordium of the universe, but denied any role to the gods, sketching an account of gradual formation which, however vague, was thoroughly physical, depending on conjunctions, articulations, infusions, and rotations.

Lucretius followed Epicurus in maintaining the plurality and self-assembly of worlds. '[W]hen an abundant supply of matter is available, when space is at hand and there is no obstruction from any object or force, things most certainly must happen and objects must be created.'[57] Our world, he declared, 'is the creation of nature: the atoms themselves collided spontaneously and fortuitously, clashing together blindly, unsuccessfully, and ineffectually in a multitude of ways, until at last those atoms coalesced which, when suddenly dashed together could always form the foundations of mighty fabrics, of earth, sea, and sky, and the family of living creatures'.[58] He went on to describe how the earth brought forth verdure, then birds, then other animals, spontaneously. '[S]he herself

[55] Epicurus, letter to Pythocles, in Diogenes Laertius, *Lives* X. 89–90; *The Epicurus Reader*, trans. and ed. Brad Inwood and L. P. Gerson (Indianapolis, Ind.: Hackett, 1994), 20–1.

[56] Ibid.   [57] Lucretius, *ONT* II. 1067 ff.; trans. Smith, p. 62.

[58] Ibid. II. 1058 ff.; trans. Smith, p. 62. Cf. Ovid: 'Ere land and sea and the all-covering sky | Were made, in the whole world the countenance | Of nature was the same, all one, well named | Chaos, a raw and undivided mass, | Naught but a lifeless bulk, with warring seeds | Of ill-joined elements compressed together' (*Metamorphoses*, bk. I; trans. A. D. Melville (Oxford: Oxford University Press, 1986), 1).

created the human race, and, almost at a fixed time produced every species of animal that ranges wildly and widely over the mighty mountains, as well as the various birds of the air.'[59] Some of the animals that formed by chance had natural qualities that enabled them to survive and live independently; others required our protection but were useful and so fell under our care; the rest died.[60] Nature made monsters and prodigies, deaf, dumb, and limbless creatures, but 'they were powerless to do anything or move anywhere or avoid danger or take what they needed'.[61] Now, however, Lucretius thought, earth is worn out, like an older woman, and has mostly ceased to bear, except for the 'multitudes of living creatures [that] spring from the earth under the influence of rains and the heat of the sun'.[62]

These striking ideas, that the world was neither eternal nor created, and that it had assembled itself with all its living inhabitants, were impossible for anyone who had come across them to ignore.[63] The most fervent and explicit Epicurean—or perhaps theo-Epicurean—was Descartes, who described himself in a letter of late November 1630 as 'in love with the fable of my World'.[64] His inquiries into cosmology, the physics of inanimate bodies, and the animal and human machines were originally intended to form three parts of a comprehensive textbook *The World*. In the *Treatise of Light*, written in the mid- to late 1620s, the first part of the planned trilogy, he showed how God might have created a material plenum, cut it up into particles, and agitated it so that various grades of particle were formed by abrasion, moved at different speeds, and in different directions according to 'the ordinary laws of nature'.

God has established these laws in such a marvellous way that even if we suppose he creates nothing beyond what I have mentioned, and sets up no order or proportion within it but composes from it a chaos the laws of nature are sufficient to cause the parts of this chaos to disentangle themselves and arrange themselves in such good order that they will have the form of a quite perfect world—a world in which we

---

[59] Lucretius, *ONT* V. 822 ff.; trans. Smith, p. 159.   [60] Ibid. V. 858; trans. Smith, p. 160.

[61] Ibid. V. 837 ff.; trans. Smith, p. 159.   [62] Ibid. V. 797–8; trans. Smith, p. 158.

[63] Kant would later write a long, worried, ambivalent book about evolution, beauty, and living forms: the *Kritik der Urteilskraft*, published in 1790.

[64] Descartes, letter to Mersenne, 25 November 1630, in *Oeuvres*, i. 179; *Writings*, trans. and ed. Cottingham et al., ii. 28. He planned to write nothing else for print, he said, 'if God lets me live long enough to finish it'.

shall be able to see not only light but also all the other things, general as well as particular, which appear in the real world.[65]

Descartes imagined, to his own delight, the gradual formation of a universe of multiple *cosmoi* or 'vortices' from the initial chaos 'as confused and muddled as any the poets could describe'. The cosmos, he maintained, while vast, was a single unified system that contained everything that existed, in a plenum of indefinite extension. 'All the bodies in the universe', he stated, 'are contiguous and interact with each other.'[66] At the same time, he held that there were many—perhaps an indefinite number of—solar systems or 'vortices'. '[S]ince our mind is of such a nature as to recognize no limits in the universe, whoever considers the immensity of God and the weakness of our senses will conclude that ... there may be other bodies beyond all the visible fixed stars'.[67] He left open the question whether there were other planets, with other minerals, plants, animals, and rational creatures.

Descartes did not publish any part of his *World*, for the condemnation of atomism of 1624 was too recent to make it safe to do so, and, in Pt. V of the *Discourse on Method*, he touched only lightly on his ideas about cosmogony. The *Meditations* that followed in 1640 managed to introduce his general ideas about the properties of corporeal substance and the mechanical body while ostensibly arguing for the immortality of the soul and the absolute dependence of everything that happened in the physical universe on the immediate agency of God. However irritating some of their comments might have been, none of the clerics and philosophers whose objections to the *Meditations* he solicited thought to charge the author with gross impiety, and Descartes felt secure enough to return to the sensitive questions of the origins of the cosmos and life, emending some of his earlier posits in his *Principles of Philosophy* of 1644.[68] There, he suggested that the initial condition of the universe was not chaotic, but rather involved equally sized particles moving at equal speed.[69] By the operation of the laws of nature 'matter must successively assume all the forms of which it is capable'. From

---

[65] Descartes, *Treatise of Light*, ch. 6, in *Oeuvres*, xi. 34–5; *Writings*, i. 91; cf. *Principles*, pt. III, § 47, in *Oeuvres*, ix. 103–4; *Writings*, i. 257–8.

[66] Descartes, *Principles*, pt. III, art. 157, in *Oeuvres*, viiiA. 202; *Writings*, i. 266.

[67] Ibid. pt. III, § 29, in *Oeuvres*, viiiA. 192; *Writings*, i. 253.

[68] See, on these emendations and their significance, John W. Lynes, 'Descartes' theory of Elements: From *Le Monde* to the *Principles*', *Journal of the History of Ideas*, 43 (1982), 55–72.

[69] Descartes, *Principles*, pt. III, § 47, in *Oeuvres*, viiiA. 102–3 f.; *Writings*, i. 257.

the initial isotropic distribution of particles of matter of equal size, all the elements of what he called the visible world, beginning with the sun, moon, and stars, would eventually emerge.[70] And if we want to understand the nature of plants or of men, Descartes urged his readers, 'it is much better to consider how they can gradually grow from seeds than to consider how they were created by God at the beginning of the world'.[71] In the earlier *Treatise of Man*, intended to form the third part of *The World*, he had proposed that living animals were purely corporeal entities. The generation and alteration of all visible form was accordingly the result of the congregation and mechanical interaction of subvisible particles. There was no difference in principle, he maintained, between the formation of inanimate patterned objects, whether grains of salt, or flakes of snow, and the formation of animate patterned objects. The baby is generated mechanically in the womb from a mixture of material fluids, just like any other object.[72] He presented his claims regarding cosmogenesis and generation as pertaining to another, alternative world in the *Treatise of Light*, as only possible in the *Discourse*, and as false in the *Principles*. There, he deferred to the account in Genesis, assuring the reader that 'There is no doubt that the world was created right from the start with all the perfection which it now has', with its sun, moon, stars, and plants, and with Adam and Eve 'created as fully grown people'.[73]

Except amongst a few Cartesians, the seventeenth- and eighteenth-century consensus was and would long remain that generation *de novo* from unformed matter was inexplicable on mechanical principles, and indeed impossible. While the crystals of various salts, Boyle maintained, could be generated mechanically and even by human effort, plants, animals, and humans could only arise from seminal principles of divine origin.[74] Glanvill, writing in 1665, considered that

though *blind matter* might reach some *elegancies* in individual effects; yet *specifick conformities* can be no *unadvised* productions, but in greatest likelyhood, are regulated by the immediate efficiency of some *knowing* agent; which whether it be *seminal Formes* ... or whatever else we please to suppose; the manner of its working is to us

---

[70] Descartes, *Principles*, in *Oeuvres*, viiiA. 103; *Writings*, i. 257–8.

[71] Ibid. § 46, in *Oeuvres*, viiiA. 99–100; *Writings*, i. 256.

[72] Descartes, letter to Mersenne, 20 February 1639, in *Oeuvres*, ii. 525; *Writings* iii. 134–5. Cf. *La description du corps humain*, pt. IV, in *Oeuvres*, xi. 252 ff.

[73] Descartes, *Principles*, pt. III, § 45, in *Oeuvres*, viiiA. 99–100; *Writings*, i. 256.

[74] Boyle, *Origin of Forms and Qualities*, § 1, in *Works*, ed. Hunter and Davis, v. 363.

unknown: or if these effects are meerly *Mechanical*, yet to learn the method of such operations may, and indeed hath been ingeniously attempted; but I think cannot be performed to the satisfaction of the severer examination[75]

At the same time, belief in the hexameral creation of the world, its main geographical features, and all its plants and animals a few thousand years earlier receded amongst the learned throughout the eighteenth century, in favour of Epicurean notions of evolutionary change.

3.4 Leibniz and the Epicureans

Leibniz's reactions to the revival of the Epicurean hypotheses of atomism, mechanism, and the plurality and self-formation of worlds were the most complex of his philosophical generation. Though he later denied that material atoms were physically possible, he began by agreeing with Bacon that theism and corpuscularianism had a special affinity for one another and with the Cartesians that everything ran according to mechanical principles alone. 'There is no wisdom in nature', he declared in an early letter to his former teacher Christian Thomasius, 'and no appetite, yet a beautiful order arises in it because it is the timepiece of God.'[76]

In his *Discourse on Metaphysics*, considered as his first presentation of a philosophical system, however, he referred to the repellent opinions of some of the 'latest innovators...whose opinion it is that the beauty of the universe and the goodness which we ascribe to the works of God are nothing but the chimeras of men who think of him in terms of themselves'.[77] Their error was to be corrected, and Leibniz would argue that the world was not only as perfect as possible, but also increasing in perfection, and that everything that happened mechanically happened at the same time in such a way as to satisfy God's requirements for a morally just world.

Leibniz was assuredly not a hexameral creationist, and his own cosmogony was a fusion of the Lucretian doctrine of natural selection and

[75] Joseph Glanville, *Scepsis scientifica* (London, 1665), 33–4.
[76] Leibniz, letter to Thomasius, 20/30 April 1669, in *Philosophische Schriften*, ed. Gerhardt, i. 25; trans. 2 and ed. Loemker, *Philosophical Papers*, p.101.
[77] Leibniz, Discourse § 2, in *Philosophische Schriften*, ed. Gerhardt, iv. 428; trans. and ed. Loemker, p. 304.

the Platonic-Christian teaching that a divinity plans and realizes the world. The world consists, he maintained, of 'the whole succession and the whole agglomeration of all existent things, lest it be said that several worlds could have existed in different times and places'.[78] This single world is composed of multiple vortices with their own inhabitants. It comes into being by a process of combination involving its simplest elements, and it is continuously developing, so that there have been dramatic changes in the appearance and constitution of our globe and in the ensemble of bodies amongst which it is situated.

Leibniz was familiar with Lucretius' poem, and, around 1680, he composed, but did not publish, a dialogue between an Epicurean nobleman and a learned hermit that engaged rather sympathetically with the proposal that random combination, and a process of variation and selection, could produce order from chaos. The marquis—an intellectual libertine—questions the hermit's adherence to the view that because 'everything fits together so well in the animal machine' it must have been specially made, reminding him of Lucretius' claim that 'feet are not made for walking, but humans walk because they have feet'. Lucretius will tell you, he continues, 'that necessity determines that badly made objects perish, and that the well-made ones are preserved... thus although there are an infinity of badly-made objects, they cannot maintain themselves amongst the others'.[79] The hermit objects that 'we see nothing that is only halfway made. How could the badly made objects disappear so quickly and how would they escape our eyes armed with the microscope?'. On the contrary, he insists, 'the more we penetrate into the interior of nature, the more we are ravished with astonishment'.[80] The marquis replies that if Epicurus is right to say that there are and have been an infinite number of worlds in the vast regions of space and time, 'it is not a great miracle if we find ourselves in a world of a passable beauty'.[81] The hermit concedes that the 'fiction' of self-assembly is not impossible, absolutely speaking, but that the ordinary way for a world to arise is not as the Epicureans say, and that that is 'as little credible as to suppose that a library forms itself one day by a fortuitous concourse of atoms'.

---

[78] Leibniz, *theodicy* § 8; trans. and ed. Farrer and Huggard, p. 128.

[79] Leibniz, *Conversation du marquis de pianese et du pere emery eremite*, in *Vorausedition*, (Münster: University of Münster, 1989–), viii. 1808.

[80] Ibid. 1808–9.   [81] Ibid. 1809.

If I found myself transported into a new region of the universe where I saw clocks, furniture, books, ramparts, I would venture everything I possessed that this was the work of a rational creature, even if it were possible absolutely speaking that it was not, and that one can pretend that there is perhaps a country in the finite extension of things where books write themselves, but one would have to have lost one's mind to think that the country in which I live is the country where books write themselves.[82]

Noteworthy is Leibniz's acknowledgement that the Epicurean hypothesis is realizable but massively unlikely. In adopting this position, he distinguished himself from the mass of critics who deemed self-assembly mad, absurd, and impossible.

In a later unpublished essay, 'on the radical origination of things', Leibniz portrayed a self-creating universe that, unlike Epicurus', was governed by ethical requirements and consistent with divine power, intelligence, and benevolence. He preserved the Epicurean notion of a struggle for survival and aggregation.

Leibniz construed the process of assembly—he referred to it as a 'metaphysical mechanism'—not as beginning with indestructible particles of matter that could aggregate into *cosmoi*, but with imperishable substances that could aggregate into coherent worlds encompassing many *cosmoi*. As Epicurus described 'seeds of the right sort ... gradually causing conjunctions and articulations and ... influxes by [atoms] which are in the right condition, until the cosmos is completed and achieves stability, [i.e.] for as long as the foundations laid can accept additional material', Leibniz maintained that the actual world was formed by the accumulation of compossible substances until the maximum of richness and variety was reached, and the world became actual. '[O]ut of the infinite combinations and series of possible things, one exists through which the greatest amount of essence is brought into existence'.[83] The patterned world that resulted was unique and ethically good. He left it unclear whether the exercise of God's will was required for the actualization of one of the possible worlds in his mind, or whether a possible world with certain qualities could leap the fence by itself, as it were, to become actual.

---

[82] Ibid. 1810.

[83] Leibniz, 'On the radical origination of things', in *Philosophische Schriften*, ed. Gerhardt, vii. 303; trans. and ed. Loemker, *Philosophical Papers*, p. 487.

Leibniz's quarrel with Newton over the introduction of Newton's principle of attraction suggests a rigid commitment to Cartesian physics, but his attitude in the correspondence with Newton's spokesman Samuel Clarke cannot be explained by his alleged disapproval of action at a distance as incompatible with his mechanism. From a metaphysical perspective, gravity was surely no more occult and obscure than Leibniz's own *vis viva*, and Leibniz was too good a mathematician and physicist not to recognize that Newton's scheme saved the celestial phenomena.[84] He had earlier commended Newton for rejecting materialism and for having 'explained so well many phenomena of nature in supposing a gravity or attraction from matter upon matter'. He even admitted in 1715 to agreeing with Newton that 'the great globes of our system, having a certain magnitude, attract each other'.

The emotional motivation for Leibniz's attacks on Newtonian attraction as 'inexplicable, unintelligible, precarious, groundless and unexampled' was doubtless his deep and justified anger over the accusations of plagiarism made against him in the calculus–priority dispute and the decision taken in favor of Newton. But his intellectual motivation was based in his doctrine of the perfection of the world, and the simplicity and elegance of its underlying structure. Boyle's universe was held together by a patchwork of mechanisms and special ordinances, and Locke glumly maintained that 'The Things that, as far as our Observation reaches, we constantly find to proceed regularly, we may conclude, do act by a Law set them; but yet by a Law, that we know not'.[85] The nature of substance was unknowable, according to Locke. The English toleration for confessional and theoretical disunity, and their accompanying skepticism seemed to presage the worst.

Now Newton had explicitly declared that the universe of his *Principia*, bound up by gravity, was not perfect, dramatically extending the Galilean thesis of the corruptibility of the heavens. In query 31 of the second edition of his *Opticks* (1704) he declared that the orderly motion of the solar system was not sustainable over the long term and that the cosmos would require divine renovation. With no other examples of corporeal perpetual-motion machines to hand, Leibniz had no particular reason, one might think, to insist that God's plans required the permanent operation

---

[84] See Catherine Wilson, *Leibniz's Metaphysics* (Princeton/Manchester: Princeton University Press/Manchester University Press, 1989), 224 ff.

[85] John Locke, *An Essay Concerning Human Understanding*, bk. IV, ch. 3 § 29; ed. P. H. Nidditch (Oxford: Clarendon, 1975), 560.

of any corporeal system, including the solar system. But his principle that 'God's ... machine lasts longer and moves more regularly than those of any other artist whatsoever'[86] was a reinvocation of Cicero's insistence in *The Nature of the Gods* that 'this world structure must either be everlasting in the same form in which we see it, or at all events extremely durable'. Clarke tried to represent the intervention needed as manifesting God's care and concern for the universe, but this banal maneuver did not impress Leibniz. The perfection of the world, like the immortality of the organism, had to be impressed into its very structure. To deny that the world was an eternally perfect clock that would never need winding was, in Leibniz's mind, tantamount to an acknowledgement of the Epicurean thesis of bounds and limits, the inevitable decay of everything. It invited the mind to consider the finitude of life, the mortality of the human soul, and to these tenets Leibniz was implacably opposed.

[86] Leibniz, second letter to Clarke, in *Philosophische Schriften*, ed. Gerhardt, vii. 357; trans. and ed. Loemker, *Philosophical Papers*, p. 678.

4

Mortality and Metaphysics

> Therefore while vitall sence thus flows through all
> Bodie and soule make but one animall;
> Which if some violence should suddenly
> Cleave in the midst, the force of soule would be
> Parted to both, in neither peice entire
> Soe would, disjoyned in severd parts exspire.
> Now immortallitie must be denied
> To all things which have parts, or can devide.
>
> (*De rerum natura*, iii. 662–9)

Aristotle's theory of substance long appeared to offer a better account of the natural world than the minimalism of atoms and void. Because souls had discernible faculties and modes of operation, the study of the soul fell, Aristotle maintained, within the science of nature.[1] Conversely, the science of nature required reference to souls—vegetative, animal, and rational—and to forms. Incorporeal forms moved celestial and animal bodies, shaped matter in generation, and lost control of it in corruption, as well as endowing primary matter with the qualities and dispositions of visible, tangible individuals. Active principles engaged in transformative work on living substances, by analogy with intelligent doctors, builders, and other craftsmen, and the genuine physicist, according to Aristotle, 'concerns himself with all the properties active and passive of bodies or materials thus or thus defined'.[2] He commented disapprovingly on Empedocles' and Democritus' disregard for form and essence and their exclusive concentration on matter. As the doctor must know both health and bile and phlegm, and the builder

---

[1] Aristotle, *On the Soul*, bk. I, ch. 1, 403ᵃ, in *Complete Works*, ed. Jonathan Barnes (Princeton, NJ: Princeton University Press, 1984), i. 643.
[2] Ibid. 403ᵇ.

the form of a house as well as bricks and beams, the physicist must know nature 'in both its senses'.[3]

Aristotle was on his firmest ground in discussing vital phenomena. The nourishment of an organism cannot be a matter of mere accretion, he pointed out; it implies the existence of some selective and directive agent.[4] Against Empedocles, he insisted that chance and mechanical necessity could not have framed animal bodies, which exhibit purposiveness in all their parts; and Democritus came in for criticism for neglecting final causes and reducing all the operations of nature to necessity. In a much-quoted passage Aristotle appeared to make short work of both atomism and the mechanical approach to explaining animate motion. Democritus, he charged, 'uses language like that of the comic dramatist Philippus, who accounts for the movements that Daedalus imparted to his wooden Aphrodite by saying that he poured quicksilver into it; similarly Democritus says that the spherical atoms owing to their own ceaseless movements draw the whole body after them and so produce its movements'.[5] Not only was the analogy absurd, but on Democritus' theory of self-moving atoms it was impossible to see how a living body could remain still. 'It is not in this way', Aristotle concluded, 'that the soul appears to originate movement in animals—it is through intention or process of thinking.'[6]

Aristotle seemed to waver on the question of immortality, as one might expect from his hylomorphic commitments and his rejection of the Platonic doctrine of separated forms. He maintained that anger, courage, appetite, and sensation were all affections of the complex of soul and body. Memory and love cease when the body decays in old age. If thinking is a form of imagination, he reflected—and according to Aristotle 'the soul never thinks without a phantasm'[7]—it too requires a body. He did not however endorse that conclusion. Thought, he mused, 'seems to

---

[3] Aristotle, *Physics*, bk. II, ch. 2, 194ᵃ, in *Complete Works*, ed. Barnes, i. 331.

[4] 'In what way...has the food been modified by the growing thing? Perhaps we should say that it has been mixed with it, as if one were to pour water into wine and the wine were able to convert the new ingredient into wine. And as fire lays hold of the inflammable, so the active principle of growth, dwelling in the growing thing...lays hold of an acceding food which is potentially flesh and converts it into actual flesh' (Aristotle, *On Generation and Corruption*, bk. I, ch. 5, 322ᵃ, in *Complete Works*, i. 526).

[5] Aristotle, *On the Soul*, bk. I, ch. 3, 406ᵇ, in *Complete Works*, i. 648.   [6] Ibid.

[7] Ibid., ch. 7, 431ᵃ14–16, in *Complete Works*, i. 685. St Thomas concurred: 'It is beyond the nature of the soul to understand without...*phantasmata*' (*Summa theologia*, bk. I q. 89 a. 1).

be an independent substance implanted within us and to be incapable of being destroyed'.[8] It is 'more divine and impassible' than memory and love, and some part of the soul might accordingly be capable of separate existence.[9]

4.1 Lucretian mortalism

Lucretius saw no need for incorporeal principles or agents. The soul, which confers life, awareness, sensation, character, and also the power of thought on animals is atomic. It is dispersed through the body and 'exceedingly subtle, being composed of the minutest particles', which are round, smooth, exceptionally mobile, and readily compacted into a small space.[10] In the living creature the fine matter of the soul 'keeps secure the vital fastenings' of the body, performing a binding and structure-preserving role. Its 'very small seeds... form a chain throughout the veins, flesh, and sinews'.[11] The mass of the body is hardly diminished at death, and its shape is unaltered; yet the soul disperses, like the scent of a perfume or the flavor of a wine.

Many observations indicate that the soul is material and perishable: the disabling effects of injury to the pupil of the eye;[12] the mental and physical incompetence associated with youth, old age, and sickness;[13] and the ridiculous behavior and emotional excesses of the drunkard.[14] The fixed instincts of various species of animal—the ferocity of lions, the cunning of foxes, and the timidity of deer—argue that their behavior has a material substratum, and that the transmigration of souls across species is impossible.[15] The mind is susceptible to disease as much as the body and responds to medicine.[16] Further, the existence of a physical threshold for perceptibility indicates that conscious feeling depends on the weight and

---

[8] Aristotle, *On the Soul*, bk. I, ch. 4, 408^b, in *Complete Works*, i. 651.

[9] 'From this it is clear that the soul is inseparable from its body, or at any rate that certain parts of it are (if it has parts)—for the actuality of some of them is the actuality of the parts themselves. Yet some may be separable because they are not the actualities of any body at all' (Aristotle, *On the Soul*, bk. II, ch. 1, 413^a, in *Complete Works*, i. 657).

[10] T. C. Lucretius, *On the Nature of Things* (*ONT*), III. 179 ff.; trans. Martin Ferguson Smith (Indianapolis, Ind.: Hackett, 2001), 72.

[11] Ibid. III. 216—17; trans. Smith, p. 73.   [12] Ibid. III. 408 ff.; trans. Smith, p. 78.

[13] Ibid. III. 445 ff.; trans. Smith, p. 79.   [14] Ibid. III. 476—7; trans. Smith, p. 80.

[15] Ibid. III. 741—2; trans. Smith, p. 87.   [16] Ibid. III. 510 ff.; trans. Smith, p. 81.

pressure of aggregated bodies.[17] We do not feel the dust clinging to our bodies, or mist, spiderwebs, feathers, or insects.

Philosophers, Lucretius pointed out, must acknowledge that there exist seeds of things, 'immune to the dangers of attack', in order to explain the persistence of life. If they did not exist, everything now alive would eventually die and nothing could grow in its place. But these indestructible seeds lie outside our experience. Every entity known to us is composite and therefore frangible, and everything we observe around us has a prescribed limit to its possible duration, a limit that depends on the kind of thing it is—bird, or mountain, or cosmos. The human soul is not exempt from the fate of dissolution, for it too is material and composite. The prospect of death should not motivate moral or immoral behavior, nor should it give rise to vain hopes. The nocturnal anxiety of the mind brooding over its oncoming demise is dispelled, Lucretius said, 'not by the sun's rays and the dazzling darts of day, but by the study of the superficial aspect and underlying principle of nature'.[18]

Carneades, the quasi-Epicurean skeptic of the New Academy, cited by Cicero in *The Nature of the Gods*, pointed out that sensibility implies receptivity, which in turn implies mortality:

No body is not liable to death, nor even indiscerptible nor incapable of decomposition and dissolution. And every living thing is by its nature capable of feeling; therefore there is no living thing that can escape the unavoidable liability to undergo impressions from without, that is to suffer and to feel; and if every living thing is liable to suffering, no living thing is not liable to death. Therefore, likewise, if every living thing can be cut up into parts, no living thing is indivisible and none is everlasting.[19]

Whatever can experience pleasure can experience pain and must be subject to death. Whatever has inclination and disinclination can be destroyed; whatever is sensitive is perishable. The ethical conclusion that followed from the materiality of the soul, according to Lucretius, was that:

[D]eath ... is nothing to us and does not affect us in the least, now that the nature of the mind is understood to be mortal.... [W]hen we are no more, when body and soul, upon whose union our being depends, are divorced, you may be sure

---

[17] Ibid. III. 381 ff.; trans. Smith, pp. 77–8.   [18] Ibid. II. 60 ff., trans. Smith, p. 37.
[19] Marcus Tullius Cicero, *On the Nature of the Gods*, bk. III, ch. 12, trans. H. Rackham (Cambridge, Mass.: Harvard University Press, 1951), p. 313.

that nothing at all will have the power to affect us or awaken sensation in us, who shall not then exist—not even if the earth be confounded with the sea, and the sea with the sky.[20]

As we approach the end, we must lose the capacity to think, feel, and remember, because all these powers depend on our having an intact and functioning living body, one in which soul atoms are intermingled with our limbs and organs. Separated from the body, detached from eyes, ears, and limbs, the soul cannot possess either sentience or life.[21] Death is not to be feared because it is inevitable, rather than a harm done to us, and because we will not experience it. As Epicurus had pointed out, 'when we are, death is not come, and, when death is come, we are not'. No one is made worse off by his own death.[22]

Although the argument that it was no misfortune to die was widely accepted in ancient philosophy, the straightforward assertion of the mortality of the soul was exceptional on the part of the Epicureans.[23] Philosophy and religion taught the contrary. There were at least four reasons why the dogma of the immortality of the soul was perceived as so worthy of defense. First, the immediate sense that life as such is a good entails a desire for its prolongation, and the impression that all human life is good was perhaps stronger in a culture in which the death of infants, children, and young adults at the peak of their physical and intellectual powers was not uncommon. Second, the depth of human relationships makes the prospect of final farewells to loved ones hard for anyone to bear.[24] Third, the justice motive in human beings induces them to impose sanctions for wickedness, and where deterrence fails, retribution must supply the want. Finally, if the resurrection and eternal life promised by Christ was not a fact, what reason might anyone have for obedience to priests?

The Epicureans had no investment in priestly institutions. As Lucretius said: 'If people realized that there was a limit set to their tribulations, they would somehow find strength to defy irrational beliefs and the threats of the

---

[20] Lucretius, *ONT* III. 830 ff., trans. Smith, pp. 89–90.

[21] Ibid. III. 624 ff.; trans. Smith, p. 84. Cf. Epicurus, letter to Herodotus, in Diogenes Laertius, *Lives of the Eminent Philosophers*, X. 64; trans. R. D. Hicks (Cambridge, Mass.: Harvard University Press, 1925), ii. 595.

[22] Epicurus, letter to Menoeceus, in Diogenes Laertius, *Lives* X. 124–5; trans. Hicks, ii. 651.

[23] See James Warren, *Facing Death: Epicurus and His Critics* (Oxford: Clarendon, 2004), esp. pp. 76 ff.

[24] See Fernando Vidal, 'Brains, Bodies, Selves, and Science', *Critical Inquiry*, 8 (2002), esp. pp. 933–4.

fable-mongers'.[25] But they could not have failed to recognize the first three inducements to belief, and Lucretius admitted that the doctrine of the mortality of the soul was hard, a bitter truth needing to be sweetened by poetry.

Amongst the Fathers of the early Church it was Lactantius who gave mortalism its most thorough consideration. The final chapter of the *Divine Institutes*, attacking Epicurus and Lucretius, characterized immortality as 'the one greatest good…for the attainment of which we were made from the beginning and for which we were born'.[26] In the absence of immortality, Lactantius thought, human affairs would be meaningless and indeed the existence of the world would have no point.[27] The immortality of the human soul was, however, very difficult to establish. It was a tenet of revealed religion, barely mentioned in the Old Testament. Although Isaiah 26: 19 prophesied that 'the dead shall live again', a prophecy was not a promise. The explicit promise of the New Testament was backed up only by Christ's performance of miracles, miracles which themselves might or might not have occurred. Introspection did not reveal an immortal soul, and while tales of ghosts and ghostly vengeance were suggestive in this regard, they were neither very conclusive nor very general. It was possible that the notions of 'the incorporeal soul' and even of 'God' were fictions generated by material minds and sustained by custom, tradition, and authority—in a word, superstition. The only ancient philosopher who had advanced a credible argument for the necessary immortality of the human soul was Plato. In the *Phaedo* he had inferred its immortality from its incorporeality, insisting that whatever is incorporeal has no parts, hence is unbreakable and 'most like the divine, deathless, intelligible, uniform, indissoluble, always the same as itself'.[28]

4.2 Descartes and the immortality of the human soul

To early modern philosophers mortalism appeared for the most part an unwanted accessory doctrine to the neo-corpuscularian philosophy and

---

[25] Lucretius, *ONT* I. 108–9.; trans. Smith, p. 6.

[26] Lactantius, *The Divine Institutes*, bk. VI, ch. 8, trans. Sister Mary Francis McDonald OP (Washington, DC: Catholic University of America Press, 1965), 492.

[27] Ibid., bk. VII, ch. 6; trans. McDonald, p. 489.

[28] Plato, *Phaedo*, 80b, in *Complete Works*, ed. John M. Cooper and D. S. Hutchinson (Princeton, NJ: Princeton University Press, 1997), 70.

the decentered world system they accepted. Even if doubts about the immortality of the soul on the part of the individual philosopher might be psychologically bearable and do him little harm—for the philosopher was capable of understanding the doctrine that virtue was to be pursued for its own sake—general acceptance of the mortality of the soul would unleash libertinage and political anarchy, or so it seemed. The realization that intellectual doubt might destroy the basis for theology and morality was the source of the actual *crise pyrrhonienne* of the early seventeenth century,[29] to which Descartes, Spinoza, and Leibniz responded as meta-physicians. The task of the philosopher was to further the revival and development of the sciences of material nature, but at the same time to support Christian doctrine, leaving room for, or even finding novel arguments for, the immortality of the soul, for his own peace of mind and security and for the good of society. Mortalism, to a far greater extent than atheism, elicited an impressive battery of philosophical counterarguments.

At the same time, the prolongation of life and health in this world were understood by Bacon and Descartes as the proper and achievable goals of philosophy. Referring to 'the law that obliges us to procure, as much as is in our power, the common good of all men', Descartes said in the *Discourse* that his train of reflections was aimed at the production of 'knowledge that would be useful in life ... by means of which, knowing the force and the action of fire, water, air, the stars, the heavens, and all the other bodies that surround us, we might be able, in the same way, to use them for all the purposes for which they are appropriate, and thus render ourselves, as it were, the lords and masters of nature'.[30] In particular, the application of true theory and sound method would lead to the invention of 'innumerable devices which would facilitate our enjoyment of the fruits of the earth and all the goods we find there, but also, and most importantly, for the maintenance of health, which is undoubtedly the chief good, and the foundation of all other goods in this life'.[31] 'Life', Descartes maintained, was the name given to the phenomena of machines that men had not

[29] See Richard H. Popkin, *The History of Skepticism from Erasmus to Spinoza* (Berkeley, Calif.: University of California Press, 1979), 1.

[30] Descartes, *Discourse*, pt. VI, in *Oeuvres*, ed. C. Adam and P. Tannery (Paris: Vrin, 1964–74), vi. 62; trans. J. Cottingham et al., in *Philosophical Writings* (Cambridge: Cambridge University Press, 1985–9), i. 142–3.

[31] Ibid. See Harold J. Cook, 'Body and Passions', *Osiris*, 17 (2002), 25–48.

constructed. Because life was mechanism, the amelioration of life implied nothing more difficult or mysterious than the improvement of any machine, except that the machines of nature were composed of more parts and were more complex than the machines of men.

In the late 1630s, as a result of the publication of his *Discourse* and the promulgation of the mechanical philosophy by his admirer Henry Regius, the prospects for the acceptance of Descartes's system of the world looked dim. He had been condemned by the Aristotelian Rector of Utrecht Gijsbert Voet or Voetius, and he saw the wisdom of demonstrating that his anti-Aristotelian ontology and his ambitious program for knowing and mastering nature posed no threat to Christian institutions and ought rather to be welcomed in the universities. Descartes was eager at this point to dissociate himself from the old atomists, and he referred in a letter to one of his critics to 'that inane philosophy conflated of atoms and the void, usually ascribed to Democritus and Epicurus, and others like it, which have nothing to do with me'.[32] The exercise of 1640, appearing under the title *Renati Des-Cartes, meditationes de prima philosophia, in qua Dei existentia et animae immortalitas demonstratur*, was written to demonstrate that the Cartesian conception of matter as mere extended substance, devoid of forms, qualities, and virtues, was consistent with the existence of God and the immortality of the soul. Its composition puzzled some of his friends who had not expected from Descartes a metaphysical treatise on incorporeal entities, framed in the scholastic language of substances, causes, perfection, and formal and objective reality.

Descartes's claim that the bodies of animals and humans might be formed without the help of a directive soul or the creative activity of God, and that 'matter takes on all the forms of which it is capable' suggested that their natural dissolution into their constituent particles without any spiritual residue was inevitable. He nevertheless evaded the Epicurean conclusion that death was the end of all thought and experience, even at the cost of baffling some of his followers and rousing charges of hypocrisy. He insisted that the human soul was an incorporeal entity, a substance affixed to each human corporeal machine, and that it could exist separated from the body in which it had once resided. He

---

[32] Descartes, letter to Fromond, 3 October 1637, in *Oeuvres*, i. 413; trans. Grene and Ariew, in Ariew (ed.), *Descartes: Philosophical Essays* (Indianapolis: Hackett, 2000), p. 84. He further devoted several paragraphs at the conclusion of his *Principles* to the topic 'Why I am not a Democritean'.

had system-internal, as well as system-external reasons for positing such a soul.

Within his system of natural philosophy Descartes could see no way of explaining the two signal capabilities that differentiated humans from animals: language and abstract thought. The particles, pores, valves, vessels, and animal spirits that constituted his physiological apparatus were wholly inadequate to this task. Nor could he explain awareness and the sense of self in these terms. Further, some forms of mental representation—of a chiliagon, of God—did not require images, or at least did not require images intuitively adequate to their objects—and so seemed independent of the corporeal imagination. This suggested to Descartes that the most exalted and the most distinctively human powers of the soul were independent of matter. It was philosophically convenient to refer these capabilities and the phenomenon of consciousness to an incorporeal soul, thereby preserving the credibility of the rest of his system—his otherwise mechanical theories of perception, memory, dreaming, and automatic movement.

In the prefatory letter to the Sorbonne giving the reasons for his debut as a metaphysician Descartes observed that

some [people] have even had the audacity to assert that, as far as human reasoning goes, there are persuasive grounds for holding that the soul dies along with the body ... But in its eighth session the Lateran Council held under Leo X condemned those who take this position, and expressly enjoined Christian philosophers to refute their arguments and use all their powers to establish the truth; so I have not hesitated to attempt this task as well.[33]

The Fifth Lateran Council, which had met between 1512 and 1517, had urged that, after five years of free study, philosophers devote themselves to theology 'for cleansing and healing the infected sources of philosophy and poetry'. The extirpation of the doctrine of the mortality of the soul, root and branch, was meanwhile the task most urgently requested of them.

The audacious people Descartes had in mind may have included Averroists, who denied personal immortality, allowing only the absorption of the human intellect into a single universal mind at death, and followers of Pietro Pomponazzi, who had maintained in his *Tractatus de immortalitate animae*, published in Bologna in 1516, that the intellectual functions of man

---

[33] Descartes, *Meditations*, in *Oeuvres*, vii. 3; *Writings*, trans. and ed. Cottingham et al., ii. 4.

depend on his sensitive and imaginative capacities, which in turn depend on his body. He also doubtless had in mind the erudite libertines of contemporary Paris. 'How vain', Gassendi had exclaimed in the preface to his *Exercitationes* of 1624, 'are the hopes with which men usually philosophize about separate substances according to the natural light of reason!'[34] It is worth remembering that Leo X, who had set the challenge to philosophers, was a frivolous and pleasure-loving pontiff, known as 'the Epicurean Pope'. His own position on the mortality question was rumored to be that 'all begins and ends in nothing'.[35]

In identifying the soul with the activity of subtle but nevertheless material particles suffusing bodily tissues, the atomists had raised the possibility that a material thinking being in a godless universe might construct and come to believe in the fiction of an incorporeal God, taking it for reality. Descartes announced that he would demonstrate both the existence of God and the immortality of the soul in his *Meditations*, and much of his argument there is concerned with the question of the origin of various ideas, including the idea of the self, ideas of corporeal things, and the idea of God. His 'method of doubt' elicited the conclusion that the thinking soul was incorporeal and did not depend on the body, and he insisted that there was no reason to suppose that an incorporeal soul that could survive the death of its body would not do so.

Descartes advanced, played with, and ultimately discarded the hypotheses that ideas of corporeal things have a source that is not itself corporeal—an evil genius—and that they are radically deceptive. Yet it is not often noticed that his *Meditations* were equally concerned with the possibility that our ideas of incorporeal things have a source that is corporeal and so are radically deceptive. His idea of himself was, he tried to show, the idea of a purely

---

[34] Pierre Gassendi, *Exercitationes paradoxicae adversus Aristotelicos* (1624), in *The Selected Works of Pierre Gassendi*, trans. and ed. Craig Brush (New York/London: Johnson, 1972), 25.

[35] As reported by Burton, *Anatomy of Melancholy*, ed. Thomas C. Faulkner, Nicholas Kiessling, and Rhonda L. Blair (Oxford: Clarendon, 1989), i. 156. The Pope, according to the article devoted to him in the *Catholic Encyclopedia*, 'had an agreeable voice, knew how to express himself with elegance and vivacity, and his manner was easy and gracious. "Let us enjoy the papacy, since God has given it to us", he is said to have remarked after his election.... [This] illustrates fairly the pope's pleasure-loving nature and the lack of seriousness that characterized him. He paid no attention to the dangers threatening the papacy, and gave himself up unrestrainedly to amusements, that were provided in lavish abundance. He was possessed by an insatiable love of pleasure, that distinctive trait of his family. Music, the theatre, art, and poetry appealed to him as to any pampered worldling. Though temperate himself, he loved to give banquets and expensive entertainments, accompanied by revelry and carousing; and notwithstanding his indolence he had a strong passion for the chase, which he conducted every year on the largest scale'.

incorporeal thing that must correspond to reality, and his idea of God, he tried to show, both derived from and accurately represented God, an omnipotent and perfect creative being who was, moreover, real. God, though certainly an idea in the mind, was not merely an idea, one caused by induction into superstition through language and social experience, as materialists maintained, but a special kind of idea that directly implied the non-fictivity and indeed the necessary existence of an object corresponding to it.[36]

Descartes's assault on the problem of skepticism about incorporeal entities necessarily set aside the observational-inductive approach he had employed in the unpublished *Treatise of Man* and even in part V of the *Discourse on Method*, where his observations about animal behavior and human language were cited as evidence for his claim that 'the rational soul…cannot be derived in any way from the potentiality of matter, but must be specially created'.[37] The first two Meditations, intended to detach the inquirer from his customary sense-based modes of inquiry, evoked St Augustine's attack on the pagan empiricists in the *City of God*, those 'thinkers…who could not conceive of anything beyond the fantasies suggested by the imagination, circumscribed by the bodily senses'.[38] But where Augustine insisted dogmatically that it was obligatory to turn away from the senses and to seek another route to knowledge of the self and God, Descartes only took pains to persuade his readers that it was risky to proceed on the unexamined assumption that sensory experiences carry reliable information. The procedure of radical doubt introduced by Descartes in this context was intended to discredit the naively intuitive, phenomenological approach of the materialist. A prohibition on extrapolation from sensory experience, the canon of truth for the Epicurean, is repeated and reformulated throughout the first three Meditations, culminating in the announcement, 'I will now shut my eyes, stop my ears, and withdraw all my senses'.[39]

'I am not', the Meditator thinks already in Meditation II—though he does not yet know that he is right—'some thin vapour which permeates the limbs—a wind, fire, air, breath, or whatever I depict in my imagination;

---

[36] Descartes, Meditations III, V, in *Oeuvres*, vii. 46 ff., 65 ff.; *Writings*, trans. and ed. Cottingham et al., ii. 25 ff., 46 ff.

[37] Descartes, *Discourse*, pt. V, in *Oeuvres*, vi. 59; *Writings*, i. 141.

[38] St Augustine, *The City of God Against the Pagans*, bk. VIII, ch. 5; trans. Henry Bettenson (London: Penguin, 1984), 306.

[39] Descartes, Meditation II, in *Oeuvres*, vii. 34: *Writings*, ii. 24.

for these are things which I have supposed to be nothing'.[40] By Meditation VI, the feeling of a minded being that it is essentially embodied has been revealed as an intellectually untenable delusion of the imagination, turning the tables on the Epicurean. Nevertheless, Meditation VI sought to prove the nonessential, logically contingent but nonetheless important fact of embodiment, and to explain the tight integration or 'union' of the human soul and its mortal body. Empirical inquiry had its place once the nature of the soul and the reliability of its intellectual faculties had been established.

Descartes's endeavor to prove, by introspection and ratiocination, that he was not and could not be a highly imaginative corporeal thinking machine in a godless universe is a masterpiece of ingenuity and philosophical architectonics. The impossibility of the task predicted its failure, however, and Descartes's reputation was not saved in his lifetime. Only the efforts of his very Christian follower Nicolas Malebranche were able to erase the suggestion of gross impiety from his physics.[41] Descartes never succeeded in proving from a consideration of the ideas he found in his mind that there were entities outside his mind that possessed substantiality and causal efficacy. The possibly fictive nature of God, a problem introduced in Meditation III, when the Meditator realizes that his ideas may be 'all made up', recurs in Meditation V, when the Meditator finds in himself 'countless ideas of things which even though they may not exist anywhere outside me still cannot be called nothing'.[42] These ideas are, in the best case, he finds, of true and immutable natures, not sheer fabrications or inventions, but critics could see that the exercise of the *Meditations* did not lead to firm conclusions about the existence of nonimaginary incorporeal and infinite substances. There were three problems with Descartes's treatment of the subject. First, the adequacy of the concept of the soul as excluding all corporeality was doubtful. Perhaps the capacity to think depended on the body in ways human beings could not conceive because they lacked knowledge or imagination. Second, even if the capacity to think did not in fact require a material substrate, the persistence of thinking after the death of the body was not assured. Finally, even if the concept of the mind as a

---

[40] Ibid., in *Oeuvres*, vii. 27; *Writings*, ii. 18.

[41] On the rehabilitation of Descartes as a good Catholic after his placement on the index of prohibited books see Thomas Lennon, *The Battle of the Gods and Giants* (Princeton, NJ: Princeton University Press, 1993), 239.

[42] Descartes, Meditation V, in *Oeuvres*, vii. 44; *Writings*, ii. 64.

separable substance was ontologically adequate, and even if the persistence of such a substance was assured, this substance might not be a fit subject for reward and punishment, and it might be that no living human being had good reason to wish for his continuation as a separated Cartesian mind. Descartes did not establish that a sensing, feeling, perceiving mind does in fact outlast the mortal body and so discharge the obligation to the Fifth Lateran Council that he had assumed in his prefatory letter.

Most philosophers could see that the immortality of the soul, in any sense in which its immortality might be desirable, did not actually follow from Descartes's claim that the concept of the soul was that of a substance that was independent of the body. His friendly critic and supporter Marin Mersenne complained about Descartes's lack of attention to the question of immortality in the *Second Set of Objections*.[43] Gassendi plagued him about the issue in the *Fifth Set of Objections*, and in the *Sixth Set of Objections* the authors—miscellaneous philosophers and theologians—cited St Paul and the author of Ecclesiastes as skeptics, insisting that Descartes had not met an acceptable standard of demonstration, and that he had not shown that 'corporeal motions' were inadequate to produce thought or that it was 'self-contradictory that our thoughts should be reducible to these corporeal motions'.[44] They observed that 'we do not know what can be done by bodies and their motions, and [that] ... you confess that without a divine revelation no one can know everything which God has imparted or could impart to any object'.[45]

Descartes admitted that he had not discharged the obligation he had appeared to take on so eagerly. In the *Synopsis to the Meditations*, presumably written after he had received the entire set of prepublication criticisms, he tried to bolster his original arguments, asserting that 'Absolutely all substances ... are by their nature incorruptible and cannot ever cease to exist unless they are reduced to nothingness by God's denying his concurrence to them'.[46] He claimed that the mind is a 'pure' substance and that

---

[43] '[Y]ou say not one word about the immortality of the human mind. Yet this is something you should have taken special care to prove and demonstrate, to counter those people, themselves unworthy of immortality, who utterly deny and even perhaps despise it ... [I]t does not seem to follow from the fact that the mind is distinct from the body that it is incorruptible or immortal' (Marin Mersenne, *Objections*, II, in Descartes, *Oeuvres*, vii. 128; *Writings*, ii. 91).

[44] *Objections* VI, in *Oeuvres*, vii. 413; *Writings*, ii. 278.

[45] Ibid., in *Oeuvres* vii. 421; *Writings*, ii. 284.

[46] Descartes, 'Synopsis', in *Oeuvres*, vii. 14; *Writings*, ii. 10.

configurational changes in its contents do not break it up.[47] '[E]ven if all
the accidents of the mind change, so that it has different objects of the
understanding and different desires and sensations', Descartes insisted, 'it
does not on that account become a different mind'.[48] But the claim that
mental substance can only be destroyed by an act of God does not entail
the indestructibility of the individual human mind. If, as the Averroists
maintained, what thinks in us is a universal mind that is indestructible
but that has particularity only so long as it informs a living body, the
proof is inadequate. Descartes ought to have shown that the thing of
which we are aware when we are aware of ourselves is a single substance,
one amongst a great multiplicity of other substances. In this connection,
his claim that configurational changes could not change the identity of
the mind merely created further problems. Why immortality would be
desirable, and how God could justly and effectively punish and reward if
identity in the mind's 'accidents' were not preserved in its substance, was
not explained.

In response to criticism, Descartes changed the subtitle of the second
edition of his *Meditations*, eliminating the reference to the immortality of
the soul. He conceded the force of Mersenne's objection that mind–body
distinctness did not imply the immortality of the soul, and he indicated that
he did not care.[49] He admitted to Mersenne that he had not proved and
could not prove that God would see to our immortality, but he insisted that
he had shown that the human mind was 'by nature entirely distinct from
the body, and consequently ... not bound by nature to die with it. This is all
that is required as a foundation for religion and all that I had any intention
of proving'.[50] To Princess Elizabeth of Bohemia he commented later: 'As
for the state of the soul after this life, I am not as well informed as M. Digby.
Leaving aside what faith tells us, I agree that by natural reason alone we can
make favourable conjectures and have fine hopes, but we cannot have any
certainty'.[51] In a late letter to Jean de Silhon he referred to the 'primary,
unearned, and certain awareness' his mind possessed and to the still greater
capacity of a future disembodied mind of 'receiving intuitive knowledge

[47] Ibid.   [48] Ibid.

[49] 'Here I admit that I cannot refute what you say' (Descartes, *Replies*, II, in *Oeuvres* vii. 153; *Writings*,
ii. 108–9; cf. 'Synopsis', in *Oeuvres*, vii. 13; *Writings*, ii. 10).

[50] Descartes, letter to Mersenne, 24 December 1640, in *Oeuvres*, iii. 266; *Writings*, iii. 163.

[51] Descartes, letter to Elizabeth, 3 November 1645, in *Oeuvres*, iv. 333; *Writings*, iii. 277. On Digby
see below, p. 137.

from God', but without suggesting that he would be an active subject of experiences in the future state.[52]

Perhaps Descartes believed that the immortality of the soul was a fact, though it could not be demonstrated with absolute certainty. More likely, his interests and ambitions were focused on this world, and on the embodied human beings living and dying within it. In any event, the Cartesian theory of sensory experience, as a 'confused mode', elaborately detailed in Meditation VI, required a body to be joined to the incorporeal mind for experiences to occur. The conclusion Descartes reached there was not just that the thinking soul was incorporeal but that all our experiences and emotions depend upon the body, and especially upon its nervous system. On this issue Descartes remained surprisingly close to the Aristotelian position: a separated soul would be unable to see colors, hear sounds, understand language, or do more than engage in pure acts of intellectual intuition. Descartes confirmed that this was his view in a letter to Henry More, indicating that there might be a distinction between angelic minds and human minds in this respect:

[T]he human mind separated from the body does not have sense-perception strictly so-called; but it is not clear by natural reason alone whether angels are created like minds distinct from bodies, or like minds united to bodies. I never decide about questions on which I have no certain reasons, and I never allow room for conjectures.[53]

The memory of material things, said Descartes, 'depends on the traces which remain in the brain after an image has been imprinted on it'. He allowed nevertheless for a form of noncorporeal memory of 'intellectual things' which he referred to vaguely as 'some other traces which remain in the mind itself'.[54]

---

[52] Descartes, letter to Silhon, March or April 1648, in *Oeuvres*, v. 137–8; *Writings*, iii. 331. Marsilio Ficino, whose views were probably known to Descartes, argued: 'Because … the substance of the human mind is completely incorporeal though united with matter, it follows that our mind understands incorporeals, but sees them, so long as it inhabits the body, in the company often of something in a way corporeal, an image of the phantasy in other words. Accordingly it usually needs such images. But once this body has been laid aside and the mind returned to itself, it will understand in itself' (*Platonic Theology*, bk. X, trans. Michael B. J. Allen, ed. James Hankins (Cambridge, Mass.: Harvard University Press, 2003), iii. 165).

[53] Descartes, letter to More, August 1649, in *Oeuvres*, v. 402; *Writings*, trans. and ed. Cottingham et al., iii. 380.

[54] Descartes, letter to Mesland, 2 May 1644, in *Oeuvres*, iv. 114; *Writings*, iii. 233. This thesis must however be reconciled with the letter of condolence to Huygens of 13 October 1642, in *Oeuvres*,

The immediate reaction to the *Meditations* in the scholarly community was varied. Descartes was pressed from both sides: to the orthodox it appeared that, while he had argued against atheistic corporealists, in failing to prove his point he had stimulated and encouraged them. To those sympathetic to the corporeal soul and interested in the naturalization of the sensory faculties he appeared to have abandoned them. The sixth set of objectors asked how Descartes could know that God had not implanted in certain bodies 'a power or property enabling them to doubt, think, etc.'.[55] Gassendi, meanwhile, to Descartes's extreme annoyance, had pushed his Epicurean agenda with vigor and persistence throughout his own lengthy set of objections to the *Meditations*, and he had reproduced the ancient arguments for the dependence of the mind upon the body, insisting that the Meditator had no reason to exclude from consideration the possibility that he was simply 'the noblest part of the soul ... the flower, or the most refined and pure and active part of it'.[56]

[W]hy is it not possible [he asked] that you are a wind, or rather a very thin vapour, given off when the heart heats up the purest type of blood, or produced by some other source, which is diffused through the parts of the body and gives them life? May it not be this vapour which sees with the eyes and hears with the ears and thinks with the brain and performs all the other functions which are commonly ascribed to you?[57]

He suggested that the Meditator might be 'some corporeal or tenuous substance', comparable to the scent wafting from a cut apple, whose particles could drift away after death. 'We would, however, have to say that, because of this dispersal, you would not continue to think, or be a thinking thing, a mind or a soul.'[58]

Although he claimed to be questioning only Descartes's arguments, not his conclusion, Gassendi hurled at him a volley of technically answerable but nevertheless compelling counterarguments, similar to those advanced

---

iii. 580; *Writings*, iii. 215–16, according to which the sense of pleasure and our capacity for happiness and tranquility, as well as our intellectual memory, will persist after death, and we will meet our relatives in heaven. I am indebted to Kurt Smith for pointing out both passages.

[55] *Objections* VI, in Descartes, *Oeuvres*, vii. 421; *Writings*, ii. 284.

[56] Gassendi, *Objections* V, in Descartes, *Oeuvres*, vii. 265; *Writings*, ii. 185.

[57] Ibid., in *Oeuvres*, vii. 260–1; *Writings*, ii. 182 f.

[58] Ibid., *Oeuvres*, vii. 343–4; *Writings*, ii. 238 f. See also his discussion in the *Syntagma philosophicum*, pt. II, § 3, ch. 17.

by Lucretius on behalf of the materiality of the soul. He denied that there was any important distinction between animal and human cogitation.[59] He cited the disturbing effects of 'foul and dense vapours or fumes' on the brain.[60] He pointed out that damage to the organ of thought that injured the imaginative faculty also impaired intelligence, concluding that 'there is surely no ready way of establishing the distinction [between thinking substance and corporeal substance]'.[61] Finally, he complained, the notion of incorporeal, thinking substance was irremediably obscure: 'You tell us nothing of the substance which performs this operation—what kind of substance it is, and what it consists of, how it organizes itself to perform so many different functions in so many different ways'.[62] The imagination and the understanding are, he said, 'the same power', whose difference in functioning is 'merely one of degree'. The ideas of God, an angel, and the human soul or mind are 'corporeal or quasi-corporeal'.[63] In the *Disquisitio metaphysica*, published in 1644, Gassendi's amplification of his *Objections*, he stated baldly that 'if the mind co-exists with a body, or an extended thing, it cannot be unextended'.[64] In his *Syntagma philosophicum*, however, published posthumously in 1658, Gassendi bafflingly posited and defended a special human soul, infused by God at conception, that was nonatomic and incorporeal, advancing arguments both physical and moral for its immortality. The physical arguments were drawn from consideration of the operations of the soul, its freedom, its ability to will what is good and honorable, preferring it to what is delicious and sensible, and its intellectual power to conceptualize without imagination, to think reflexively on itself, and to consider universals and incorporeal things.[65] The moral arguments

[59] Gassendi, *Objections* V, in Descartes, *Oeuvres*, vii. 270–1; *Writings*, ii:188–9f. On Gassendi's theory of the soul see Emily Michael, 'Renaissance Theories of Body, Soul, and Mind', in P. Potter and J. Wright (eds.), *Psyche and Soma: Physicians and Metaphysicians on the Mind–Body Problem from Antiquity to Enlightenment* (Oxford: Oxford University Press, 2000) and 'Gassendi's Method Illustrated by His Account of the Soul', in *Pierre Gassendi 1592–1992*, (Digne-les-Baines, Société Scientifique et Littéraire des Alpes de Haute-Provence: 1994), 1: 181–93.

[60] Gassendi, *Objections* V, in Descartes, *Oeuvres*, vii. 263; *Writings*, trans. and ed. Cottingham et al., ii.183.

[61] Ibid., in *Oeuvres*, vii. 267; *Writings*, ii. 186.

[62] Ibid., in *Oeuvres*, vii. 266; *Writings*, ii.185–6.

[63] Ibid., in *Oeuvres*, vii. 332 ff.; *Writings*, ii. 230 ff.

[64] Pierre Gassendi, *Disquisitio metaphysica*, Contra Meditation VI; Doute III, Inst. XI, Dubitatio IV, trans. and ed. Bernard Rochot (Paris: Vrin, 1962), 584–5.

[65] Pierre Gassendi, *Syntagma philosophicum*, in *Opera omnia* (Lyon: 1658, repr. Hildesheim: Olms, 1968), ii. 398–9, 440 ff. As Antonia LoLordo points out, these arguments are peculiar, insofar as Gassendi

comprised in turn the universal consent of all men of all ages, nations, and religions to the doctrine of an afterlife, the desire or appetite for immortality naturally inherent in all men, and the necessity of divine justice.[66]

Regius, later described by Descartes's biographer as his 'denatured disciple',[67] was baffled and outraged by what appeared to him a hypocritical volte-face. Regius had had access to Descartes's manuscripts on animal life, and he went on to create a furore by suggesting that the soul 'is a certain attribute which belongs to a single subject jointly with extension, even though the attributes of one are not comprised in the idea of the other'.[68] He maintained that the idea of God was a corporeal idea, and, in 1647, he published an anonymous broadsheet of the sort that was typically affixed to church doors to be read by passers-by, in which, while seemingly allowing for an incorruptible and substantial soul, he repeated his view that the mind might be a mode of a corporeal substance, rather than a substance, 'a sort of attribute co-existing in the same subject'. As long as the mind is in the body it is 'organic in all its actions', he suggested, and it could be affected by imaginary as well as real things. All common notions, including the idea of God, had their origin in either observation of things or verbal instruction. Regius' views were angrily rejected by Descartes, who insisted that his arguments absolutely excluded any such interpretation. He was furious at having been made a subject of controversy when his intention in writing the *Meditations* had been to render appropriate assurances.

Voetius, writing in the wake of the 'Regius affair', the vicious exchanges of letters and public denunciations of the early 1640s at the University of Utrecht, compared Descartes with Cesare Vanini, who had been burned at the stake for writing dialogues pretending to oppose atheism that he knew would instead encourage skepticism with bad arguments.[69] These accusations were unjust, insofar as Descartes had not intended to promulgate

appears to reverse his mode of argumentation when challenging Cartesian arguments (*Pierre Gassendi and the Birth of Modern Philosophy* (Cambridge: Cambridge University Press, 2006), 235).

[66] Gassendi, *Syntagma*, in *Opera omnia*, ii. 628 ff. See Margaret Osler, 'Baptizing Epicurean Atomism: Pierre Gassendi on the Immortality of the Soul', in Margaret J. Osler and Paul Farber (eds.) *Religion, Science and Worldview* (Cambridge: Cambridge University Press, 1985), 163–83.

[67] 'Before Spinoza, some of whose errors he shared', commented the Cartesian De Raey, in 1692, 'Regius corrupted philosophy'. Descartes's biographer Adrien Baillet was largely responsible for the infamy of Regius (*La vie de Monsieur Descartes* (1691; repr. Geneva: Sklatine, 1970), i. 270–1).

[68] Henry Regius, *Philosophie naturelle de Henry le Roy* (Utrecht: Rodolphe van Zyll 1687), 428.

[69] Descartes responded in his letter to Voetius of May 1643, in *Oeuvres*, viii B.175; *Writings*, trans. and ed. Cottingham et al., iii. 223.

skepticism, but he had assuredly laid the groundwork for a corporeal theory of mentality in his depiction of the animal machine. Although he had directly attacked the Epicurean theory that the soul was composed of tiny particles that would disperse at death, his intervention made the Epicurean thesis ever more visible by drawing out criticism that might have remained unvoiced.

Malebranche devoted *The Search after Truth* of 1675 to trying to improve the status of Cartesianism amongst Christians and to reconciling as far as possible the mechanical philosophy, the ubiquity of laws of nature, the plurality of worlds, and the Cartesian theory of the bodily machine with the doctrine of personal salvation through Jesus Christ. Malebranche insisted on Descartes's Jesuit credentials, and inveighed against the stupidity of Voetius and all detractors who thought that 'those who denied pain to animals were libertines'. Still, he had to make substantial modifications to Cartesianism to rehabilitate it, which he did by extending Descartes's physical program but simultaneously reviving the old theological doctrine of the impotence of created substances. We look at the world, Malebranche claimed, but we see all things in God; we will to move our arms and legs, and to utter words, but it is God, the only causal power capable of initiating or altering motion, who enables us to act, speak, and understand.[70] The materialists' hypothesis that the idea of God was a social fiction, indoctrinated through language and superstitious ritual, was impossible according to Malebranche, for God could be shown to be the direct cause of all life, experience, and communication, the ground of the world appearing to the senses, and the necessary condition of all human society. God was active everywhere in the universe, in every instant, and nothing else was, except the human mind, though Malebranche was unclear about the extent to which we initiate and control the course of our own thinking.

Malebranche's piety, enthusiasm, and literary style were much admired and his version of Cartesianism was reassuring to the orthodox. Yet acceptance of his visionary metaphysics was widely viewed as too high a price to pay for the rescue of the incorporeal and immortal soul. Meanwhile, Descartes's other students, Spinoza and Leibniz, addressed the question of human immortality, retaining, as Locke conspicuously did not, Descartes's

---

[70] Nicolas Malebranche, Dialogue VIII § 13, in *Dialogues on Metaphysics*, trans. Willis Doney (New York: Abaris, 1980), 119.

commitment to a metaphysics of substance. Twenty years later the issue was very much alive. Henry Oldenburg noted in his third letter to Spinoza that '[t]he controversy about what Thought is, whether it is a corporeal motion or some spiritual act, entirely different from the corporeal, is still unresolved'.[71] God might, he allowed, be merely an idea, conjured up by the mind, corresponding to nothing outside itself.

4.3 The calculated ambiguity of Spinoza

Spinoza's philosophy is difficult to understand, characterized by abrupt changes in style and mode of address, and replete with apparent contradictions. His ethical ideas regarding the need to extirpate disturbing emotions by employing one's rationality had obvious affinities with Stoicism, as did his doctrine of the world as characterized by both thought and extension. Spinoza had no place, however, for the Stoics' providence, or for their all-pervading vital pneuma. His metaphysics entailed a thoroughgoing rejection of the existence of any purely incorporeal substance, finite or infinite, human or divine, and he was accordingly read as a materialist. His ethical writings fused the Epicurean doctrine that men ought to be freed from distress and fear by an understanding of natural causes with the doctrine of Plato that some persons can transcend the fate of the vulgar man and achieve immortality by acquiring ethical knowledge. Like other early modern philosophers, he tried to effect a reconciliation between a mechanical theory of nature recognizing only physical causes and the aspirational elements of theology and morality. Spinoza's tempering of his rejection of providence, and his scorn for anthropomorphism and superstition with strong doses of Plato's theory of the transcendence of mundane reality account for the somewhat peculiar fascination this philosopher exercises over some readers.

Spinoza had no personal investment in Christianity, and he was under no pressure to defend the Christian revelation or to make good philosophically on its promise of salvation. His separation from Judaism and the Jewish community left him with no need to uphold specific theological premises,

---

[71] Henry Oldenburg, letter to Spinoza, 27 September 1661, in Baruch Spinoza, *Collected Works*, trans. Edwin Curley (Princeton, NJ: Princeton University Press, 1985), i. 168–9.

and no motive to mount arguments to maintain his good standing. Several commentators have drawn attention to his early skepticism regarding the immortality of the soul and the personhood of God, as well as the reliability of prophetic testimony.[72] However, the notion of 'salvation' continued to play a role in his physical-moral system, and Spinoza did not fully dispense with the notions of grace, or divine favor, or a special future for the virtuous. He succumbed unavoidably, as Margaret Wilson puts it, to 'the temptation to exalt mind over body'.[73]

In the early *Short Treatise* Spinoza indicated that ethics and theology depended upon a proper understanding of nature and body, which were accordingly primary in the order of reasons leading up to ethics and salvation. The first step was 'to show that there is in Nature a body by whose form and actions we are affected, so that we perceive it'. Then, he promised, 'we shall...find the first and principal cause of all those passions, and at the same time the means by which all these passions can be destroyed'.[74] He avoided stating any agreement with Hobbes, whom he admired, to the effect that everything in the universe was body and that God was unknowable, maintaining instead that extension and thought are copresent attributes of a single, universal substance, and that the mind is the 'idea' of the body. He denied that God had anything like a human body, a human mind, and human passions. '[E]veryone who has to any extent contemplated the divine nature denies that God is corporeal'.[75] He went on, however, to criticize philosophers who regarded God as wholly incorporeal.[76] The claim that God does not have a body was clearly aimed at anthropomorphists; Spinoza did not insist on any incompatibility between the divine nature and corporeal substance, only between divinity and its embodiment in a particular figure. If corporeal substance is recognized as infinite, there is no incompatibility of the sort mooted. And because there cannot be two substances, either infinite or limited, God cannot be the creator of corporeal nature. All this was explained briefly in the *Short*

---

[72] See Jacqueline Lagrée, 'Spinoza "Athée et épicurien"', *Archives de Philosophie*, 57 (1994), 541–58, and Steven Nadler, *Spinoza's Heresy: Immortality and the Jewish Mind* (Oxford: Clarendon, 2001).

[73] Margaret Wilson, 'Spinoza's Theory of Knowledge', p. 130. Wilson describes his theory of knowledge as 'a strange and hybrid creature...[blending] highly distinctive, original (even bizarre) formulations with both 'modern'—especially Cartesian—influences, and ideas and aspirations rooted in much older thought' (ibid. 89).

[74] Spinoza, *Short Treatise*, ch. 19, in *Works*, trans. Curley, i. 130.

[75] Spinoza, *Ethics*, pt. I; prop. 15, scholium, in *Works*, i. 421.   [76] Ibid.

Treatise, and more cumbersomely in scholium I to proposition 14 of the first book of the *Ethics*, in which Spinoza insisted that God could not create another, material substance outside of and supplementary to Itself.

God is accordingly an extended, thinking thing, whose basic attributes, insofar as they are explained in the *Ethics*, are more corporeal than psychological. God is unique—the only substance—infinite, uncreated, and indivisible. God is perfect, that is exhaustive of what there is and of what happens, but devoid of ethical qualities, including goodness. Like jealousy and liability to anger, the trait of benevolence ascribed to God by the tradition is merely anthropomorphic projection, according to Spinoza. God has all the power of corporeal nature to produce effects, but no will, choice, or intention; and all objects and all events flow from Its fixed nature. Having neither freedom of choice nor ethical qualities, God has no intentions or purposes with respect to human beings and pays them no heed. Nothing can happen in a way other than it does; there are no unrealized possibilities. Matter and God are the same substance, though differently conceived; one is the object of perception and manipulation, the other the object of reverence for Its magnitude, power, and implacability. Spinoza does not describe the infinite individual that has intellect, will, and body as an organism, or as an animal, but the world-animal animated by a world-soul was a familiar, if heretical, concept.[77]

Spinoza's system, like Descartes's, was technically incompatible with atomism, for he denied that corporeal substance, 'insofar as it is a substance', was divisible,[78] and whether he should be classified as a materialist depends on whether the denial of the existence of incorporeal substance is taken as a sufficient or as an insufficient qualification. He most certainly accepted corpuscularianism as a scientific posit, and his early *Principles of Cartesian Philosophy* (1663) was, as the title suggests, a presentation of Cartesian mechanism. There, Spinoza commended the hypothesis of *Principles* (iii. 47) concerning the self-formation of the world from particles in motion or 'seeds', on the grounds that it was noncontradictory, maximally simple, easy to know, and that it could account for everything observed in the whole of nature.[79] Nevertheless, individual persons, stones, dust particles, animals,

[77] See Plato, *Laws*, X. 980d and *Timaeus*, 30b ff.
[78] Spinoza, *Ethics*, pt. I, props. 12–13, in *Works*, trans. Curley, i. 419–20.
[79] Spinoza, *The Principles of Cartesian Philosophy*, pt. III; in *Works*, i. 296–7.

and so on were for him 'finite modes' of the single divine substance, and the same apparently held of the particles or 'seeds' that were the concern of the physical scientist. The individuality of all such things is a kind of illusion—a point to which Leibniz took worried exception. Yet because the unique corporeal-divine substance could think (as the human body can think without the superaddition of a mental substance), as well as undergo change, God could be said to possess ideas of singular, finite things. Because there are no unrealized possibilities, and because God's power is fully exerted at all times, these quasi-individual things cannot be mere ideas; they exist and interact. Moreover, they are bound together in a chain of cause and effect that is rigorously mechanical. 'Every singular thing ... can neither exist nor be determined to produce an effect unless it is determined to exist and produce an effect by another cause, which is also finite and has a determinate existence.'[80] Thus 'all things have been determined from the necessity of the divine nature to exist and produce an effect in a certain way'.[81]

His monism enabled Spinoza to reject the Cartesian posit of an incorporeal, separable thinking soul without having to endorse the doctrine of corporeal thinking machines. Human beings, on his view, were extended, thinking things, modes of the single substance. The undated *Treatise on the Improvement of the Understanding* claimed that it was as false and confused to believe 'that there are bodies from whose composition alone the intellect is made',[82] as to believe that corpses reason, walk about, and speak. In the *Short Treatise*, however, Spinoza stated that the mind (wherever it existed) was an idea generated by the body: 'The Soul is an Idea which is in the thinking thing, arising from the existence of a thing which is in Nature'.[83] It 'has its origin from the body', and its changes depend '(only) on the body'.[84] Mind and body, Spinoza went on to say in the *Ethics*, are 'one and the same Individual'.[85] The mind cannot perceive, imagine, or remember anything without the body: 'The human Mind does not perceive any external body as actually existing, except through the ideas of the affections of its own Body'.[86] Sensation results from changes in 'proportions' between motion and rest in the sensory organs. More motion in a certain respect can

---

[80] Spinoza, *Ethics*, pt. I, prop. 28; in *Works*, i. 432.   [81] Ibid., prop. 29; in *Works*, i. 433.
[82] Ibid., *On the Improvement of the Understanding*, in *Works*, i. 30.
[83] Ibid., *Short Treatise*, ch. 23; in *Works*, i. 140.   [84] Ibid., app. 2, prop. 3; in *Works*, i. 152.
[85] Ibid., *Ethics*, pt. II, prop. 21; in *Works*, i. 467.   [86] Ibid., pt I, prop. 26; in *Works*, i. 469.

produce sensations of heat, less motion produces sensations of cold.[87] Every alteration in first-order sensory experience corresponds to some change in the external world, and the idea of the 'mind' arises from our second-order experience of ourselves as first-order sensory experiencers. 'Because we have now explained what feeling is', Spinoza says, 'we can easily see how from this there arises a reflexive Idea, or knowledge of oneself, experience, and reasoning.'[88]

Final causes were rejected by Spinoza in more scornful terms than by Descartes, and he developed the Lucretian critique of superstition, explaining the error of positing a providential supervisor with definite plans. Human beings project the structure of intention and beneficence onto nature as a whole:

[T]hey find, both in themselves and outside themselves—many means that are very helpful in seeking their own advantage, e.g., eyes for seeing, teeth for chewing, plants and animals for food, the sun for light, the sea for supporting fish.... Hence they consider all natural things as means to their own advantage. And knowing that they had found these means, not provided them for themselves, they had reason to believe that there was someone else who had prepared those means for their use.... [T]hey had to infer that there was a ruler, or a number of rulers of nature, endowed with human freedom, who had taken care of all things for them, and made all things for their use.[89]

Spinoza was clear that there is little difference between individual human constitutions, and even between men and animals, where their basic propensities and all that concerns their vitality and drive to reproduce themselves are concerned. Every finite object, whether it is a particle, an organ, or an animal body, seeks to preserve itself, exercising conatus, a tending or striving, which appears under different circumstances as inertia, resistance, force, appetite, or desire.[90] The obedience of inanimate objects to the Cartesian law of inertia can be understood as their pursuit of their own trajectory of motion, provided no *force majeure* intervenes.[91] Analogously, animate objects strive to preserve their physical integrity and to eliminate pain. 'After we know the origin of the Mind [in the body]', Spinoza says,

---

[87] Spinoza, *Short Treatise*, app. 2, prop. 15, in *Works*, i. 155.
[88] Ibid., prop. 17; in *Works*, i. 156.   [89] Spinoza, *Ethics*, pt. I, app., in *Works*, i. 440–1.
[90] Spinoza, *Ethics*, pt. III, prop. 6, in *Works*, i. 498.
[91] Ibid., pt. II, prop. 13, lemma 3 Corollary, in *Works*, i. 459.

'we cannot in any way doubt that the lower animals feel things.'[92] Animal emotions differ from human 'as much as their natures differ from human nature…. [T]he Lusts and Appetites of Insects, fishes, and birds must vary'.[93] Yet all creatures—horse, bird, fish, drunkard, philosopher—according to the ontological doctrines of parts I and II of the *Ethics* are aggregates of solid and fluid parts, retaining a stable organic relationship, animated by desire, subject to the pains and pleasures of the transitions it induces. Lucretius had suggested that life required the assimilation of particles that form connections with and that 'respond sympathetically to the vital motions within the body [and] imitate them',[94] and being just such a relational unity of parts is, for Spinoza, a precondition of being a functional unity with conatus: 'The Individual thus composed preserves its nature, whether it be, as a whole, in motion or rest, whether it be moved in this or that direction; so long as each part retains its motions, and preserves its communication with other parts as before'.[95]

Spinoza did not consider the world as a neutral place, neither especially good nor especially bad for us, but as a dangerous and painful place. As Carneades stressed, the liability to feeling, the result of 'impressions from without', was a sign of mortality. Pain is the harbinger of death, or nonexistence in time, and must be very widely experienced in complex individuals. Spinoza's superficially objective stance towards the world was in fact value-laden. He saw animals as fragile systems, with delicate and unstable ratios of motion and rest in the particles composing them. He interpreted the passions as the means by which the relentless abrasions of living—the infinite power of the rest of nature, with whom we exist in an impossibly unequal competition—become manifest to consciousness. The world acts on our organized bodies in such a way as sometimes to facilitate, but mainly to impede our actions. The struggle to persevere in one's being is costly and ultimately futile, for, as we are told, 'The force by which a man perseveres in existing is limited, and infinitely surpassed by the power of external causes'.[96] Even simple acts of perception are mild assaults by the environment on our sensory systems. Spinoza dramatized the Cartesian account of vision as produced by impulse and pressure, referring

---

[92] Spinoza, *Ethics*, pt. III, prop. 57, in *Works*, i. 528.
[93] Ibid., pt. II, prop. 49, in *Works*, i. 485.   [94] Lucretius, *ONT* II. 716–17; trans. Smith, p. 53.
[95] Spinoza, *Ethics*, pt. II, prop. 13, lemma 7, in *Works*, trans. Curley, i. 461.
[96] Ibid., pt. IV, prop. 3, in *Works*, i. 548.

to the different ways we can feel pain 'when we are struck with a little stick in the eyes or on the hands'.[97] Where the emotions, according to Descartes, help us to preserve our lives by informing us of what is harmful and beneficial, in Spinoza's system they are essentially messengers bringing us the bad news that we are already losing our individual contests with the world.

The tradition held the emotions to be psychic and somatic disturbances, caused by the perceived good and evil inherent in events and situations, that descended on people without warning and that tended to promote irrational and imprudent actions. Parts III and IV of the *Ethics* revised the account of the origins and significance of human emotions along naturalistic Cartesian lines, while retaining the view that they were apt to leave us, as Spinoza put it, helpless with dejection or burning with uncontrollable desires.[98] Our emotional lives unfold according to 'the laws and rules of nature, according to which all things happen, and change from one form to another, [which] are always and everywhere the same'.[99] As the aim of the Epicureans was to eradicate men's fears and anxieties by revealing the true mechanical causes of events that seemed to the ignorant to indicate the favor or disfavor of the gods, Spinoza's aim was to eradicate dangerous and disturbing emotions generally by revealing the true mechanical causes of our judgements of good and evil. He refrained, however, from drawing the ethical conclusions that the pleasures of the senses and freedom from bodily pain were the greatest goods for living, sensitive creatures, and that the death of the human body was the end of all its thoughts and experiences. Instead Spinoza constructed his *Ethics* to build, on an ontological foundation not very different from Hobbes's, an ethics promising joy and beatitude in this life, but urging, at the same time, detachment for the sake of tranquility, and even hinting at the promise of another life.

The ethics that should replace our spontaneous way of acting when we are ignorant of causes is alternately pragmatic and detached. We ought to pursue those things that are needful and conducive to the integrity of the body and the tranquility of the mind, but avoid pursuits that speed up the inevitable process of disintegration. The emphasis on romantic love as a source, in the words of Spinoza's recent editor, of 'dangers, disturbances,

---

[97] Spinoza, *Short Treatise*, app. 2, prop. 16, in *Works*, i. 155.
[98] Spinoza, *Ethics*, pt. III, props. 11–19 ff., in *Works*, i. 500 ff.
[99] Ibid., preface to pt. III, in *Works*, i. 492.

insatiability, and futility', is prominent in part IV of the *Ethics*, 'Of Human Bondage', which seems addressed to 'the person lying in bonds of love', as Lucretius describes him, 'torn by winged creatures'.[100] 'Love, desire and everything that is proper to love', Spinoza had claimed earlier, are 'of such a kind and nature that without them we can neither be nor persist, and they belong to us, as it were, essentially'.[101] Yet 'love falling on a certain object' that is mutable and corruptible, 'hate and sadness' follow necessarily. Love of God alone prevents us falling into this 'bog'. By coming to understand oneself as an organism, a physical machine acted upon by the environment, one frees oneself from romantic illusion and obsession and the helplessness that accompanies them.

The thesis that the mind is an idea of the body, and that the conatus of each individual thing is eventually exhausted, might be taken to imply mortalism. Substance considered en masse is eternal; its properties do not change, and there is nothing external to it that can create or destroy it, but its modes do not endure. Spinoza appeared to concede the mortality of the human soul in the *Short Treatise*,[102] and the priority of the body was restated in the *Ethics*: 'Our mind can be said to endure, and its existence can be defined by a certain time, only insofar as it involves the actual existence of the body'.[103] Further, 'The Mind can neither imagine anything, nor recollect past things, except while the Body endures'.[104] Puzzlingly, however, Spinoza also asserted both that every human mind was in some way immortal, and also that immortality was the natural accompaniment of virtue, and permanent extinction the sequel to a vicious life. The ignorant man is driven by his appetites and constantly distracted, and 'as soon as he ceases to be acted on, he ceases to be', whereas the wise man 'is hardly troubled in spirit, but being, by a certain eternal necessity, conscious of himself, and of God, and of things, he never ceases to be'.[105]

---

[100] Lucretius, *ONT* III. 992–3; trans. Smith, p. 95.

[101] Spinoza, *Short Treatise*, ch. 14, in *Works*, trans. Curley, i. 118.

[102] Ibid., ch. 23, in *Works*, i. 140–1.   [103] Spinoza, *Ethics*, pt. V, prop. 23, in *Works*, i. 608.

[104] Ibid., pt. V, prop. 21, in *Works*, i. 607.

[105] The notion that sagacity induces immortality is advanced by Plato: '[I]f a man has become absorbed in his appetites or his ambitions and takes great pains to further them, all his thoughts are bound to become thoroughly mortal. And insofar as it is at all possible for a man to become thoroughly mortal, he cannot help but fully succeed in this, seeing that he has cultivated his mortality all along. On the other hand, if a man has seriously devoted himself to the love of learning and to true wisdom, if he has exercised these aspects of himself above all, then there is absolutely no way that his thoughts can

In the *Short Treatise* the immortality of one and all was held to follow from the fact that 'the Soul can be united either with the body of which it is the Idea or with God, without whom it can neither exist nor be understood'.[106] In a section headed *The human Mind cannot be absolutely destroyed with the Body, but something of it remains which is eternal*, Spinoza asserted that 'though it is impossible that we should recollect that we existed before the Body—since there cannot be any traces of this in the body...still, we feel and know by experience that we are eternal'.[107] It is clear that the 'something' which remains cannot be a sector of our mental faculties, for instance, the intellectual ones. This would have collapsed Spinoza's position into Descartes's, against his manifest intentions. His gnomic dicta on this subject suggest that what remains of me after the death of my body is simply the divine idea of my body and the personality it expresses. After his death, Peter's mind is no longer an idea of his body, but Peter is an idea in Paul's mind.[108] As the individual human mind perceives all that happens in its individual human body,[109] so the divine mind perceives all that happens in its body, and it can anticipate, perceive, and remember the human body that generated a distinct human mind and personality. The divine idea of my personhood is a thought or memory attributable to God; that is, to extended-thinking nature taken as whole. And as God is the totality of what is and cannot be affected by anything external, the divine body is immortal and its ideas are inextinguishable.

At the end of the *Ethics*, however, Spinoza appeared abruptly to change tracks and to insist that even if we did not know that our mind was eternal, we would still regard as of principal importance 'the things we showed to be related to Tenacity and Nobility'.[110] The enlightened subject perceives that the traditional apparatus of theology and ethics is superstitious delusion and

---

fail to be immortal and divine...And to the extent that human nature can partake of immortality, he can in no way fail to achieve this' (*Timaeus*, 90b–c, in *Complete Works*, ed. Cooper and Hutchinson, 1289.

[106] Spinoza, *Short Treatise*, ch. 23, in *Works*, trans. Curley, i. 141.

[107] Spinoza, *Ethics*, pt. V, prop. 23, in *Works*, i. 607–8.

[108] Ibid., pt. II, prop. 17, in *Works*, i. 464–5.

[109] Ibid., pt. II, prop. 12, in *Works*, i. 456–7. Susan James takes this to be the principal reading of the claim that the mind is the idea of the body (see *Passion and Action: The Emotions in Seventeenth-century Philosophy* (Oxford: Clarendon, 1997), 142–3.)

[110] Spinoza, *Ethics*, pt. V, prop. 41, in *Works*, trans. Curley, i. 615.

yet maintains his commitment to virtue. Reason can determine the rules of and find the grounds for appropriate conduct even if death ends personal experience. It is absurd for someone, 'because he does not believe he can nourish his body with good food to eternity, [to] ... prefer to fill himself with poisons and other deadly things, or because he sees that the Mind is not eternal, *or* immortal, [to] ... prefer to be mindless, and to live without reason'.[111] Spinoza accordingly took pains to insist that the continuity between human and animal life and the impossibility of personal immortality in any conventional sense did not justify libertinage. He endorsed the Stoic position that a virtuous life is intrinsically a better life than a pleasure-seeking one, and he maintained that the pursuit of knowledge is appetitive in humans, though he did not manage to explain, any more than his predecessors had, why all humans in that case were not observed to pursue it. Insofar as scientific knowledge was an object of quest, it could constitute a 'new goal' and part of a 'new plan', that could substitute not only for the demeaning goals and plans of the libertine, but for the pursuit of the phantom subjects of theology and for participation in the absurd observances of religion.

The free man—that is to say the man released from the bondage of obsession with finite things, not the man possessed of free will in any traditional metaphysical sense—values intellectual pursuits over the comfort of the body, and 'there is no small difference between the gladness by which a drunk is led and the gladness a Philosopher possesses'.[112] However, the multitude do not understand this, Spinoza conceded, and cannot conduct themselves properly, except through their hopes and fears for the hereafter.[113] The improvement of society required, in his view, both the rejection of superstition and the appreciation of the true basis of morals. Then men could live free, in a friendly, tolerant democracy, and they would pose no danger to one another. Learning the true basis for morals as outlined in the *Ethics* would tend to the destruction of moral deontology, though merely unlearning religion would be disastrous.

Spinoza's simultaneous endorsement of psychological determinism and, at the same time, a normative theory of individual liberty created a

---

[111] Spinoza, *Ethics*, pt. V, prop. 41, in *Works*, i. 616.
[112] Ibid., pt. III, prop. 57, in *Works*, i. 528. 'I wished to mention this in passing', Spinoza adds.
[113] Ibid., pt. V, prop. 41, scholium, in *Works*, i. 615.

noticeable tension in his work, a tension that is predicted by the coexistence of fatalistic and voluntaristic elements in classical atomism. Lucretian psychology implied the rigid dependence of all thought and experience on interaction with the environment mediated by atoms. Yet the Epicureans were curiously unperturbed by the problem of determinism that so exercised their successors. Their relative fecklessness is easily explained: they did not feel the force of the machine analogy, or the appeal to inviolable laws of nature, and the alleged foreknowledge of God did not concern them either. The atoms' free and spontaneous movement in empty space might be grasped as a model for the social and political freedom of agents moving about unimpeded in their life world, occasionally meeting and interacting in ways that left their integrity fully intact.[114]

4.4 Leibniz's immortal organisms

The impression that the *Meditations*, for all their brilliant intellectual artifice, had not established and to some extent had even undermined the thesis of the immortality of the human soul did not generate a frank critique of the powers of pure reason in the early modern period. Nevertheless, Leibniz's approach to the problem of immortality was marked by a return to empirical observation and induction. He saw that a frontal assault on the problem of immortality by Cartesian a priori methods could not succeed. His own theory steered a middle course between the adoption of Kenelm Digby's and Robert Boyle's palingenetical models of resurrection, models which Descartes had dismissed with scorn,[115] and conceptual argument.

At a time when he was still favorably disposed towards Hobbes's mechanical philosophy, Leibniz became acquainted with Spinoza's unpublished *Ethics* through conversations with Spinoza's friend Ehrenfried Walther von Tschirnhaus, in the winter of 1675–6. He noted its chief doctrines, including the unique substantiality of God and the mind as the idea of the body, and he commented on Spinoza's not very robust notion of

---

[114] Kroll, *The Material Word: Literate Culture in the Restoration and Early Eighteenth Century* (Baltimore, Md.: Johns Hopkins University Press, 1991), 160.

[115] Descartes, letter to Elizabeth, 3 November 1645, in *Oeuvres*, iv. 333; *Writings*, trans. and ed. Cottingham et al., iii. 277.

immortality.[116] He read it, very reasonably, as a kind of Averroism, a peculiar and remarkable variant of ancient world-soul theories,[117] and he commented disapprovingly that 'it is completely alien to every sort of reason that a soul should be an idea.... [I]t is a mockery to call souls immortal because ideas are eternal'.[118]

Probably provoked by Spinoza, Leibniz seems to have tried out his own proof of the immortality of the soul, endeavoring to apprehend a priori and directly his continuing identity. He tried, for example, to infer from the possibility of a recursive function applied indefinitely to his thinking (thinking of his thinking, thinking of his thinking of his thinking, etc.) to his infinite prolongation as a thinking being.[119] But this line of speculation was quickly given up as unprofitable, and his most developed answers to the problem of mortality were not based on the analysis of ideas and thinking, but on physical and biological considerations. He decided that 'speaking as natural scientists', we can be sure that 'souls cannot fail to awake from the state of torpor into which death... may place them'.[120]

The formation of the Arbor Dianae in the chemist's glass, the phenomena of solution and recrystallization, and especially the recovery of niter from solutions offered intriguing proofs of the possibility of reconstructing complex forms that had earlier vanished from sight. Leibniz noted with special interest Boyle's speculations on the relevance of chemical redintegration to the resurrection of the body, citing as well observations on preformation and the precipitation of salts.[121] In the essay 'Some Physico-theological Considerations about the Possibility of the Resurrection' Boyle had discussed a

[116] 'I do not accept the view of Spinoza, that the individual mind is extinguished with the body; that the mind in no way remembers what has gone before; that there remains only that which is eternal in the mind, i.e. the idea or essence of the body.... For that ultimate perfect essence, which is all that will survive when we die, is nothing to us' (G. W. Leibniz, 'Über Spinozas Ethik,' in *Sämtliche Schriften*, ed. Akademie der Wissenschaften (Berlin: Akademie-Verlag, 1923–), vi. iv. 385.

[117] Leibniz, 'On Truths, the Mind, God, and the Universe', in *Sämtliche Schriften*, vi. iv, 510; trans. G. H. R. Parkinson, in *De summa rerum*, ed. Parkinson (New Haven, Conn.: Yale University Press, 1992), 61–3.

[118] Leibniz, 'Comments on Spinoza's Philosophy', in *Philosophical Essays*, trans. and ed. Roger Ariew and Daniel Garber (Indianapolis, Ind.: Hackett 1989), 277.

[119] Margaret Wilson, 'Self-Consciousness and Immortality in the *Paris Notes* and After', repr. in *Ideas and Mechanism* (Princeton, NJ: Princeton University Press, 1999), 382.

[120] Leibniz, 'On the Seat of the Soul', in *Sämtliche Schriften*, vi. iv. 478 ff.; *De summa rerum*, ed. Parkinson, pp. 33–5; cf. *New Essays*, in *Sämtliche Schriften*, vi. iv. 58–9.

[121] Ibid. See L. E. Loemker, 'Boyle and Leibniz', *Journal of the History of Ideas*, 16 (1955), 22–4.

palingenetical experiment in which a colleague 'took some ashes of a plant, just like our English red poppy, and having sow'd these Alcalizate Ashes in my Friends Garden, they did, sooner than was expected, produce certain Plants larger and fairer than any of that kind, that had been seen in those parts'. Boyle inferred that either some 'Plastick Power' remained in the ashes, 'inabling them to contrive disposed Matter, so as to reproduce such a body as was formerly destroyed', or else that 'an External and Omnipotent Agent' performed the resuscitation by direct means.[122] Kenelm Digby had claimed in his treatise on plants that the essential substance of a plant is contained in its fixed salt, and that washed and boiled crayfish, distilled, filtered, evaporated, and the result left to putrefy, would give rise to many little animals, which 'being fed of river water and ox blood, you may bring them on to what bignesse you please'.[123]

Leibniz accepted the Carneadean premise that if every living thing can be cut into parts, no living thing is everlasting. He speculated at first that there was an indestructible core to the organism, analogous to the rabbinical *luz* or bone of irrefrangible hardness that God uses to reconstruct the same human body. He proposed a version of the Boyle-Digby palingenetical model, according to which a plant or an animal continues in subvisible existence, with the power of rebuilding itself, even when most of its body has been burned or ground up. In his 'Notes on Science and Metaphysics', from March 1676, he considered the problem of immortality from an atomistic perspective and ventured a highly original opinion. Any divisible object is indeed impermanent, he conceded: 'Whatever is divisible, whatever is divided, is altered—or rather, is destroyed'. But this only implies that any persisting and indestructible element, any atom, must be possessed of a mind that serves as some kind of cement or glue. Were there no indestructible minds, there could not be atomic bodies either, and were there no atomic bodies, then, as Lucretius thought, everything would slip into nothingness and there would be no renewal and reconstruction in the universe. Thus:

[F]rom all this it follows that thought enters into the formation of matter, and there comes into existence a body which is one and unsplittable, i.e., an atom, of

---

[122] Robert Boyle, 'Some Physico-theological Considerations about the Possibility of the Resurrection', in *Works*, ed. Michael Hunter and Edward B. Davis, (London: Pickering and Chatto, 2000), viii. 303.

[123] Kenelm Digby, *A Discourse Concerning the Vegetation of Plants* (London: 1661), 81–2.

whatever size it may be, whenever it has a single mind.... From this it can easily be understood why no mind can be dissolved naturally, for if it could, it would have been dissolved long ago. For the whole universe constantly exerts itself to destroy any mind.[124]

This new idea—ensouled atoms—was pursued in his notes of April 1676, in which each body was conceived as a 'vortex' animated and made indivisible and indestructible by a mind, whose resistance to external forces produced sensation and which continued to register its history of encounters forever.[125] By this means Spinoza's conclusion that the individual mind is extinguished at death and that the mind can remember only what is eternal was circumvented. Leibniz accepted, for the time being, the atomists' view that there was 'some solid and unbreakable portion of matter' that could compose complex, fissile objects, though later he insisted that the material atom was a scientific fiction. It followed from his conception of an atom, whose cohesion is attributable to the mind holding it together, that an aggregate of atoms, like a rock, could be ground up or reduced to powder and scattered, but that each minute fragment was possessed of its own mind.

Leibniz abandoned the vortex theory of mind-bound atoms, but he retained the notion of living atoms in his metaphysics,[126] and he went on to argue, in his correspondence with Arnauld, and in his later monadological writings, that a corporeal substance, like an animal or a person, is made into a coherent and unified thing by the presence of a non-material 'entelechy'. He appealed to the new microscopical discoveries of the 1660s and 1670s. 'Those who grasp that there is almost an infinity of animals in the least drop of water, as the observations of Mr Leeuwenhoek have shown', he declared, 'will not find it strange that there is something animated even in ashes, so that fire can transform an animal and reduce it to a small size instead of destroying it entirely',[127] and he compared the seemingly dead organism to the chrysalis in which the

---

[124] Leibniz, 'Notes on Science and Metaphysics', *Sämtliche Schriften*, vi. iv. 392 ff.; *De summa rerum*, ed. Parkinson, pp. 45–7.

[125] Leibniz, 'On Truths, the Mind, etc.', *Sämtliche Schriften*, vi. iv. 509–10; *De summa rerum*, pp. 59–61.

[126] See Stuart C. Brown, 'The Proto-monadology of the *De summa rerum*', in Brown (ed.), *The Young Leibniz and his Philosophy* (Dordrecht: Kluwer, 1999).

[127] Leibniz, letter to Arnauld, 9 October 1687, § 6, in *Die Philosophische Schriften von Leibniz*, ed. C. I. Gerhardt (Berlin: 1875–90; repr. Hildesheim: Olms, 1965), ii. 122.

future butterfly sleeps. The entire creature remains enucleated in a small particle of its old body; its organs are 'merely enveloped and reduced to a small volume'.[128]

The soul, Leibniz thought, can never abandon the body entirely, and it cannot be destroyed, any more than can the entire universe. '[I]t is impossible that the changes in this extended mass called our body should do anything to the soul or that the dissolution of this body should destroy what is indivisible.'[129] Because a soul requires nothing else for its existence except God, it qualifies as a substance, an 'individual substance'; and an organism, like a limited version of Spinoza's universal substance, manifests itself both as an extended thing, or, more broadly, an extended thing endowed with force, and as a thinking thing, or, more broadly, a perceiving, appetitive thing. The threatened absurdity of a Cartesian mind that could perceive, feel, and remember without a body was forestalled, and the problem of specifying the 'part' or subset of faculties of the mind that could survive the death of the body disappeared. A Leibnizian eternal mind remembers everything, however dimly, not some subset of its experiences; it is not restricted to intellectual memory. Every substance, as Spinoza intimated of the individual, bears marks and traces of everything that ever has happened to it and that will happen to it, though these are not entirely legible to the substance itself.[130] At the same time, it does not undergo destructive interaction with any external thing; a Leibnizian soul is 'windowless'. Its causal isolation 'shelters it absolutely from all external things, since the soul alone makes up its whole world and is sufficient to itself with God'.[131]

Lucretius had admitted that his doctrine of the mortality of the soul was harsh, the equivalent of medicinal wormwood. '[M]ost people recoil back from it.'[132] The honey-coating of poetry was needed to get it down. The

---

[128] Leibniz, 'Reflections on the Doctrine of a Single Universal Spirit', in *Philosophische Schriften*, ed. Gerhardt, vi. 533; Leibniz, *Philosophical Papers and Letters*, trans. and ed. L. E. Loemker, 2nd edn. (Dordrecht: Reidel, 1969), 557.

[129] Leibniz, *Discourse on Metaphysics*, § 32, in *Philosophische Schriften*, ed. Gerhardt, iv. 458; *Philosophical Essays*, trans. Ariew and Garber, p. 104. Cf. *Monadology*, §§ 4, 5, in *Philosophische Schriften*, vi. 60; *Philosophical Essays*, p. 213. 'There is ... no dissolution to fear, and there is no conceivable way in which a simple substance can perish naturally'.

[130] Ibid., § 61, in *Philosophische Schriften*, ed. Gerhardt, vi. 617; *Philosophical Essays*, trans. Ariew and Garber, p. 221.

[131] Leibniz, *Discourse on Metaphysics*, § 32, in *Philosophische Schriften*, iv. 458; *Philosophical Essays*, p. 104.

[132] Lucretius, *ONT* I. 946; trans. Smith, p. 29.

notion that life could be extinguished forever by a few days of fever, that a vital, aware personality would become nothing more than a stinking, maggot-ridden corpse, that there were no reunions, no second chances, no opportunities for rectification of broken relationships, was difficult to bear. The wicked whom the law of man was unable to touch were safe from retaliation; the good men and women whom fortune had dealt hard blows could receive no compensation. No God could come to anyone's aid in times of danger and affliction, and politics was an unsupervised arena of power-grabbing. But *On the Nature of Things* concerns not only limits—the prize discovery Lucretius ascribes to Epicurus, 'the knowledge what can arise and what cannot, and again by what law each thing has its scope restricted and its deeply implanted boundary stone'[133]—but renewals. Death is compensated for by new life.[134] The atoms are the requisites for renewal, as well as the reason for the limited term of every animal, plant, monument, or geographical feature, and to die is to make a contribution to life and its flourishing.

Renewal, for Lucretius, was to be found in the 'mutual exchange' of all living creatures, in the circulation of atoms, which join and part, collect and disperse, and in the cycle of generations, whether we participate as runners who 'pass on the torch of life from hand to hand', or only as spectators, like the childless poet himself. The cries of newborn infants in the city streets at night mingle with the cries of lamentations for the dead.[135] Lucretius' confidence in the renewing and reconstructive powers of nature complemented his theory of limits and dissolution, leading him to ascribe powers and even a divine status to nature seemingly at odds with the anti-theology underlying his text. 'Lucretian optimism' was barely registered by philosophers of the seventeenth century, focused as they were on the question of individual survival.

Philosophical enlightenment historically implied a detachment from everyday concerns, a redirection of the mind to incorporeal entities, higher things, and to the prospects of a future life in which the mundane preoccupations of the present one, along with its troubles, conflicts, temptations, and pleasures, were to be superseded by another kind of happy existence. Plato's figure of the ladder is the memorandum for this

---

[133] Lucretius, *ONT* I. 75, trans. Smith, p. 5.   [134] Ibid. I. 262–3 f.; trans. Smith, p. 10.
[135] Ibid. I. 577 ff., trans. Smith, p. 50.

aspirational character of philosophy. The pupil must be shown how to climb it and must be shown what reward awaits him at the top. If a person could master his emotions and live a just life, Plato thought, 'he would at the end return to his dwelling place in his companion star to live a life of happiness that agreed with his character'.[136] Christian authors described in turn the bliss of the beatific vision. The new philosophers detached themselves partially—but only partially—from ancient and medieval ideals of transcendence. They perceived that human beings were enmeshed in corporeal nature, that their perceptions and feelings were the causal effect of, or at least corresponded to, the shifting configurations of particles that impacted on them through their sensory organs. They made our corporeality central in a way it had never been to most ancient and medieval philosophers, and Descartes conceived his contribution to ethics to be the introduction of a physiological component to the theory of the emotions, ignorance of which had, he said, vitiated the ethical systems of the ancients.

This grounding in nature did not, however, erase all the otherworldly aspirations inherent in their projects. Something of individuality and personality, they insisted, could survive the death of the material entity this personality had been associated with in life. If it was not clear from their accounts exactly what qualities and capabilities would remain after death, this was because they were attempting an impossible grafting, not of a new science onto an old metaphysics, but of an old scientific philosophy onto the synthesis of metaphysics and theology that had passed for centuries as the most exalted form of human knowledge.

---

[136] Plato, *Timaeus*, 42b, in *Complete Works*, ed. Cooper and Hutchinson, p. 1245.

5

Empiricism and Mortalism

Now all that suffer, bodies be
And all that gives them space, vacuitie
    Wherefore besides, there is no third
Which sence can reach or nature can afford.
For unto these, whatever elce we see
Either conjoyned, or accidentall be
Those are conjunctions which at no time force
Without pernicious injury can divorce
As wett, heate, weight, from water, fire and stone
From bodies touch, from incorporealls none.

(De rerum natura, i. 448–57)

The claim that organized matter can think and that the mind does not survive the death of the body is often attributed to Locke. Despite his provision of a carefully contrived account of resurrection in the first edition of his *Essay Concerning Human Understanding* (1689), and the casual nature of the proposal, tossed out in a late chapter of the second edition (1694), that suitably organized matter might be endowed by God with the power of thought, he is sometimes considered the boldest of the seventeenth-century opponents of the incorporeal, separable soul posited by Descartes. Yet his suggestion that matter might think was timid compared with Gassendi's attacks on the incorporeal soul and the rough challenges to it of interregnum radicals, including Overton, whose *Mans Mortalitie* was in Locke's father's library,[1] and Hobbes. It was undeveloped by contrast with the materialist tracts of his contemporary Henry Layton. His suggestions nevertheless attracted considerable attention, and brought him both fame and notoriety, because of Locke's status as a well-connected,

---

[1] Roger Woolhouse, *Locke: A Biography* (Cambridge: Cambridge University Press, 2007), 7.

high-ranking bureaucrat under William and Mary. As knowledge of the authorship of the *Two Treatises of Government* and *The Reasonableness of Christianity*, published anonymously between 1689 and 1695, became known, it was increasingly difficult to see the *Essay* as the innocent work of an under-labourer who intended merely to explain the foundations of morality and the epistemological basis of the experimental sciences, leaving more contentious matters to others.

5.1 English mortalism

Hobbes, who had spent much of the 1630s and 1640s in Paris, where Gassendi's influence was strong, had presented a materialist theory of mind in his treatise *Humane Nature*, fashioned in 1640. Hobbes was perfectly definite that while Christians must 'acknowledge' spirits, no one actually had any knowledge of them:

We that are Christians *acknowledge* that there be Angels good and evil, and that there are Spirits, and that the Soul of Man is a Spirit, and that those Spirits are immortal: *but*, to *know* it, that is to say, to have natural Evidence of the same, it is *impossible*: For, all *Evidence* is *Conception* … and all Conception is *Imagination*, and proceedeth from *Sense* … And *Spirits* we suppose to be those Substances which work *not* upon the *Sense*; and therefore not conceptible…. To me therefore it seemeth, that the Scripture favoureth them more, who hold Angels and Spirits corporeal, than them that hold the contrary. And it is a plain *Contradiction* in natural Discourse, to say of the Soul of Man, that it is *tota in toto, & tota in qualibet Parte Corporis*, grounded neither upon Reason nor Revelation, but proceeding from the Ignorance of what those Things are which are called *Spectra*, Images, that appear in the dark to Children, and such as have strong Fears, and other strange Imaginations[2]

In *Leviathan* Hobbes expressed almost without reserve his views on religious delusion, and what he referred to as misinterpretation of Scripture, and there he presented an exceptionally complicated and eccentric position on life and death.[3] Human beings do not possess immortal souls according

---

[2] Thomas Hobbes, *Humane Nature*, in *Human Nature* and *De corpore politico*, ed. J. C. A. Gaskin (Oxford: Oxford University Press, 1999), ch. 11, §5.

[3] Thomas Hobbes, *Leviathan*, ed. Richard Tuck (Cambridge: Cambridge University Press, 1996), chs. 38, 44.

to Hobbes. Rather, Adam, before the Fall, was a naturally immortal but otherwise ordinary corporeal entity, and human death entered the world as a result of his sin. Men who die in the ordinary way will remain dead until the resurrection. This will take place on earth, for heaven is not a place located in the celestial realm or anywhere other than here, the future kingdom of heaven. The faithful will thenceforth enjoy newly awarded 'glorious and spirituall Bodies' in perpetuity, as will those virtuous persons happening by chance to die at the exact moment of the general resurrection. The reprobate will find themselves in hell, which is no more a location out of this world than heaven; the place name designates 'metaphorically a grief, and a discontent of mind, from the sight of that Eternall felicity in others, which they themselves, through their own incredulity, and disobedience have lost,' a state considered to be physically painful. After enduring the torments of hell, the reprobate will then die a second death, which is permanent. Milton's treatment in *Paradise Lost* published in 1667 has obvious affinities with Hobbes's view that hell is a psychological condition; Milton, however, treats heaven symmetrically.[4]

The most thorough philosophical discussion of the immortality question in England was the contribution of Walter Charleton. Charleton was an important conduit for Epicureanism in natural and moral philosophy through his *Physiologia Epicuro-Gassendo-Charletoniana* (1654). Boyle and Newton studied him closely, and Kargon notes that passages of Boyle's *History of Fluidity and Firmness* are taken almost verbatim from Charleton's *Physiologia*, which are borrowed in turn from Gassendi's *Animadversions*.[5] After issuing an edition of J. B. van Helmont's semi-corpuscularian treatises under the heading *A Ternary of Paradoxes* in 1650, Charleton had discovered French philosophy, and he defended, or at least discussed, immortality along unoriginal Cartesian lines in the *Darknes of Atheism*.

---

[4] 'The mind is its own place, and in itself | Can make a Heaven of Hell, a Hell of Heaven' (John Milton, *Paradise Lost*, i. 258–9). On English mortalism see Burns, *Christian Mortalism from Tyndale to Milton* (Cambridge, Mass.: Harvard University Press, 1972).

[5] R. H. Kargon, 'Walter Charleton, Robert Boyle, and the Acceptance of Epicurean Atomism', *Isis*, 55 (1964), 188–9. Charleton was a pupil of John Wilkins in logic and philosophy at Magdalen Hall (later Hertford College), Oxford. His original interests were in anatomy and iatrochemistry; he later turned to natural history, metaphysics, and morals. He became one of the king's physicians, attending both Charles I and Charles II, and held various honorific posts, dying, however, 'in very poor Circumstances' at the age of 87. (See Sabina Fleitmann, *Walter Charleton (1620–1707), 'Virtuoso': Leben und Werk* (Frankfurt/Berlin, Lang, 1986), pp. 8–9 and Lindsay Sharp, 'Walter Charleton', *Annals of Science*, 30 (1973), 311–40.)

Following his apparent Epicurean turn, he published *Epicurus's Morals* (1656), in which he maintained that the greatest evils to befall man concern his body, and he later compiled a *Natural History of the Passions* (1674). His *Immortality of the Human Soul* of 1657 turned away from a priori demonstration and showed a real engagement with the arguments for the mortality of the human person, as well as considerable ambivalence about the possibility of actually knowing anything about this subject.

The *Immortality* took the form of a dialogue between 'Athanasius', an experimental philosopher, fresh from Oxford, who is also the author of an unpopular treatise in natural philosophy corresponding to Charleton's *Physiologia*, and 'Lucretius', probably representing the friend of Charleton's youth, John Evelyn. Evelyn had associated with Gassendi's circle of freethinkers in Paris in the early 1650s, and he had embarked on the translation of and commentary on *De rerum natura* mentioned earlier on his return. While, according to Michael Hunter, Evelyn eventually repudiated most aspects of Lucretius' philosophy and abandoned his translation project for moral reasons after publishing only the first book of the poem, he was briefly attracted by mortalism during the period of composition of Charleton's dialogue.[6]

In the dialogue, Athanasius and Lucretius both avow themselves admirers of nature. They agree that 'who so enquires into the operations of Nature, by no other light than that of Books and solitary speculations, shall in the end find his head full of specious Termes, but empty of true and solid Science'.[7] Lucretius, unlike his forebear, describes himself as believing in the immortality of the soul 'as firmly as you, or any person living can', though desirous of arguments 'as might for ever silence all Doubts and Contradictions and make a convert of my old master Epicurus'. 'I am', he says, 'an Epicurean, in many things concerning Bodies; yet, as a Christian, I detest and utterly renounce the doctrine of that Sect, concerning Mens Souls.'[8] He has laid on 'the disguise of a Contrary opinion... only to experiment the strength of your Allegations'.[9] Athanasius, for his part, notes that Christians divide into two kinds. For some, faith is so powerful

---

[6] See Michael Hunter, 'John Evelyn in the 1650s', in *Science and the Shape of Orthodoxy* (Woodbridge: Boydell, 1995).

[7] Walter Charleton, *The Immortality of the Soul* (London: 1657), 5.

[8] Ibid. 185.   [9] Ibid. 152.

that they have no need and no use for the assistance of reason. The rest, while not lacking in faith, 'yet are glad, when they can bring up the Forces of their Reason to assist them in the conquest of their fleshly oppositions'.[10]

Athanasius and Lucretius also agree that the immortality of the soul is 'the grand Base of Religion', the keystone of its arch. 'For, if the Soul be mortal, & subject to utter dissolution with the body; to what purpose doth all Piety and Religion serve? What issue can we expect of all our Prayers, of all our Adorations, of all our Self-denying acts of obedience, of all our unjust Sufferings? Why should we worship God at all? Nay, more, why should we consider whether there be a God or no?'[11] Lucretius points out that the doctors of the Church and the schoolmen have confessed that their arguments on behalf of the immortal soul are 'not rigorously Convincing, or such as constrain assent as inevitably as *Mathematical Demonstrations*'.[12] Athanasius demurs mildly; some doctors, he says, 'stiffly maintained' that their demonstrations were apodictical, and, in any case, it is possible to provide reasons which, though not equal in force to geometrical demonstrations, are such 'as import either a Physicall or Moral evidence, sufficient to perswade a mind well affected toward truth, and free from the obstruction of prejudice'. As long as they are more clear and certain than proofs that have been urged to the contrary, they are, when added to holy writ, 'ineluctable'.[13] Athanasius cites the arguments for the immortality of the soul familiar from Plato's *Phaedo*: whatever is immaterial has no parts, hence is not dissoluble, and hence 'must of perfect necessity alwayes continue to be what it is'. This conclusion is contested by Lucretius, who suggests that incorporeal entities may well be subject to destruction in some other way.[14] He goes on to insist that 'substances Immaterial' are either an absurdity or 'somewhat too sublime for the comprehension of so humble and short-sighted a reason as mine is'.[15] He cites Pomponazzi and Kenelm Digby (though not Hobbes!) to the effect that 'cognition is made by the working of our Phansy', demanding, 'some more pregnant testimony, of the intellects knowing, without the immediate help of Images, pre-admitted by the Senses'.

---

[10] Charleton, *The Immortality of the Soul* 57.   [11] Ibid. 58–9.
[12] Ibid. 61.   [13] Ibid. 62.   [14] Ibid. 78–9.   [15] Ibid. 84.

Athanasius' counterarguments for the incorporeality and immortality of the soul are borrowed from the puzzling sections of Gassendi's *Syntagma philosophicum*, but here, too, Lucretius seems to gain the upper hand, for he points out that belief in the immortality of the human soul is not universal—Epicurus for one did not hold it—and that foolish opinions are common among men. Athanasius concedes that 'erroneous Conceits many times spread themselves abroad, and diffuse by what subtle contagion I know not; especially when they have first been taken up upon presumption of Authority, Antiquity, Utility, and the like Inducements to belief'. He goes so far as to introduce the suggestion, already bruited in antiquity, that the immortality of the soul is a deception of priests, 'it being at all times true, that such audacious Malefactors, as are not moved by the whole arme of the Civil Magistrate, will yet tremble at the finger of Divinity'.[16] Is it not possible, Lucretius asks, 'that Men, casting about for various devices and imaginations to palliate and sweeten the sowernesse of their Miseries, in this life, may have both invented this comfortable opinion of a state of future Immortality; and introduced the supposition of this provident justice of God; relating only to mens actions, on purpose to support it?'.[17] Athanasius rejects the possibility that religion is a 'meer politique Fiction' on the grounds that 'the first Law-Makers we read of in History...found this Tenent [*sic*] of the Soul's Immortality settled and radicated in the hearts of the people, from the very beginning of Mankind'.[18] He admits the belief might have been manipulated by them, but he denies that it is instilled by the powerful.

Charleton's dialogue ends officially with a victory for Athanasius. Lucretius concludes that Athanasius has satisfied all his doubts and solved all his objections about the immortality of the soul. 'Yet whether you have so Demonstrated it, as to exclude all Dubiosity, and compell assent...in a pure Natural Philosopher, who refusedth to admit any other conviction, but from the Light of Nature' has to be left to the judge, Isodiocastes, to decide.[19] Isodiocastes insists that demonstration *more geometrico* is, of all forms, the 'most convincing and scientificall', but that for certain metaphysical and even physical matters 'we ought not to require absolute Demonstrations'. Yet the book seems to advertise its own failure to prove the case for the immortality of the soul, and Charleton's dedicatory epistle

---

[16] Ibid. 131.   [17] Ibid. 147.   [18] Ibid. 147; cf. p. 132.   [19] Ibid. 186.

confesses that even if his readers cannot fail to approve the dedication 'many may chance to dislike the book it self'. For, he admits, his reasonings

Perhaps... have not attained to that perfection and exquisite Rigour, as to satisfie those immoderately Curious Wits of our Age, who think it much beneath them, to acquiesce in any other Evidence but that of Demonstrations Geometrical (of which notwithstanding, the Argument of these my Discourses is absolutely uncapable).[20]

These 'immoderately Curious Wits' are probably not the loose talkers of the coffeehouses, the libertines and poets of the Stuart court.[21]

Malebranche remarks acutely that the crux of a philosopher's doctrine is to be found in those passages where he defends an unpopular thesis; his defense of accepted theses has no informational value. It is difficult to gauge the impact of Charleton's dialogue. The form he chose was ideally suited to the airing of heterodox views. It had been vigorously exploited by Valla and by J. C. Vanini, whose *Amphitheatrum* of ancient philosophers was observed to have 'presented many seductive heresies with very feeble refutations'.[22] In any event, the prospect of a 'Demonstration Geometrical' of the immortality of the soul seemed remote by the end of the seventeenth century. If Cartesian arguments for the essential incorporeality and indestructibility of the human soul seemed increasingly unconvincing, and if physico-theological arguments might at most prove the existence of a benign creator but leave the specific promises of Christianity in doubt, where was one to turn? The most one could do was to argue, on the basis of our faculties and powers, that there *must be* an incorporeal soul in man, active during his lifetime, and then to recommend *faith* in its persistence. Both Boyle and Richard Bentley suggested that faith in God and the existence of a future state in what William James would call a situation of forced and momentous choice is life-sweetening and so well warranted. Locke, to be sure, would depart markedly and conspicuously from this common strategy by arguing that the immortality of the person, not his soul, was what was in question, that it was assured by Scripture, and

---

[20] Charleton, *The Immortality of the Soul*, epistle dedicatory.

[21] On coffeehouse culture, with its the mockers and scoffers, see John Redwood, *Reason, Ridicule and Religion* (Cambridge, Mass.: Harvard University Press, 1976).

[22] Don Cameron Allen, 'The Rehabilitation of Epicurus and His Theory of Pleasure in the Early Renaissance', *Studies in Philology*, 41 (1944) 13.

that personal immortality did not require the existence of an incorporeal soul active in the operations of life.

The reaction to Hobbes's theory of the corporeal mind had been furious on the part of the divines, especially the Cambridge Platonists. Henry More said that it was as absurd to imagine that we could find the basis for 'such noble operations as free Imagination and sagacious collections of Reason' in the 'loose Pulp' inside our crania as to imagine them in 'a Cake of Sewet or a bowle of Curds'.[23] Only Thomas Tenison, later Archbishop of Canterbury, adopting the posture of a student in his dialogue *The Creed of Mr Hobbes Examined* (1670), allowed Hobbes an exposition of his views and treated them with real consideration.[24] Bentley's *Confutation of Atheism from the Faculties of the Soul, alias Matter and Motion cannot think*, one of his Boyle Lectures, delivered in 1692 and published in the following year, tried to establish that matter could not generate thought and perception, and that the soul must be incorporeal. He backed up his metaphysical arguments with the pragmatic argument that materialism was depressing. Suppose men are told, he ventured,

that all about them is dark senseless Matter, driven on by the blind impulses of Fatality and Fortune; that Men first sprung up, like Mushrooms, out of the mud and slime of Earth; and that all their Thoughts, and the whole of what they call Soul, are only various Action and Repercussion of small particles of Matter, kept a-while a moving by some Mechanisms and Clock-work, which finally must cease and perish by death[25]

The sweetest enjoyments of life, Bentley said, 'will become flat and insipid, will be damp'd and extinguish'd, be bitter'd and poison'd by the malignant and venomous quality of this Opinion'. It is a 'firmer foundation for Contentment and Tranquillity', he went on, 'to believe that All things were at first created, and since are continually order'd and dispos'd for the best, and that principally for the Benefit and Pleasure of Man'.[26]

---

[23] Henry More, *An Antidote Against Atheism* (London: 1653), bk. I. ch. 11, p. 137.

[24] Though he considered that ideas of universals must be 'estranged from all corporeal matter' and defended Descartes's distinction between reason and imagination, Tenison raised a number of more interesting points, asking, for example, how the body could remember the same things if, like the ship of Theseus, it was being continually rebuilt (Thomas Tenison, *The Creed of Mr Hobbes Examined* (London: 1670), 93).

[25] Richard Bentley, *The Folly and Unreasonableness of Atheism* (London: Mortlock, 1693), 11–12.

[26] Ibid. 24.

Bentley's claim that no mere assemblage of atoms could produce human thought was immediately challenged in the year of its enunciation by Henry Layton, who brought the skeptical charge of 'not proved' against Bentley's confutation, appealed to the voluntaristic conception of God as omnipotent and not limited by human reason, and, at the same time, advanced his own views on the material substrate of thinking. '[H]e who made Matter out of nothing, can make anything out of Matter, and many other things than Men can imagine.'[27] Thomas Willis, the anatomist of the brain, had dismissed with scorn, Layton said, the Cartesian hypothesis of animal insensibility. 'Although we do not thorowly know the Substance and Operation of the brain, nor the *ubi* or, *quomodo* such things are wrought in it' we can agree with Melancthon that the brain is the seat and office of cogitation.[28] Men are not 'bare machines', Layton urged, for they have sense and reason. Like the beasts, however, they are made of matter 'pulverized and rarified into the tenuity of a Cloud, impregnated with steams and juices no less, but more fine and active than the Vegetable Souls or Spirits of Plants.... Matter, thus constituted, impregnated, irrigated, and enlived, may, by Divine Power, be made cogitative'.[29] Human art, he pointed out, can 'communicate to dead and hard Matter a fixed and regular Motion: Witness *Architas* his Dove, and *Regiomontanus* his Eagle ... Men would not then believe [this] could be done without an Immaterial Spirit'.[30] And just as 'those Atoms which we call Motes in the Sun.... of their own nature maintain a perpetual Motion', he observes, 'a Compositum of such active Particles impregnated with rorid Steams and Juices apt to ascend by adhering to any solid Body, are not apt alone for Motion, but ... by the hand and skill of a Divine Architect there may be made of such like Ingredients, a Cogitative Matter'.[31]

5.2 Locke and thinking matter

Locke owned two copies of Diogenes Laertius' *Lives* and three copies of *On the Nature of Things*.[32] He was associated with two well-known Gassendists,

[27] Henry Layton, *Observations upon a Sermon Intitulated,* A Confutation of Atheism from the Faculties of the Soul (London: 1692), 18.

[28] Ibid. 7.   [29] Ibid. 13.   [30] Ibid. 4.   [31] Ibid. 7.

[32] Richard W. F. Kroll, 'The Question of Locke's Relation to Gassendi', *Journal of the History of Ideas*, 45 (1984), 339–59.

François Bernier and Gilles de Launay. Despite ongoing controversy over whether Locke derived his basic ontology and epistemology from one or more of these sources, or from direct acquaintance with Gassendi's texts above and beyond the *Objections*, or through the mediation of Stanley's *History*, or the Port-Royal logicians, or through Hobbes and Boyle, there is no question that his skepticism about thinking substance was stimulated by his familiarity with ancient and modern atomism. The parallels between Gassendi's views about the acquisition of knowledge and Locke's are sufficiently strong to sustain claims for some as yet imperfectly understood causal chain linking the two.[33] In any case, Locke's evasive strategy with respect to the question of incorporeal substances is a key to the interpretation of his *Essay Concerning Human Understanding*. Evidently, Locke wanted to fit the frame of a Gassendist science of appearances to theology and morals, and if his was not a critical idealism in the sense of Kant, it was assuredly a 'critical idea-ism'. Locke carefully avoided asserting the incorporeality of the soul, but he arranged his main philosophical theses so as to leave the foundations of morality and the rationale for religious indoctrination intact even if the incorporeal soul was a fiction. His eventual suggestion that the power of thought was a 'superaddition' by God to the organic body was a technical maneuver. It afforded a compromise between the position that the motion and arrangement of matter could directly produce the powers falling under the headings of perception, will, and thought, as Boyle had suggested was the case for all the powers whose operations were observed in medicine, chemistry, and physiology, and the position that such powers could only reside in an immaterial substance.

By 1683 Locke's reflections on personal identity had, according to Michael Ayers, veered away from his early mind–body dualism, and assumed 'a starting point more favourable to the materialists'.[34] The first edition of the *Essay*, though organized around the corpuscularian

---

[33] Fred and Emily Michael quote many parallel passages in 'The Theory of Ideas in Gassendi and Locke' (*Journal of the History of Ideas*, 51 (1990), 379–99), while J. R. Milton, in 'Locke and Gassendi: A Reappraisal' (in M. A. Stewart (ed.), *English Philosophy in the Age of Locke* (Oxford: Oxford University Press, 2000)), argues that there is little evidence for a close study by Locke of either Gassendi's *Exercitationes* or his *Syntagma philosophicum*. See also Richard W. F. Kroll, *The Material Word: Literate Culture in the Restoration and Early Eighteenth Century* (Baltimore, Md.: Johns Hopkins University Press, 1991).

[34] Michael J. Ayers, *Locke* (London: Routledge, 1991), ii. 255.

philosophy and a Democritean causal theory of perception, did not mention thinking matter. But the second edition, published two years after the Bentley–Layton controversy in 1694, appeared to take Layton's side.[35] Locke's argument was virtually identical to Layton's; our faculties and understanding are so limited that we cannot be certain that God, rather than joining to our bodies a thinking, immaterial substance, has not 'given to some Systems of Matter fitly disposed, a power to perceive and think', in virtue of which such suitably organized systems might exhibit not only vegetable life, but also animal perception, and human reason. What certainty can anyone have, Locke asked, 'that some perceptions, such as *v.g.* pleasure and pain, should not be in some bodies themselves, after a certain manner modified and moved, as well as that they should be in an immaterial Substance ... Body as far as we can conceive being able only to strike and affect body; and Motion ... being able to produce nothing but Motion?'.[36]

At times, to be sure, Locke sounded open-minded in the *Essay* with respect to the truth of Cartesian dualism. It is, he said, 'as rational to affirm, there is no Body, because we have no clear and distinct *Idea* of the *Substance* of Matter; as to say, there is no Spirit, because we have no clear and distinct *Idea* of the *Substance* of a Spirit'.[37]

It is for want of reflection, that we are apt to think, that our Senses shew us nothing but material things. Every act of sensation, when duly considered, gives us an equal view of both parts of nature, the Corporeal and Spiritual. For whilst I know, by seeing or hearing, *etc.* that there is some Corporeal Being without me, the Object of that sensation, I do more certainly know, that there is some Spiritual Being within me, that sees and hears. This I must be convinced cannot be the action of bare insensible matter; nor ever could be without an immaterial thinking Being.[38]

Locke was not, however, claiming in this context that an incorporeal soul existed and was certainly known to exist. If God has superadded the power of thought to bare insensible matter, the spiritual being of which I am aware is just my own purely material, thinking self.

---

[35] Layton, Woolhouse reports, later sent one of his books to Locke 'as a very good judge upon this argument, and as one who has suffered some measure of persecution, for but saying the thing was possible' (*Locke: A Biography*, p. 427).

[36] John Locke, *An Essay Concerning Human Understanding*, bk. IV, ch. 3, §6, ed. P. H. Nidditch (Oxford: Clarendon, 1975), 541.

[37] Ibid. bk. II, ch. 23, §5; ed. Nidditch, p. 298.   [38] Ibid. §15; ed. Nidditch, pp. 305–6.

Henry More had maintained that 'the *nature* of a *Spirit* is as conceivable and easy to be defin'd as the nature of anything else', and he had gone on to list all the essential properties of spirit as known by ratiocination, including self-penetration, self-motion, self-contraction and dilation, indivisibility, and the powers of penetrating, moving, and altering matter.[39] That the properties of corporeal and thinking substance were easily conceived and known, as Descartes too had insisted in his *Meditations*, Locke firmly denied. We have no immediate and direct insight into the essential properties of either corporeal or incorporeal substance. We have access only to the appearances that are caused by the motion and impression on our organs of the bodies around us.[40] As Hobbes had argued, we form concepts by joining various simple ideas together, and even if we can be assured that our simple ideas have a basis in reality, we have no assurance that these composites exist in reality. They may be chimeras. The ideas of thinking and willing, which we acquire by introspection, joined to substance, 'of which we have no distinct *Idea*', give us the idea of an immaterial spirit; and the ideas of having coherent solid parts and a power of being moved, joined with substance, 'of which likewise we have no positive *Idea*', give us the idea of matter. So we have ideas of corporeal and incorporeal substance, but both are constructed by us. We can say nothing decisive about their properties unless it is on the basis of our own immediate, lived experience. With his double negation—we cannot know that God has not given the power of thought to matter—Locke avoided brute affirmations. Denying that his aim was to 'anyway lessen the belief of the Soul's Immateriality', he emphasized that 'it becomes the Modesty of Philosophy, not to pronounce Magisterially, where we want that Evidence that can produce Knowledge'.[41] He responded in a mocking tone to Bishop Stillingfleet, who harassed him in numerous letters over thinking matter: 'I gratefully receive and rejoice in the light of revelation, which sets me at rest in many things, the manner whereof my poor reason can by no means make out to me: omnipotency, I know, can do anything that contains no contradiction'.[42]

Locke's constant references to ideas might have evoked Cartesianism, and even surrounded the *Essay* with an aura of spirituality. These impressions

---

[39] More, *Antidote Against Atheism*, bk. I, ch. 4, p. 11.
[40] Locke, *Essay*, bk. II, ch. 1, §§1–25; ed. Nidditch, pp. 104–18.
[41] Ibid., bk. IV, ch. 3, §6; ed. Nidditch, p. 541.
[42] John Locke, 'Second Reply to the Bishop of Worcester', in *Works* (Aalen: Scientia, 1923), iv. 492.

were initially misleading—and perhaps still mislead. Lockean ideas are only Epicurean appearances internalized; like Gassendi and Hobbes, Locke chose to begin his exposition not with material first principles, working his way up to sensation, imagination, and judgement, but with sensory appearances whose existence strongly suggested corpuscular causes.

Locke harped in book IV of the *Essay* on the impossibility of our ever coming to understand how corpuscles produce sensory experiences, or how their motions and configurations explain the powers and appearances of particular substances, by which he meant only natural kinds, and indeed on the impossibility of knowing that the corpuscular hypothesis was true. '[A]s to a perfect *Science* of natural Bodies, (not to mention spiritual Beings,) we are, I think, so far from being capable of any such thing, that I conclude it lost labour to seek after it.'[43] His sacrifice of the ideal of science as knowledge of the inner nature of corporeal substances was not, however, very heavy in his eyes. The theory of ideas posited that beliefs can be credentialed by their generation in experience.

By locating both unsensed corporeal things and unsensed incorporeal things outside the realm of practical, efficacious human knowledge, Locke articulated the form of two new sciences, natural and moral, that would require no reference to unexperienced entities. Because all sensory experiences were, in Locke's view, caused by corporeal objects, and because all 'ideas of reflection' presupposed experience, the existence of matter endowed with causal powers was consistent with his epistemology, his psychology, and his moral theory, while the existence of incorporeal entities was logically irrelevant to all of them, save only that the existence of the world, and of thinking creatures, could not be the effects alone, he maintained, of 'incogitative Matter'.[44] By acknowledging an eternal, cogitative, incorporeal being—God—Locke was able to construct a system that in fact privileged matter, absolutely requiring it as an explanatory principle. He could now sketch a conception of scientific and moral knowledge based on Epicurean-Gassendist premises, corresponding to what he took to be the actual practice of his most admired contemporaries, especially Boyle in chemistry, Newton in applied mathematics, and Thomas Sydenham in medicine. His critical stance enabled him to elude charges of

---

[43] Locke, *Essay*, bk. IV, ch. 3, §29; ed. Nidditch, p. 560.
[44] Ibid., ch. 10, §§9 ff; ed. Nidditch, pp. 622 ff.

materialism—though vigilant guardians of theology and morals professed to see through his skepticism to his underlying commitments. The mere reference to the impossibility of ruling out thinking matter prompted, as noted, the attacks of the longtime scourge of Epicureanism, Edward Stillingfleet, the Bishop of Worcester.[45] John Edwards as well was convinced that Locke was a 'Hobbist', denouncing him from the pulpit in a sermon at Cambridge in July 1699:

It is *probable*, that as in *other* very considerable Points, so *here* he Symbolizes with the Philosopher of *Malmsbury*, in whose steps he affects to tread, and borrows some of his Thoughts. For…he follows him in his Opinion of the *Necessity* of only *One Fundamental Article of Christian Faith*, and in his notion of *Thinking matter*, and particularly in that of the likelyhood or possibility of the *Materiality of Humane Souls*, and of their tendency (on that Principle) to *Mortality*, and in his *Contempt of some parts of the Holy Scripture*, and in his avow'd disbelief of the *Resurrection of the same Body*, and in his ridiculing of the *receiv'd Explication of the Doctrine of the Holy Trinity*, and in his general favouring of *Scepticism* and *Infidelity*, and his denial of *Natural* and *Inbred Notions*[46]

Leibniz, in turn, considered Locke a follower of Gassendi who held persons to be purely material machines. He employed the text of his *New Essays on the Human Understanding*, completed in 1704 but not published during his lifetime, to track materialist themes through the *Essay* and to argue that Locke's antiquarian system should be shelved in favor of Leibniz's own 'new system' of monads and preestablished harmony, a system he had been pondering and developing ever since he first became alarmed at the encroachment of Epicurean naturalism.

---

[45] Locke replied at length, but only restating his claim that we could not know that God had not superadded the power of thought to matter; see esp. his 'Second Reply', in *Works*, iv. 459 ff.

[46] John Edwards, *The Eternal and Intrinsick Reasons of Good and Evil* (Cambridge: 1699), 27–8.

6

Some Rival Systems

Because I first greate misteries disclose,
And souls from superstitions fast knotts loose;
And next, because in such sweet verse I sing,
With easie words, soe difficult a thing,
Nor is this labour spent in vaine; soe strive
Phisitians childrens weake age to deceive
And when they give a bitter potion, baite
The verges of the cup with honie, that
While th'outward sweetnesse doth their lips invite,
They may receive their cure with their delight.

(*De rerum natura*, i. 937–46)

Aristotle's arguments in favor of incorporeal principles and their agency in corporeal things were more complex and more difficult to challenge than his physical and mathematical arguments against material atoms. As observed earlier, his positive theory of life and substance contributed as much or more to the subsequent rejection of Epicureanism as did his specific arguments against the Democritean atom. The animal soul became a conceptual battleground in the late seventeenth century, for, if an incorporeal soul initiated motion in the bodies of animals, an incorporeal will could evidently initiate motion in human bodies, and an incorporeal God could initiate motion in the corporeal world as well. Descartes tried to show that animals—paradigms of a natural entity for Aristotle—were mere machines, and he indicated that the whole corporeal world was a grand machine, devoid of life and intelligence, in which everything happened according to the laws of motion and the principles of mechanics. He credited God with the construction of this machine, to be sure, and he denied that men were individual machines like animals, but his account of the incorporeal human soul, its capabilities and its mode of operation in the bodily machine to which it was joined, was not sufficiently clear and compelling to make his system acceptable to more than a small group of followers. Virtually no one could be found to agree both that animals had no sensory experiences and that the fetus was mechanically generated in the womb from a mixture of seminal fluids.

Atomism was difficult to square with metaphysical intuitions about the activity of incorporeal directive agents. Moreover, the parsimony indicated by Lucretius' appeal to the alphabet analogy, in an era in which the richness of nature was repeatedly contrasted with the poverty of theory, might not be perceived as an advantage. Margaret Cavendish, like a number of philosophers of her period, rapidly grew disenchanted with what she perceived as atomism's limitations. She expanded her view of nature as an active worker, endowed with more than mechanical means for accomplishing her range of stunning effects. Observation proves, she said, 'the infinite variety in nature, and that nature is a perpetually self-moving body, dividing, composing, changing, forming, and transforming her parts by self-corporeal figurative motion'.[1] She saw this 'infinite variety' in the coloration of birds, the differences in human understandings, fancies, conceptions, imaginations, judgements, wits, memories, affections, passions, flesh, gems, and skies, and even if the atomic realm was characterized by continuous movement, recombination, and change, the phenomena could not, she thought, be grounded in mindless particles. 'Perception', she maintained against Hobbes, 'is properly made by way of patterning and imitation, by the innate, figurative motions of those animal creatures, and not by receiving either the figures of the exterior objects into the sensitive organs, or by sending forth some invisible rays from the organ to the object; nor by pressure and reaction.'[2] Everything is alive, aware, and sensitive. '[T]here is no part of nature that has not sense and reason, which is life and knowledge; and if all the infinite parts have life and knowledge, infinite nature cannot be a fool or insensible.'[3] Further, although there are no supernatural souls, 'nothing is perishable or subject to annihilation in nature ... but what is called by the name of death is only

---

[1] Margaret Cavendish, *Observations upon Experimental Philosophy*, ed. Eileen O'Neill (Cambridge: Cambridge University Press, 2003), 85.

[2] Ibid. 15. On 'patterning out', see Susan James, 'The Philosophical Innovations of Margaret Cavendish', *British Journal for the History of Philosophy*, 7 (1999), 235.

[3] Cavendish, *observations*, p. 82.

an alteration of the corporeal natural motions of such a figure to another figure'.[4]

Cavendish's critique of atomism was thoughtful and even inspired, but it was not influential. Many however agreed with her that experience could never be explained mechanically, by motion or pressure, and that there was more variety in nature than could ever be explained by the doctrine of *corpus et inane*, among them Leibniz and Berkeley. Both were committed critics of Epicurean atomism, and their systems and motives are usefully compared.

6.1 Leibniz and atomism

Leibniz saw metaphysical opportunities in the weaknesses of Cartesianism. He restored souls to animals—though not, as Gassendi had done, by awarding them vaporous, ethereal, atomic souls—and he made the pre-existence of every organism from the creation of the universe a feature of his system. He populated the cosmos with these eternal animals, denying that any entity in the natural world, however small, was insensible, passive, or unperceiving. His contestation of the Epicurean image was the most thoroughgoing of any of the early modern philosophers, and it was, at the same time, the most modern. While, like Cudworth and other opponents of 'Atheistic Corporealism', he constantly referenced the ancients, especially Plato, Plotinus, and Cicero, Leibniz anchored both his critique and his constructions in the observational and mathematical sciences of the seventeenth century. This lent his metaphysics its special distinction.

Towards the end of his life, Leibniz explained his intellectual development to his friend Louis Remond. He had been taken with Gassendi's theories, he said, in his schooldays, and he had rejected the scholastic metaphysical fare on which he had been brought up. 'Since the atomic theory satisfies the perceptual imagination, I gave myself to it, and it seemed to me that the void of Democritus or Epicurus, together with their incorruptible atoms, would remove all difficulties.'[5] Later, however, having pushed his own

---

[4] Margaret Cavendish, *Philosophical Letters* (London: 1664), 223.

[5] G. W. Leibniz, letter to Remond, 14 July 1714, in *Die Philosophische Schriften von Leibniz*, ed. C. I. Gerhardt (Berlin: 1875–90; repr. Hildesheim: Olms, 1965), iii. 618; *Philosophical Papers and Letters*, trans. and ed. L. E. Loemker, 2nd edn. (Dordrecht: Reidel, 1969), 657.

thinking further, he had found 'that the void and atoms cannot subsist at all'.[6] Neither the atoms of Democritus nor the 'perfect globes of the Cartesians' actually existed. They were figments of the imagination, 'the incomplete thoughts of philosophers who have not inquired sufficiently well into the natures of things'.[7]

Without the atoms, Lucretius had said, everything would slip away into nothing, for if nothing was indestructible, everything could and would eventually be destroyed. Spinozism, the posit of an eternal, indestructible substance, invulnerable from attack from anything outside it because nothing could logically be outside it or oppose it, offered an escape route from the threat of annihilation. It implied, however, that all the objects of experience, from particles to animals to men, could be only the fluctuating and impermanent modes of this all-inclusive substance, and this conclusion was as repugnant to Leibniz as Gassendi's atomism. His solution to the dilemma preserved the plurality, substantiality, and indestructibility of things, but rejected the doctrine of *corpus et inane*. The true 'atoms of nature' that Leibniz recognized were uncuttable but unextended. They were not endowed with the innate motion of the Epicurean atom, but with innate force and appetition. To self-selecting aggregations of material particles he opposed self-selecting combinations of predicates; to chance, the ubiquity of law and design. The cosmos is not morally neutral and largely empty, he declared, but, on the contrary, as good as it can possibly be, and densely packed with created beings. Providential regulation runs in parallel with the ordinary operation of the laws of nature. These modifications enabled him to sail between the Scylla of Epicurean atomism and the Charybdis of Spinoza's monism. He conceded the Epicurean theses of the existence of indivisible least elements, the infinity of world systems, their self-creation through combinatorial processes, and the ubiquity and exclusivity of mechanism, while upholding the existence of a God who creates and judges and the immortality of the human soul.

Leibniz's first acquaintance with Epicurean and Lucretian doctrine is difficult to pinpoint, but it is easy to imagine the effect of Lucretius' poem

---

[6] Ibid.

[7] Leibniz, letter to de Volder, 20 June 1703, in *Philosophische Schriften*, ed. Gerhardt, ii. 250; *Philosophical Essays*, trans. and ed. Roger Ariew and Daniel Garber (Indianapolis, Ind.: Hackett, 1989), 175.

on a youth with his curiosity and intellectual dispositions. A quick and voracious reader who knew how to take advantage of a good library, he had access to classical and modern sources. He cited Diogenes Laertius' *Lives* Cicero's *De natura deorum*, and Lucretius' poem in his early sketches and letters, and in his letter to Thomasius of 1669, Leibniz insisted that the 'reformed philosophy', which he associated with Descartes, Gassendi, Bacon, Galileo, Boyle, Hobbes, and Digby, could be reconciled with the teachings of Aristotle's *Physics*; only magnitude, figure, and motion need be appealed to to explain corporeal properties. Generation, corruption, increase, decrease, and alteration are all effects of a subtle motion of parts. Forms, in the traditional sense, and qualities, including colors, arise from the motion of matter. More corpuscularian essays followed. The 'concrete' parts of his ambitious *Hypothesis physica nova* of 1671 employed material corpuscles. The *Paris Notes* of 1676 pondered vortex motion and raised the question whether fluidity was explicable in corpuscularian terms or, as Hobbes thought, primitive.

Yet Leibniz never subscribed wholeheartedly to what he termed 'naturalism'. He stated in his 'Confession of Nature against Atheists' also of 1669 that

We must agree with those contemporary philosophers who have revived Democritus and Epicurus that so far as can be done everything should be derived from the nature of body and its primary qualities—magnitude, figure, and motion. But what if I should demonstrate that the origin of these very primary qualities themselves cannot be found in the essence of body? Then indeed, I hope, these naturalists will admit that body is not self-sufficient and cannot subsist without an incorporeal principle.[8]

Gassendi's explanation of the hardness of bodies as following from the cohesion of their corpuscles, and cohesion as following from entanglement did not satisfy him. Leibniz pointed out that entanglement presupposes hardness.[9] The indivisibility of atoms could only be explained by reference to a miracle, and 'the hypothesis of small bodies of infinite hardness', he decided early on, 'cannot be sustained without recourse to God or the angels who, by a perpetual miracle, occupy themselves in holding them

---

[8] Leibniz, 'Confessio naturae', in *Philosophische Schriften*, ed. Gerhardt, iv. 106; *Philosophical Papers*, trans. and ed. Loemker, p. 110.
[9] Ibid.

together'.[10] God, the young Leibniz concluded, 'endows with firmness these ultimate elements of things' and he argued that because a variety of physical systems were all equally possible, there must be some reason, stemming from the power, intelligence, and goodness of God, for the existence of some magnitudes, figures, and motions as opposed to others.[11] A consideration of the problem of the continuum suggested to him at one point that motion required God's re-creative action from instant to instant. He was dissatisfied with the claim that the motion of bodies could explain 'true sensation such as we experience in ourselves',[12] and he was committed to the personhood of God and the immortality of the soul.

Leibniz was prodded into further philosophical action by the appearance of Spinoza's *Ethics* in 1677, of which he had had advance notice from Tschirnhaus. Though he claimed to find Spinoza's earlier *Tractatus theologico-politicus* shocking, he did not associate its doctrines with a specific natural philosophy. But the *Ethics* worried him. Sensing a threat to religion and political peace, he began to lump, to employ William James's term, ranging Hobbes with Descartes and Spinoza. They all rejected final causes, maintaining that God exercises neither wisdom, nor justice, nor benevolence, and they all ascribed everything that happens in the universe to mechanical necessity. A passage written during this period sums up his moral reaction to Descartes's Epicurean hypothesis of world formation in his *Principles of Philosophy* (pt. III, sect. 47):

A God like Descartes's allows us no consolation other than that of patience through strength. Descartes tells us in some places that matter passes successively through all possible forms, that is, that his God created everything that can be made, and [that it] passes successively through all possible combinations, following a necessary and fated order. But for this doctrine, the necessity of matter alone would be sufficient, or rather, his God is merely this necessity or this principle of necessity acting as it can in matter. Therefore, it is impossible to believe that this God cares for intelligent creatures any more than he does for the others; each creature will be happy or unhappy depending upon how it finds itself engulfed in these great currents or

[10] Leibniz, *Nouvelle lettres et opuscules inédites de Leibniz*, ed. A. Foucher de Careil (Paris: Durand, 1857), 8.

[11] Leibniz, 'Confessio naturae', in *Philosophische Schriften*, ed. Gerhardt, iv. 109; *Philosophical Papers*, trans. and ed. Loemker, p. 112.

[12] Leibniz, letter to Hobbes, July 1670, in *Philosophische Schriften*, vii. 574; *Philosophical Papers*, p. 107.

vortices. Descartes has good reason to recommend, instead of felicity, patience without hope.[13]

He referred to Epicureanism as 'the view that there is no happiness other than the tranquility of a life here below content with its own lot, since it is madness to oppose the torrent of things and to be discontented with what is immutable'.[14]

In the *Discourse on Metaphysics*, his first attempt to systematize his thoughts on matter, perception, God, and the laws of nature, Leibniz attacked Spinoza and asserted divine creation and the perfection of the world. His aim, he explained, was to 'reconcile those who hope to explain mechanically the formation of the first tissue of an animal and the whole machinery of its parts, with those who account for this same structure using final causes. Both ways are good, and both can be useful'.[15]

I see that those who apply themselves to explaining the beauty of the divine anatomy laugh at others who imagine that a movement of certain fluids that seems fortuitous could have produced such a beautiful variety of limbs, and call these people rash and profane. And the latter, on the other hand, call the former simple and superstitious, comparing them to the ancients who regarded physicists as impious when they maintained that it is not Jupiter that thunders, but some matter present in the clouds.[16]

The reconciliation of finality and mechanics, culminating in the theory of the preestablished harmony, became one of his principal tenets. Leibniz did not merely surround mechanism with a theistic frame as Descartes and Gassendi had, or supplement it with the additional posit of an incorporeal soul. For Leibniz, the entire system of Epicurean morals and physics had to be demolished, and the most effective attack on the Epicurean image was directed at the material atom and the claim that atoms, void, and motion were the fundamental terms of physics.

In 1684, on the basis of Galileo and Huygens's earlier investigations into falling bodies, Leibniz had determined that physical bodies were endowed with 'force', a quantity that could not be reduced to 'motion', and he

[13] Leibniz, letter to Molanus, *c*.1679, in *Philosophische Schriften*, iv. 299–300; *Philosophical Essays*, trans. and ed. Ariew and Garber, p. 242.
[14] Leibniz, *On the Two Sects of Naturalists*, in *Philosophische Schriften*, vii. 334; *Philosophical Essays*, p. 282.
[15] Leibniz, *Discourse on Metaphysics*, § 22, in *Philosophische Schriften*, iv. 447; *Philosophical Essays*, p. 54.
[16] Ibid.

later argued that because motion is relative, the true elements of nature could not have motion, but only force. 'It is ... possible to demonstrate', he decided further, 'that the notions of size, shape, and motion are not so distinct as is imagined and that they contain something imaginary and relative to our perception'.[17] If space, time, motion, and matter are somewhat imaginary, the world cannot be composed of uncreated material atoms that have always existed and that have always possessed the power of movement. Leibniz proposed instead two ontologies of intrinsically, rather than arbitrarily, uncuttable least entities. One was based on the notion of a hylomorphic 'corporeal substance' composed of a soul and an organic, mechanical body from which it could never be separated. Seemingly inanimate substances, such as rocks and diamonds, consisted, on this view, of infinite collections of living, sensitive organisms, each organism containing within its body an infinite series of organisms of increasing smallness. Rocks and diamonds derived what reality they had from the real substances composing them, and these organisms could grow, shrink, and change. Their souls could retreat to one part of their corpses, but the organism could not be destroyed. The other ontology posited fundamental units, extensionless, and so indestructible, metaphysical points that possessed the power of representing states of the world clearly or confusedly, depending on the quality of the 'monad' involved and the remoteness of the stimulus. The monads' sequences of perceptions were determined from the creation, and each represented the entire universe from its own particular point of view. Lactantius had insisted that 'it is clear that nothing is produced from the atoms since every single thing has its own peculiar and fixed nature, its own seed, its own law given from the beginning'.[18] A Leibnizian monad has just such a peculiar and fixed nature, a law of development impressed into its substance.

The perceptiveness and appetition of every individual substance, on either ontology, not only secured their individuality, but made sense of divine reward and punishment, which had necessarily to be addressed to a determinate, percipient, and motivated individual. Particles do not agitate locally in a void; rather, everything in the universe acts upon and perceives

---

[17] Ibid., §12, in *Philosophische Schriften*, ed. Gerhardt, iv. 436; *Philosophical Essays*, trans. and ed. Ariew and Garber, p. 44.

[18] Lactantius, *The Wrath of God*, ch. 10, in *The Minor Works*, trans. Sister Mary Francis McDonald, OP (Washington, DC: Catholic University of America Press, 1965), 79.

everything else; a complete description of anything involves reference to everything. '[T]here is no individual created substance so imperfect that it does not act on all the others and is not acted upon by all others, no substance so imperfect that it does not contain the entire universe, and whatever it is, was, or will be, in its complete notion'.[19] We are each aware of and reciprocally influence, however faintly and delicately, everything that is taking place on Jupiter.

While insisting that there was one universe in which every entity perceived and appeared to adjust itself to every other identity, Leibniz depicted, as no metaphysician had ever done, self-contained multiple worlds existing on a cosmic, microscopical, and temporally extended scale. The notion of little worlds within worlds that he aired in his early notes on the 'Secrets of the Sublime'[20] charmed him, as it had Cavendish some years earlier, and to Arnauld in 1687 he wrote, 'There is no particle of matter which does not contain a world of innumerable creatures, organized as well as massed together'.[21] In his *Monadology*, he depicted a fishpond, dense with living creatures, the water between the visible fish carrying its own allotment of smaller living organisms, with no creature the smallest. In these speculations he followed Cyrano, who, thirty years earlier, and well before the great enthusiasm surrounding Leeuwenhoek's and Hooke's discoveries with the microscope that began with the publication of *Micrographia* in 1665, had argued that 'there are infinite worlds within an infinite world'. Picture the universe as a vast organism, he urged. 'We, in our turn, are also worlds from the point of view of certain organisms incomparably smaller than ourselves, like certain worms, lice, and mites. They are the earths of others, yet more imperceptible.'[22]

Leibniz seemed to hope his hylomorphic corporeal substance might be integrated with his theory of unextended monadic individuals existing

[19] Leibniz, 'On Freedom', in *Philosophical Essays*, trans. and ed. Ariew and Garber, p. 95.

[20] 'If one imagines creatures of another world, which is infinitely small, we would be infinite in comparison with them. From which it is evident that we, conversely, can be imagined to be infinitely small in comparison with the inhabitants of another world, which is of infinite magnitude and yet is limited' (Leibniz, 'Secrets of the Sublime', in *Sämtliche Schriften und Briefe*, ed. Akademie der Wissenschaften (Berlin: Akademie-Verlag, 1923–), vi. iv. 478; *De summa rerum*, ed. C. H. R. Parkinson (New Haven, Conn.: Yale University Press, 1992), 27).

[21] Leibniz, letter to Arnauld, 9 October 1687, in *Philosophische Schriften*, ed. Gerhardt, ii. 128; *Philosophical Essays*, trans. and ed. Ariew and Garber, p. 347.

[22] Cyrano de Bergerac, *Other Worlds*, trans. Geoffrey Strachan (London: Oxford University Press, 1965), 75.

outside of space and time. '[S]ince I am truly a single indivisible substance, unresolvable into many others', he reflected, 'it is necessary that there be a persisting individual substance over and above the organic body. This [substance] is completely different... from... body, which, assuming that it is in a state of continual flux of parts, never remains permanent, but is perpetually changed.'[23] He was unable, however, to show how this reconciliation might be effected. Both ontologies nevertheless excluded materialism and satisfied Leibniz's anti-atomic principle of the identity of indiscernibles. 'Two drops of water or milk, viewed with a microscope', he claimed, echoing a point previously made by Hooke and by Cavendish, 'will appear distinguishable from each other. This is an argument against atoms, which are confuted, as well as the void, by the principles of true metaphysics.'[24] Lucretius, it might be observed, had found no two ears of corn or seashells exactly alike, but he did not regard this as an argument against identical atoms, but only as an argument for atomic diversity.[25] If the atoms had an infinity of different shapes, he argued, they would have to be composites of shapes, and so some would be of infinite magnitude; Leibniz concluded only that every shape is infinitely complex.

Leibniz's universe was accordingly unique and limitless, though not, thanks to his doctrine of the subjectivity of space and time, infinitely extended. Its entities were bound together by perception and accommodation. The individual substances he posited were 'windowless' (noninteracting), and their appetitions could only transform them, leading them to better states. Individuals, accordingly, did not attack, abrade, or destroy each other, as finite modes did in Spinoza's pitiless vision of the consequences of conatus—or their doing so was only an appearance, disguising a hidden and harmonious monadic reality. He allowed nevertheless that the atomic hypothesis could satisfy 'mere physical scientists, and assuming that there are such atoms, and giving them suitable motions and figures, there are few material qualities which they could not explain if we knew enough of the

---

[23] Leibniz, 'Notes on Comments by Michelangelo Fardella', in *Sämtliche Schriften*, vi. iv. B. 1669; *Philosophical Essays*, trans. and ed. Ariew and Garber, p. 104.

[24] Leibniz, fourth letter to Clarke, in *Philosophische Schriften*, ed. Gerhardt, vii. 372; *Philosophical Essays*, p. 328.

[25] Lucretius, *On the Nature of Things (ONT)*, II. 371; trans. Martin Ferguson Smith (Indianapolis, Ind.: Hackett, 2001), 44.

details of things'.[26] He insisted that his insensible perceptions and subvisible corpuscles were both essential posits, the one to pneumatology, the other to natural philosophy, and that 'it is just as unreasonable to reject the one as the other on the pretext that they are beyond the reach of our senses'.[27] 'The multitude of souls', he said, 'should not trouble us, any more than does the multitude of Gassendi's atoms, which are as indestructible as these souls.' He accepted the radical Epicurean distinction between the macroworld of objects with qualities—colors, tastes, and other phenomenological properties—and the microworld of corpuscles invisible to the naked eye. Like Cavendish, however, he insisted that perception was an irreducible mental power. '[W]e should seek perception in the simple substance and not in the composite or in the machine.'[28]

Leibniz was alarmed by Descartes's claim that all possible configurations of matter are actualized at some time or other in the history of the universe, and by Spinoza's Epicurean assumptions that the universe is ethically neutral, that God has no concern for human beings, and that values are projected onto objects and situations by emotionally agitated human beings in accord with their needs and desires. Besides depriving God of any substantial role in constructing and populating the universe, Descartes's account implied that moral and aesthetic values were ungrounded, and that God was morally indifferent to everything. Everything that can possibly happen is either happening now, or has happened, or will happen. Leibniz was equally horrified by Spinoza's claim in *Ethics* (pt. I, prop. 16) that 'From the necessity of the divine nature there must follow infinitely many things in infinitely many ways'. Spinoza begins where Descartes leaves off, he commented, '*in naturalism*'.[29] Ethically, Leibniz remained implacable in his belief that justice must be served by God, and the world must give evidence of its selection by a morally well-intentioned being. His conviction that the universe was constantly improving excluded the Epicurean doctrines that life and sense are emergent properties and that time brings only cycles of disintegration and renewal.

---

[26] Leibniz, letter to Remond, 14 July 1714, in *Philosophische Schriften*, ed. Gerhardt, iii. 618; *Philosophical Papers*, trans. Loemker, p. 657.

[27] Leibniz, *New Essays*, in *Sämtliche Schriften*, vi. vi. 56; trans. Peter Remnant and Jonathan Bennett, in *New Essays in Human Understanding* (Cambridge: Cambridge University Press, 1981).

[28] Leibniz, *Monadology*, §17, in *Philosophische Schriften*, ed. Gerhardt, vi. 209; *Philosophical Essays*, trans. and ed. Ariew and Garber, p. 215.

[29] Leibniz, *Comments on Spinoza's Philosophy*, in *Philosophical Essays*, p. 277.

Repeatedly in his essays Leibniz echoed Cicero's attack on the Epicureans in *On the Nature of the Gods*: 'If the structure of the world could not have been better whether in point of utility or beauty, let us consider whether this is the result of chance ... or whether the parts of the world could not possibly have cohered together if they were not controlled by intelligence and by divine providence'.[30] He argued persistently that God was the designer and author of the world we inhabit and responsible for all its beauties, and that we have excellent reason to believe, from an observation of nature, that our good and evil deeds must be compensated and punished in the hereafter. He insisted, conventionally, that 'reason and will ... lead us towards happiness, whereas sensibility and appetite lead us only towards pleasure'.[31] Nevertheless, in making representation and appetite the two basic faculties of souls or monads, under which reason and will were subsumed as special cases, Leibniz departed markedly from Descartes and the Augustinian tradition and revealed his affinity for Hobbes's and Spinoza's conatus-based animal psychology. He retained the Hobbesian conviction that tranquility is a state psychologically unattainable by human beings, that their passions are not beliefs, as the Stoics maintained, but impulses or endeavors, which 'like ... so many springs trying to unwind ... [drive] our machine along'.[32] He defined 'happiness' in terms of pleasure: happiness is 'a lasting pleasure, which cannot occur without a continual progress to new pleasures', and he commended especially the higher pleasures, 'which occur in the knowledge and production of order and harmony'.[33] Despite an undeniably authoritarian streak, he was perturbed by the doctrine of the damnation of the majority of the human race.

Leibniz saw himself as the synthesizer and reconciler of all past systems. He had read and annotated Plotinus' *Enneads*, which he admired greatly, as well as Cudworth's *True Intellectual System*. Scraps of Platonic and Neoplatonic idealism, along with remnants of Aristotelian hylomorphism, and of Bruno's immaterial atomism, went into the construction of his metaphysics. Modestly, Leibniz claimed that he never wished to be the founder of a sect. Immodestly, though not untruthfully, he represented his

[30] Marcus Tullius Cicero, *On the Nature of the Gods*, bk. II, ch. 34; trans. H. Rackham (Cambridge, Mass.: Harvard University Press, 1951), p. 207.

[31] Leibniz, *New Essays*, in *Sämtliche Schriften*, vi. vi. 194, trans. Remnant and Bennett.

[32] Ibid. vi. vi. 166; trans. Remnant and Bennett.

[33] Ibid. vi. vi. 194–5; trans. Remnant and Bennett.

metaphysical system as equal in profundity to the systems of Democritus, Aristotle, and Descartes. He told Remond that he had compared the mechanists with the formalists (Platonists and Aristotelians) and was the first to have 'penetrated into the harmony of these different realms and to have seen that both sides are right'.[34]

[W]ith Aristotle and Descartes, and against Democritus and Gassendi, I admit no vacuum, and even though, against Aristotle, and with Democritus and Descartes, I consider all rarefaction or condensation to be only apparent, nevertheless, with Democritus and Aristotle, and against Descartes, I think that there is something passive in body over and above extension…. Furthermore, with Plato and Aristotle, and against Democritus and Descartes, I acknowledge a certain active force or entelechy in body…. However, I agree with Democritus and Descartes, against the multitude of Scholastics, that the exercise of motive power and the phenomena of bodies can always be explained mechanically, except for the very causes of the laws of motion.[35]

In some passages Leibniz echoed Plotinus: 'Bodies in themselves are no self-states, but shadows which flow away. Corporeal things are but shadows which flow away, glimpses, shapes, truly dreams'.[36] Yet he saw nothing in his metaphysics that might be in any way incompatible with the approach to physics and chemistry of Galileo, Descartes, Huygens, and Boyle, or with his own contributions to analytical mechanics, and his enthusiastic interest in geology and microscopy. His reconciliation of idealism with physical science amounted to simultaneous acceptance of two different images of the world, satisfying different and incommensurable criteria of desirability, linked by the metaphysical language of reality and appearance. This form of juxtaposition reappeared in Berkeley's mature philosophy, as presented in his *Siris*. It was developed to perfection, and, some might think, to the point of absurdity in Immanuel Kant's so-called critical idealism, in which Newtonian mechanics and the ubiquity of causal relations were reconciled with free will, moral aspiration, and the idea of a supernatural creator of the universe and judge of men.

[34] Leibniz, letter to Remond, 10 January 1714, in *Philosophische Schriften*, ed. Gerhardt, iii. 607; *Philosophical Papers*, trans. and ed. Loemker, p. 655.
[35] Leibniz, 'On Body and Force', in *Philosophische Schriften*, iv. 393; *Philosophical Essays*, trans. and ed. Ariew and Garber, p. 250.
[36] Leibniz, 'On the True Theologia Mystica', in *Philosophical Papers*, trans. and ed. Loemker, p. 368.

6.2 Berkeley's desperate remedies

Berkeley embarked on his philosophical career as an opponent not simply of the corpuscularian philosophy but of matter itself. Unimpressed by Locke's lengthy musings on the impossibility of an eternal incogitative being, Berkeley scented doubts and evasions in his theology. 'Matter once allowed, I defy any man to prove that God is not matter',[37] he wrote in *Notebook* A, composed in about 1707, when he was twenty-two. 'If Matter is once allow'd to exist Clippings of beards & parings of nails may Think for ought that Locke can tell.'[38] Like Leibniz, he considered an attack on the foundation of the atomic philosophy necessary, and he boasted that with his own teaching 'all that Philosophy of Epicurus, Hobbs, Spinoza etc. wch has been a Declared Enemy of Religion comes to ye Ground'.[39] Berkeley's contribution to metaphysics lay in his refusal to dismiss sensory qualities as fluctuating, and unstable, and so as unreal in the manner of the Platonists. He insisted that qualities, together with the incorporeal spirits in which they resided, were robustly real, that objects were ensembles of qualities. The word *matter*, his spokesman Philonous maintains, need not be employed in common talk and ought to be expunged from philosophical discourse 'since there is not perhaps any one thing that hath more favoured and strengthened the depraved bent of the mind towards *atheism* than the use of that general confused term'.[40] While his attentiveness to the flux of experience resulted in Berkeley's being labeled an empiricist in the historiographical tradition, he is more appropriately seen as another rationalist critic of Epicurean atheistic corporealism. Few empiricists would endorse his statement that 'The existence of matter, or bodies unperceived, has... been the main support of *atheists* or *fatalists*' as well as of idolators.[41]

Descartes, amongst other early modern theorists of vision, had rejected, in his *Optics* of 1637, the theory of *idola*—colored atomic films that peeled off from visible objects and floated through the air to the perceiver—insisting that the visual image was occasioned by pressure, specifically the pressure generated by the spin of colorless corpuscles, propagating an impulse

---

[37] George Berkeley, *Notebook* A, 625, in *Works*, ed. A. A. Luce and T. E. Jessop (London/New York: Nelson, 1948–57), i. 77.

[38] Ibid. 718, in *Works*, ed. Luce and Jessop, i. 87.   [39] Ibid. 824, in *Works*, i. 98.

[40] Berkeley, *Dialogue* III, in *Works*, i. 261.   [41] Berkeley, *Principles*, pt. I § 94, in *Works*, ii. 82.

through the ambient aether, impacting on the retina, and then propagating
further through the animal spirits to the brain, the mind subsequently
adjoining a qualitative experience to the impression on the brain to which
it was united. To see a color is to read certain motions in the brain as
phenomenological colors, just as in hearing we 'conceive the motion of the
parts of the air which is then vibrating against our ears'.[42] Hobbes advanced
a related account, allowing, however, for the momentary generation of
phantasms in nonliving objects, denying only that they were retained in
consciousness, and Spinoza mooted something similar. In *Humane Nature*
Hobbes challenged what he referred to as the long-received theory of
vision, according to which color and shape, sound and noise are '*the very
Qualities themselves*', though he conceded that the long-received contrary
opinion that they were only effects 'must needs appear a great Paradox',[43]
giving Berkeley something of an opening. The images and colors of things
were 'but an *apparition* unto us of the *Motion*, Agitation, or Alteration, which
the *Object* worketh in the *Brain*, or Spirits, or some internal Substance of
the Head'.[44] Light coming through the eyes 'by Reflection from *uneven*,
rough, and coarse Bodies, ... then we call it *Colour*';[45] Boyle would later cite
reports of people who were able to discriminate colors via their fingertips
according to their roughness, an observation he took to count in favor of
his similar theory of qualities. We are to conceive colors, he thought, as
existing in bodies as latent 'ruggednesses' as revealed by the microscope.
The surface of an opaque body is made up of 'a multitude of singly
insensible Corpuscles, but ... giving these Surfaces that disposition, which
makes them alter the Light that reflects thence to the Eye, after the manner
requisite to make the Object appear Green; Blew, & c'.[46]

Though the neo-Democritean analysis of qualities as mind-dependent
had been widely accepted for nearly a century in Berkeley's youth,
it could still seem 'paradoxical' on several grounds. It could not be
explained in ordinary causal terms how particles in motion could produce

[42] René Descartes, *Treatise of Light*, ch. 1, in *Oeuvres*, ed. C. Adam and P. Tannery (Paris: Vrin,
1964–76), xi. 5; *Philosophical Writings*, trans. and ed. Cottingham et al. (Cambridge: Cambridge
University Press, 1985–9), i. 82.

[43] Thomas Hobbes, *Humane Nature*, in *Human Nature* and *De corpore politico* (Oxford: Oxford
University Press, 1999), ch. 2, § 4.

[44] Ibid.   [45] Ibid. § 8.

[46] Boyle, *Experiments and Considerations Touching Colours*, in *Works*, ed. Michael Hunter and Edward
B. Davis (London: Pickering and Chatto, 2000), iv. 35–6.

visual experiences in sensitive creatures, such modes of generation being impossible to observe or to analyze. Consequently, it could not be explained why particular textures in bodies produced the experience of particular colors. Boyle and Locke had bemoaned the fact that they could see no evidence of any intrinsic relation between colors and their causes in the asperity or roughness of the surface of bodies. Boyle mused:

I would further Know why this Contemperation of Light and Shade, that is made, for Example, by the Skin of a Ripe Cherry, should exhibit a Red, and not a Green, and the Leaf of the same Tree should exhibit a Green rather than a red; and indeed…why since the Light that is Modify'd into these Colours consists but of Corpuscles…. it should there not barely give a Stroak, but produce a Colour; whereas a Needle wounding likewise the Eye, would not produce Color but Pain[47]

Locke echoed him: 'Besides this Ignorance of the primary Qualities of the insensible Parts of Bodies, on which depend all their secondary Qualities, there is yet another and more incurable part of Ignorance … and that is, that there is no discoverable connection between any *secondary Quality and those primary Qualities* that it depends on'.[48] Boyle, though his piety was never in question, thanks to assiduous cultivation of his persona as a 'Christian Virtuoso', expressed the bafflement of the philosopher of the minute: '[W]hensoever I would Descend to the Minute and Accurate Explication of Particulars, I find my Self very Sensible of the great Obscurity of things'.[49] For all his appeals to God's omnipotence, Locke's expressions of bewilderment over the nature of substances and the ground of their qualities looked more sinister.

Berkeley had to concede that his experimentalist contemporaries who occupied themselves with matter had made astonishing progress in the sciences, and he had to concede that the interiors of plants and animals as revealed by dissection and microscopical examination were artfully wrought, suggesting that the material world was robustly real and complex. He was however able to capitalize on the philosophical helplessness of the corpuscularians to relate the latent image to the manifest. 'The sillyness

[47] Ibid. iv. 59–60.
[48] Locke, *An Essay Concerning Human Understanding*, bk. IV, ch. 3, §12; ed. P. H. Nidditch (Oxford: Clarendon, 1975), 545.
[49] Boyle, *Experiments and Considerations Touching Colours*, in *Works*, ed. Hunter and Davis, iv. 192.

of the Currant [*sic*] Doctrine makes much for me', he decided. '[The corpuscularians] commonly suppose a material world, figures, bulks of various sizes etc according to their own confession to no purpose, all our sensations may be & sometimes actually are without them. Nor can we so much as conceive it possible that they should concur in any wise to the production of them.'[50] If, he thought, he could show that qualities—all qualities—could only exist in minds and not in material things, 'an infinite mind should be necessarily inferred from the bare existence of the sensible world'.

You may now, without any laborious search into the sciences, without any subtilty of reason, or tedious length of discourse, oppose and baffle the most strenuous advocate for atheism. Those miserable refuges, whether in an eternal succession of unthinking causes and effects, or in a fortuitous concourse of atoms; those wild imaginations of Vanini, Hobbes, and Spinoza; in a word, the whole system of atheism, is it not entirely overthrown by this single reflection on the repugnancy included in supposing the whole, or any part, even the most rude and shapeless of the visible world, to exist without a mind? Let any one of those abettors of impiety but look into his own thoughts, and there try if he can conceive how so much as a rock, a desert, a chaos, or confused jumble of atoms; how any thing at all, either sensible or imaginable, can exist independent of a mind, and he need go no further to be convinced of his folly.[51]

Berkeley's spokesperson, Philonous, ascribes to his corpuscularian opponent Hylas the doctrine that '*the red and the blue which we see are not real colours, but certain unknown motions and figures which no man ever did or can see*'.[52] This is a shocking view, he suggests, and one leading to ridiculous inferences. He goes on to attack the distinction between primary and secondary qualities, insisting that the former are as relative to perception as the latter. All 'things' are bundles of perceptual qualities, and perceptual qualities are ideas that cannot exist outside of minds. Malebranche had urged against the materialists that 'Everything by itself is invisible', for we see all things in God,[53] and Berkeley took up the latter part of the suggestion, registering the absurdity of supposing that everything we see, or for that matter everything we look at, is, as Malebranche had proposed, invisible. Because there is a

---

[50] Berkeley, *Notebook* A, 476, in *Works*, ed. Luce and Jessop, i. 60.
[51] Berkeley, *Dialogue* II, in *Works*, ii. 212–13.   [52] Berkeley, *Dialogue* I, *Works*, ii. 193.
[53] Nicolas Malebranche, *Dialogue* II, trans Scott, p. 19.

world external to the mind, and because everything in the external world exists even when no particular person is observing it, the entire external world exists in the mind of God. Hylas, though distressed at having to do so, is forced to admit that 'Material substance was no more than an hypothesis, and a false and groundless one too'.[54]

Berkeley's 1732 dialogue *Alciphron* is a lengthy and comprehensive attack on the 'minute philosopher', probably a reference to Cicero's *On Old Age*, in which the mortalist *minuti philosophi* are criticized. Crito, speaking for the author, summarizes the position of the modern *minuti*, or freethinkers. There is no God, no providence, happiness consists in obeying animal instincts, appetites, and passions; guilt and remorse are prejudices of education; religion is a 'State trick'; vice is beneficial; the soul of man is corporeal and goes out like a flame or disperses like a vapor; and man is a machine, played upon by sensible objects, a ball 'bandied about by appetites and passions'.[55]

Certain particles, [says Alciphron] issuing forth in right lines from all sensible objects, compose so many rays, or filaments, which drive, draw, and actuate every part of the soul and body of man, just as threads or wires do the joints of that little wooden machine, vulgarly called a *puppet*: with this only difference, that the latter are gross, and visible to common eyes, whereas the former are too fine and subtile to be discerned by any but a sagacious free-thinker. This admirably accounts for all those operations, which we have been taught to ascribe to a thinking principle within us.[56]

Alciphron and his friends reject religious notions as 'follies of childhood'. Religion is a conspiracy, they think, between the priest and the magistrate. Belief in God lies 'amongst other old lumber in some obscure corner of the imagination, the proper receptacle of visions, fancies, and prejudices of all kinds'. The notions of conscience, duty, and principle enslave men and embitter all their pleasures. Atheism, by contrast, according to Alciphron, 'that bugbear of women and fools, is the very top and perfection of free-thinking. It is the grand arcanum to which a true genius naturally riseth'. The atheistical sage

looks upon himself, or his own bodily existence in this present world, as the centre and ultimate end of all his actions and regards. He considers his appetites as natural

---

[54] Berkeley, *Dialogue* I, in *Works*, ed. Luce and Jessop, ii. 229.
[55] Berkeley, *Alciphron*, Dial. 2, § 25, in *Works*, iii. 107.   [56] Ibid., Dial. 7, § 16, in *Works*, iii. 310.

guides directing to his proper good, his passions and senses as the natural true means of enjoying this good. Hence, he endeavours to keep his appetites in high relish, his passions and senses strong and lively.[57]

Alciphron's friend Lysicles, a libertine and a follower of Bernard de Mandeville's theory that private vices are conducive to the public good, defends hedonism:

We make men relish the world, attentive to their interests, lively and luxurious in their pleasures, without fear or restraint either from God or man. We despise those preaching writers, who used to disturb or cramp the pleasures and amusements of human life.... With us it is a maxim, that a man should seize the moments as they fly. Without love, and wine, and play, and late hours we hold life not to be worth living.[58]

He goes on to pronounce his view that the advantages of his atheism 'extend to the tenderest age and the softer sex: our principles deliver children from terrors by night, and ladies from splenetic hours by day'.[59]

Instead of these old-fashioned things, prayers and the bible, the grateful amusements of drams, dice, and billets-doux have succeeded. The fair sex have now nothing to do but dress and paint, drink and game, adorn and divert themselves, and enter into all the sweet society of life.... We will set down in the life of your fine lady rich clothes, dice, cordials, scandal, late hours, against vapours, distaste, remorse, losses at play, and the terrible distress of ill spent age increasing every day: suppose no cruel accident of jealousy, no madness or infamy of love, yet at the foot of the account you shall find that empty, giddy, gaudy, fluttering thing, not half so happy as a butterfly or a grasshopper on a summer's day.[60]

'We are a merry nation indeed,' observes the moralist Crito, 'young men laugh at the old; children despise their parents; and subjects make a jest of the government: happy effects of the minute philosophy!'[61]

In his youth Berkeley had been an aesthete, a pre-Romantic worshipper of landscape and animal forms, enchanted by the fields, the ocean, the mountains, the 'agreeable wildness of rocks and deserts', as well as by the delicacy, beauty, and contrivance of animal bodies. 'Sensual Pleasure is the Summum Bonum', he had stated unapologetically in his *Notebooks*.[62]

---

[57] Berkeley, *Alciphron*, Dial. 1, §§ 6–9, in *Works*, iii. 40 ff.
[58] Ibid., Dial. 2, § 13, in *Works*, iii. 84.   [59] Ibid., Dial. 2, § 24, in *Works*, iii. 106.
[60] Ibid., Dial. 2, § 25, in *Works*, iii. 107.   [61] Ibid., Dial. 2, § 25, in *Works*, iii. 107.
[62] Berkeley, *Notebook A*, 769, in *Works*, i. 93.

'Foolish in Men to despise the senses',[63] says *Notebook* A; 'Vain is the Distinction twixt Intellectual and Material World.'[64] It is not altogether surprising that he seems to endorse the views—a sort of amalgamation of Valla and Plato—on beauty, pleasure, and moral excellence that he puts in the mouth of the minute philosopher.[65] Like the alleged freethinker Shaftesbury, Alciphron supposes 'a certain vital principle of beauty, order and harmony diffused through the world'[66] that is distinct from providence and does not presuppose punishment and reward. Natural beauty, he maintains, has an attraction for the mind of man, as do moral excellence, justice, and all the virtues.[67] For all his scorn for religion and his view of man as a mechanical puppet, Alciphron is committed to the existence of faculties of moral sense and moral judgement. 'Make an experiment on the first man you meet. Propose a vilanous or unjust action. Take his first sense of the matter, and you shall find he detests it.... How can we account for this but by a moral sense, which, left to itself, hath as quick and true a perception of the beauty and deformity of human nature as the eye hath of colours?'[68]

It is difficult not to read the author as concurring in this opinion rather than rejecting it. His view that sensory experience constitutes a 'divine visual language', through which God communicates with us, is thoroughly in accord with it. The discriminatory faculty posited in the aesthete, his capacity to judge truly, and the close relationship that exists between the moral sense and the sense of beauty redeem the visible world from the charge that it is a delusion and a snare. It is as though Berkeley's rejection, first of the existence of material things outside the mind, later only of the mechanical philosophy, was the price he had to pay to purchase a permission for his belief that sensory pleasure was the *summum bonum*.

In any event, the staunch refusal to believe in a world external to the mind manifested in his youthful *Dialogues* and his *Principles of Human*

---

[63] Ibid., 539, in *Works*, i. 67.   [64] Ibid., 538, in *Works*, i. 67; cf. Locke, *Essay*, bk. IV, ch. 3, § 27.

[65] '[T]here is an idea of beauty natural to the mind of man. This all men desire, this they are pleased and delighted with for its own sake, purely from an instinct of nature.... And as this beauty is found in the shape and form of corporeal things, so also is there analogous to it a beauty of another kind, an order, a symmetry, and comeliness in the moral world.... And more or less there is of this taste or sense in every creature that hath reason' (*Alciphron*, Dial. 3, § 3, in *Works*, iii. 117).

[66] Ibid., Dial. 3, § 10, in *Works*, iii. 129.   [67] Ibid., Dial. 3, § 3, in *Works*, iii. 117.

[68] Ibid., Dial. 3, § 6, in *Works*, iii. 121.

Knowledge was relaxed after Berkeley discovered Newton's wave theory of color and his dynamical physics. 'Nature', he declared, 'seems better known and explained by attractions and repulsions than by those other mechanical principles of size, figure and the like; That is, by Sir Isaac Newton than Descartes.'[69] 'In strict truth', he continued to insist, in his *Siris* of 1744, 'all agents are incorporeal, and as such are not properly of physical consideration.'[70] He quoted with approval Plotinus' alleged remark that 'the soul is not in the world, but the world in the soul'.[71] The Platonists had grasped that whatever real things existed independent of the soul 'were neither sensible things nor clothed with sensible qualities'.[72] But he now describes the philosopher as climbing a ladder extending from the grossly sensible to the purely intellectual.[73] At the lowest rung he behaves like an experimental philosopher; he is concerned only with the 'outward forms of gross masses which occupy the vulgar'. At the next rung he becomes a naturalist, physiologist, and physicist, for he directs his attention to the 'inward structure and minute parts of bodies' and aims to discover the laws of motion. At the next level he becomes a mathematical physicist, reflecting on the laws of motion and their status as rules. Continuing his inquiry, 'he ascends from the sensible into the intellectual world, and beholds things in a new light and a new order, he will then change his system, and perceive that what he took for substances and causes are but fleeting shadows; that the mind contains all, and acts all, and is to all created beings the source of unity and identity, harmony and order, existence and stability'.[74]

Even while approving this beatific vision, however, Berkeley now accepted that color, odor, and flavor, rather than existing only in minds, 'seemeth to depend on peculiar particles of light or fire'.[75] The 'different modes of cohesion, attraction, repulsion, and motion appear to be the source from whence specific properties are derived, rather than different shapes or figures'.[76] Newton's active principles,[77] the cause of gravity, and the cause of 'fermentation', or vital warmth and motion, as well as of the solar radiance, fire, putrefaction, generation, and vegetation, enliven the

---

[69] Berkeley, *Siris*, § 243, in *Works*, ed. Luce and Jessop, v. 116.
[70] Ibid., § 247, in *Works*, v. 118.
[71] Ibid., § 270, in *Works*, v. 127.   [72] Ibid., § 316, in *Works*, v. 146.
[73] Ibid., § 295–6, in *Works*, v. 137. Cf. his poem 'On Tar', in *Works*, v. 225.
[74] Ibid., § 295, in *Works*, v. 137.   [75] Ibid., § 165, in *Works*, v. 86.
[76] Ibid., § 162, in *Works*, v. 85.
[77] Newton, query 31, in *Opticks*, ed. I. B. Cohen, 4th edn. (New York: Dover, 1952), 399.

'whole mass' or 'gross corporeal system'. Berkeley depicted the soul as weighed down and encumbered by the body, reproducing the old Platonic incoherence: matter is both unreal *and* evil. We are like persons wading up and down in the shallows of a river, and we long for 'the lot of pure souls ... happy, free and unchained from those bodies wherein we are now imprisoned like oysters'.[78] These metaphors of effort and imprisonment stand in sharp contrast to the earlier image of a brilliantly colored world of fluctuating and evanescent sensory ideas.

[78] Berkeley, *Siris*, § 164, in *Works*, v. 164.

7

The Social Contract

> Slaine kings, thrones, scepters, orewhelmd majestie,
> All, then did in contemned ruins lie;
> The bloodie crowne the fate of greatenesse mournd
> Beneath the feete of the base vulgar spurned;
> Who most insultingly trampled upon those
> They lately feard. Thus did those falls expose
> Soveraigne powers, which everyone persued,
> To the base dreggs of men, the multitude.
> By whose tumultuous sway, mortalls were taught
> To sett up magistrates, and laws were brought
> In publike use, when mankind stir'd with strife,
> Languishing in a sad contentious life,
> Bound up themselves, of their owne free accord
> Within strict laws, which will not now afford
> A libertie to such revengefull rage,
> As causd a loathing of that violent age.
>
> *(De rerum natura,* v. 1180–95)

Slavery and freedom, poverty and riches, war and concord, said Lucretius, are accidents; they are not properties of matter or void.[1] Their doctrine that only the atoms were eternal, and that all forms of life and all social structures emerged in time and altered over time, forced and enabled the Epicureans to give constructive accounts of the origins of civilization, beginning with the gradual emergence from the state of nature and then from a condition of war of all against all. Existing social and political arrangements, they maintained, were both contingent on accidents of development and at the same time relatively stable, thanks to the elimination of more fragile

---

[1] Lucretius, *On the Nature of Things* (*ONT*), I. 450 ff.; trans. Martin Ferguson Smith (Indianapolis, Ind.: Hackett, 2001), 15.

forms. As nature proceeded experimentally towards the creation of viable organisms, men found their way by trial and error. There were no models of civic order in the celestial realm.

Atomism did not preclude the possibility of defining moral concepts or identifying better and worse conditions of life. Justice, according to Epicurus, was not a virtuous condition of the just person; it was a relation obtaining between two individuals, or two classes of individuals, who were potentially dangerous to one another, a 'symbol or expression of expediency', as he put it, 'to prevent one man from harming or being harmed by another'.[2] Such restraints were the condition of a good life, and men who had found their way to such just arrangements 'passed the most agreeable life in each other's society'.[3] Unjust behavior, Epicurus thought, departing from the Platonic teaching, did not necessarily worsen the agent's internal equilibrium, but the pangs of conscience and the fear of discovery and punishment were sufficient to keep men in check; fear of divine wrath was superfluous. Epicurus' conventionalism and Lucretius' depiction of the state of nature acquired a new relevance in the early modern period, as jurists debated whether the authority of the prince and the magistrate and the duty of subjects arose from divine dispensation, from the law of nature, or from the voluntary submission of subjects for their own good.

7.1 Hobbes and the ancients

Gassendi had planned, but failed to complete, a seventh book for his *Exercises against the Aristotelians* of 1624 that was intended to show 'in what way the greatest good depends on pleasure and how the reward of human deeds and virtues is based upon this principle'.[4] He did, however, recapitulate the main points of the Epicurean theory of justice as a protective institution in his *Syntagma philosophiae Epicuri* in a manner that suggested his endorsement of it. To his 'Romance', Thomas Tenison

---

[2] Epicurus, saying 31, in Diogenes Laertius, *Lives of the Eminent Philosophers*, X. 150; trans. R. D. Hicks (Cambridge Mass.: Harvard University Press), ii. 675.

[3] Epicurus, saying 40, in Diogenes Laertius, *Lives* X. 154; trans. Hicks, ii. 677.

[4] Pierre Gassendi, *Exercitationes paradoxicae adversus Aristotelicos*, in *The Selected Works of Pierre Gassendi*, trans. and ed. Craig Brush (New York/London: Johnson, 1972), 25.

noted, 'he subjoyneth no Essay of Confutation'.[5] Epicurus denies, Gassendi explained, that some things are just of their own nature and unchangeably so.[6] According to his exposition, men agreed amongst themselves that 'if any wrong'd his Neighbours, the rest were to punish him for it'.[7] 'I suppose', Gassendi said, elucidating a utilitarian criterion and a contractualist procedure,

that which is Profitable and that which is Good, to be but one and the same thing; and therefore to the making up of what is Just and Right, two things are prerequisite, The First, That it be Useful, or that it hath Usefulness on its side. The second that it be prescribed and ordained by the common Consent of Society; for there is nothing perfectly Just but what the Society by common Agreement or Approbation hath thought fit to be observed.

Hobbes's Epicurean leanings were in turn evident to his contemporaries. Thomas Creech noted in the preface to his translation of *De rerum natura* that 'the admirers of Mr Hobbes may easily discern that his Politics are but Lucretius enlarged; His State of Nature is sung by our Poet: the rise of Laws; the beginning of Societies; the Criterions of Just and Unjust exactly the same, and Natural Consequents of the Epicurean origin of Man; no new adventure'.[8]

Like Bacon, who complained that the philosophical systems of the Greeks had brought forth nothing by way of works, Hobbes took a dim view of the 'vain and erroneous Philosophy' of Plato and Aristotle, and he drew for inspiration on the political theory of the atomists. Echoing Bacon, he described the natural philosophy of the two main schools of antiquity as 'rather a Dream than Science, and set forth in senseless and insignificant language'.[9] The Platonic philosophy, which had launched the pernicious

---

[5] Thomas Tenison, *The Creed of Mr Hobbes Examined* (London: 1670), 133.

[6] Pierre Gassendi, *Three Discourses of Happiness, Virtue and Liberty*, trans. F. Bernier (London: 1699), 315; cf. *Syntagma philosophiae Epicuri*, pt. III, ch. 26; *Selected Works*, trans. and ed. Craig Brush, 238−9.

[7] Gassendi, *Three Discourses*, p. 317.

[8] Thomas Mayo, *Epicurus in England 1650−1725* (Dallas, Tex.: Southwest Press, 1934), 64; see Bernd Ludwig, 'Cicero oder Epikur: Über einen "Paradigmenwechsel" in Hobbes' politischer Philosophie', in Gábor Boros (ed.), *Der Einfluss des Hellenismus auf die Philosophie der frühen Neuzeit* (Wiesbaden: Harrassowitz, 2005). A more tentative view was taken by Albert Haas, 'Über den Einfluss der epikureischen Staats- und Rechtsphilosophie auf die Philosophie des 16. and 17. Jahrhunderts', Ph.D. thesis (University of Berlin, 1896).

[9] Thomas Hobbes, *Leviathan*, pt. IV, ch. 46; ed. Richard Tuck (Cambridge: Cambridge University Press, 1996), 461 f.

study of incorporeals, was born, according to Hobbes, in the idleness of imperial peace, and his condemnation of Aristotle extended beyond his natural philosophy to his normative philosophy. 'I beleeve that scarce any thing can be more absurdly said in naturall Philosophy, than that which now is called Aristotles *Metaphysiques*; nor more repugnant to Government, than much of that hee hath said in his *Politiques*; nor more ignorantly, than a great part of his *Ethiques*.'[10]

Hobbes's originality consisted in his substitution of the question *What is the function of the ruler and what powers enable him or it to fulfill that function?* for the question *Who should the ruler be?* The ancients focused largely on the second question; while each one of the powerful thought that he should rule, the philosophers thought that the virtuous should rule. Both answers to the question who should rule presupposed differences of quality amongst men, whereas Hobbes's question, and his treatment of it, presupposed that people were very much alike. The sovereign fulfilled a role not because he or it was powerful, but only because authority had been ceded to the contingent occupant of the role.

The ancients, in Hobbes's view, had failed to theorize any stable basis for government, and their political behavior was reprehensible. Having no appropriate and common conception of the rationale for political authority and obedience, they jostled for power, and then they assassinated the powerful. History was the absurd story of regicide after regicide, and the classical emphasis on resistance to tyranny became especially dangerous, in Hobbes's view, when mixed up with the Christian conviction that God was a higher moral authority than any temporal ruler, that His will, as concerned mundane politics, could be revealed to men, and that much that happened in the world was the result of demonic agency. Men in ancient times and in modern times as well were usually to be found at war, recovering from war, or preparing for war. The historian Thucydides, whom Hobbes admired and translated, was the *locus classicus* for the description of the war-centered oscillating condition of society, and he had made his opinion of 'the imbecility of ancient times' clear. Before it was exhausted by the Peloponnesian War and the plague that followed, according to the memorable speech Thucydides put into the mouth of Pericles, Athens had been a cosmopolitan trading center of law-abiding citizens, with the

---

[10] Ibid.

right proportions of labor, recreation, games, and sacrifices to ensure 'the daily delight whereof we expel sadness'.[11] Thucydides described movingly and memorably the breakdown of this society, the loss of virtue, and the perversion of the language of morals, as men's passions were inflamed, and they took up arms and mobilized troops. For Thucydides, 'the nature of man is wont even against law to do evil', and the horrors of war 'have been before and shall be ever as long as human nature is the same'.[12] Unlike Thucydides, Hobbes did not think of war as stemming from the human disposition to do evil, or as an aberration that turned good, rational people into destructive madmen. Rather, war, punctuated by intervals of peace, was the condition into which human society, in the absence of an adequate political philosophy and an effective sovereign, naturally and so inevitably slipped. The propensity to war was obvious as well from the recent terrifying struggles with Spain, the Thirty Years War on the Continent, and the savage conflicts in Ireland. The political philosophy available to his contemporaries had not prevented, and had in fact been taken to legitimate, the assassination of King Charles I in Hobbes's own lifetime, and it had precipitated the collapse of his own country into civil war.

Hobbes rejected all notions of natural authority, natural submissiveness, and natural sociability as the foundations of civil society. Man is not a self-sacrificing animal like the bee, but one 'continually in Competition for Honour and Dignity'.[13] He did not accept Epicurus' view that conscience deters men from performing unjust actions, but he agreed that fear of discovery did so, and, like the Epicureans, he insisted that private and political morality involved the imposition of protective conventions whose rationale was in principle evident to all. The Aristotelian dictum that 'political and military actions are distinguished by nobility and greatness'[14] had no place in his system. The responsibility of the sovereign was clearly defined and delimited. It was to keep the peace internally and rebuff external threats; other possible kingly roles go unmentioned in Hobbes's

---

[11] Thucydides, *The Peloponnesian War*, bk. II, § 38; trans. Thomas Hobbes (Chicago, Ill./London: University of Chicago Press, 1989), 110.

[12] Ibid., bk. III, § 82; trans. Hobbes, pp. 204–6.

[13] Hobbes, *Leviathan*, pt. I, ch. 17; ed. Tuck, p. 119.

[14] Aristotle, *Nicomachean Ethics*, bk. X, ch. 7, 1177^b; in *Complete Works*, ed. Jonathan Barnes (Princeton, NJ: Princeton University Press, 1984), ii. 1861.

account. No political or theological emotions, moreover—not reverence, love, admiration, or esteem—had, in his view, to be directed towards the sovereign and his deputies, only fear.

Yet Hobbes's theory of political right and power is poorly categorized as positivism. The power of the Hobbesian sovereign resembles only superficially the despotic authority of the divinely appointed ruler; it is tightly constrained by the sovereign's role as the protector of its subjects one from another and as the enforcer of decent civil relations. His theory was naturalistic, insofar as the legitimacy of authority and the duty of obedience were held to follow from the characters, tendencies, needs, and desires of human beings. It was modern in several respects. First, universal participation and majority rule in the selection of the sovereign are envisioned.[15] Second, equality, impartiality, and even randomness are posited as guiding principles of distribution where things that are used and needed by all are concerned, as well as in the administration of justice.[16] Third, keeping the peace implied far more, for Hobbes, than keeping men from each other's throats; the sovereign was responsible for providing a safe environment for human industry. On the surface Hobbes denied the contribution of the state to the realization of human perfection, but in a sense to be explored below he recognized it.

7.2 The problem of obedience in a corporeal world

The Greeks were naturalists, taking experience as their guide, in the sense that they found in the cosmos and in the immediate environment models of regulation, dominance, and obedience. 'The state', Aristotle said, 'is a creation of nature and...man is by nature a political animal.'[17] The scientific understanding of the natural world seemed to confirm the existence of natural hierarchies; higher entities ruled lower entities, and form, the superior principle, mastered matter. The control of the many by the excellent and wise few mirrored the control of nature by God or the gods, of his slaves by the master, of the body by the soul.

The analogy of nature is especially evident in Aristotle's theory of slavery. Granted that the physical labor of a society, its agriculture, mining, weaving,

---

[15] Hobbes, *Leviathan*, pt. I, ch. 18; ed. Tuck, pp. 122–3.   [16] Ibid., ch. 15; ed. Tuck, pp. 108–9.
[17] Aristotle, *Politics*, bk. I, ch. 2, in *Complete Works*, ed. Barnes, ii. 1987.

and manufacture, had to be accomplished, Aristotle had to explain why
some human beings who appeared under their clothes to be no different
from any others, and who were undeniably equipped with some degree of
rationality and language, were subordinated to others who did not perform
this work. 'That some should rule and others be ruled', he declared, 'is
a thing not only necessary, but expedient; from the hour of their birth,
some are marked out for subjection, others for rule'.[18] Matter needs to be
controlled and directed by form, and in the social world as well bodies
must be seized and directed by intelligent authority if useful work is to be
accomplished. '[I]n all things which form a composite whole and which
are made up of parts...a distinction between the ruling and the subject
element comes to light. Such a duality exists in living creatures, originating
from nature as a whole; even in things which have no life, there is a
ruling principle, as in a musical mode.'[19] For Aristotle, men had always
experienced dominance and subordination; conquest and submission were
patterns of behavior natural for them. While a household is composed
of slaves and the master, together with his wife and children, a state is
composed of rulers and subjects, whose relationship exemplifies the cosmic
dualities just noted, the complementarities of form and matter, soul and
body, heaven and earth. Such relationships were stable, in Aristotle's view,
in a way that conventional relationships based on force or agreement were
not. The state, considered as a whole, was 'a union of people who need
each other'. It originated to meet the bare needs of life, but continued 'for
the sake of a good life'.[20]

   The introduction of theology into politics as rulers became Christians and
as religious leaders assumed temporal power introduced new complications
into the old theories of justice and obedience. The possibility of conflict
between religious duties and the commands of a tyrant was recognized
by pagan writers, but it did not influence their political theories either by
providing a justification for resistance or by necessitating a theory of divine
right. In the early Christian era, however, the problem of two sources
of authority, spiritual and temporal, became acute. Temporal authority,
according to the New Testament, was ineluctable and had to be patiently
borne; divine authority commanded genuine respect. This posture reflected

---

[18] Aristotle, *Politics*, bk. I. ch. 4, 1254ᵃ, in *Complete Works*, ed. Barnes, ii. 1990.   [19] Ibid.
[20] Ibid., bk. I. ch. 2, 1252ᵇ, in *Complete Works*, ed. Barnes, ii. 1987.

the origins of Christianity as the religion of an oppressed subject people in the context of the Roman empire, but it was unsuited to the subsequent marriage of Christian doctrine and worldly power. The problem of split and possibly conflicting obligations to God and to Caesar was partly addressed, not by rendering differently to God and to Caesar, but by taking Caesar as God's chosen representative. Though Christianity commands men to serve God, Augustine said in *The City of God*, God has appointed kings for the protection of his kingdom on earth, so people should obey the divinely appointed ruler and assume that God's choice has its reasons, however inscrutable they may seem. The construction of a theory of divine right built upon this premise was memorably articulated by James I of England:

Kings are justly called Gods, for that they exercise a manner or resemblance of Divine power upon earth: For if you will consider the Attributes to God, you shall see how they agree in the person of a King. God hath power to create, or destroy, make, or unmake at his pleasure, to give life, or send death, to judge all, and to be judged nor accomptable to none: To raise low things, and to make high things low at his pleasure, and to God are both soule and body due. And the like power have Kings: they make and unmake their subjects: they have power of raising, and casting downe: of life, and of death: Judges over all their subjects, and in all causes, and yet accomptable to none but God onely.... So is it sedition in Subjects, to dispute what a King may do in the height of his power.[21]

Hobbes's task, as he saw it, was to rid the theory of government of superstition and to make it compatible with the new naturalism of the mechanical philosophy, to construct a theory of obedience for a purely material world. He announced his intention to 'look at men as if they had just emerged from the earth like mushrooms and grown up without any obligation to each other'.[22] Atomism forecloses on the possibility that intelligent and incorporeal entities shape, manage, and discipline the material world. The atomist recognizes no natural rulers or natural subjects; there are only particles constantly in motion, some of which have coalesced into living bodies moved by appetite and aversion. Differences in abilities and competencies correspond to differences in physique and

---

[21] James I, *A Speach to the Lords and Commons of the Parliament at White-Hall on Wednesday the XXI of March Anno 1609*, repr. in *King James VI and I, Political Writings*, ed. Johann P. Somerville (Cambridge: Cambridge University Press, 2007).

[22] Thomas Hobbes, *On the Citizen*, ed. Richard Tuck and Michael Silverthorne (Cambridge: Cambridge University Press, 1998), 102.

the organization of the brain, and human beings are not in fact very different from one another—no more so, one might say, than crows or wolves. If the visible order emerges out of purposeless interactions, political relations cannot be modeled on natural ones. If 'power' does not name an incorporeal thing that can be insufflated into an ordinary atomic human being from a higher source, the holding of power by the ruler implies that the enthralled have decided or have been forced to submit. Such de facto relations are not necessarily just or beneficial, nor are they ineluctable.

Hobbes denied that there were slaves by nature.[23] As well, he ridiculed the notion of the natural sociability of man. The Stoics maintained that civic and national feeling were innate and they envisioned a widening circle of affection, 'all mankind united in one society',[24] that begins with 'family...bound together by marriage and parenthood', embracing first blood relationships, then friendships, then neighbors and fellow citizens, then political allies, 'and lastly...embracing the whole of the human race'.[25] Cicero's spokesman in *On Ends* found that 'there is nothing more glorious nor of wider range than the solidarity of mankind, that species of alliance and partnership of interests and that actual affection which exists between man and man'.[26] This was all wishful thinking in Hobbes's view: didn't men lock their doors at night and arm themselves for journeys? The Stoic doctrine of natural sociability was refuted, in Hobbes's view, by the facts of ordinary criminality and nationalist aggression. Cicero's statement in any case obscured the deep division in Roman society between *optimates* and *populares*, with their markedly different roles and interests, just as Aristotle's appeals to the complementarity of matter and form obscured the coercive and disagreeable aspects of Greek slavery.

To the question whether human beings are linked in any way by incorporeal souls to a supersensible reality or a divinity Hobbes answered in the negative. 'The Universe', he maintained, the whole mass of all things that are, 'is Corporeall, that is to say, Body; and hath the dimensions of

---

[23] Hobbes allowed that slavery was legitimate, but not natural. 'Aristotle...maketh men by Nature, some more worthy to command, meaning the wiser sort (such as he thought himselfe to be for his Philosophy); others to Serve, (meaning those that had strong Bodies, but were not Philosophers, as he;) as if Master and Servant were not introduced by the consent of men, but by difference of wit: which is not only against reason, but against experience' (*Leviathan*, pt. I, ch. 15; ed. Tuck, p. 107).

[24] Ibid. 471.   [25] Ibid. 467.

[26] Marcus Tullius Cicero, *On Ends*, bk. V, ch. 23; trans. H. Rackham (Cambridge, Mass.: Harvard University Press, 1931), 467.

Magnitude, namely, Length, Breadth, and Depth: also every part of Body, is likewise Body, and hath the like dimensions; and consequently every part of the Universe, is Body, and that which is not Body, is no part of the Universe.'[27] In a manner that can only be described as provocative, Hobbes discussed the idea of God under the chapter heading 'What Imaginations and Passions Men have at the Names of Things Supernatural', in which he considered 'what Thoughts and Imaginations of the Mind we have, when we take into our Mouths the most blessed Name of GOD, and the Names of those *Vertues* we attribute unto him'.[28] Thus theology was reduced to the study of religious ideation and dealt, by implication, with an imaginary object, an inference Hobbes left to the reader. He maintained only that we could have no conception or image of God and that 'all his attributes signify our inability and defect of power to conceive any thing concerning his nature ... excepting only this: "That *there is a God*" ';[29] that is, a power producing the effects men ascribe to God. God cannot be treated by philosophy, being neither an effect nor an appearance of bodies in motion, but, on the contrary, 'Eternal, Ingenerable, Incomprehensible', and immune to division and composition.[30] God is, however, a body, body in general, or bodies; and in calling God 'Incorporeall' we express our desire to honor Him, not our comprehension of His nature.[31]

The doctrines of essences, forms, and other incorporeal principles, he urged, are not only absurd and supportive of absurd practices; they are socially and politically pernicious and keep men in a state of fear and awe. A set of chapters in the *Leviathan* devoted to animism and to religious psychology and culture combined penetrating analysis of the cognitive springs of belief in gods—a desire for explanation, the need for succor in times of crisis—with ridicule of religious observance. Hobbes moved rapidly over the deification of animal and vegetable forms, conjuring, the interpretation of dreams, horoscopes, and temples built to honor qualities such as fever and rust.[32] 'The Enemy ... has sown the tares of Spirituall Errors ... by ... their fabulous Doctrine concerning Daemons, which are but Idols, or Phantasms

---

[27] Hobbes, *Leviathan*, pt. IV, ch. 46; ed. Tuck, p. 463.

[28] Thomas Hobbes, *Humane Nature*, in *Human Nature* and *De corpore politico*, ed. J. C. A. Gaskin (Oxford: Oxford University Press, 1999), Ch. 11, § 1.

[29] Ibid. § 2.   [30] Hobbes, *Elements of Philosophy* (London: 1656), pt. I, ch. 1, § 8.

[31] Hobbes, *Leviathan*, pt. IV, ch. 46; ed. Tuck, p. 464.

[32] Ibid., pt. I, chs. 11–12; ed. Tuck, pp. 75 ff.

of the braine, without any reall nature of their own, distinct from humane fancy; such as are dead mens Ghosts, and Fairies... [and] by mixing with the Scripture divers reliques of the Religion.'[33] The ideology of incorporeal spirits promotes fear of ghosts and demons, and makes men seek protection from nonexistent helps and submit to priests. At the same time, a belief in transcendental authority that can dictate directly to conscience renders them unruly and unwilling to submit to legitimate temporal powers. Those who obey their consciences imagine that they can know God to be the author of moral laws without knowing what, beyond lack of conformity to divine law, can make an action wrong or unjust.

7.3 Justice as convention

Historical awareness of an idyllic hunting and gathering past, followed by the discovery of agriculture and metallurgy, followed by weapon making and the collapse into war and chaos, was common in Greek and Latin literature. Lucretius' poem described a number of stages traversed in prehistoric times as the human race experimented with different forms of coexistence. Ovid, following him, depicted a golden age, without swords or helmets, cities or agriculture, when men lived on milk, honey, wild strawberries, and acorns. It had been succeeded by a silver, agricultural age of climatic extremes, and then the bronze and the iron ages, when

> Men lived by spoil and plunder;
> Friend was not safe from friend, nor father safe
> From son-in-law, and kindness rare between
> Brother and brother; husbands plotted death
> For wives and wives for husbands; stepmothers
> With murderous hearts brewed devlish aconite,
> And sons, importunate to glut their greed,
> Studied the stars to time their fathers' death.
> Honour and love lay vanquished.[34]

The Lucretian account of the formation of the state upon which Hobbes as well was able to draw began with solitary humans existing in a state

---

[33] Hobbes, *Leviathan*, pt. IV, ch. 44; ed. Tuck, p. 418.
[34] Ovid, *Metamorphoses*, bk. I, trans. A. D. Melville (Oxford: Oxford University Press, 1986), 5.

of nature and ended with the imposition of law and order. As the first four books of *On the Nature of Things* made the gradual formation of the cosmos visualizable to Lucretius' seventeenth-century readers, book V made the historical emergence of a social contract narratively compelling, and provided a rationale for obedience to authority that rested on the desire for peace. The primitive condition of human life *ante legem* and the gradual formation of civil society were exceptionally well drawn. Lucretius described early men as large, shaggy, and tough, as living 'random-roving lives like wild beasts'.

No sturdy farmer guided the curved plow; no one knew how to work the field with iron implements or plant young saplings in the earth or cut the old boughs from tall trees with pruning hooks. What the sun and rains had given them, what the earth had spontaneously produced, were gifts rich enough to content their hearts. For the most part they nourished their bodies among the acorn-bearing oaks and arbute berries.[35]

Living in the woods and caves, without fire or clothing, they were 'unable to look to the common interest, and had no knowledge of the mutual benefits of any customs or laws. Individuals instinctively seized whatever prize fortune had offered to them, trained as they were to live and use their strength for themselves alone'.[36] Nevertheless, they could not forge weapons, and they did not perish in shipwrecks or die of surfeits. Though they were painfully torn by wild beasts and succumbed to starvation, 'never... did a single day consign to destruction many thousands of men marching beneath military standards'.[37]

With the accidental discovery of fire, warfare, but also family life, according to the narrative, became possible and appealing; lovemaking and proximity to children rendered early humans less fierce. Those living side by side 'began to form mutual pacts of friendship', and indicated 'by means of inarticulate cries and gestures, that everyone ought to have compassion on the weak'.[38]

Although it was not possible for concord to be achieved universally, the great majority kept their compacts loyally. Otherwise the human race would have

---

[35] Lucretius, *ONT* V. 933 ff.; trans. Smith, p. 162. [36] Ibid. V. 958 ff.; trans. Smith, pp. 162–3.

[37] Ibid. V. 999 ff.; trans. Smith, p 163. See Michael Miller, 'Epicureanism in Renaissance thought and Art: Piero di Cosimo's Paintings on the Life of Early Man' (Lecture, Boston: American Philological Association, 2005).

[38] Ibid. V. 1022–3 f.; trans. Smith, p. 164.

been entirely extinguished at that early stage and could not have propagated and preserved itself to the present day.[39]

The era of village life, and informal cooperation and regulation, came, however, to an end with the invention of wealth and the laying up of gold. Where beauty and strength had brought prestige, now riches did so. Kings consolidated power, built cities, and awarded domains. The pursuit of gain led to the slaying of kings, and 'the sovereign head, now blood-bespattered beneath the feet of the rabble, mourned the loss of its high prerogative... The situation sank to the lowest dregs of anarchy, with all seeking sovereignty and supremacy for themselves'. At last, 'utterly weary... of leading a life of violence and worn out with feuds', the human race was 'ready to submit voluntarily to the restraint of ordinances and stringent laws'.[40]

Hobbes's account in *Leviathan* chapter 13 identified only one state of nature, in which rough and roving individualism, civil war, the predation of warlords, and regicide were collapsed into a single form of anarchy. His notion of the conflict-suppressing social contract differed from the Epicurean pact in several respects. Most important, Hobbes did not posit a direct agreement amongst men to refrain from hostilities against one another, or to help one another. Epicurus and Lucretius had regarded men as capable of policing their peers and as internalizing the voice of conscience. 'Violence and injustice enmesh all who practice them; they generally recoil on the wrong-doers, and it is not easy for those who by their actions violate the mutual pacts of peace to pass a placid and peaceful life; for even if their crime goes undetected in heaven and on earth, they are bound to fear that it will not remain hidden forever.'[41] On Hobbes's less sanguine view, conscience is not so powerful, and human malevolence will render any compacts amongst the principal actors nugatory; they will be broken whenever it is to the stronger party's advantage to break them. A system of punishment that depends on the retaliatory vengeance of neighbours, rather than on a powerful sovereign, furthermore, is unreliable and only provokes more violence. Hobbes did not imagine that men could build a commonwealth spontaneously, without philosophical direction, which, he came to realize, required persuasiveness. No matter how exhausted they

---

[39] Lucretius, *ONT* V. 1024 ff.; trans. Smith, p.164.   [40] Ibid. V. 1145 ff.; trans. Smith, p. 168.
[41] Ibid. V. 1152–7; trans. Smith, p. 168.

are by 'irregular justling and hewing one another' they cannot 'without the help of a very able Architect, be compiled into any other than a crasie building' that will fall on the heads of posterity. While the atomists insisted on the eventual perishing of every composite thing, from rocks to animals, to civilizations, to planets, Hobbes was convinced that, 'though nothing can be immortall, which mortals make', the rationally constructed commonwealth could be secured from perishing by 'internall diseases'.[42]

Hobbes tried to arouse mundane fear for their persons, as opposed to transcendental fear for their souls in his readers. In proportion as he released men from their terror of hell and their fear of ghosts and demons, he sought to impress on them their bodily vulnerability, and to rouse their desire for material comfort in this world. The felicity of heaven is as unknown as it is remote, he said, and 'the word of Schoole-men *Beatificall Vision* is unintelligible'.[43] He appealed to the universal aspiration to be active in the world and at the same time secure in one's enjoyments. Cooperative lives of building and making are unconditionally good, and to the extent that the power of the sovereign is a necessary and sufficient condition of realizing such lives, the sovereign can command our unconditional obedience. Hobbes's recognition that all humans, not merely a dissipated few, desire 'Ease and sensuall Delight', that delight is intrinsically related to vitality, and that this desire along with the desire to be free from pain is the only possible ground for political authority, is unprecedented. So the duty of obedience was grounded after all in the nature of men. Hobbes had, he boasted, derived 'the Rights of Soveraigne Power, and the duty of Subjects hitherto, from the Principles of Nature onely; such as Experience has found true, or Consent ... has made so'.[44]

Hobbes implicitly took issue with Thucydides, as well as with the entire Christian tradition, in denying that men are evil by nature.[45] There is no good or evil in the state of nature, only what men deem good and evil in light of their vigorous and understandable desire to preserve themselves and advance their interests. In some places Hobbes even suggests that nothing really is good or evil: '[T]hese words of Good, Evill, and Contemptible, are ever used with relation to the person that useth them: There being nothing simply and absolutely so; nor any common Rule of Good and Evill, to be

---

[42] Hobbes, *Leviathan*, pt. II, ch. 29; ed. Tuck, p. 221.   [43] Ibid., pt. I, ch. 6; ed. Tuck, p. 46.
[44] Ibid., pt. III, ch. 32; ed. Tuck, p. 255.   [45] Hobbes, preface to *On the Citizen*, p. 11.

taken from the nature of the objects themselves'.[46] He charged the ancients with passing off their own passions as virtues,[47] by which he meant that they praised various qualities—justice, temperance, magnanimity, and so on, as well as intellectual activities—but failed to show why they had objective value for everyone. Nevertheless, without calling peace objectively good and war objectively bad, Hobbes effectively appealed to the reader to acknowledge them as such. The condition of men *ante legem* is one of unremitting want and suffering, and anything but neutral. '[A]ll men', he insists, 'by necessity of their nature, want to get out of that miserable and hateful state, as soon as they realize its misery.'[48] By submitting to the despotic authority who could guarantee their peace, men stood to gain all 'the Felicity of this life'.[49] In arguing that the mere incongruity between a law and an action could not make the action wrong or unjust, Hobbes departed from positivism: good is what promotes human capability, evil is what hinders it. While men even in civic society consider various things good for them, no reasonable person doubts that civil life is better than the state of nature. Though Hobbes is not commonly considered a pacifistic and Utopian thinker, he was concerned as much as the ancients were with the contribution of the state to the realization of human perfection; his underlying view was that wasteful internecine conflict is inevitable in the absence of centralized power. The hope of prosperity and enjoyment as well as fear of loss, injury, and death ought to motivate men's submission to the sovereign.

Officially Hobbes rejected all teleological notions of human purpose. Because of the 'diversity of passions' in men and the 'difference of knowledge or opinion' each one has of what suits them and how to achieve it, everyone will and should pursue his or her own personal ends.[50] Scientific knowledge is reserved for an elite, but material production is natural to men in general. The atomic machines that we are cannot have an essence, but if they had one it would be as manufacturers. The subject of philosophy is, accordingly, 'Effects and Appearances', as they are generated or produced by the 'Powers of Bodies'.[51] The aim of philosophy, Hobbes

---

[46] Hobbes, *Leviathan*, pt. I, ch. 6; ed. Tuck, p. 39.   [47] Ibid., pt. IV, ch. 46; ed. Tuck, p. 461.

[48] Hobbes, preface to *On the Citizen*, p. 12.   [49] Hobbes, *Leviathan*, pt. I, ch. 11; ed. Tuck, p. 70.

[50] '[T]here is no such *Finis ultimus*, (utmost ayme,) nor *Summum Bonum* (greatest Good) as is spoken of in the Books of the old Morall Philosophers' (Hobbes, *Leviathan*, pt.I, ch. 10; ed. Tuck, p. 70).

[51] Hobbes, *Elements of Philosophy*, pt I, ch 1, §§ 2–4.

declared, echoing Bacon once again, is 'that we may make use to our benefit of effects formerly seen; or ... by application of Bodies to one another, we may produce the like effects of those we conceive in our minde, as far forth as matter, strength, and industry will permit, for the commodity of humane life'.[52] The greatest inventions are the arts of measurement and the mechanical arts—building, architecture, and navigation.

The renunciation of the right to strive for all that one can obtain, to attack and retaliate against other strivers, and the transfer of the right to punish to the sovereign is not grounded merely in what Hume later called 'stable possession'. Sovereign power is the necessary and sufficient condition of a truly agreeable existence by which we are permitted to live 'elegantly, happily securely'; to make, use and enjoy, as Lucretius said, 'ships, tillage, walls, laws, travel, weapons, clothes | Whatere like them from mans invention flows, | All the delights that humane life can find, | Poetrie, painting, sculpture'.[53] To that end, human beings require safe and commodious travel, well-ordered trade, the availability of workers, and restrictions on luxurious consumption, as well as 'peace amongst ourselves' and defence against foreign power.[54] Eliminating the negations of the state of nature, the condition humans can achieve *post legem* is the one in which there is:

Culture of the Earth ... Navigation ... use of the commodities that may be imported by Sea ... commodious Building; Instruments of moving and removing such things as require much force ... Knowledge of the face of the Earth ... account of Time ... Arts ... Letters ... Society.[55]

Hobbes's 'laws of nature'—the essential pacts of civil society—that he articulated in sections 14 and 15 of his *Leviathan*[56] are assuredly not the laws of nature of Pauline Christianity and St Thomas Aquinas. They are not descriptions of behavior that is typical of the species, often observed in other living creatures, that corresponds to an innate disposition, or that can be violated in the case of the *crimen contra natura*—choosing a marriage partner

---

[52] Ibid. § 6.

[53] Lucretius, *De rerum natura*, trans. Lucy Hutchinson, in *Lucy Hutchinson's Translation of Lucretius* De rerum natura, ed. Hugh de Quehen (London: Duckworth, 1996), v. 1502–4.

[54] Hobbes, *De corpore politico*, ch. 28, in *Human Nature* and *De corpore politico*, ed. J. C. A. Gaskin (Oxford: Oxford University Press, 1999), 173–4.

[55] Hobbes, *Leviathan*, pt. I, ch. 13; ed. Tuck, p. 89.

[56] Ibid., chs. 14–15; ed. Tuck, pp. 91 ff.

of the opposite sex, caring for one's children, obeying authority. Nor are they moral beliefs imprinted on the heart of man, innate, universally agreed upon, or observed by men in all nations. They are the conditions of a decent existence as disclosed by philosophy, the constitutive rules of a well-ordered society that is remarkably egalitarian in its distribution rules, impartial and corruption-free in its dispensation of justice, and mannerly with respect to individual relations. The laws of nature are infused with pacifistic spirit, a spirit shared by Pufendorf, who comments that 'Their force is not realized by children or the unlearned, or their advantages by those who have never experienced the losses consequent upon their nonexistence'.[57]

Hobbes was capable of holding two conflicting images of humanity in his mind at once. One image was, as is often noted, 'atomistic'. Human beings, on this view, are self-propelled material units in often violent collision, saturated with personal aims, ambitions, and desires, but without aspirations to the common good. These men are not political by nature; they have no spontaneous inclination to act as citizens, or even to cooperate with their fellows. This is the image that seems historically innovative in Hobbes, and that supports his critique of ancient political philosophy. The other image, however, is surprisingly classical. It is a benign image of the species, its collective achievements, and its cooperative potential, differing from the images of Plato, Aristotle, and Cicero in its egalitarianism and its emphasis on manufacture, two conditions antithetical in their view to the spirit and practice of philosophy.

7.4 Some critics and some admirers

Though *De Cive* and *Leviathan* were admired in France, Hobbes's materialism aroused attacks from English theologians, mathematicians, and natural philosophers.[58] *Leviathan* was censured in Parliament as promoting atheism,

---

[57] Pufendorf, *De Jure naturae et gentium* (1672), bk. VII, ch. 1, trans. Oldfather and Oldfather (1934), iii. 952, quoted by Ian Hunter, *Rival Enlightenments* (Cambridge: Cambridge University Press, 2001), 183.

[58] Samuel I. Mintz, *The Hunting of Leviathan* (Cambridge: Cambridge University Press, 1962). This study contains an extensive bibliography of anti-Hobbes literature. On favorable views of Hobbes, see Noel Malcolm, 'A Summary Biography of Hobbes', in Tom Sorell (ed.), *The Cambridge Companion to Hobbes* (Cambridge: Cambridge University Press, 1996) 37; Skinner, *Visions of Politics*, ii. *Hobbes and Civil Science* (Cambridge: Cambridge University Press, 2002), 316.

profaneness, and blasphemy, and Hobbist ideas were denounced from the pulpit. John Smith, in sermons of the 1640s, complained that the Epicurean 'allows no Natural Morality, nor any other distinction of Good and Evil, Just and Unjust; than as Human Institution and the Modes and Fasshions of various Countries denominate them'. The atheist, he said, denies 'the eternal and essential Difference between Virtue and Vice'.[59] Unable to grasp that Hobbes had posited a third way between a divine-command theory of justice and morals and relativism or nihilism, late seventeenth-century moralists turned to a defense of natural authority, divine command, punishment, and reward, and utility-independent standards of right and wrong, everything Hobbes had bravely set himself against. Thomas Tenison, in *The Creed of Mr Hobbes Examined*, insisted that 'Some primary rules of good and evil carry a reason with them so immutable in the eternal connexion of their terms that they can never be abolished or destroyed'.[60] Tenison objected to the hypothesis of the state of nature without government, maintaining that, while speculative astronomical hypotheses concerning the stars were matters of indifference, insofar as nothing in human life depended on their truth, 'fancied Schemes and Models of Polity' threaten 'the Temporal and Eternal safety of mankind.... Hypotheses, framed by imagination, and not by reason assisted with Memory, touching the past state of the World, [are] as exceedingly dangerous as they are absurd'.[61]

We are born and grow up under paternal authority, Tension declared, and Cicero was right to call wedlock the beginning of the city. Records of ancient times suggest that even nomadic people observed familiar moral codes, and even if 'every Man [were] supposed loose even from the yoke of Paternal Government, yet in such a state, there would be place, for the Natural Laws of good and evil'.[62] Henry More said that Hobbes's views were 'the Foundation of all Sin and Error'. The notion that good and evil are relative to persons was 'a deep Stream of that Fountain of all Uncleanness'.[63] More insisted on a concept of the '*Moral Perfection of*

---

[59] John Smith, *Select Discourses* (London: 1660), 3.

[60] Tenison, *The Creed of Mr Hobbes Examined*, p. 143. Locke tried to supply this want in his hastily abandoned attempt to create a morality capable of demonstration.

[61] Ibid. 131.   [62] Ibid. 136.

[63] Henry More, 'Animadversions on Hobbes', in *Letters on Several Subjects by the Late Dr Henry More* (London: 1694), 80.

human nature *antecedent* to all Society'.[64] Cudworth declared that '[T]he *Laws* and *Commands* of *Civil Sovereignty*, do not make *Obligation*, but presuppose it, as a thing in Order of Nature *Before* them'.[65] John Edwards maintained that 'The Rules and Measures of what is Just and Right were determin'd and fix'd from Eternity.... [T]hey are of Perpetual and Eternal Obligation.... [W]hat is Good or Evil in its own nature, can at no time, or upon any account be alter'd'.[66] The rules of righteousness, thundered Edwards, 'are no imaginary and precarious things, nor do they depend upon humane Institution and Arbitrement; but they are Real and True in themselves, they are Solid and Substantial, there being an Intrinsick Goodness and Excellency in them'.[67]

Cudworth took particular issue with Hobbes's moral empiricism. He pointed out that sensory experience cannot impress the rightness or wrongness, the beauty or ugliness, of situations, events, and objects on us. If the soul were *tabula rasa*, 'there could not be any such thing as moral good and evil, just and unjust, forasmuch as these differences do not arise merely from the outward objects or from the impresses which they make upon the senses'.[68] Our evaluations, Cudworth maintained, presuppose an intrinsic quality in the thing perceived, and 'an inward and active energy of the mind itself',[69] as well as a native disposition towards the good. Morality, he insisted, cannot be theorized without reference to incorporeal entities, and it involves the apprehension of timeless truths regarding the right and the good that have no direct connection with power, benefit, and social esteem, and that may in fact be at odds with their pursuit.

Why, one might wonder, did Hobbes's critics focus on issues peripheral to the central issue he raised: the locus of, justification for, and responsibilities attaching to power in a civil society composed of equals? Why did they fail to detect, or at least to comment on, the presence of a clearly

---

[64] More, letter to John Norris, 13 April 1685, in Norris, *The Theory and Regulation of Love* (Oxford: 1688), 173.

[65] Ralph Cudworth, *True Intellectual System of the Universe* (London: Royston, 1678), 697.

[66] John Edwards, *The Eternal and Intrinsick Reasons of Good and Evil* (Cambridge: 1699), 1–2.

[67] Ibid. 2.

[68] Ralph Cudworth, *A Treatise Concerning True and Immutable Morality*, with *A Treatise of Freewill*, ed. Sarah Hutton (Cambridge: Cambridge University Press, 1996), 73. This work was not published in Cudworth's lifetime.

[69] Ibid.

delineated vision of human welfare and the norms objectively conducive to it? Locke alone made objections that were to the point, perceiving that Hobbes's effort to minimize the evils of tyranny was unsuccessful; for his scheme allowed for the ruler to 'retain all the liberty of the state of nature, increased with power, and made licentious by impunity'.[70]

The neglect and misunderstanding of his critics is perhaps best explained by the Epicurean ontology in which Hobbes embedded his main propositions, and the unfamiliar character of the norms he designated as laws of nature. His corporeal God, his bizarre theory of the Last Judgement and the General Resurrection, his hostility to priests, and his quarrels with university mathematicians and Royal Society philosophers, especially Boyle, were scandalous. His rejection of the admired classical authorities in politics and ethics, Plato, Aristotle, and the Stoics, in favor of Epicurus and Lucretius, was so patent that critics, with the exception of Tenison, expended little effort trying to come to terms with his remarkable vision. Hobbes's writings nevertheless enjoyed a delayed, displaced, and significant influence on the evolution of both British moral philosophy and Continental political philosophy. The critique of kingship and kingly privilege as mystification was powerfully developed by the *philosophes* of the eighteenth century, and divine right replaced by a functionalist view of political authority and the grounds of obedience.[71] Not only the utilitarian presumption of equality and its hedonic framework, but the distaste for corruption and privilege manifested by eighteenth- and nineteenth-century political theorists including Mill and Bentham can be traced to Hobbes.

'Probity and honour', Hume remarked in his *Enquiry*, 'were no strangers to EPICURUS and his sect.... And among the moderns, HOBBES and LOCKE, who maintained the selfish system of morals, lived irreproachable lives, though the former lay not under any restraint of religion, which

---

[70] Locke, *Second Treatise of Government*, ch. 7, § 93, in *Two Treatises of Government*, ed. Peter Laslett (Cambridge: Cambridge University Press, 1960).

[71] Samuel Pufendorf, writing well after Hobbes, satirized ontological monarchy as follows: 'Men such as Hornius have conceived majesty to be a physical entity, which, upon being created by God, wanders about over the world with no home or resting-place, until it lights upon a king, who has been selected by a people, and invests him with this august splendour ... [But] when was it created, at the beginning of the world or later? Is there also but one majesty in the entire world, bits of which are distributed to individual kinds? Do kings have their own special and entire majesty? When a king dies does his majesty perish with him? Or does it survive him?' (*De Jure naturae et gentium*, bk. VII, ch. 3, trans. Oldfather and Oldfather, ii. 1005–6, quoted by Hunter, *Rival Enlightenments*, p. 189 (see also p. 68).

might supply the defects of his philosophy.'[72] Hume, like Hobbes, was convinced of Epicurus' claim that there can be no relations of justice obtaining between creatures that are unable to make contracts regulating harm.[73] Although he submerged the materialist hypothesis in skepticism and veiled his atheism, he endorsed Hobbes's view of human dispositions in the state of nature. 'This avidity... of acquiring goods and possessions for ourselves and our nearest friends', is, he said, 'insatiable, perpetual, universal, and directly destructive of society. There is scarce any one, who is not actuated by it; and there is no one, who has not reason to fear from it, when it acts without any restraint'. No affection of the human mind, he went on 'has both a sufficient force, and a proper direction to counter-balance the love of gain and render men fit members of society, by making them abstain from the possessions of others'.[74] He resumed the pursuit of the Epicurean metaethical program, agreeing with Hobbes's principle that there is 'no common Rule of Good and Evil, to be taken from the nature of the objects themselves', and he sharply criticized the doctrine of the 'eternal fitnesses and unfitnesses of things, which are the same to every rational being that considers them'.[75]

[M]orality consists not in any relations that are the objects of science [nor] in any *matter of fact*, which can be discover'd by the understanding... nothing can be more real, or concern us more, than our own sentiments of pleasure and uneasiness; and if these be favourable to virtue, and unfavourable to vice, no more can be requisite to the regulation of our conduct and behaviour.[76]

The cultivation of the virtues followed, according to Hume, from our interest in our living conditions and our ability to improve, refine, and embellish them, not from our cognitive powers and our knowledge-seeking impulses. Though Hume considered benevolent feelings and motives as

---

[72] David Hume, *An Enquiry Concerning the Principles of Morals*, ed. Tom Beauchamp (Oxford: Oxford University Press, 1998), app. 2, p. 165.

[73] Epicurus, saying 31, in Diogenes Laertius, *Lives* X. 150; trans. Hicks, ii. 675. This might be the basis of Hume's famous remark that 'Were there a species of creatures, intermingled with men, which, though rational were possessed of such inferior strength, both of body and mind, that they were incapable of all resistance', we would 'lie under no restraint of justice' with regard to them. They might deserve gentle usage but could possess neither rights nor property (*Enquiry* § 3, pt. I; ed. Beauchamp, p. 88). Hume says that this applies to animals; in his part of the world, women are able to make their disapproval felt.

[74] David Hume, *Treatise of Human Nature*, bk. III, pt. II, § 11, ed. L. A. Selby-Bigge (Oxford: Clarendon, 1978), 492.

[75] Ibid. bk. III, pt. I, § 1; ed. Selby-Bigge, p. 456.   [76] Ibid. 468–9.

original dispositions of mankind—he borrowed that much from Hobbes's sentimental critics—and although he seemed persuaded that, even without the threats of terror and the sword, or the control of a single architect, men could build a stable moral-political structure rather than only a 'crasie' one, his conception of morality was, like Hobbes's, relational and utilitarian.

Hume's writings abound in metaphors of human manufacture and commodious and incommodious domesticity. Where the ancients appealed to the heavens as the model for civic order and personal decorum, Hume had the audacity to compare the universe with a poorly built, drafty, sloping house in his posthumously published *Dialogues Concerning Natural Religion*. 'A machine, a piece of furniture, a vestment, a house well contrived for use and conveniency, is so far beautiful, and is contemplated with pleasure and approbation', he said in his chapter on benevolence in the *Enquiry Concerning the Principles of Morals*, and 'in all determinations of morality, this circumstance of public utility is ever principally in view'.[77] In chapter 5 of the *Enquiry* he described the pleasure we feel in entering a 'convenient, warm, well-contrived apartment'. The good feelings aroused are comparable to the feelings we experience in the presence of, or when contemplating good actions. They contrast with the feelings of indignation and horror we feel at the recitation of the story of 'an oppressive and powerful neighbour' who has enslaved provinces, depopulated cities, and made the field and scaffold stream with human blood.[78] Constructing a set of normative practices is like building a house:

All birds of the same species, in every age and country, build their nests alike: In this we see the force of instinct. Men, in different times and places, frame their houses differently: here we perceive the influence of reason and custom...How great soever the variety of municipal laws, it must be confessed that, their chief outlines pretty regularly concur; because the purposes, to which they tend are everywhere exactly similar. In like manner, all houses have a roof and walls, windows and chimneys; though diversified in their shape, figure and materials[79]

Human convenience, guided by necessity and utility, dictates the basic form of the building, the rest is embellishment.

---

[77] Hume, *Enquiry*, § 2; ed. Beauchamp, pp. 80–1.   [78] Ibid. § 5; ed. Beauchamp, p. 110.
[79] Ibid. § 3; ed. Beauchamp, p. 97.

8

The Problem of Materialism in the *New Essays*

> Even you your selfe attempts have sometimes made,
> Vanquisht with terror, when the priests did tell
> Their frightfull tales, from our truths to rebell.
> For I could easily many dreames invent,
> Which would quite overthrow and change th'intent
> Of all your life, perplexing with just feare
> Your whole estate; for if men saw there were
> A certeine bound to there calamitie
> Then superstitious formes and threats would be
> Withstood by all, which none dares now oppose.
> Since after death, they dread eternall woes.
>
> (*De rerum natura*, i. 104–14)

Leibniz commented in 1715 that 'natural religion itself seems to decay [in England] very much'.[1] His remark was prompted not only by his concern over Newton's depiction of a prone-to-breakdown solar system, but by his suspicion that Newton and many of his co-nationals considered the soul and God corporeal beings. Leibniz was referring to the dissemination of materialism and mortalism that had begun in the anti-authoritarian upheavals and sectarian fragmentation of the English Civil War, when a flood of publications idealized nature, showed contempt for status, urged a more liberal approach to sex and marriage, and promoted theologies

---

[1] Leibniz, first letter to Clarke, in *Die Philosophische Schriften von Leibniz*, ed. C. I. Gerhardt (Berlin: 1875–90; repr. Hildesheim: Olms, 1965), vii. 352; *Philosophical Essays*, trans. and ed. Roger Ariew and Daniel Garber (Indianapolis, Ind.: Hackett, 1989), 430.

with minimal doctrinal content.[2] After the Restoration treasonous plots and anti-monarchical writings reinforced the sense of moral and political breakdown, and the discrepancy between court manners and Christian teachings was all too evident. 'Dead we become the Lumber of the World', rhymed the clever and dissipated Lord Rochester, 'And to that Mass of Matter shall be Swept, | Where things destroyed with things unborn are Kept'. Restoration comedy was frivolous and lewd, and the decline of morals was associated with Hobbism and antitrinitarianism.[3] In his *History of My Own Time*, Gilbert Burnet commented on the recent death, in 1697, of the Socinian Thomas Firmin, a good friend of Locke's, as follows:

Books were printed against the Trinity which he dispersed over the Nation, distributing them freely to all who would accept of them. Profane Wits were much delighted with this; it became a Common Topick of Discourse, to Treat all Mysteries in Religion, as the Contrivances of Priests, to bring the World into a blind submission to them. Priestcraft grew to be another word in fashion, and the Enemies of Religion vented all their Impieties under the cover of those words.[4]

Efforts at containment were ongoing. The Blasphemy Act of 1650 forbade denials of the holiness and righteousness of God, as well as the expression of any favorable or even neutral attitudes towards 'the acts of lying, stealing, cozening and defrauding others, or the acts of murder, adultery, incest, fornication, uncleanness, sodomy, drunkenness, filthy and lascivious speaking'. Preachers proclaimed the necessity of 'reforming...the prodigious wickedness & immorality of the nation, never so enormously & universally over-spread with Atheisme, Murders, Robbing, Blasphemy & prophaneness'.[5] John Evelyn, who had lost his enthusiasm for Lucretius after 1657, reported in his diary the sermons he had heard against atheism, Arianism, Socinianism, Quakerism, libertines, and other aberrations.

---

[2] J. R. Jacob, 'Boyle's Atomism and the Restoration Assault on Pagan Naturalism', *Social Studies of Science*, 8 (1978), 211–33. Jacobs's claim that Boyle's target in his *Free Inquiry* was Charles Blount is controversial.

[3] See Warren Chernaik, 'Hobbes and the Libertines', in his *Sexual Freedom in Restoration Literature* (Cambridge: Cambridge University Press, 1995), 22–51.

[4] Gilbert Burnet, *A History of My Own Time* (London: 1753), iii. 292.

[5] John Evelyn, entry for 10 July 1698, in *Diary*, ed. E. S. De Beer (London: Oxford University Press, 1959), 102.

8.1 Leibniz and the English

Grotius' invocation of Carneades as his foil in *The Laws of War and Peace* introduced a new, though doxographically incorrect, association between Epicureanism and a kind of Carneadean-Thrasymachean moral egoism, and Hobbes's more cynical-sounding declarations probably helped to reinforce it. Virtue for virtue's sake was as inane a creed, in Hobbes's view, as knowledge for the sake of knowledge, or rule by the natural rulers. Virtue, in his view, had to be a means to an end, just as knowledge-seeking had to aim at the production of something we want.[6] Honor and worth, he asserted, derive from the exercise of a man's powers and are measured by the value attached to those powers by others, not by reference to any absolute standard. Thus:

The *Value* or WORTH of a man, is as of all other things, his Price; that is to say, so much as would be given for the use of his Power; and therefore is not absolute; but a thing dependent on the need and judgement of another.... A learned and uncorrupt Judge, is much Worth in time of Peace; but not so much in War. And as in other things, so in men, not the seller, but the buyer determines the Price.[7]

Although Leibniz never directly accused his old master of holding views destructive of good morality and true religion, Hobbes's naturalism and his doctrine that justice was established by human agreement were antithetical to Leibniz's own convictions regarding the harmony of the spiritual and corporeal worlds. His spokesman in the *New Essays*, Théophile, complains that ethics has been reduced by many of his contemporaries to a principle of honor which amounts to no more than a concern for external reputation.[8] There are some actions, Théophile insists, that absolutely recommend themselves as morally fine while not being useful or even tranquility-inducing. The category of the honorable and virtuous does not reduce to any variety of the pleasant, though divine justice ensures that all good actions are in fact rewarded. If there are performances we value and strive to encourage even though they do not satisfy hedonic criteria, and

---

[6] Hobbes, *Leviathan*, pt. I, ch. 10; ed. Richard Tuck (Cambridge: Cambridge University Press, 1996), 63.

[7] Ibid.

[8] G. W. Leibniz, *New Essays*, in *Sämtliche Schriften und Briefe*, ed. Akademie der Wissenschaften (Berlin: Akademie-Verlag, 1923–), vi. vi. 462; trans. and ed. Peter Remnant and Jonathan Bennett (Cambridge: Cambridge University Press, 1981).

performances we condemn even though they do, then, while social forces might explain how we acquire our moral beliefs, those beliefs do not reflect merely our interest in pleasure and tranquility, 'the goods of this life'. We must, like God, have other, irreducibly moral, interests. In insisting that ethical distinctions—better and worse, perfection and imperfection—were carved into the fabric of the universe, in no way dependent on the divine will or on human preferences, Leibniz recalled to the minds of his educated readers the elevating discourse of Platonic-Ciceronian moral realism.

Justice, according to Cicero, is a personal virtue bearing a close relationship to other personal virtues, including generosity, equity, dutiful affection, kindness, liberality, goodwill, courtesy, 'and the other graces of the same kind'.[9] It does not fluctuate, or depend on the needs and judgements of perceivers, and it bears no relation to the expedient. The Stoics posited laws of nature in an ethico-legal sense, rules of right conduct that they held pertained to all humanity and that were superior in force of obligation to any positive and merely local law. 'True law', according to Cicero, 'is right reason in agreement with nature; it is of universal application, unchanging and everlasting.'[10] What is good and right, Leibniz urged in turn, is not whatever men prefer and choose, or even whatever they perceive will bring them the most tranquility, security, and happiness. It is not even the set of arrangements God prefers and chooses because it can ensure our tranquility, security, and happiness. Rather, God prefers what is, in itself absolutely, and independently of us, good and just. As Cicero said, 'True law…summons to duty by its commands, and averts from wrongdoing by its prohibitions.…And…there will be one master and ruler, that is, God, over us all, for he is the author of this law, its promulgator, and its enforcing judge'.[11] The image of a community of spirits in Leibniz's *Monadology* and his *Principles of Nature and Grace* is indebted to Cicero's idealizations: God is said to stand to created things as a prince to his subjects and a father to his children, 'whence it is easy to conclude that

---

[9] Marcus Tullius Cicero, *On Ends*, bk. V, ch. 23; trans. H. Rackham (Cambridge: Mass.: Harvard University Press, 1951), 469. The long speech of the climactic book V is assigned to Piso, representing the Old Academy, but it is regarded as persuasive by its auditors and its eloquence would seem to justify the identification.

[10] Marcus Tullius Cicero, *On the Republic and On Laws*, bk. III, ch. 22, § 33; trans. Clinton W. Keyes (Cambridge, Mass.: Harvard University Press, 1928), 211.

[11] Ibid.

the totality of all spirits must compose the City of God, that is to say, the most perfect State that is possible, under the most perfect of Monarchs'.[12]

The conventional opinion that Leibniz's *Nouveaux essais sur l'entendement humain,* a page-by-page analysis of Locke's *Essay,* set the empiricist teaching that experience is the touchstone of truth against the rationalist doctrine that demonstration is the touchstone of truth reflects an anachronistic, post-Kantian perspective. The methods of philosophy and natural science are not the principal subjects of discussion in the *New Essays.* A more fundamental set of differences between Leibniz and Locke attaches to their respective ontological and metaethical stances. By 1698 Leibniz had studied the controversy between Locke and Edward Stillingfleet, the long-time critic of Epicureanism,[13] and he had selected Locke to serve as the new target of his extended criticisms of materialism, which in the past he had aimed at Descartes and Spinoza. The contest between Locke's version of Epicurean corporealism and Leibniz's Platonic theory of the intelligible substratum in the *New Essays* is often veiled and usually nuanced. Leibniz insisted that he did not hold Locke for a heretic. He contrasted Locke with 'those who wished to destroy natural religion, and reduce everything to revelation, as if reason had nothing to teach us in this area', and he credited him with the view that the immateriality of the soul was a 'probability in the highest degree'.[14] Nevertheless, Leibniz spent approximately half the preface to the *New Essays* ruminating on material atomism and thinking matter. In Leibniz's response to book I, chapter 1 of Locke's *Essay* Théophile observes that

This author is pretty much in agreement with M. Gassendi's system, which is fundamentally that of Democritus: he supports vacuum and atoms, he believes that matter could think, that there are no innate ideas, that our mind is a *tabula rasa,* and that we do not think all the time; and he seems to agree with most of M. Gassendi's objections against M. Descartes.[15]

---

[12] Leibniz, *Monadology,* § 85, in *Philosophische Schriften,* ed. Gerhardt, vi. 621. Cf. Cicero: '[T]hose who share Law must also share Justice; and those who share these are to be regarded as members of the same commonwealth.... Hence we must now conceive the whole universe as one commonwealth of which both gods and men are members' (*On the Republic and On Laws,* bk. I, ch. 7; trans. Rackham, p. 323).

[13] 'Remarques sur le sentiment de M. de Worcester et de M. Locke, des idées, et principalement de l'idée de la substance, etc.' (*Nouvelles lettres et opuscules inédites de Leibniz,* ed. Foucher de Careil (Paris: Durand, 1857), 1–26).

[14] Leibniz, preface to *New Essays,* ed. Akademie der Wissenschaften, vi. vi. 68; trans. Remnant and Bennett.

[15] Ibid. vi. vi. 70–1.

Leibniz's summary of the position of 'Philalèthe' converted Locke's scattered suggestions, and qualified endorsements into hard doctrine in order to deal with them effectively. While reputable historians shrink back from ascribing atomism and the doctrine of thinking matter outright to Locke, there can be no doubt that he was not simply toying with these philosophical theses, but concerned to mount a defense of science and morals that would be secure even if they were true. This would not have been worth doing unless Locke had strongly suspected that the corpuscularian philosophy was true, and that individual incorporeal substances, Cartesian mental substances, were fictions, or at least that others might find it plausible to think so.

Locke's hostility to innate ideas, his teaching that the causal influence of external objects and the mind's own operations upon its ideas were the only sources of knowledge, his skepticism about knowledge of essences, and his view that pain and pleasure were the springs of all human action were more salient features of his *Essay* than his disavowal of Hobbes's assumptions and arguments elsewhere. He took care not to link his understated commitment to Epicurean corpuscularianism to his semi-hedonistic views about morality. The hypothesis of thinking matter, bruited in book IV of the *Essay*, that aroused the wrath of Bishop Stillingfleet, who had been writing against Epicureanism for almost thirty years, was thrown out in a seemingly casual manner, as though unrelated to anything else in his book. Locke's contemporaries were, however, shrewd readers. And if they ungenerously overestimated Locke's heterodoxy, they also detected features of his position that escaped later interpreters. Locke claimed in the first instance to be advancing a theory about our experiences, our ideas, and our knowledge, not about ontology. However, his 'idea-ism' had a skeptical, ground-clearing function similar to Hobbes's and Gassendi's epistemology of appearances and their Lucretian critique of imaginary notions. Where Hobbes brought concreteness into moral and political philosophy by considering historical reality and human desires and appetites, Locke brought in concreteness by considering ideas. As ideas are either caused by corpuscles or are generated by reflection, Locke, too, could claim to found a moral philosophy on principles wholly natural.

When Locke voiced his view in the *Essay* that good and evil were 'only the Conformity or Disagreement of our voluntary Actions to some Law', backed by the mundane or supernatural punitive force of the lawmaker,[16] Leibniz was shocked and chagrined. 'I for one', Théophile says, 'would prefer to measure moral worth and reason by the unchanging rule of reason which God has undertaken to uphold.'[17] One of the longest and most emotional speeches Théophile delivers in the *New Essays* concerns the necessity of suppressing evil doctrines, and Epicureanism—conventionalism, hedonism, and 'living apart'—qualified as such in Leibniz's mind. While Epicurus himself had led a blameless life, Théophile concedes, this was not true of his disciples, who 'believing themselves to be relieved of the inhibiting fear of an overseeing Providence and of a threatening future ... give their brutish passions free rein and apply their thoughts to seducing and corrupting others'.[18] There was no basis for resisting tyrants, Leibniz maintained, reversing Hobbes's argument that religion and moral realism led to criminal assassinations, unless one recognized God as the author of justice.[19]

Leibniz was aware of two important facts relevant to the standing of Epicurean moral and political theory. First, he acknowledged that it was possible to be a good man while subscribing to dangerous falsehoods, including atheism, and he allowed that Spinoza, as well as Epicurus, had been a person of moral probity.[20] Second, he recognized that there was room for doubt about the dogmas of revealed religion, and that theological controversies over minute points of doctrine were basically undecidable. In some texts he asserted a theology so minimal and unmysterious that it could not have failed to please an English deist. 'The wisest course is to take no position regarding things of which so little is known, and to be satisfied with the general belief that God can do nothing which is not entirely good and just.'[21] Adherence to two chief doctrines—the goodness, wisdom, and justice of God, and the immortality of the soul and its liability to reward and punishments in the afterlife—was, in Leibniz's view, a sufficient foundation for morality and public order. It was also

---

[16] Locke, *An Essay Concerning Human Understanding*, bk. II, ch. 23, § 5; ed. P. H. Nidditch (Oxford: Clarendon, 1975), 351.

[17] Leibniz, *New Essays*, vi. vi. 250; trans. Remnant and Bennett.   [18] Ibid. vi. vi. 462–3.

[19] According to a letter of 1683–91, translated in Patrick Riley, *Political Writings* (Cambridge: Cambridge University Press, 1972), 187.

[20] Ibid. vi. vi. 462. Gassendi had defended Epicurus' virtue in the preface to his *De vita et moribus Epicuri libri octo* of 1647, and Pierre Bayle had insisted on the probity of atheists in his popular *Penseés sur la comete* of 1683.

[21] Leibniz, *New Essays*, vi. vi. 502–3; trans. Remnant and Bennett.

necessary. Leibniz endeavored, as a philosopher, to convince his readers of their truth, but he also considered, as a politician, that religious skepticism should not be freely promulgated and that censorship was necessary.

8.2 Locke's hedonism

'[N]othing can be more evident to us, than our own Existence', said Locke. '*I think, I reason, I feel Pleasure and Pain.*'[22] Pleasure and pain were the universal motives to human action, and it was better to be active than idle. 'The business of man', he mused in 1677, 'is to be happy in this world by enjoyment of the things of nature subservient to life, health, ease and pleasure and the comfortable hopes of another life.'[23] These views were at odds with the view expressed in Genesis that pain and labour were punishments for sin, and with the Augustinian notion that concupiscence was the cause of sin, and that happiness was to be obtained by making union with God the sole object of our desires. Happiness could be obtained in many ways, Locke thought, insofar as there were so many objects and states in the world capable of providing legitimate pleasure.

Locke's remarkably favorable attitude to pleasure, his assumption that it was a central ethical concept, was evident in his early journal entries as well as in the *Essay*. Drinking, gaming, and vicious activities ruin health and torment conscience, he decided in 1668, but 'innocent diversions and delights', including hunting and theatergoing, are to be pursued. Locke wavered somewhat in his criteria, austerely citing reputation, knowledge, and doing good as sources of lasting pleasure, whereas 'the perfumes I smelt yesterday now no more affect me with any'. But health, 'without which no sensual pleasure can have any relish', was also in his view a condition of a happy life.[24] 'The expectation of eternal and incomprehensible happiness in another world', he assured himself, 'is that also which carries a constant pleasure with it.'[25] It might appear that empiricism was here decisively

---

[22] Locke, *Essay*, bk. IV, ch. 9, § 3; ed. Nidditch, p. 618.

[23] Locke, journal entry for Mund. 8 February 1677, in *An Early Draft of Locke's Essay*, ed. Richard Aaron and Jocelyn Gibb (Oxford: Clarendon, 1936), 88.

[24] Locke, quoted in Maurice Cranston, *John Locke: A Biography* (London: Longmans, 1957), 123, from British Library MSS Locke, c. 28, fos. 143–4.

[25] Ibid.

set aside in order to make room for faith, but Locke's emphasis was already being placed on a psychological attitude—expectation—not on the certainty of this 'incomprehensible' state.

The early draft of his *Essay* known as 'Draft A', together with his journal entries for the late 1670s and early 1680s, gives a clear picture of Locke's original preoccupations. Draft A begins with an affirmation of the mechanical theory of perception, and this account of the generation of ideas balances the skeptical account of the boundaries of knowledge suggestive of Gassendi's influence. 'Our mindes are not made as large as truth nor suited to the whole extent of things amongst those that come within its ken it meets with a great many too big for its graspe, and there are not a few that it is faine to give up as incomprehensible.'[26] Locke transformed his doubts about the existence of God into a doctrine concerning the limits of knowledge, avoiding Hobbes's aggressive posture. Even if, he decided in his journal, 'anyone should so far be prevailed on by prejudice or corruption as to phansy he found in the wild inconsistent thoughts of Atheisme less contrariety to reason and experience then in the beliefe of a deity', and even if the 'seeming Probability' lies on the atheist's side, he will consider the risk of infinite misery he runs if his prediction that death brings annihilation proves false. In the absence of 'plain, undeniable demonstration' of either alternative, he will choose to believe. He will believe, however, no more than is necessary to eliminate his excess risk.

Within the epistemological space remaining, Locke proposed to found an ethics: a general design for living and a stance to adopt towards religion, religious dissent, and religious fanaticism. While his views on the substance of theology and on toleration changed over his lifetime, Locke always considered religion from a psychological and social perspective. The enjoyment of eternal bliss was not a goal in and of itself; rather the hope of bliss and the fear of eternal torment were disincentives to immorality, and so constituted indispensable pieces of mental furniture in oneself and in others. After stating his position that the business of man was to be happy and hopeful, Locke expressed his opinion that 'we need noe other knowledg for the attainment of those ends but of the history and observation of the effects and operations of naturall bodies within our power, and of our dutys in

---

[26] Locke, journal entry for Mund. 8 February 1677, in *An Early Draft*, ed. Aaron and Gibb, p. 84.

the management of our owne actions as far as they depend on our wills.'[27] In his *Essay*, Locke first argued that pain and pleasure were necessary spurs to action; then he tried to show that pleasure and pain are the grounds of morality. If we experienced no sensations connected with the exercise of our wills, he argued, 'we should have no reason to prefer one Thought or Action to another; Negligence, to Attention; or Motion, to Rest.... In which state Man, however furnished with the Faculties of Understanding and Will, would be a very idle, unactive Creature, and pass his time only in a lazy, lethargick Dream'.[28] Pain and pleasure are indicators of what to pursue and what to avoid.[29] Consequently, Locke thought, the human will was never motivated by an intellectual perception of the good alone. '[W]hatever good is propos'd, if its absence carries no displeasure nor pain with it; if a Man be easie and content without it, there is no desire of it, nor endeavour after it; there is no more but a bare *Velleity*, the term used to signifie the lowest degree of Desire, and that which is next to none at all.'[30]

As examples of pleasure and pain, Locke referred to 'the Pain of *Hunger* and *Thirst*, and the Pleasure of Eating and Drinking to remove them; The pain of tender Eyes, and the pleasure of Musick; Pain from captious uninstructive wrangling, and the pleasure of rational conversation with a Friend, or of well-directed study in the search and discovery of Truth'.[31] Elsewhere, he mentioned the pains of heat, cold, weariness, and the mental anguish of infertility; correspondingly, delight in the taste of grapes, poignant sauces, delicious wine, and delight in the acquisition of knowledge. We can also, he thought, take pleasure in the happiness and well-being of others. '*Love*, to Beings capable of Happiness or Misery, is often the ... Delight, which we find in our selves arising from a consideration of their very Being, or Happiness.... Thus the Being and Welfare of a Man's Children or Friends, producing constant Delight in him, he is said constantly to *love* them.'[32] Where the Stoics argued against the identification of philosophical happiness with pleasurable experiences and sensations, Locke identified them: '*Happiness* then in its full extent is the utmost Pleasure we are capable of, and *Misery* the utmost Pain. And the lowest degree of what can be called *Happiness*, is so much ease from all

---

[27] Ibid. 88.   [28] Locke, *Essay*, bk. II, ch. 7, § 4; ed. Nidditch, p. 129.   [29] Ibid.

[30] Ibid., ch. 20, § 6; ed. Nidditch, p. 230. The point is considerably amplified in Locke's celebrated discussion of 'uneasiness' in bk. II, ch. 21, §§ 32 ff.

[31] Ibid., ch. 20, § 18; ed. Nidditch, p. 233.   [32] Ibid., § 5; ed. Nidditch, p. 230.

Pain, and so much present Pleasure, as without which any one cannot be content.'[33]

Locke went on to argue that the terms 'good' and 'evil' are understood only in reference to pleasure and pain:

That we call *Good*, which is *apt to cause or increase Pleasure, or diminish Pain in us; or else to procure, or preserve us the possession of any other Good, or absence of any Evil*. And on the contrary we name that *Evil*, which *is apt to produce or increase any Pain, or diminish any Pleasure in us; or else to procure us any Evil, or deprive us of any Good*.[34]

At the same time, Locke maintained that moral good and evil were 'the Conformity or Disagreement of our voluntary Actions to some Law, whereby Good or Evil is drawn on us, from the Will and Power of the Law-maker'.[35] This left him with the task of making his view that the concept of goodness was understood through the concept of pleasure, and that motivation depended on the prickings of discomfort and the promise of happiness, consistent with his deontological criterion of the right.

In order to link up these disjoint views, Locke first emphasized the Epicurean point that pursuit of many pleasures results in long-term pain, and that well-informed and rational persons shun them:

I lay it for a certain ground, that every intelligent Being really seeks Happiness, which consists in the enjoyment of Pleasure, without any considerable mixture of uneasiness; 'tis impossible any one should willingly put into his own draught any bitter ingredient, or leave out any thing in his power, that would tend to his satisfaction, and the compleating of his Happiness, but only by a *wrong Judgment*.[36]

Unlike the Epicurean, however, Locke maintained that the pains and pleasures of a future life were assured (even if only by faith). The God-given hedonic motive accordingly guides us towards our ultimate happiness in the afterlife. '[F]inding imperfection, dissatisfaction, and want of complete happiness, in all the Enjoyments which the Creatures can afford us', God intended that we 'might be led to seek it in the enjoyment of him, *with whom there is fullness of joy, and at whose right hand are pleasures for evermore*.'[37] Though men's ordinary psychology incorporates a bias towards the present that is difficult to overcome, no person aware of the prospects of heaven

---

[33] Locke, *Essay*, bk. II, ch. 21, § 42; ed. Nidditch, p. 258.
[34] Ibid., ch. 20, § 2; ed. Nidditch, p. 229.
[35] Ibid., ch. 28, § 5; ed. Nidditch, p. 351.   [36] Ibid., ch. 21, § 62; ed. Nidditch, p. 274.
[37] Ibid., ch. 7, § 5; ed. Nidditch, p. 130.

and hell will purchase a temporary worldly pleasure at the cost of eternal torment.[38]

'[M]oral principles', Locke decided, 'require Reasoning and Discourse, and some Exercise of the Mind, to discover the certainty of their Truth.'[39] Effort is necessary to discover them, even if it is not always sufficient. The need for effort does not, however, condemn us to overscrupulousness and repression. Though some aspects of our conduct are fixed by Scripture, by the law of nature, or simply by reason, and while other aspects are constrained by local custom and convention, a good deal is up to the individual. That we have considerable moral liberty and need not 'clog every action of our lives, even the minutest of them ... with infinite Consideration before we begin it and unavoidable perplexity and doubt when it is donne' was the substance of the letter Locke wrote to the neurotically worried Denis Grenville in 1678.[40] The actions forbidden or mandated as a matter of real obligation are few. Many performances are elicited and constrained by the regard or scorn of men, and while maintaining a good reputation is important, we still enjoy considerable freedom in deciding how to live. Though this rather existentialist message is muted in the *Essay*, it comes through in Locke's rejection of perfectionism. Our inability to demonstrate the existence and uniqueness of a *summum bonum* by philosophical argument allows us a certain latitude in pursuing what appears and feels good to us:

Hence it was, I think, that the Philosophers of old did in vain enquire, whether the *Summum bonum* consisted in Riches, or bodily Delights, or Virtue, or Contemplation: And they might have as reasonably disputed, whether the best Relish were to be found in Apples, Plumbs, or Nuts; and have divided themselves into Sects upon it.... So the greatest Happiness consists, in the having those things, which produce the greatest Pleasure; and in the absence of those, which cause any disturbance, any pain. Now these, to different Men, are very different things.[41]

---

[38] 'For since nothing of Pleasure and Pain in this Life, can bear any proportion to the endless Happiness, or exquisite Misery, of an immortal Soul hereafter, Actions in his Power will have their preference, not according to the transient Pleasure or Pain that accompanies, or follows them here; but as they serve to secure that perfect durable Happiness hereafter' (ibid., ch. 21, § 60; ed. Nidditch, p. 274).

[39] Ibid., bk. I, ch. 3, § 1; ed. Nidditch, p. 66.

[40] John Locke, *The Correspondence of John Locke*, ed. E. S. De Beer (Oxford: Clarendon, 1976), i. 558.

[41] Locke, *Essay*, bk. II, ch. 21, § 55; ed. Nidditch, p. 269.

Our pursuits are constrained only by what God or the law of nature explicitly prohibits.

Because we have a powerful drive towards happiness, moral steering requires only the correction of false beliefs concerning what will make us happy, and Locke's prescriptive ethics are based on a kind of sophisticated personal-utility calculus. We wrongly minimize the evil consequences of our actions, or suppose that they can be avoided or compensated for.[42] We make wrong judgements of our long-term interests since 'Objects, near our view, are apt to be thought greater, than those of a larger size, that are more remote'.[43] We estimate present pains as needing immediate removal even if suffering them is conducive to greater happiness in the long run. The pain of deprivation of a desired object 'forces us, as it were, blindfold into its embraces', and we pursue the very objects that make us miserable.[44] Further, our emotions make us impervious to moral reasoning and blind us to our own true interests. We are liable to 'extreme disturbance' that 'possesses our whole Mind, as when the pain of the Rack, an impetuous *uneasiness*, as of Love, Anger, or any other violent Passion, running away with us, allows us not the liberty of thought, and we are not Masters enough of our own Minds to consider thoroughly, and examine fairly'.[45] Yet, so long as we forbear from 'too hasty compliance with our desires', aim for 'the moderation and restraint of our Passions', and engage in sober reflection on our true happiness, God, 'who knows our frailty, pities our weakness, and requires of us no more than we are able to do, and sees what was, and was not in our power, will judge as a kind and merciful Father'.[46]

As he explained to his critic James Lowde, Locke was not interested in 'laying down moral Rules' in the *Essay* but rather in 'shewing the original and nature of moral *Ideas*, and enumerating the Rules Men make use of in moral Relations, whether those Rules were true or false'.[47] Writing in an era in which there had been astonishing progress in the physical sciences, in mathematics, optics, and experimental philosophy, Locke hoped to show that moral objectivity was consistent with the new natural philosophy, and above all with a Gassendist epistemology according to which the mind dealt only with appearances or ideas, insofar as it was either unable to grasp the essences of extra-mental things, or there were

---

[42] Locke, *Essay*, bk. II, ch. 21, § 66; ed. Nidditch, p. 278.   [43] Ibid., § 63; ed. Nidditch, p. 275.
[44] Ibid., § 64; ed. Nidditch, p. 277.   [45] Ibid., § 53; ed. Nidditch, pp. 267–8.
[46] Ibid. 268.   [47] Ibid., ch. 28, § 11 n.; ed. Nidditch, p. 354.

no such essences. He modified Hobbes's epistemology to make reflection a contributory source of ideas independent of sensation, leaving it open to the reader to understand reflection either as a corporeal process in Hobbes's fashion, or as the activity of an incorporeal mind in Descartes's fashion, just as that reader might think appropriate. He dispensed altogether, however, with the Cartesian notion that God imprints ideas of Himself directly on an incorporeal soul, where they serve subsequently as objects of the incorporeal understanding. Without asserting that religious beliefs and emotions concern mere phantasms attached to names, Locke turned to a consideration of the origin of moral and theological ideas. Moral ideas, he maintained, arise from social experience, not from sources within. To learn about virtue and vice is to learn from our elders and peers the actions to which certain names attach and to experience conforming reactions of approbation, dislike, esteem, and blame when those actions are performed. He was accordingly the first philosopher to give sustained attention to moral epistemology, comparing and contrasting our limited ability to discover facts about the natural world with our somewhat better ability to discover the truths of morality.

Locke criticized the theory of innate moral notions in terms reminiscent of Hobbes's earlier criticisms of the scholastic, and for that matter Grotian, notion of natural law. The alleged universality of the moral laws of nature in the minds of all but children and fools is refuted by observation. Further, he maintained, appeals to innate ideas by preachers and philosophers had been counterproductive. The Platonists had overplayed their hand, for, failing to find innate moral ideas in themselves, or impressed by their apparent absence in others, disillusioned readers reacted by rejecting all idealistic apparatus and concluded that they were mere machines that could not help what they did: '[T]hey take away not only innate, but all Moral Rules whatsoever, and leave not a possibility to believe any such' in the name of mechanism.[48] Locke was no libertine, and he had a strong sense of agency and moral responsibility. Recognizing that the two notions were 'not very easy to be reconciled, or made consistent' he signaled to the reader that, rather than denying either mechanism or morality, he might attempt a difficult task: to *'put Morality and Mechanism together'*.[49] Putting them together would mean providing an account of personhood that did not

---

[48] Ibid., bk. I, ch. 3, § 14; ed. Nidditch, p. 76.   [49] Ibid. 77.

depend on the notion of incorporeal mental substance, and an account of agency that was psychological rather than metaphysical. The latter involved for Locke a Hobbesian reduction of human liberty to the power to do whatever it is you prefer to do.[50]

Locke was, like Hobbes, too worldly to consider the Epicureans' pained conscience and fear of the neighbors' retaliation sufficient to restrain men's egoism or capable of curing sheer moral blindness. He appeared to offer theological foundations for main norms in his references to God's commands and his approval of the basic tenets of Christian ethics. But the thrust of the *Essay* was that morality is to be understood in terms of men's ideas—ideas of God and the future state—and that, beyond a moral core given by the prescriptions of the New Testament, moral regulations are arbitrary. Though some forms of behavior are unconditionally prohibited—and Locke could not really come up with any good reason for his strong intuitions about which these were, except the will of God—his rejection of the *summum bonum* licensed men to strive for the realization of different worthwhile ends. So Locke supplied a minimal moral framework in which, the basic ethical postulates of Christianity assumed to be satisfied, the rest was left up to the individual, his tolerance for social sanctions and for potential loss of reputation. Where social pressure was insufficient, ideas of God and the life to come were efficacious. Though we have no experience of the rewards of heaven and the torments of hell, the thoughts of them are motivating. Civic harmony thus depends by implication on indoctrination into a culture of religious ideas.

Locke followed the Epicurean tradition in noticing the relativistic aspects of the language of virtue. '[W]hatever is pretended', he declared, the terms 'virtue' and 'vice' are employed differently 'through the several Nations and Societies of Men in the World', and are 'constantly attributed only to such actions, as in each Country and Society are in reputation or discredit'.[51] He referred to the 'secret and tacit consent' established in 'Societies, Tribes, and Clubs of Men in the World: whereby several actions come to find Credit or Disgrace amongst them, according to the Judgment, Maxims, or Fashions of that place'.[52] Numerous illustrations of this social fact were given in book I of the *Essay*, which began with a report, editorially tinged

---

[50] Locke, *Essay*, bk. II, ch. 21, § 15; ed. Nidditch, pp. 241–2.
[51] Ibid., ch. 28, § 10; ed. Nidditch, p. 353. [52] Ibid.

with disgust, of the behavior of the inhabitants of the New World, who allegedly practiced cannibalism and bestiality, kept concubines, and killed their own children. Locke was not endorsing a broad form of moral relativism in relaying these horror stories, but rather pointing to the variety of moral customs taken for granted at home and abroad, some of which were in his eyes morally unacceptable however routine they might be. The occurrence of such practices decisively refuted, in Locke's view, the claim that consciousness of morality was impressed into the human mind by God, that observance of natural law was universal in humankind, and that the human heart possessed an instinctive appetite for the good.

Locke's assertions and denials aroused consternation; their antecedents were quickly recognized.[53] Even his close friends thought that Locke had not made his distance from Hobbes sufficiently clear. The third Earl of Shaftesbury complained that the attack on innate ideas in the *Essay* 'struck at Fundamentals, threw all *Order* and *Virtue* out of the World',[54] and that Locke had 'fairly told us that virtue and vice, had, after all, no other law or measure than mere fashion or vogue'.[55] Newton had later to apologize to Locke for giving out that 'you struck at ye roots of morality in a principle you laid down in your book of Ideas'.[56] Locke's fiercest critic, John Edwards, attacked him for a range of vices, including social snobbery, antifeminism, irreligion, and sexual misconduct. In his sermon on *The Eternal and Intrinsick Reasons of Good and Evil* of 1699, Edwards called attention to Locke's claims in the first edition of the *Essay* that the terms 'virtue' and 'sin' have a significance that is very hard to understand, and that we judge of virtue and vice according to the 'consent of Private Men'—which words, he noted, were corrected in subsequent editions. Locke 'thrusts this Conceit upon the world, that Experimental Observation is the Standard of all Goodness and Morality'. His belief in '*the precarious and arbitrary nature of Morality*', said Edwards, and his references to the role of public esteem in maintaining moral conduct, 'may pass for *the Leviathan*

---

[53] See Samuel I. Mintz, *The Hunting of Leviathan* (Cambridge: Cambridge University Press, 1962), esp. ch. 5.

[54] Lord Shaftesbury, *Several Letters Written by a Noble Lord to a Young Man at University* (London: 1716), 39.

[55] Lord Shaftesbury, 'Sensus Communis', in *Characteristics of Men, Manners, Opinions, Times*, ed. Lawrence Klein (Cambridge: Cambridge University Press, 1999), 38.

[56] Isaac Newton, letter to Locke, in *Correspondence of Isaac Newton*, ed. H. W. Turnbull et al. (Cambridge: Cambridge University Press, 1959–77), ii. 280.

Epitomiz'd. The design and project of Hobbes, Locke, and their followers is, he declared, to undermine virtue, 'to put all out of order', to 'expose Religion itself, and to make sport for the Atheistical and Scoffing part of the World'.[57]

8.3 Morality and mechanism

Leibniz understood Locke's account of personal identity in book II of the *Essay* not implausibly as an attempt to construct a theory of identity for atomic thinking machines. On Locke's view, as Leibniz discerned, it is possible that we are material constructions with the divinely superadded power of thought, and our 'selfhood'—including our moral identity—is simply an idea the machine has, a way in which the machine represents itself. On Locke's theory, the idea of the self—for we cannot know 'the self', as Descartes thought we could, by introspecting a substance—is composed of a bundle of memories, including memories of agency and memories of experience, that exhibit continuity and narrative linkages. The thought that I am so-and-so, a unique person, and, what's more, the selfsame person as the person who performed certain acts and had certain experiences, can occur even if the 'I' referred to and the 'me' in whom the thought occurs are not substances, or indeed anything over and above a corporeal machine. For divine reward and punishment to occur, all that is required is the existence of that same self in the afterlife, not the persistence of anything substantial. Surely it is within God's power to reconstitute the bundle of memories that is me, and to attach it to an organic body that I can experience as 'mine' at some distant future date.

'If a man could be a mere machine and still possess consciousness', Théophile concedes to Philalèthe, 'I would have to agree with you [that psychological identity is sufficient for moral identity]'. But this state of affairs, Leibniz insisted, is just not possible, 'at least not naturally'. Rather, '[a]n identity which is apparent to the person concerned ... presupposes a real identity'.[58] I can lose my psychological sense of who I am, though I remain the same person. I can suffer various illusions or delusions about my

---

[57] John Edwards, *The Eternal and Intrinsick Reasons of Good and Evil* (Cambridge: 1699), 28.
[58] Leibniz, *New Essays*, vi. vi. 236; trans. Remnant and Bennett.

identity. But I cannot, Leibniz insisted, be nothing more than a collection of material corpuscles organized for thought.

The hypothesis of material thinking machines was disturbing in many ways. Even if Locke had shown that it did not preclude the possibility of bodily resurrection and subsequent rewards and punishments, the logical mind of Leibniz was not satisfied by what looked like the creation of an identical psychological counterpart in a similar body to experience punishment and reward. Worse, Locke could be understood as raising the possibility that we are atomic thinking machines that generate, in addition to delusory ideas of ourselves as immaterial substances, delusory ideas of God and a life beyond the grave. In that case, the whole notion of a 'moral identity'—of being the person who deserved punishment or reward for performing certain actions—was nugatory. No machine could really be the subject of desert, though it might represent itself in a delusory way as such. Accordingly, to the extent that we regard the atomic thinking machine hypothesis as even *possibly true*, Leibniz thought, we have to regard it as possibly true as well that morality and justice can only be upheld by the threat of temporal punishment, and that, once this is grasped, human beings will, following the worst examples, recklessly pursue pleasure wherever they think they can escape retribution. He quoted Locke's remark that 'If there be no prospect beyond the grave, the inference is certainly right, *Let us eat and drink*, let us enjoy what we delight in, *for to morrow we shall* die',[59] implying that Locke considered the inference to be possibly warranted.

'[O]nly a regard for God and immortality makes the obligations of virtue and justice absolutely binding', Théophile declares,[60] and this means that there must really be a God and that the soul must really be incorporeal and immortal. The mere idea of God and the mere idea of immortality is inadequate to ground moral obligation. Indeed, Locke's treatment could only arouse the most profound skepticism, insofar as postmortem retribution presupposed the persistence of psychologically integrated units. Since experience indicates that the transition from babyhood to adult life, and from adult life to senility, involves no such thing, to believe in immortality and just compensation is to believe that God can preserve or reconstitute psychologically integrated units, despite their nonexistence in

---

[59] Locke, *Essay*, bk. II, ch. 21, § 55; ed. Nidditch, p. 270.
[60] Leibniz, *New Essays*, vi. vi. 201; trans. Remnant and Bennett.

nature. Locke's psychological account, then, insofar as it specified precisely what was required by way of continuity of memory, set the bar rather high for rational belief in immortality and divine justice. We are thrown back on faith, which, he maintained in his lengthy discussion of belief and opinion, is never as certain as what we can reason out for ourselves.[61]

The word 'arbitrary', whenever it was used to characterize a relation in the natural world or in the social world, was a red flag for Leibniz. 'I don't know why you and your associates always want to make virtues, truths and species depend upon our opinion or knowledge', Théophile complains to Philalèthe. 'They are present in nature, whether or not we know it or like it.'[62] Leibniz's mistrust was evident in his critique of Locke's teaching on secondary qualities. When Philalèthe states that particular *qualia*, such as the color yellow or the scent of violets, have no discernible relationships to the conditions of the external world that give rise to them, Théophile pegs him as one of those Cartesians who 'regard it as arbitrary what perceptions we have of these qualities, as if God had given them to the soul according to his good pleasure, without concern for any essential relation between perceptions and their objects' and promptly contradicts him: 'This is a view which surprises me and appears unworthy of the wisdom of the author of things, who does nothing without harmony and reason'.[63] He repeats his point later: 'It must not be thought that ideas such as those of colour and pain are arbitrary and that between them and their causes there is no relation or natural connection: it is not God's way to act in such an unruly and unreasoned fashion. I would say, rather, that there is a resemblance of a kind'.[64] When Philalèthe muses that God might, at his discretion, have given organized matter the power to think, Théophile declares that 'within the order of nature (miracles apart) it is not at God's arbitrary discretion to attach this or that quality haphazardly to substances. He will never give them any which are not natural to them, that is, which cannot arise from their nature as explicable modifications'.[65] And when Philalèthe advances

---

[61] Locke, *Essay*, bk. IV, ch. 18, § 4; ed. Nidditch, pp. 690–1.
[62] Leibniz, *New Essays*, vi. vi. 327; trans. Remnant and Bennett.
[63] Ibid. vi. vi. 56.   [64] Ibid. vi. vi. 131.
[65] Ibid. vi. vi. 66. Cf. p. 379. Leibniz remarked in a dialogue of 1712–15: 'A follower of Epicurus would say that … if we knew the corpuscles that form thought and the motions necessary for this, we would see that thoughts are measurable and are the workings of some very subtle machines—just as the nature of colour does not seem to consist internally of something measurable. And yet, if it is true that the reason for these qualities of objects comes from certain configurations and certain motions, as,

the view that ideas of right and wrong depend on social learning, Théophile sets him straight: '[T]here are *fundamental Maxims* which constitute the very law itself; they make up the actions, defences, replications etc. which, when they are taught by pure reason and do not come from the arbitrary power of the state, constitute natural law'.[66]

In a set of related comments on Samuel Pufendorf, Leibniz amplified his view that divine justice, not human agreement, was the foundation of the law. The state of nature posited by Hobbes and Pufendorf might be 'imagined by somebody for a didactic purpose', but it was an error, insofar as 'everybody is naturally subordinated to God'. Leibniz professed himself scandalized by Pufendorf's claim that 'The end of the science of natural law is backed by the limit of this life alone'.[67]

Leibniz held views that were in some respects close to Locke's. He agreed that the human being was in some respects a corporeal machine, though he denied that there were any machines of nature that were not ensouled. He was committed to the position that perception could be explained mechanically;[68] this too was required by his principle that everything that happened could be explained simultaneously in terms of final and efficient causes. He had no compelling account of free will, and he denied liberty of indifference. Leibniz further agreed with Locke that our actions are often determined by unease or *inquiétude*, and he pressed the point further in insisting that we are very delicate machines, easily set aflutter, and in showing how we are often unaware of many of the little shocks and impacts on the machine that determine our actions. But consciousness, Leibniz maintained, cannot be a power enjoyed by a purely material structure. If no experience can be causally generated in and through matter, experiences must preexist in an immaterial soul and flow spontaneously from it.

Philalèthe, speaking for Locke, tries to convince Théophile that morality can be firmly grounded without recourse to the unobservables of

---

for example, the whiteness of foam comes from little hollow bubbles that are polished like so many small mirrors, then these qualities would, in the end, reduce to something measurable, material, and mechanical' ('Conversation of Philarète and Ariste', in *Philosophische Schriften*, ed. Gerhardt, vi. 587; *Philosophical Essays*, trans. and ed. Ariew and Garber, p. 263). Leibniz insists that he is not thereby committed to the materiality of the soul; indeed, he can 'perfect' proofs for the distinction between soul and body.

[66] Leibniz, *New Essays*, vi. vi. 425; trans. Remnant and Bennett.
[67] Leibniz, 'The Principles of Pufendorf', § 2; *Political Writings*, trans. Riley, p. 66.
[68] Leibniz, *New Essays*, vi. vi. 131; trans. Remnant and Bennett.

metaphysics. 'Although ... the foundations of morality may not extend so far if they do not have a natural theology like yours at their base, still, merely by considering the goods of this life, we can establish inferences which are important for the ordering of human societies.'[69] Though this piece of invented critique goes unanswered by Théophile, Leibniz meant to insist on a firm, extensive, and deep metaphysical substructure. As he saw it, the philosopher was faced with a problem of theory choice between two packages of natural and moral philosophy.

Locke's package encompassed the following train of thought. We cannot really know anything about fundamentals, but the corpuscularian account of the nature of reality is most likely the true one. It is evident that we think, feel, experience, and perform voluntary actions, but we cannot infer from these data that we have immaterial souls or immortal personalities. The hidden truth about matter and about ourselves has no bearing on the question of our duties, and it is a waste of time to pursue it; our minds and our senses are not really suited to such inquiries. A better grasp of ontological issues is not the key to the improvement of men's morals. Once we have reasoned out the existence of a supreme being, however, and once we have granted, on the basis of our faith, that this being has absolute power over us and certain expectations of us, we can ground the basic duties of morality as they are found in Scripture. Reflection will reveal other connections, such as the conceptual connection between property and justice. All this is accessible to the mediocre human intellect. For the rest, we must conform to the expectations of our society to avoid censure, though we are otherwise free to choose courses of conduct that seem to us best. To uphold morality, we need good classical and biblical educations. We should read Aristotle, Cicero, Pufendorf, 'and above all the New Testament'.[70]

Leibniz's preferred package encompassed the following train of thought. A philosopher who acknowledges the material corpuscle as the basic unit of nature must end by denying the natural and certain immortality of the person and the existence of the purely spiritual substance, God. He will be led, as Hobbes was, first to the doctrine that all is body, then to the view that names are arbitrary, and truth is man-made, then to a

[69] Leibniz, *New Essays*, vi. vi. 383–4.
[70] John Locke, letter to Carey Mordaunt, September/October 1697 (no. 2320), in *Selected Correspondence*, ed. Mark Goldie (Oxford: Oxford University Press, 2002), 253.

conception of good and evil, justice and injustice, as conventional, or as analyzable in terms of pleasure and power, then to mortalism and atheism. Even if he does not become personally depraved as a result of holding these philosophical views, he ought to consider their influence on weak minds and on powerful men before publishing them abroad. A society of materialists will be corrupt and dangerous. Fortunately, however, the notion of a purely material corpuscle is incoherent, so it is impossible that we are merely material thinking machines, with all that this implies for morals and politics. It can be shown that the fundamental units of nature must be spiritual substances, and by pulling up the root of Hobbist physics, we starve its ethical and political branches. On Leibniz's view, Locke was blind to the existence of the realm of truths, factual and moral, independent of ideas caused by the percussive effects of corporeal objects, for he never really grasped the power of mathematical reasoning, and the ability of our minds to grasp such truths.[71]

The *New Essays*, then, had as its target a materialism that Leibniz believed was taking hold with sinister effects, and that he perceived, along with a number of his contemporaries, as the platform of Locke's *Essay*. Leibniz presented himself as a naturalist and a defender of natural immortality. He had a clear notion of what it was and was not in the nature of substances to do and experience, but his conception of nature was not the autonomous and material nature of his opponents. His beliefs and desires explain the undue attention given to the theme of thinking matter in the *New Essays*, the surprising vehemence of Leibniz's attack on dangerous men, his challenges to every form of Democritean or Hobbesian conventionalism that he detected in Locke's work, including conventionalism about the boundaries of species and conventionalism about qualities, his sensitivity to any reference to the word 'arbitrary'. They explain the care Leibniz took to remind the reader of his monadic ontology and his system of preestablished harmony, despite the fact that he was commenting, not on a book about the fundamental units of nature, about which Locke claimed to have nothing certain to say, but on a book about 'Ideas'.

---

[71] As the Platonist Benjamin Whichcote maintained, the mathematicians 'do only Contemplate and Speculate upon the Idea's and Forms of Things: Thus they propose to take Men off from Matter, and to subtilize Men's parts, and to raise them to more Noble and generous Apprehensions' (*Several Discourses*, ed. John Jeffery (London: 1701–4), ii. 400).

The seventeenth-century theory of ideas was, as observed, one of the fronts upon which Epicureanism advanced.[72] In Descartes's hands the theory of ideas not only enabled him to carve out a philosophical theology of divine goodness and power that was independent of revelation. It cleared away all confusion about matter, so that his accounts of corporeal nature could be simply and appropriately grounded. His system allowed for a realm of 'true and immutable natures' and innate ideas, as well as a realm of fleeting and constantly metamorphosing corpuscular composites that caused sensory experiences. Hobbes used ideas more ruthlessly. Thoughts, according to Hobbes, are all appearances. They are caused directly, in the case of perception, by external objects pressing on material sense organs, and indirectly, in the case of imagination, by residual or 'decaying' motions in the brain and heart. Reasoning does not require an incorporeal soul, as it is simply an organized form of imagination, while dreaming and other forms of reverie are less coherent forms of imagination.[73] Hobbes knew that human minds were stocked with apparitions—ideas corresponding to nothing outside themselves, including ideas of spiritual, divine, and demonic entities, as well as ideas of color, odor, and taste, when all that existed either inside or outside the material human body was more matter. 'Whatsoever accidents or qualities our senses make us think there be in the world, they are not there, but are seemings and apparitions only. The things that really are in the world without us are those motions [in matter] by which these seemings are caused.'[74]

Leibniz, as usual, tried to reconcile everything he had learned with everything else. He accepted the percussively generated ideas of the materialists. They appeared in the mind in sequence, according to the rules of mechanics, but the corpuscularian theory of perception, like the rest of physics and physiology, might be considered as only a theoretical apparatus for predicting and explaining the appearances, not as a fundamental account.

---

[72] See, on the significance of the contrast between Cartesian intellectual ideas and Gassendist corporeal ideas, and the 'reflective' conception of the soul associated with the latter, Emily Michael and Fred S. Michael, 'Corporeal Ideas in Seventeenth-century Psychology', *Journal of the History of Ideas*, 50 (1989), 31–48 and 'Two Early Modern Concepts of Mind', *Journal of the History of Philosophy*, 27 (1989), 29–47.

[73] Thomas Hobbes, *Human Nature*, in *Human Nature* and *De corpore politico*, ed. J. C. A. Gaskin (Oxford: Oxford University Press, 1999), pt. I, chs. 1–5.

[74] Thomas Hobbes, *Human Nature*, pt. I, ch. 2. § 10; ed. Gaskin, p. 26.

All ideas flowed spontaneously from the depths of the unextended, active monadic soul selected by God for its contribution to the perfection of the world. Leibniz saw himself as the philosopher who had disproved the very possibility of the material atom without sacrificing theoretical rigor in physics. Speaking of himself in the third person, he says that

[I]n letters exchanged with Hartsoeker, inserted in the *Mémoires de Trévoux*, you can also find how he destroyed the void and atoms through higher considerations, even making use of part of his *Dynamics* for this; others who occupy themselves instead with matter alone cannot settle the question. That is why the new philosophers, who are ordinarily too materialistic and not trained to combine metaphysics with mathematics, have not been in a position to decide whether or not there are atoms and void; and several have even been led to believe in them, that is, to believe that there is either a void with atoms, or at least, that there are atoms swimming in a fluid that excludes the void. But he shows that void, atoms, that is, perfect hardness, and finally, perfect fluidity, are equally opposed to fitness and order.[75]

By understanding the true nature of the indivisible unities that compose the natural world, 'one is transported into another world, so to speak; from having existed entirely amongst the phenomena of the senses, one comes to occupy the intelligible world of substances'.[76] From the demolition of the Epicurean atom, Leibniz derived the existence of a commonwealth of spirits, a divine legislator, and absolute standards of justice.

---

[75] Leibniz, *Conversation of Philarète and Ariste*, in *Philosophische Schriften*, ed. Gerhardt, vi. 588; *Philosophical Essays*, trans. and ed. Ariew and Garber, p. 264.
[76] Ibid., *New Essays*, vi. vi. 378; trans. Remnant and Bennett.

9

Robert Boyle and the Study of Nature

> where
> Can colours in the darke exist, which are
> So oft varied in the light,
> When the beames fall on things, oblique or right
> As the bright plumes, with which are deckt
> The doves faire neck, when the sun shines reflect
> The rubies glorious red, the emeraldes greene
> With which the mixtures of pale blews are seene,
> And as, in Peacocks traines, with much light filld
> All sorts of glorious colours are beheld.
>
> (*De rerum natura*, ii. 803–11)

Robert Boyle's insightfulness as a metaphysician and epistemologist is increasingly recognized. Many philosophical notions usually ascribed to Locke—the doctrine of primary and secondary qualities, nominal and real essences, concepts made by the mind, the bounds of knowledge, and the psychological basis of personal identity—were derived from Locke's reading of, and sometimes his reaction to, Boyle. As the principal apologist for the new experimental philosophy in England, Boyle repeatedly voiced his commitment to what he called the 'Corpuscularian or Mechanical' philosophy in language emulating Gassendi's, though his source was Charleton's *Physiologia Epicuro-Gassendo-Charletoniana*, which had appeared in 1654.[1]

I plead...for such a Philosophy, as reaches but to things purely Corporeal, and distinguishing between the first *original of things*; and the subsequent *course of Nature*,

---

[1] R. H. Kargon, 'Walter Charleton, Robert Boyle and the Acceptance of Epicurean Atomism in England', *Isis*, 55 (1964), 184–92.

teaches...not onely that God gave Motion to Matter, but that in the beginning He so guided the various Motions of the parts of it, as to contrive them into the World...(furnish'd with the *Seminal* Principles and Structures or Models of Living Creatures,) and establish'd those *Rules of Motion*, and that order amongst things Corporeal, which we are wont to call the *Laws of Nature*...[T]he Phaenomena of the World thus constituted, are Physically produc'd by the Mechanical affections of the parts of Matter, and...operate upon one another according to Mechanical Laws.[2]

His moral and philosophical writings were concerned to a large extent with Epicureanism—the natural and moral philosophy—and with Epicurism—the pursuit of sensory pleasure. References to the philosophy and to the mode of life associated with it appear in virtually every one of Boyle's essays, and they worried him for several reasons. First, he was troubled by his adoption of an ontology associated with atheism and libertinism.[3] Second, he was troubled by the natural philosopher's evaluation of the material objects of this world as worthy of sustained attention and effort, and by the utilitarian, this-world focus of the experimental philosophy. Third, he was bothered by the discrepancy between the standards of evidence employed in the theological realm and those employed in the experimental realm.

9.1 The Christian Virtuoso

To reconcile his scruples with his attractions to both Epicureanism and Epicurism, Boyle invented and commended to his readers the figure of the Christian Virtuoso, and he endowed the Boyle Lectures to confute atheists and libertines. The creation of this model figure, and the subsequent defense of the corpuscularian or mechanical philosophy as intellectually more supportive of the Christian religion than scholastic philosophy, helped to secure legitimacy for the somewhat insecure enterprises of the early Royal Society. The recovery and interpretation of some of Boyle's many lost and suppressed manuscripts confirms the suggestion that the

---

[2] Robert Boyle, *Excellency and Grounds*, in *Works*, ed. Michael Hunter and Edward B. Davis (London: Pickering and Chatto, 2000), viii. 104.

[3] See J. J. MacIntosh, 'Robert Boyle on Epicurean Atheism and Atomism', in Margaret J. Osler (ed.), *Atoms, Pneuma, and Tranquillity: Epicurean and Stoic Themes in European Thought* (Cambridge: Cambridge University Press, 1991).

Christian Virtuoso is an imaginary figure Boyle created to fulfill his own psychological needs and that he was able to enlist others in the task of creating an appropriate image of the natural philosopher.[4]

Boyle repeated the old refrain of Bacon and Gassendi. Atomism and mechanism implied the existence and activity of a God. '[A] Machine so Immense, so Beautiful, so well-contrived, and, in a word, so Admirable as the World cannot have been the effect of mere Chance, or Tumultuous Justlings and Fortuitous Concourse of Atoms, but must have been produced by a Cause exceedingly Powerful, Wise, and Beneficent.'[5] He termed his theory of nature 'Anaxagorean' to distinguish it from Epicureanism, and also to distinguish it from Cartesian mechanism, which, though it introduced God as the cause and maintainer of corpuscular motions, posited that the cosmos and plant and animal life had emerged spontaneously.[6] According to the Anaxagorean, the frame of the world, and its original plants and animals, or at least their 'seeds or seminall principles', had been intelligently and beneficently designed and created, though thereafter the laws of motion, the structure of objects, and the dispositions of seeds sufficed for the production of all, or almost all, effects.[7] Still, the creator was present to and watchful over his creation and occasionally intervened in it or 'intermeddled' with it.[8]

The Anaxagorean system, one might think, reconciled religion and natural philosophy easily, provided one accepted the notion that the laws of nature could in some sense be prescribed to and obeyed by inanimate particles. Yet Boyle was not intellectually or emotionally secure in his adoption of the basic framework of a pagan and aggressively anti-theistic system. He believed himself to be living in an exceptionally dissolute age, and he considered the neo-Epicurean threat to religion and morals more

---

[4] Michael Hunter maintains that Oldenburg, Glanvill, Burnett, and Birch contrived an image of Boyle as 'a paragon of civility and moderation with a clear and unproblematic strategy for the vindication of a mechanistic view of nature by profuse experimentation, and an accompanying combination of deep piety'. Boyle was, Hunter suggests, more 'mixed-up' than his Christian Virtuoso (Michael Hunter, *Robert Boyle: Scrupulosity and Science* (Woodbridge: Boydell, 2000), 8).

[5] Boyle, *Christian Virtuoso*, in *Works*, ed. Hunter and Davis, xi. 299–300.

[6] The term 'Anaxagorean' appears in the suppressed or discarded sections of the *Free Inquiry*, in *Works*, ed. Hunter and Davis, xiv. 148.

[7] On Boyle's theory of generation see Peter Anstey, 'Boyle on Seminal Principles', *Studies in History and Philosophy of Biological and Biomedical Sciences*, 33 (2002), 597–630; Hiro Hirai, 'Le Concept du semence de Pierre Gassendi', *Medicina nei secoli arte e scienza*, 15 (2003), 205–26.

[8] God 'hath not Abandoned a Masterpiece so worthy of him, but does still Maintain and Preserve it' (Boyle, *Christian Virtuoso*, in *Works*, ed. Hunter and Davis, xi. 300).

serious and less easily defended against than other atheist and mortalist versions of Aristotelianism and pagan naturalism, such as those represented by Pomponazzi and Vanini. 'Libertines', he said, 'own themselves to be so upon the account of the *Epicurean* or other *Mechanical Principles of Philosophy*,'[9] and they fail to pay due regard to Aristotle, Duns Scotus, Aquinas, and Augustine. Yet one cannot say that Boyle paid due regard to Aristotle or to his scholastic followers. He complained of being taken for an Epicurean himself,[10] and no wonder, as there are over one hundred references to Epicurus and Lucretius and quotations from *On the Nature of Things* in his writings. If Boyle was sincere in maintaining that he had read little of Lucretius and lacked conversancy with Epicureanism in 1661,[11] he made up for his neglect later.

Two points relentlessly driven home by Lucretius were that the gods do not concern themselves with affairs on our earth and that fear of them is an oppressive and needless burden. They are happy immortals existing in the spaces between *cosmoi* where they do not interfere with the goings on in any actual world, and if they cannot help us they cannot harm us either. This view was at odds with the Christian conviction that divine and demonic intervention are manifested in political and meteorological turns of events and in personal life. According to Boyle's third-person account of his youthful self, he had been roused as a boy from religious indifference by a terrifying thunderstorm.[12] Thereafter, he perceived the saving intervention of God in several astonishing escapes, in one case when he was nearly killed by falling from a horse, in another case when collapsing bedroom walls nearly ended his life, and in a third when a careless apothecary administered a dangerous drug. '*Philaretus*', Boyle recalled in his memoir, 'would not ascribe any of these rescues unto chance, but would be still industrious to perceive the hand of heaven in all these accidents; and he indeed would profess, that in the passages of his life, he had observed so gracious and so peculiar a conduct of providence, that he

---

[9] Boyle, *About the Reconcileableness of Reason and Religion*, in *Works*, ed. Hunter and Davis, viii. 237.

[10] Boyle, *The Sceptical Chymist*, in *Works*, ed. Hunter and Davis, ii. 354.

[11] 'If you knew how little Conversant I have been with Epicurean authors', says the Boylean chemist to his interlocutor, 'and how great a part of Lucretius himself I have not yet had the curiosity to read', [you would be free of suspicion] (Boyle, *The Sceptical Chymist*, in *Works*, ed. Hunter and Davis, ii. 354).

[12] Boyle, 'An Account of Philaretus in his Minority', in *Works* (London: Millar, 1744), i. 12.

should be equally blind and ungrateful, should he not both discern and acknowledge it.'[13]

All his life, however, Boyle was troubled by religious doubts. He read many pagan authors, including Seneca, whom he admired.[14] And when the young Boyle visited a Carthusian monastery in the wild, snow-covered mountains near Grenoble he was nearly driven to suicide by worries over Christian dogma, as he brooded on the reclusive founder of the order, St Bruno.[15] After months of 'tedious perplexity', God restored 'the withdrawn sense of his favour', and Boyle came to see 'these impious suggestions, rather as temptations to be suppressed, than doubts to be resolved; yet never after did these fleeting clouds cease now and then to darken the clearest serenity of his quiet'. They were, he says, like a toothache—very troublesome, though not fatal. But they were chronic, 'a disease to his faith'.[16] Hunter has provided transcripts of Boyle's end-of-life confessions to Gilbert Burnet, Bishop of Salisbury, in which Boyle referred to the 'Impious or Blasphemous Suggestions or Injections' that pursued him, which Burnet reassured him were 'mere Effects of Distempers of the Body or the Brain... Mechanical Effects'.[17] To be sure, religious doubt can be construed as a test of faith for a convinced Christian, or as a temporary derangement. But doubt can also reflect a veridical glimpse of things as they are, and a flash of understanding that the religious imaginary is a source of needless anxiety and apprehension. Biblicism, piety, and morality are equally traits consistent with certain forms of doubt or outright unbelief.[18] Newton, it is reported, for all his own religious deviance, could not bear to hear anyone—including Halley and Bentley—speak lightly of religion. Boyle's condition would not have been the condition of someone who simply wonders whether everything he was taught is really true. Another complete account of the world, that he accepted as sane in many of its

---

[13] Boyle, 'An Account of Philaretus in his Minority', in *Works* (1744), i. 8.

[14] Seneca, the most Epicurean of all the Stoics, insisted in his *Questiones Naturales* that thunderstorms have no theological significance and are naturally caused.

[15] '[T]he devil taking advantage of that deep raving melancholy, so sad a place, his humour and the strange stories and pictures he found there of Bruno, the father of that order, suggested such strange and hideous thoughts, and such distracting doubts of some of the fundamentals of Christianity, that, though his looks did little betray his thoughts, nothing but the forbiddenness of self-dispatch hindered his acting it' (Boyle, 'An Account of Philaretus in his Minority', in *Works*, (1744), i. 12).

[16] Ibid.   [17] Hunter, *Robert Boyle: Scrupulosity and Science*, p. 90.

[18] Steven Snobelen, 'Isaac Newton, Heretic: The Strategies of a Nicodemite', *British Journal for the History of Science*, 32 (1991), 411.

fundamentals, was available to him in the Lucretian text. In any case, when a clerical career was proposed to him at the age of thirty-three, Boyle realized that he was not called by the Holy Ghost.[19]

In his tract on the Christian Virtuoso, Boyle explained that an experimental philosopher is not 'a libertine, though ingenious, a sensualist, though curious', nor a mere empiric or a 'vulgar chemist'. His engagement with the material world leads his mind to higher things: '[T]he study of the creatures may justly produce in a *virtuoso*, 1st, a profound *admiration* of the majesty, and some of the attributes of God. Secondly, An external *celebration* of him, for them, by hymns and praises. Thirdly, a deep *humility* in the view of his immense greatness and majesty, and the distance of our nature, as we are human creatures, from his'. Gratitude towards and trust in God follow.[20] Boyle was concerned, in this connection, to distinguish the physico-theology of the Christian from that of the pagan nature-worshipper.

Three years before his execution, in 1616, the unfortunate Vanini had published a dialogue, *De admirandis naturae reginae deaeque mortalium arcanis*. This worship of divine or semidivine 'Natura', the 'filia Dei, semper … actuosa', as Comenius called her,[21] was easily amalgamated with the Venusian paratheology of Lucretius. Without suggesting that Venus manipulates the atoms, Lucretius had nevertheless presented the goddess as the embodiment of the whole of nature, as representing the capacity for vitality and renewal that the atomic system intrinsically contained. Boyle's purpose in writing his *Free Inquiry into the Received Notion of Nature* (1686) and his *Tractatus de ipsa natura* (1687) was to extract nature from the Venusian frame of reference and to place it firmly within the Christian theo-mechanical system.[22] As Descartes had reanalyzed the behavior of

---

[19] Boyle, 'An Account of Philaretus in his Minority', in *Works* (1744), i. 37.

[20] Boyle, *Christian Virtuoso*, in *Works*, ed. Hunter and Davis, xii. 481.

[21] Amos Comenius, *Pansophia*, in *Opera didactica* (Amsterdam: 1657), i. 449. Under the heading 'What is Nature?' Comenius lists fourteen axioms on nature's ways of acting. The *locus classicus* for nature worship was probably Galen. In his treatise on the human body, *De usu partium*, Galen had combined detailed descriptions of the functions and uses of its parts with praise for the skill, wisdom, economy, and foresight of the designing intelligence behind them. He sometimes directed his worshipful attitude to 'the Creator', but more usually to 'Nature', whom he apotheosized as a clever and habile *artifex*.

[22] John Evelyn, who had erected what was virtually a temple to Venus on his estate, noted in the introduction to his translation of book I of *On the Nature of Things* (London: Collins, 1656): 'The poet invocates *Venus*, by whom, as a Philosopher, he understands the Goddess *Nature* or rather nature it self'.

animals in mechanical terms, Boyle would show how the tendencies and appetites that seemed to reside in corporeal things could be reduced to mechanical interaction, and the phenomena addressed without reference to nature's powers of generation, nurturing, and healing.

However, Boyle still needed to provide reasons for accepting the Christian message of the Fall of Man, the redemption of the world through Christ's martyrdom, and the existence of heaven and hell, insofar as the Anaxagorean conception of mechanism had nothing to say about such matters. Boyle could not endorse a deistic religion that did not posit an afterlife, or that did not allow for what he called the 'intermeddlings' of the deity with the corporeal world. His ontology and theory of science had to be carefully constructed to accommodate these possibilities, and his epistemology enlarged beyond the plain experimental method. There were really three worlds, he decided. Besides the corporeal world, and the present state of things, consisting of 'objects proportioned to our unassisted sight', there was a 'dioptrical world... which consists of all those creatures, that lay concealed, in former ages, from mortal eyes, and are not now discovered, without dioptrical glasses', and also a spiritual world of 'good angels, and other intelligent beings, as devils, and separate human minds, that have either no bodies, or none that we can see'.[23] How this world was to be accessed, and how far it could be accessed, without flying in the face of sense and reason—for Boyle disdained fideism—was a problem he addressed in many of his essays.

9.2 Pleasure and the material world

Many English aristocrats faced a crisis of occupation after the Restoration. They had returned from abroad to their estates, and without military affairs to occupy them they filled their hours with intrigue, sport, gaming, and dissipation. As Mayo remarks, with Buckingham and Rochester in mind, among them were 'men of restless and itching minds, endowed... tragically... with intellectual powers for which the frivolous viciousness of their lives offered little outlet'.[24] Thomas Birch

[23] Boyle, *Christian Virtuoso*, in *Works*, ed. Hunter and Davis, xii. 502.
[24] Mayo, *Epicurus in England 1650–1725* (Dallas, Tex.: Southwest Press, 1934), 130.

explained Boyle's choice of a career in natural philosophy as motivated by a powerful wish to divert the upper classes from their customary pursuits.

He set himself to phylosophise, and to persuade the nobility and gentry of the nation, who had the means and leisure to pursue such sorts of studies, to follow his example. He was convinced, that it would be of inestimable use to mankind to engage them in these enquiries; it would divert them from those impertinent and criminal amusements, with which most of them busied themselves, and would make them not only better Christians, but likewise more useful members of society.[25]

Other studies emphasize the physico-theological over the moral and socially altruistic motive.[26] But the motives and incentives that led Boyle to adopt the experimental life were far more personal and circumstantial than his rationales. Boyle too needed something to do, and the experimental life was a source of pleasure for him, relatively free of the guilt and distaste that attached to other sources of pleasure. Relatively free; for Boyle, always a moralist, experienced periods of self-doubt and ambivalence in which he was inclined to trivialize what he most loved.

Boyle's early writings reveal a rich and romantic imagination, an aesthetic sensibility; he was once a sort of Epicurist, though often a self-censoring and censorious one.[27] His memoir of his childhood is a surprisingly unguarded account of his experiences of being indulged by his elders, and of the gustatory pleasures and temptations he enjoyed and endured. One of his first memories was of eating half a score of plums. Little Boyle was given toys, fruits, and candies, instructed in an 'affable, kind and gentle way', and cajoled into love of study by Mr Harrison, who 'would often as it were cloy him with fruit and sweetmeats, and those little dainties, that age is greedy of... He would

---

[25] Birch, 'Life of the Honourable Robert Boyle', in Boyle, *Works* (1744), i. 33.

[26] Reijer Hooykaas, *Robert Boyle: A Study in Science and Christian Belief* (Lanham, Md.: University Press of America, 1997).

[27] See Malcolm Oster, 'Biography, Culture, and Science: The Formative Years of Robert Boyle', *History of Science*, 31 (1993), 177–226; also John T. Harwood's introduction to *The Early Essays and Ethics of Robert Boyle* (Carbondale, Ill.: Southern Illinois University Press, 1991) and Lawrence Principe, 'Style and Thought of the Early Boyle: The Discovery of the 1648 Manuscript of Seraphic Love', *Isis*, 85 (1994), 247–60. An entire issue of the *British Journal for the History of Science*, 32 (1999), is devoted to the topic of Boyle and psychoanalysis.

sometimes give him unasked play-days and oft bestow on him such balls, and tops, and other implements of idleness'.[28] But Boyle always understood the importance of moderation and self-control. He tells a number of stories in which, when Philaretus, the young lover of virtue, is faced with some delicious but wrong prospect, his inner self-restraint triumphs.

> During his stay at Stalbridge all [one] summer, his father, to oblige him to be temperate, by freely giving him the opportunity to be otherwise, trusted him with the keys of all his gardens and orchards. And indeed Philaretus was very little given to greediness, either in fruits or sweetmeats; in the latter he was almost abstemious, and in the former, he was very moderate: so valuing such niceties and dainties, that although he enjoyed them with delight, he could want them without the least regret.[29]

His ascetic tendencies again came to the fore when the sweetmeats of adolescence dangled before him. '[T]hough his boiling youth did often very earnestly solicit to be employed in those culpable delights, that are usual in, and seem so proper for that season; and have repentance adjourned till old age; yet did its importunities ever meet with denials.'[30] He visited brothels—and brothel imagery reappears in his later writings—but remained aloof.

As he approached maturity, Boyle began to write clever, misanthropic satires on foppishness, gaming, flirtation, and the vain and foolish boasting of the members of his social class.[31] His *Occasional Reflections* are concerned with pleasure and its regulation, and the theme of the sugary again appears in an entry on 'Sweetmeats offer'd him after a Banquet'. As a surfeit of sweets nearly turns his stomach, he decides to 'use them, that they shall be ever Noveltys to me; & so, tho' Sensualists enjoy more Pleasure (then I) yet Ile enjoy the Greater, & make amends for their Discontinuance with the Freshnes of my Delihts'.[32] His tracts against face-painting and

---

[28] Boyle, 'An Account of Philaretus in his Minority', in *Works* (1744), i. 8.   [29] Ibid. i. 10.

[30] Ibid. i. 12.

[31] For example, 'A Mere fine Gentleman', in *Works*, ed. Hunter and Davis, xiii. 139–40. 'Scaping into his Study out of a Crowd of extraordinarily vaine Company of both Sexes', at xiii. 141–5. 'As a young man', John Clay remarks, 'Boyle started avoiding things.' He became more 'choosy, fastidious, and pernickety' ('Robert Boyle: A Jungian Perspective', *British Journal for the History of Science*, 32 (1999), 288). See also Michael Hunter (ed.), *Robert Boyle by Himself and by his Friends* (London: Pickering & Chatto, 1994), 88.

[32] Boyle, *Occasional Reflections*, in *Works*, ed. Hunter and Davis, v. 116.

décolletage suggest that exaggerated femininity was extremely aversive,[33] but the homosexual aggression that he had experienced in an episode from his childhood was also recollected with a shudder. The common element in these pleadings is heightened sensitivity. Too much visual and emotional stimulation was experienced as deeply unpleasant, and Boyle even empathically ascribed a delicacy and acuity of the senses to dogs and apes.[34]

Boyle was scholarly. His meditation on 'Scaping into his Study out of a Crowd of extraordinarily vaine Company of both Sexes' to the works of Heraclitus, Democritus, Plato, Hermes, Zeno, and other ancient writers hinted at a literary career, and indeed Boyle's career turned out to be largely literary. But he needed a *via tertia* between the 'world'—tiresome visits and parties, love affairs, debauchery, idleness, hunting, gambling, swearing, and politics, all of which he despised or which bored him—and theology. Ethical inquiry and the investigation of nature provided it. 'The other humane studies I apply myself to', he reported of his time on his father's Stalbridge estate in 1646–7, 'are natural philosophy, the mechanics, and husbandry, according to the principles of our new philosophical college, that values no knowledge, but as it hath a tendency to use.'[35] At the age of twenty-two he set up a laboratory, and reported to his sister that he was now happy. '*Vulcan* has so transported and bewitched me, that...the delights I taste in it, make me fancy my laboratory a kind of Elysium.'[36]

Boyle made contact with Samuel Hartlib's London group of pansophists, the Invisible College, and with John Wilkins's society of subscriber-experimentalists, which moved from London to Oxford and back between 1645 and 1660, eventually receiving a charter as the Royal Society. His membership offered a 'scape' from ordinary social life and at the same time a convivial circle of friends he could respect. He found the members of the College impressive, describing them as

[33] The texts are printed as 'Letter to Lady Drury' 12 February 1647, in *Works*, xiii. 564 and in the letter that follows, on breast-feeding. Malcolm Oster refers in this connection to a 'theatrical imagination that enacts a polarized view of virtue and vice' (Oster, 'Formative Years', pp. 200 ff.).

[34] See Malcolm Oster, 'The Beame of Divinity', *British Journal for the History of Science*, 22 (1990), 151–79, and J. J. MacIntosh, 'Animals, Morality, and Robert Boyle', *Dialogue*, 35 (1996), 435–72. Boyle expressed scruples regarding the vivisection of animals, though his practice was later at variance with his declarations (see MacIntosh, 'Animals', p. 447).

[35] Boyle, 'An Account of Philaretus in his Minority', in *Works* (1744), i. 20.   [36] Ibid. i. 27.

men of so capacious and searching spirits, that school-philosophy is but the lowest region of their knowledge; and yet, though ambitious to lead the way to any generous design, of so humble and teachable a genius, as they disdain not to be directed to the meanest, so he can but plead reason for his opinion; persons that endeavour to put narrow-mindedness out of their countenance, by the practice of so extensive a charity, that it reaches unto everything called man, and nothing less than an universall good-will can content it. And indeed they are so apprehensive of the want of good employment, that they take the whole body of mankind for their care[37]

The social incentive for Boyle to engage in natural philosophy was powerful. His early treatise on ethics, the *Aretology*, had been poorly received, dashing his hopes of becoming a respected moralist. In the laboratory the presence of helpful assistants created a cooperative human environment in which one could at the same time enjoy the absorption and reverie offered by manual industry. Boyle could forget about the dissonance between his Christian ideals and the behavior of his social set.[38] The experimental life delivered the pleasures of acting and experiencing, without the depressing side effects of vulgar hedonism. The suggestion that scientific pursuits are a substitute for, and equivalent to, conventional amorous exploits had been laid out very elegantly in Walter Charleton's dialogue on the mortality of the soul, in which Athanasius recalls to the friend of his youth Lucretius 'our ancient Caresses in the days of youth, innocence, and peace'. 'Since that day I first ventured abroad in to the World', he continues, 'I have had no Mistress that held any considerable room in my thoughts but One, and that the very same I have observed you to court with the strongest desires imaginable... Her, upon whom women usually transfer the blame for all their imperfections, Nature.' Lucretius agrees that, although conscious of the vast difference between himself and nature, and his inability to satisfy his desire in the knowledge of the least part of her, still, 'I discover such an infinite variety of fresh beauties and excellencies in her every day, that but to gaze upon them at a distance and view her in the weak and pale reflection

[37] Boyle, letter to Francis Tallents, 20 February 1646–7, in *Works* (1744), i. 20.

[38] On this phase of his life see R. E. W. Maddison, 'Studies in the Life of Robert Boyle, 6. The Stalbridge Period, 1645–55, and the Invisible College', *Notes and Records of the Royal Society*, 18 (1963), 104–24, and Steven Shapin, 'Personal Development and Intellectual Biography: The Case of Robert Boyle', *British Journal for the History of Science*, 26 (1993), 335–45.

made in the glasse of my own Reason, I find the most pleasant and ravishing employment'.[39]

Boyle's Epicurist leanings were already evident in his *Aretology*, in which he had opposed the Platonic doctrine that all pleasure is evil. The garden of Eden, the original paradise, he points out, was pleasant, and if pleasure were evil, it would have been no punishment to be thrown out of it. God has 'seasoned and as it were sweetened all the Necessary actions of our life with certain pleasures'.[40] His sensuality is evident in his *Experiments Touching Colours* (1664), written, he said, 'to divert and recreate, as well as to excite … by the delivery of matters of fact' assisted by experiments that are easy and delightful.[41] The color essay is a recitation of beautiful experiences and productions, beginning with a description of the glorious colors appearing to persons in a fever or about to suffer a stroke, and lovingly going on to describe the whiteness of beaten eggs, the green of leaves and emeralds, the nap of cornfields and fields of peas, the color of heated steel as it changes from yellow, to red, to blue, and a kind of glass that, when held at various angles, turns from gold to a pale blue or turquoise. There are 'experiments' with the juice of blackberries, cochineal, and cherries, and Boyle describes the revival of the color of dried rose leaves fixed with oil of sulfur. Copper, he found, turns the flame in which it is held green; sulfur produces a blue flame; and salt a yellow. Acids turn syrup of violets from blue to red; alkalis from blue to green.

The world of the chemist is a painted and scented world of graceful and protean forms, very unlike the sub-dioptrical world of atoms, possessed of bulk, figure, and motion alone, that characterized Boyle's official ontology. In his reflections 'Upon the sight of N.N. making of Syrup of Violets' Boyle observed that one might suppose 'N.N.' a very great 'Friend to *Epicurism*'. His employment seems 'wholly design'd to gratifie the senses', as the things

[39] Walter Charleton, *The Immortality of the Soul* (London: 1657), 3–4. In *The Excellency of Theology* Boyle refers to natural philosophy as a 'Mistris', and to the Virtuoso as '(if not a Passionate) an Assiduous Courter of Nature', *Works*, ed Hunter and Davis, viii. 9.

[40] Boyle, *Aretology*, in John T. Harwood (ed.), *The Early Essays and Ethics of Robert Boyle* (Carbondale, Ill.: Southern Illinois University Press, 1991), 30. Boyle personally identified with certain dramatic heroines. He explored the themes of sensibility, amorous folly, and lust in the remarkable letter he composed, as a personal exercise, to Joseph from Potiphar's Wife, and in the early, suppressed version of 'The Martyrdom of Theodora', in *Works*, ed. Hunter and Davis, xiii. 3–41, composed after a play by Corneille.

[41] Boyle, *Experiments and Considerations Touching Colours*, in *Works*, ed. Hunter and Davis, iv. 25.

'he deals with are Flowers and Sugar'.[42] But regardless of the color and scent of the one and the sweetness of the other, the distiller of violets is in fact, Boyle insists, manufacturing a useful remedy. Flowers, sugar, and the colors and textures of things—changeable taffeties, velvet, the blue and golden necks of pigeons, rainbows, little birds and mice—these were the charming components of the experimental life, reminiscent of the fish, dogs, looking-glasses, clocks, and medicines that Boyle described in his journalistic musings on the trifles of everyday life, the *Occasional Reflections*.

Inevitably, however, guilt attached even to these pure and seemingly innocent enjoyments. The *Occasional Reflections* often turn to pastoral and natural beauty, but typically in a spirit of self-correction. Describing the paring of an apple—'fresh and lively Vermillion ... emulation at Rubies themselves ... the Platonick definition which styles Beauty the *Lustre and Flower of Goodness*', Boyle reflected that the 'gay outside' of the fruit is 'cut and thrown away' and urged that we 'strip and devest [things] of all those flattering Ornaments (or cheating Disguises) which so often conceal or misrepresent their true and genuine nature'.[43] They are like the sweetmeats that turned out to be modeled in wax.[44] We must learn to look upon 'the curiosest Productions of Nature ... with a Philosopher's and a Christian's eyes', so that we can gaze on her 'bright objects' with pleasure but also turn away from them without trouble and disquiet.[45] Boyle's appreciation of the conflict between Christian morality and English life was replaced by a more threatening perception of a conflict between Christian theology and the experimental life of involvement not only with small, dirty, and low objects, but with beautiful and transitory ones. This problem had surfaced

[42] Boyle, *Occasional Reflections*, in *Works*, ed. Hunter and Davis, v. 148. The comment evokes John Evelyn's youthful suggestion that a gentleman devote himself to the study of 'many excellent receipts to make perfumes, sweet powders, pomanders, antidotes, and divers such curiosities'. Such receipts, he notes, are commonly possessed by persons of mean condition, 'but if men of quality made it their delight also, arts could not but receive infinite advantages ... and there is nothing by which a good man may more sweetly pass his time' (*Diary*, 10 January 1656/7, quoted in Walter B. Houghton, Jr., 'The English Virtuoso in the Seventeenth Century', *Journal of the History of Ideas*, 3/1 (1942), 56).

[43] Ibid. v. 60−1.

[44] Ibid., in *Works*, v. 169. Cf. Bach: 'Despicable sins | Are indeed lovely from outside | But afterwards in grief and chagrin | One is condemned to remorse | From outside sin is gold | Yet look within | You see only an empty shadow | And a whited sepulcher' (Cantata BWV 54, 'Widerstehe doch der Suende').

[45] Boyle, *Occasional Reflections*, in *Works*, ed. Hunter and Davis, v. 60−1.

by 1664, when he composed his paradoxical essay on the *Excellency of The-ology Compared with Natural Philosophy*.

The frivolous, self-indulgent, and unchristian character of experimental science had for some time been a theme of theologians and metaphysicians.[46] John Smith, the Cambridge Platonist, echoed the Fathers of the early Church in criticizing in his sermons those men who, 'spending themselves about Bodily and Material acts, and conversing only with Sensible things…are apt to acquire such deep stamps of Material phantasms to themselves, that they cannot imagine their own Being to be any other than *Material & Divisible*, though of a fine Aetheriall nature'. Their minds, he thought, are not 'fully abstracted while they have contemplated the highest Being of all'.[47] Thomas Browne's *Religio medici* (1643) was written to defend doctors from the charge of atheism, but it did not remove the suspicion that persons who engage too much with the material world come to attach too much respect to the powers of material things. Kenelm Digby pounced on the book on its first appearance.

[It cannot] be expected that an excellent Physitian whose fancy is always fraught with the materiall drugs that hee prescribeth his *Apothecary* to compound his Medicines of; and whose hands are inured to the cutting up, & eies to the inspection of anatomised bodies; should easily, and with successe, flye his thoughts at so towring a *Game*, as a pure intellect, a Separated and unbodyed Soule[48]

Robert South, the prolific and irascible Canon of Christ Church, and Orator of the University of Oxford, in a sermon of 1678 described the Royal Society as 'sons of Epicurus, both for Voluptuousness and Irreligion'.[49] Though Hobbes was in fact excluded from the Society, South saw it as a hotbed of 'Hobbism'. He availed himself of the religious contrast between knowledge and love of God and the knowledge and love of World: '[A]lthough there is vanity, a sorrow and dissatisfaction in the knowledge of created, inferior objects, yet we are assured it is life eternal to know God'.[50]

---

[46] See R. H. Syfret, 'Some Early Critics of the Royal Society', *Notes and Records of the Royal Society*, 8 (1950), 20–64.

[47] John Smith, *Select Discourses* (London: 660), 65.

[48] Kenelm Digby, *Observations upon Religio Medici* (London: 1643), 3.

[49] Quoted in R. H. Syfret, 'Some Early Reactions to the Royal Society', *Notes and Records of the Royal Society*, 7 (1950), 234.

[50] Ibid. 244.

A more subtle critic was Méric Casaubon, who agreed that experimental philosophy was 'very destructive to true Religion and Christianity'. The appeal to what is normally invisible led by a chain of associations, he claimed, to the 'blinde atomes' of '*Epicurus* and his mates' and raised the spectres of atheism, mortalism, and hedonism. 'High curiosities', such as human flight, the possibility of which had been proposed by John Wilkins in 1638, are dangerous and their pursuit distracts the mind from higher and nobler entities and mysteries. 'Men that are much fixed upon matter and secondary causes and sensual objects … forget that there be such things in the world as *Spirits*, substances really existing and of great power, though not visible, or palpable by their nature … and consequently discredit *supernatural operations*: and at last, that there is a God, and that their souls are immortal.'[51] Casaubon professed to see through the experimentalists' rhetoric of appreciation, contrasting their esoteric physico-theology with that available to the ordinary man who appreciates the sun and moon, the tides, and the seasons. 'We do not find by any of these admirable Psalms that are written of the subject, that any other works of God are specified, but those that are visible to all men.'[52]

Casaubon insisted on the value of the traditional university curriculum, emphasizing logic, history, and morals, which furnished the pupil with the arts of reasoning, of detecting fallacies, moral and political philosophy, history, and languages. Man, he said, has a soul as well as a body and we do not live by bread—the promotion of works and trades—alone, but need studies conducive to virtue and holiness. The reading of histories and military exercises offers a better education than 'attending on furnaces, or raking into the entrails of men, or beasts, to find somewhat, which it may be will never make them much wiser when they know it, nor prove of any great use'.[53] He professed alarm at Gassendi's account of the life of the virtuoso Peiresc, who was apparently moved to moral reflection and control of his own passions by observing the battle of a louse and a fly 'shut in a microscope'. One would do far better, he thought, to read the many philosophers who had written on the subject of self-control. Deriving one's morality from observations of the animal world would in any case lead to no good results. Casaubon cited the story told by

[51] Méric Casaubon, *A Letter of Meric Casaubon DD. &c. to Peter du Moulin … Concerning Natural Experimental Philosophy* (London: 1669), 30.
[52] Ibid. 23.   [53] Ibid. 24.

Peiresc of the man who, observing the behavior of a sparrow—'the most lascivious of all creatures, as is observed by some naturalists'—towards its mate, reproached God with having made him a man and not a sparrow.[54]

Henry Stubbe quoted Sprat's description of Wren's instrument for demonstrating the effects of collision between globous bodies, professing his unhappiness with Sprat's deduction that 'not onely ... the Material part of every thing in the Corporeal Universe is *Body*, or *Corpuscularian*, but ... the Vicissitudes and *Phaenomena* occurring therein, even in the Generation of *Man*, are the result of *Corpuscles* moving *Mechanically*'.[55] Sprat referred everything to a 'Geometrical Necessity arising from the Fabrick'.[56] Stubbe expressed dismay at Sprat's remarkable suggestion that where mastering, naming, and looking into the nature of all creatures were concerned, '[t]his had bin the only *Religion*, if men had continued innocent in *Paradise* and had not wanted a *Redemption*'.[57] He twisted Sprat's meaning somewhat to imply that Adam's fall was a consequence of his insufficient attention to natural philosophy. 'No man ever taught', Stubbe complained, 'that *Adam's* fall was a deficiency from the study of *Experimental Philosophie*; or that *he* was not ejected *paradise* for the breach of a *positive command*, but for not minding the *cultivation of the Garden* and *natural curiosities*.'[58]

Sprat had insisted that there was no reason why the experimentalist should be prone to deny the existence and properties of God and his providence.[59] Far from leading him to reject the possibility of incorporeal spirits, his involvement with material things, he declared, 'puts his thoughts into an excellent good capacity to believe them'. Corpuscularianism expands his imagination and raises his thoughts from unseen atoms to unseen angels:

In every *work* of *Nature* that he handles, he knows that there is not only a gross substance, which presents itself to all mens eies; but an infinite subtilty of *parts*, which come not into the sharpest sense. So that what the *Scripture* relates of the Purity of *God*, of the Spirituality of his *Nature*, and that of *Angels*, and the *Souls* of men, cannot seem incredible to him, when he perceives the numberless particles

[54] Ibid. 34.   [55] Thomas Sprat, *A History of the Royal Society* (London: 1667), 312.
[56] Henry Stubbe, *A Censure upon Certain Passages Contained in the History of the Royal Society* (Oxford: 1670), 66–7.
[57] Sprat, *History of the Royal Society*, p. 350.   [58] Stubbe, *Censure*, pp. 38–9.
[59] Sprat, *History of the Royal Society*, p. 348.

that move in everymans *Blood*, and the prodigious streams that continually flow unseen from every *Body*.[60]

Experimentalism and libertinism nevertheless remained associated in the minds of critics, enhanced by moral disgust with the behavior of the King and the aristocracy. All this put Boyle in a state of conflict, but also afforded an opportunity for him to express the moral-religious side of his personality in a defense of his preferred activities. The difficulty was in finding the language and concepts in which to do so. As Karl Figlio acutely remarks, the problem of its justification, in face of the destructive potential and resource-consuming wastefulness of experimental science, is still actual, but the financial and institutional power of modern science have strengthened its position. Its language of justification, even where useless, speculative, or lethal activities are concerned, has been developed and polished in the wake of some genuinely useful and humane results and applications. Boyle, with some assistance from Bacon and Descartes, had to think out his rationale for experimental activity for the first time.[61]

Boyle attempted to resolve the problem presented by the hedonistic incentive to natural philosophy first by insisting that his experimental practice was not merely accompanied by, but actually served to establish the truth of, the Anaxagorean system that he presented in his programmatic works. He was not, he maintained, a mere empiric—even an empiric who happened to be a nobleman—but a philosopher attaining knowledge of reality. The changes of color and form in the glass had, he implied, shown him the reality underneath the colored surface of the world, the latent image of the creation, and through the vagaries of experiment he had somehow detected the institution of a system of laws of nature.

But was experimentation really useful? In the sketch 'Of Naturall Philosophie' of the early 1650s, which rehearsed the themes of the later *Usefulness of Natural Philosophy* (1671), Boyle cited as rationales for the pursuit of experimentation the satisfaction of curiosity, the exciting of religious devotion, and applications in medicine, husbandry, navigation, and the trades, the latter mainly consisting, it seems, of solvents and paint

---

[60] Sprat, *History of the Royal Society* p. 348.
[61] Karl Figlio, 'Psychoanalysis and the Scientific Mind: Robert Boyle', *British Journal for the History of Science*, 32 (1999), 314.

additives.[62] He reminded himself that the experimental philosopher must not scorn what seems trivial, or expect too much from experiments, or give way to frustration when they failed. When properly conducted, without excessive fondness and hope, involvement with nature is legitimate and productive. But the utilitarian rationale for experimental philosophy was not entirely satisfying to Boyle. His essay on the *Excellency of Theology*, published in 1674, was ostensibly addressed to a virtuoso inclined to atheism who, closely involved in experimental practice, sees no need for supplementing his studies with the texts of revealed theology. It is tempting to read this essay not as reflecting a debate Boyle is having with some unidentified Royal Society colleague, but as a debate he is having with himself. In any event, he acknowledged very strong reasons in favor of the opponent's position, yet came to the conclusion that the experimentalist must and can take on more than a minimal religious commitment to the existence of a wise and provident creator. A remarkable feature of this tract is that every reason Boyle gave for practicing experimental philosophy in the *Usefulness* was subverted, and true felicity deemed an effect of theological studies, by contrast with experimental philosophy.

The first part of the *Excellency* assumed the naturalist's tendency to skepticism and his lack of concern for Christian doctrine. The philosopher who values the study of nature and its canons of evidence will wonder, Boyle agreed, about the warrant for claims concerning supersensible beings and the events and promises recorded in Scripture. Was Christ's sacrifice necessary? Might not God have remitted all the penalties of sin? Does the soul remain in suspension until judgement day or does she go immediately to heaven or hell? Will we know one another in the afterlife and see our mistresses, relatives, princes, and subjects? Or just be annihilated?[63]

'Reason is not much to be trusted when she wanders far from Experiments', Boyle had remarked in 'Of Naturall Philosophie'.[64] He shrewdly noted that Descartes was unconvinced by his own arguments for the immortality of the soul, those cited so favorably by John Smith, for Descartes himself wrote sarcastically to Princess Elizabeth 'my knowledge of [eternal life] is far inferiour to that of Monsieur Digby. For, setting aside that which Religion teaches us of it, I confess, that by meer Natural Reason we may indeed

---

[62] The text is given in Hunter, *Robert Boyle: Scrupulosity and Science*, pp. 30–1.
[63] Boyle, *Excellency of Theology*, in *Works*, ed. Hunter and Davis, viii. 27–8.
[64] Hunter, *Robert Boyle: Scrupulosity and Science*, p. 31.

make many conjectures to our own advantage, and have fair *Hopes*, but not any Assurance'.[65] The Cartesian argument for the incorporeality of the soul, Boyle noted, is telling against Epicureans and atheists who consider the soul to be a modification of the body, but it doesn't prove her immortality.

Meer Reason [Boyle declared] cannot inform us what will become of [the soul] in her separate state, whether she will be vitally united to any other kind of Body or Vehicle; and if to some, of what kind that will be, and upon what terms the Union will be made. For possibly she may be united to an unorganiz'd or very imperfectly organiz'd body, wherein she cannot exercise the same Functions she did in her Humane Body.[66]

Just as the soul's incorporeality does not guarantee her immortality, Boyle recognized, her immortality does not guarantee the possibility of happiness. What if the soul is reinstalled at the resurrection in a body that only feels pain and that cannot move? How can such a soul experience felicity? Philosophers from Aristotle to Descartes had maintained that even a disembodied, unsensing soul can be happy, because she can always think and contemplate, and those are her favourite activities. But, Boyle reflected, men would grow weary of thinking 'if they received no supply of Objects from without, by Reading, Seeing, or Conversing; and if they also wanted the opportunity of executing their thoughts, by moving the Members of their Bodies, or of imparting them, either by Discoursing, or Writing of Books, or by making of Experiments'.[67] He described the unfortunate case of a nobleman who was imprisoned for a year in Spain and furnished with a diet befitting his station, but deprived of books, light, and company. The prisoner could reminisce and contemplate without interruption, but he fell victim to an extreme melancholy: his chief impulse was to drink himself into a stupor and fall asleep.[68]

Happiness, as proponents of the experimental philosophy implied or insisted, comes from engagement with material things that can be seen, tasted, and handled, and from investigating these things and discoursing of them with others. The worry Boyle placed in the mouth of the naturalist was a serious one:

Among thinking men, whose thoughts run much upon that future state, which they must shortly enter into, but shall never pass out of; there will frequently

---

[65] Quoted by Boyle, *Excellency of Theology*, in *Works*, ed. Hunter and Davis, viii. 24–5.
[66] Ibid. viii. 25.   [67] Ibid. viii. 26.   [68] Ibid.

and naturally arise a distrust, which, though seldom owned, proves oftentimes disquieting enough. For such men are apt to question, how the future condition, which the gospel promises, can afford them so much happiness as it pretends to; since they shall in heaven but contemplate the works of God, and praise him and converse with him; all which they think may, though not immediately be done by men here below, without being happy.

So Boyle suggested that in heaven we must not only meet our relatives and lovers, and converse with God, the saints, and the angels, but also re-encounter our erstwhile friends and colleagues. This allowed, the naturalist who subscribes to the Epicurean doctrine of universal destruction faces the loss of 'the pleasure of his knowledge, by losing those Senses and that World, which are the Instruments and Object of it', as well as facing the threat of eternal punishment. The pious naturalist is not only 'freed from the wracking Apprehensions of having his soul reduc'd to a state of Annihilation or cast into Hell',[69] but can look forward to even better working conditions: 'Those things, that do here most excite our Desires, and quicken the Curiosity and Industry of our searches, will not onely there Continue, but be Improv'd to a far greater measure of Attractiveness and Influence'.[70] We will be free of those interests, passions, and lusts that here below impede us in these pursuits. In his early essay *Seraphic Love*, Boyle had argued that the beatific vision of God would not, as was sometimes intimated, bore us with its monotony, but stimulate us with iridescence and sparkle, offering 'Variety in further knowledge of the fixed object', such as arises 'from the fixt Beholding of the changing-necks of Doves, or such as we may see in the diversifi'd Refractions of the same sparkling Diamond'.[71]

The conceptualization of heaven and the beatific vision, it might be noted in this connection, was increasingly problematic. Heaven, according to Valla's Christian spokesman in *On Pleasure* (also known as *The True Good*), is like our own beautiful world, only far better:

If peacocks and some other birds are distinguished for their lovely colors, and if lilies and roses and other flowers of briefest lifespan surpass Solomon in all his glory, what may we then think are the adornments of angels? And of men? The appearance of what may be called the angels' bodies will be such as to declare

---

[69] Ibid. viii. 51.   [70] Ibid.

[71] Boyle, *Some Motives and Incentives to the Love of God* ('*Seraphic Love*'), in *Works*, ed. Hunter and Davis, i. 129.

at a glance their blessed state and to set your spirit on fire to gain an equal happiness.[72]

Where the bodily senses are concerned, 'either we shall continue to enjoy the use of the same ones, or if some of these are no longer present, we shall be given much better ones in their place'.[73] In Valla's heaven we will smell wonderful, enjoy marvellous food and drink, have wings, be able to move at great speed, and be indefatigable, indulging in 'a great variety of splendors, adornments, delights', and listening to the loveliest 'voices, conversations, songs'. Only there will be no hunting, bird catching, or fishing, insofar as there are herbs and flowers, but no animals, in heaven.[74] Either, it seemed, one was forced to the Platonic-Cartesian conclusion that in heaven we will be free of bodies and free of the corporeal imagery they produce, or else to the position that heaven offers unmitigated sensory delight, though no hunting or sex. The former option left it less than fully desirable—the Cartesian separated soul was barely capable, after all, of mathematics—the latter, however, implicitly reinforced the worthiness of terrestrial forms of happiness, which, even if somewhat inferior in quality and quantity, were at least available and assured.

Part II of Boyle's *Excellency* seems in any case infected by second thoughts. Rather than reinstalling the laboratory in heaven and lending an element of Vallaesque materiality to the beatific vision, Boyle sought to persuade his skeptical naturalist that the laboratory was not so heavenly. 'I shall, without Preamble', he announced, 'begin this Discourse, by considering the Delightfulness of Physicks, as the main thing, that inveigles your Friend, and divers other Virtuosi, from relishing as they ought, and otherwise would, the pleasantness of Theological Discoveries.'[75] The experimental life brings, indeed, 'sincerer Pleasures, than those the more undiscerning part of Mankind is so fond of', but it is still inferior to a life of devotion and theological study. Boyle set out to 'weaken the Argument, that is drawn from delightfulness' by showing the inconveniencies of natural philosophy.

The utilitarian arguments for experiment and the devotion to the common good that he had cited earlier were considerably discounted in

[72] Lorenzo Valla, *On Pleasure*, bk. III, §23, trans. A. Kent Hieatt and Maristella Lorch (New York, Abaris, 1977), 293.

[73] Ibid., §24; trans. Hieatt and Lorch, p. 299.   [74] Ibid. 303.

[75] Boyle, *Excellency of Theology*, in *Works*, ed. Hunter and Davis, viii. 55.

this tract. 'The boasted use of Natural Philosophy, by its advancing Trades and Physick', he says, 'will still be to serve the Body, which is but the Lodging and Instrument of the Soul.'[76] Even if the chemist were to discover a method of extracting gold from ore, this would not benefit mankind by much; the discoveries of the Americas have enriched the Spaniards but made many multitudes of men miserable from working in mines.[77] Prolongation of life is a small thing in relation to eternity; 'all the Remedies, and Reliefs, and Pleasures, and Accommodations that Philosophical Improvements can afford a man, will not keep him from the Grave, (which within a few days will make the body of the greatest *Virtuoso* as hideous and loathsome a Carcase, as that of any ordinary man)'.[78] Experimental practice is full of frustration, as the naturalist is dependent on 'such a Variety of Mechanick People (as Distillers, Drugsters, Smiths, Turners, &c.)'.[79] He must seek out apparatus, wait upon tradesmen, and repair losses from his own pocket. Natural philosophy is not the best route to fame and reputation. It is subject to fashion, 'wanes and eclipses', vicissitudes and prejudices.[80] It is difficult to make new discoveries, to write books, to be right. The virtuoso is interrupted by visitors and letters, and he acquires a bad reputation if he puts people off.[81]

So Boyle appeared to downgrade the experimental life, dismissing both charitable and physico-theological motives, in order to correct the view that it was a life needing no supplementation with the study of the world of bodiless intelligent agents and the secrets of the future state. Boyle referred repeatedly to 'mere Reason', 'mere Matter', and to the 'merely Corporeal', 'mere Naturalists', and the 'Phaenomena of meer Nature'. Yet his downgrading was at the same time an ennobling. By seeming to diminish nature and the activities of the naturalist, and by portraying corporeal nature as supplemented and patterned by spiritual agents and the investigator as necessarily led to appreciate the mysteries of theology, Boyle conferred dignity and worth on these objects and roles.

In the second part of *The Christian Virtuoso*, published in the last years of Boyle's life, the attempt to represent heaven as a superior form of earth and heavenly intercourse as a superior form of human sociability was abandoned. Years of trouble with his eyesight, and perhaps some

---

[76] Ibid. viii. 62.   [77] Ibid. viii. 62.   [78] Ibid. viii. 64.
[79] Ibid. viii. 57.   [80] Ibid. viii. 85.   [81] Ibid. viii. 82–3.

degree of social fatigue, may have been as much responsible as increasing philosophical sophistication. In the future state, he mused, 'the nature of things corporeal, may be very differing from those that obtain in the present world', and our science may be accordingly useless.[82] God, he says, can give the soul a purely rational form of happiness 'though it have no remembrance or knowledge of the world or any corporeal creature'. The sweetness of life will have come to seem insipid to it and its former inquiries into nature worthwhile only insofar as they involved 'laudable industry'.[83]

9.3 Evidence and belief

Boyle insisted that God could not have made our salvation dependent on our acceptance through faith alone of any manifest irrationality. But he also insisted that we should not reject claims merely because they seem contrary to reason. He also claimed that Scripture contains matters of fact, known by experience and through testimony.[84] This triad of beliefs was not easy to maintain consistently.

For the harmonization of standards of evidence in science and religion Boyle employed various strategies, including concession, *ad hominem* attacks, prudential reminders, and metaphysical and epistemological argument. He argued that some doubts were excusable, for the doubtful doctrines had not been clearly delivered in Scripture or proved.[85] He charged that Epicurean atheists were biased by their sensuality, lust, and passion.[86] He pointed out that the dictates of prudence mostly coincided with divine command, and that self-interest might encourage us to require a lower standard of proof when eternal life was at stake.[87] He argued that competent testimony can compensate for apparent irrationality; many initially implausible things reported by travellers and experimenters have turned out since to be well grounded.[88] He reminded readers that the experimental philosophy had revealed many

[82] Boyle, *Christian Virtuoso*, in *Works*, ed. Hunter and Davis, xii. 521.
[83] Ibid. xii. 521.   [84] Ibid. xi. 308–9.
[85] Boyle, *About the Reconcileableness of Reason and Religion*, in *Works*, ed. Hunter and Davis, viii. 284–5.
[86] Boyle, *Christian Virtuoso*, in *Works*, ed. Hunter and Davis, xi. 294.
[87] Boyle, *Reconcileableness*, viii. 282–5.
[88] Boyle, *Christian Virtuoso*, in *Works*, ed. Hunter and Davis, xi. 309 ff.

surprising things concerning the magnet, and that instruments like the telescope had revealed much that was previously unknown.[89] He insisted that belief in the resurrection was supported by observation of plants and animals and by experiments involving the redintegration of chemical substances.[90]

But because the realm of souls was invisible and intangible, the experimental method was somewhat difficult to apply to the investigation of the future state, its different corporeal order, and its possibly non-sensory minds. Boyle tried to turn a minus into a plus. We do not need 'anatomical knives, or geometrical globes, or optical telescopes or microscopes... or elaborate instruments' to explore theological questions. But what do we need? Boyle was not very clear on this point. The experimental life implied the imposition of strict standards for distinguishing competent testimony from the ubiquitous doubtful testimony surrounding it. Hunter rightly points to 'the ingenuity Boyle displayed in devising and executing trials',[91] but Boyle could not settle on a method for the investigation of incorporeals. As a kind of epistemological last resort, he looked for evidence of angelic, demonic, and ghostly activity in the world; if these beings were not to be captured and proved in the laboratory, at least their effects might be witnessed in the world.

Proof of the existence of ghosts would settle the issue in favor of separable souls. This was agreed to by More, and by Boyle's contemporary Richard Baxter, who explained in the preface to his own collection of stories of apparitions, that 'There are in this City of *London*, many Persons that profess their great unbelief, or doubt of the Life to come, the Immortality of the Soul, and therefore much more of the truth of the Gospel, and Christian Faith, and Supernatural Revelations'. These doubters, according to Baxter, take all reports of spirits, apparitions, witchcraft, and miracles to be the effects of 'Error, Deceit, and easie Credulity', but admit that if they could be certain of the phenomena 'it would do

[89] Boyle, *Reconcileableness*, in *Works*, ed. Hunter and Davis, viii. 275 ff.

[90] Boyle, 'Some Physico-theological Considerations about the Possibility of the Resurrection', in *Works*, ed. Hunter and Davis, viii. 305 ff.

[91] Michael Hunter, 'Robert Boyle: A Suitable Case for Treatment?', *British Journal for the History of Science* 32 (1999), 263. In their 'over-greedy' desire to learn whether there are other spiritual substances besides the souls of men, Boyle maintained, many have 'chosen rather to venture the putting themselves within the power of Daemons', a temptation he may have experienced but evidently withstood (*Excellency of Theology*, in *Works*, ed. Hunter and Davis, viii. 13).

more to convince them than the Assertions of the Scriptures'.[92] Baxter attempted to rise to the challenge of convincing them. Within a course of nature regulated by exact and exceptionless laws, occasionally suspended by God for the performance of physical miracles, there is room left for the free agency of devils, as well as of humans, and God refrains from intervening.

The God that fixeth the Course of Nature, so as that he will not for the Prayers of any make the Sun alter a Minute of its rising and setting time, nor alter the Spring and Fall, Summer and Winter, &c. Hath setled also a Subordinate order of *Free-agents* for Moral Government, and though he dispose of the Events of all Mens Acts, without causing their Sin, yet will he not usually violate that free order. It's Marvellous the Devils have so much power over Children and Men, as I have here proved, if but a silly wretched *Witch* consent; And how much more mischief may he do to Church and Kingdom, if he can but get Bishops, Priests and Princes, and Law-makers to consent.[93]

While early modern philosophers in the Cartesian tradition appear to have abandoned the notion that God could do anyone personal favors in this life,[94] this was not altogether true of Boyle, though his later views suggested a more mechanical view of causation and signification, one in which chance might indeed play a role, and particular, as opposed to general, providence could not be so easily inferred—or at least not as many instances of particular providence as he had noted in the course of one small person's early life. The dominant position in his *Free Inquiry* resembles the views of Malebranche and Leibniz. The universe is a perfectly working clock, and God does not need to intervene in the ordinary course of nature, for he clearly discerns 'what would happen in consequence of the Laws by Him establish'd, in all the possible Combinations of Them, and in all the Junctures of Circumstances wherein the Creatures concerned in them may be found'.[95] A secondary point was, however, that God himself causes many 'irregularities and exorbitances' and extends favor and punishment to individuals.[96] Anyone of a certain age, Boyle remarked sagely in *The Christian Virtuoso*, who has escaped the perils and misfortunes that befall

[92] Richard Baxter, *The Certainty of the Worlds of Spirits* (London: Parkhurst and Salusbury, 1691), 17.
[93] Ibid. 246.
[94] Though, judging by some passages in his *Discourse on Method*, Descartes seemed in his youth to consider himself a sort of favored son.
[95] Boyle, *Free Inquiry*, in *Works*, ed. Hunter and Davis, x. 567.   [96] Ibid. x. 529; cf. 518.

so many, must realize his indebtedness to God 'for particular and personal preservations'.[97]

The philosophers' dogged adherence to schemes of postmortem punishment and reward, their refusal to abandon deontological Christian ethics for the sophisticated accounts of moral virtue as self-regulation available in Greek and Roman texts, even when they had adopted so much else from them, is a feature of the period that differentiates it sharply from the rather more pagan century following. Against a background of civil war, libertinage, peasant unrest, and constant plotting and maneuvering, a secular conception of morality was perhaps thinkable for oneself, but not for men in general. The *puer robustus sed malitiosus*, as Marx and Engels later called him, was not going to be transformed into a Platonic, Epicurean, or Stoic sage. In Boyle's view, pagan moralists lacked the emotional intensity, the insistence and earnestness, of Christian moralists, who offered 'shining examples, pathetical exhortations, sweet consolations, great and precious promises, and powerful though secret assistances'.[98]

Boyle's mature position on knowledge of the sacred and the profane was that typically ascribed to Locke, and deriving from Gassendi via Charleton.[99] The powers of human reason do not extend as far as might be thought, either in natural philosophy or in theology, and our best course of action is 'nobly attempting to surmount Difficulties that are superable, and wisely submitting... to those that are not so'.[100] We cannot fully understand our own minds, Boyle thought, and the book of nature is, he said, like a romance—a mystery novel whose 'parts have such a connection and relation to one another, and the things we would discover are so darkly or incompletely knowable by those that precede them, that the mind is not satisfied 'till it come to the end of the Book'[101]—though we cannot in fact do so. In the last pages of *The Christian Virtuoso*, he appeared to approach, the position of Immanuel Kant, or even William James, in his references

---

[97] Boyle, *Christian Virtuoso*, in *Works*, ed. Hunter and Davis, xii. 492.   [98] Ibid. 519.

[99] Jan Wojcik has argued that we ought to read Boyle not as a 'confident and single-minded advocate both of the corpuscularian philosophy and rational religion', but as a philosopher who expected to keep running up against the limits of knowledge (Wojcik, *Robert Boyle and the Limits of Reason* (Cambridge: Cambridge University Press, 1997), 212). Cf. Boyle, *Christian Virtuoso*, in *Works*, ed. Hunter and Davis, xii. 475.

[100] Quoted by Wojcik, *Robert Boyle*, p. 296.

[101] Boyle, *Excellency of Theology*, in *Works*, ed. Hunter and Davis, viii. 57.

to an 'extrinsick Motive', meaningful in the present order of things, for belief. The excellence of religion, he said there, consists in the fact that, regardless of the truth status of its claims, faith and religious contemplation and study make this life agreeable. If (however implausibly) 'all those *great and precious promises* ... should prove illusory', if he can only set aside his doubts, the experimentalist will 'sweeten all his hardships and sufferings in this life'.[102]

The Christian Virtuoso followed the pattern of earlier tracts written specifically for the confutation of those given to 'Prophane Discourses and Licentious Lives'. It was meant to be a literary scourge to those occupied by 'Secular Affairs and Sensual Pleasures'.[103] Yet Boyle himself was passionately occupied with secular and sensual things. He insisted that the appreciation of the complexity of natural machines and their beauty was a form of sincere worship, and that his discovery of the manifold of qualities producible by his efforts enhanced the naturalist's admiration for God's power, wisdom, and benevolence. The Christian Virtuoso constructed by Boyle and presented to the world was at once a reproach to his more light-minded colleagues, the 'erring Virtuosi', a reply to the charge that the experimental philosophy undermined society and morals, and an idealized version of Boyle himself, one free of the doubts and conflicts that were expressed elsewhere in his essays and autobiographical writings. His attempt to reconcile reason and religion, the experimental life with the devotional life, was protracted and intelligent, if not altogether consistent or convincing to the modern eye. He was chronically unable to banish all dangerous ideas from his own mind.

As a young man Boyle had worried about his tendency to give way to imaginative 'roving' or 'raving',[104] and it is perhaps significant that his paper on the 'Atomicall Philosophy', for all its seemingly innocuous theo-mechanical content, was amongst the papers Boyle ordered to be destroyed, along with all his papers concerning the romance of Theodora—a richly detailed story of romantic ardor, villainy, sex slavery, heroism, and martyrdom composed in his youth. Boyle wanted to assure posterity that he was not a friend to Epicureanism—nor to Epicurism. 'Corpuscularian Principles', he never tired of insisting, 'may not only be admitted *without*

---

[102] Boyle, *Christian Virtuoso*, in *Works*, ed. Hunter and Davis, xii. 511.   [103] Ibid. xi. 284–5.
[104] Harwood (ed.), *The Early Essays*, p. xlviii ff.

Epicurean Errors, but be employ'd *against* them'.[105] Scholasticism, he assured his readers, was closer to pagan naturalism and to materialism than the atomical hypothesis of the moderns. But his own complex reactions to the possibility that Epicurean mortalism was true, and to the question of the permissibility of Epicurist sensual enjoyment, cannot be read off from his portrayal of the Christian Virtuoso, regardless of the degree to which this imaginary figure's beliefs and motives in their certitude, fixity, and purity represented an intellectual and personal ideal to him.

[105] Boyle, 'Some Physico-theological Considerations about the Possibility of the Resurrection', in *Works*, ed. Hunter and Davis, viii. 297.

10

The Sweetness of Living

When thou (O Goddesse) comest stormes flie away
And heaven is no more obscur'd with showres.
For thee the fragrant earth spreads various flowers
The calmed ocean smiles, and att thy sight
The serene skie shines with augmented light.
Then doth the spring her glorious days disclose
And the releast, life-giving westwind blowes.
Thy power possessing first birds of the ayre
They thy approach with amorous noates declare

. . . .

Since all things thus are brought to light by thee,
By whom alone their natures governd bee,
From whom both lovelinesse and pleasure springs.
Assist me while the nature of these things
I sing.

(*De rerum natura*, i. 6–25)

'We', announced Lorenzo Valla's Epicurean Vegio, 'holding to Nature's own laws, declare that pleasure should be pursued; they recommend purposeless labors, we recommend mirth; they propose torments, we propose pleasure; finally, they advocate death, we advocate life. You already see clearly what is in dispute.'[1] Beauty, he went on to remind his interlocutors, is everywhere around us, and it is there for us to enjoy and to create. Nature makes gold, jewels, choice wools, marble, fields, vines, gardens, horses, and dogs; men make statues and paintings. '[M]en are

---

[1] Lorenzo Valla, *On Pleasure*, bk. I, § 16; trans. A. Kent Hieatt and Maristella Lorch (New York: Abaris, 1977), 91.

superior to all other animals on two counts; we can express what we feel, and we can drink wine, sending out the one and ushering in the other.'[2]

Ancient philosophers considered ethics as the theoretical study of how to live a happy life, from the age of autonomy to the grave. Their disagreements concerned the characterization of happiness, the means by which it was to be procured, the most effective ways of minimizing one's exposure to misfortune or recovering from it, and the cognitive attitudes most conducive to bearing with the inevitabilities of pain and death.[3] Within this framework, the role of pleasure was disputed between Epicureans and Stoics. The former insisted that pleasure and freedom from psychological and physical pain were identical with the condition of human happiness; the latter that the employment of reason and the exercise of virtue were both necessary and sufficient for the enjoyment of that condition. The claims of both sects were acknowledged by their opponents, and the difference between them could seem narrow; for the Stoics conceded that the virtuous man experienced pleasure in his honest comportment, and the Epicureans insisted that they did not identify pleasure with dissipation but with frugality and restraint. Nevertheless, when their ethical doctrines were considered within the framework of their physical, cosmological, and political doctrines, the divergent features of the two sects, and their divergence from the other great ethical systems of antiquity, were evident. Leibniz brought out these differences expertly in the sections of the *New Essays* devoted to moral philosophy.

The Christian conception of ethics that took hold after the collapse of the Roman empire was based on a rejection of the ancient eudaimonistic premise, and it reorganized the conceptual terrain in a number of ways. The condition of human beings was posited as irremediably miserable from the age of autonomy to the grave, and the ethical life was not construed as a happy life, nor as one lived in accordance with human nature, but rather as a life lived in accordance with God's commands. Insofar as these had been revealed to the prophets and to God's son, philosophical exploration of the terms of the good life was unnecessary. Happiness—indeed eternal

---

[2] Ibid., bk. I, § 24; trans. Hieatt and Lorch, p. 105.

[3] See Maximilian Forschner, *Über das Handeln im Einklang mit der Natur* (Darmstadt: Wissenschaftliche Buchgesellschaft, 1998), 120 ff.

bliss—was a condition promised for the afterlife to those whom God favored, but its experiential character was, in view of both its deontological status and its deferral to an unexperienced future state, hardly a matter for rational argument. The ancient debates about the necessary and sufficient conditions of a happy life were accordingly replaced by a new set of debates centering on the puzzles of the obedient life: Did obedience guarantee salvation, or was God above all influences, arbitrary and inscrutable? Was faith necessary for salvation, along with obedience, or perhaps sufficient on its own? How was obedience possible in light of such confounding factors as original sin, hereditarily transmitted to every member of the species, and God's foreknowledge of all human actions? Early modern philosophers continued to be preoccupied with the problem set of the theory of obedience, especially the problems of sin, the will, justification by faith or works, and divine inscrutability. At the same time, their improved access to ancient texts and their growing familiarity with Cicero's lengthy explorations of the Epicurean and Stoic positions encouraged a reconsideration of happiness and pleasure and their relation to ethics, as Locke's persistent attention to those questions shows. The philosophers' reconstruction of cosmology, physics, and psychology along the lines laid down by the ancient atomists, and their recognition that, for all that human reason could determine, it was possible that the soul was after all mortal and that there would be no life beyond the grave, made the question of the happy life actual once again.

Epicureanism accordingly furnished an alternative to Stoic and Christian rigorism, and it brought the issue of basic human welfare, understood as the satisfaction of non-intellectual needs, into focus. Hobbes's insistence that morals and manners were explained and justified by their utility for social life indicated the possibility of a new grounding for ethics, even when he was misinterpreted as a pessimist and when philosophers of benevolence, like Richard Cumberland, counted themselves amongst Epicureanism's critics. The lengthy compilation of Gassendi's writings published by François Bernier in 1699 under the title *Three Discourses of Happiness, Virtue and Liberty* began confidently and warmly: 'Mankind having a natural Inclination to be happy, the main bent and design of all his Actions and Endeavours tend chiefly that way. It is therefore an undeniable Truth, that Happiness, or a Life free from Pain and Misery, are such things as influence and direct all our Actions and Purposes to the obtaining of them'.[4]

10.1 Beauty and danger

In early modern moral discourse, women assumed a new status and a new importance, as Augustinian *askesis* was replaced by the more respectful views of the passions that characterize early eighteenth-century French and English letters. The dethronement of Aristotle encouraged a renewed interest in the Platonic metaphysics of love, now applied in a heterosexual context, and, at the same time, the acceptance of a Democritean naturalism regarding the human body. While the moral worth and dignity of personal love, and the legitimacy of the enjoyment of beauty were themes perhaps more often supported in English philosophy by references to Plato than by references to Epicurus, the case of Ficino in the fifteenth century shows how the transit from the concepts of one system to those of the other could be effected. A conceptually distinct, but sometimes interleaved, movement was the trend just mentioned towards explaining and justifying moral rules in terms of their social utility. If all legal and moral restraints on human beings were artificial, as Hobbes and Pufendorf maintained, made by and for their subjects and requiring justification, new questions concerning social equality and the entitlements of women could be raised. Luxury, curiosity, and emotionality—the conceptual accoutrements of the female sex—could even be defended by the bolder writers as having a place in the overall economy of nature and society.

To be sure, Epicurus, like all philosophers, had warned against excesses of emotion and the complications of marriage. Lucretius, too, advised readers that escape from the 'tight bonds of Venus', once they have fastened themselves, is difficult. He described the solitary torment of the lover whose mistress has 'thrown out an ambiguous word and left it embedded in his passionate heart, where it burns like living fire',[5] and he

---

[4] Pierre Gassendi, *Three Discourses of Happiness, Virtue and Liberty*, trans. F. Bernier (London: 1699), 1.

[5] Lucretius, *On the Nature of Things (ONT)*, IV. 1137–8; trans. Martin Ferguson Smith (Indianapolis, Ind.: Hackett, 2001), 131.

proposed remedies for the victim of scorn or betrayal, the most useful of which is the reminder that we have managed to survive up to now without possessing that person. Yet the love-as-bondage metaphor in Lucretius is circumscribed in his text and is overwhelmed by a positive vision of Venus as the ruler of all animate life.[6] The cyclicity of the seasons, the cresting and collapse of human emotions, the courtship of animals, and the affection of mothers for their young[7] all enter his purview. With the exception of the atom, every object exists temporarily; nothing can be eternal—not God, the forms, the heavens, the world, or any species, certainly not any individual life, or social institution, or indeed any relationship between human beings. The philosopher must acknowledge limits and boundaries, and put his faith not in permanence but in the eternal possibility of renewal. The power of women to produce and tend new life is a visible manifestation of the power of nature to create form and value, and the female is the necessary condition of the only eternity that is thinkable in an atomic universe. Her beauty and attractive power are the means by which she accomplishes her generative work. Not only does the female have, in Lucretian metaphysics, a genuine role to play, her role is dominant. The purpose of man, according to the tradition, is cultivation of his higher powers, those he does not share with animals, including formal reasoning and the contemplation of divinities and incorporeals. Epicureanism, disdaining such notions of higher purpose, found beauty and value in the subhuman world; the generative powers humans share with animals lent value to them both, rather than degrading the one.

The common ground for Christian moralists, whatever differences their various positions on sin, the will, and grace reflected, was Augustinian theology, specifically its relentless prosecution of the notion of a gulf separating love of God and love of the creature. Everything beautiful, enchanting, or absorbing in the visible world, though the beauty of the creation in general might be appreciated as proof of the divine goodness and power, was, according to Augustine, to be kept at a distance, lest it distract

---

[6] Lucretius, *ONT* II. 70 ff.; trans. Smith, p. 37; cf. 1. 250–64. David Sedley comments that the poem's opening hymn to Venus is puzzling in an atheist: 'It would scarcely be an exaggeration to say that he spends the remainder of the poem undoing the damage undone by the first forty-three lines' (*Lucretius and the Transformation of Greek Wisdom* (Cambridge: Cambridge University Press, 1998), 16).

[7] Lucretius memorably describes the bereavement of the cow, 'her heart transfixed with longing for her calf' (*ONT* II. 352; trans. Smith, p. 44).

the mind from its special and all-important relationship to God. In the fallen world the beauty of women was a reminder of Eve's temptation, Adam's fatal disobedience, and all the evil and suffering that ensued, including the torture and martyrdom of Christ. The old intuition, shared to some degree by all the ancients, that one ought to avoid entanglement with beings who complicate masculine life was dramatically reinforced by the introduction of this mythology and by Augustine's elaboration of it. While Christian theology acknowledged the goodness of female saints, it took a less favorable view of ordinary females, and pleasure-seeking behavior was degraded as martyrdom was exalted.

The historical narrative of Augustine's *Confessions* described the transition of the young man from love of the creature to love of God, and his commentary explained the role of the Platonic philosophy as he understood it in rescuing him from confusion and despair. 'To Carthage I came', he tells us:

where a whole frying-pan full of abominable loves crackled round me, and on every side. I was not in love as yet, yet I loved to be in love. I sought for something to love, loving still to be in love, security I hated and that way too that had no snares in it: and all because I had a famine within me, even of that inward food (thyself, O God) though that famine made me not hungry.... For this cause my soul was not very well, but miserably breaking out into blotches, had an extreme itch to be scratched by the touch of those sensible things.... It was very pleasurable to me, both to love and to be loved; but much more, when I obtained to enjoy the person whom I loved.[8]

Pleasure was attended with disgust and numerous torments. 'I defiled therefore the spring of friendship with the filth of uncleanliness, and I besullied the purity of it with the hell of lustfulness.... I was with much joy bound with sorrow-bringing embracements, even that I might be scourged with the iron burning rods of jealousy, and suspicions, and fears, and angers, and brawls.'[9] To Augustine, the contrast between the ungrateful and perishable things of the visible world and the invisible things of God presented itself with increasing starkness. Two chapters of book X of the *Confessions*, devoted to 'Enticements coming in by the Eyes', and

[8] St Augustine, *Confessions*, bk. III, ch. 1; trans. William Watts (Cambridge, Mass.: Harvard University Press, 1912), i. 99.

[9] Ibid. pp. 99–100.

'Curiosity in knowing', treated as equivalent 'delight in fair forms … in beautiful and pleasant colours', love of toys, apparel, shoes, vessels, and pictures, sadomasochistic pleasure in torn carcasses, carnal temptations in general, the theater, experiment, the observation of nature, and the investigation of hidden powers:

Curiosity for trial's sake pries into objects … merely out of an itch of gaining the knowledge and experience of them … Hence also men proceed to investigate some concealed powers of that nature which is not beyond our ken, which it does them no good to know, and yet men desire to know for the sake of knowing.[10]

Even a seemingly innocent interest in animate nature in the safety of one's own room threatened perdition. A lizard or a spider catching flies could capture attention without warning. 'One thing it is to get up quickly and another thing not to fall at all. And of such toys my life is full; and my only hope is thy wonderful great mercy.'[11] In book XIII of the *Confessions*, Augustine praised the creation, and described creatures, including animals and women, as 'all severally Good and all together Very Good',[12] rejecting hatred for the world as Manichaean. But this conclusion, with its expressed admiration for natural woman, did not take hold as did his implied critique of artificial woman, and his notion that curiosities, beauties, and entertainments are false corporeal goods from which we flee to the truly good and incorporeal. Amorous suffering—usually caused by artificial woman—has a purpose. It is chastisement and aversive therapy.

Seventeenth-century theologians borrowed heavily from the patristic theory of women. Pierre Du Moulin's devotional work *Théophile ou l'amour divin* described women's adornment as Satan's most deadly weapon. The faithful eye sees through their costume to the devil's very image:

A soldier having a sword that hath surely served him in many combats, will be carefull to scowre & polish it: and doe we marvell if the woman having served Sathan to overthrow *Adam*, bee carefully decked & embellished by him; and that women are curious in ornaments by the suggestion of the devil?[13]

Other religious writers, like Jean Senault in *Man Become Guilty, or, The Corruption of Nature by Sinne, According to St Augustines Sense*, translated

---

[10] St Augustine, *Confessions*, bk. X. ch. 35; trans. Watts, ii. 177.   [11] Ibid. ii. 181.
[12] Ibid., bk. XIII, ch. 32; trans. Watts, ii. 465.
[13] Du Moulin, *Theophilus, or Loue Diuine*, trans. Richard Goring (London: 1610), 117.

into English in 1650, represented love of particular women as slavery, an inversion of the natural order. According to theological authority, said Senault, 'the face of the world was changed when man altered his condition... the earth lost his beauty when man lost his innocency, and... thorns were mingled with roses when concupiscence was mingled with nature'. From that time forward, he declared, 'divine Justice did fit our abode to our desert, and thought it not reasonable that guilty man should be lodged in a Palace prepared for the innocent. She punisheth man in his state, after having punished him in his person, and altering the inclinations of all creatures, made them the Ministers of her vengeance'.[14] In his sixth treatise, 'On the Corruption of all Creatures', Senault observed that love makes slaves of everybody it possesses, rendering them pale, trembling, and incapable of action, causing them to languish with vague hopes.[15]

Du Moulin's *Theophilus*, as a tract of consolation and a manual for improvement, made the same points. 'God humbleth us by his affliction and pricketh the swelling of our pride. He cutteth and loppeth us, to the end we may bring forth the more fruit. He filleth us with bitternesse in this life to the end we might long for the life to come.'[16] Du Moulin rejected the study of philosophy and of the natural world as well as the love of women. In *Heraclitus, or Meditations upon the Vanity and Miserie of Humane Life* he expressed a Solomonic weariness and skepticism. 'Man cannot by all his Philosophy attaine to the perfect knowledge of a small fly, or garden Lettice, much less of his owne composition. We desire to traverse our spirits through all things, but remain strangers to ourselves.'[17] The fallen world outside this chamber of meditation is vividly described. There 'corruption doth encrease, as a cancer or ulcer. Quarrels, vanity, superfluity in apparel, avarice, ambition and sumptuousness' are in the ascendant; Europe is overrun with brothels; in the east, churches have become mosques; the West Indies are 'afflicted and tormented with evil spirits', the north with ghosts and demons, with 'lying deceipts' and 'strange shapes'. The ordinary preoccupations of women reveal their dedication to the devil. They employ

[14] Jean-François Senault, *Man Become Guilty, or, The Corruption of Nature by Sinne, According to St Augustines Sense* (London: 1650), 330.

[15] Ibid. 356.   [16] Pierre Du Moulin, preface to *Theophilus*.

[17] Pierre Du Moulin, *Heraclitus, or Meditations upon the Vanity and Miserie of Humane Life*, trans. R. S. (Oxford, 1609), 37.

'the fourth part of their life, in attiring themselves: wearing haire bought out of *Tyre-women's shoppes*, painting their faces, Idolatrizing their own bodies ... viewing themselves in a looking glasse a thousand times in a daie'.[18] Love was classified by Du Moulin as a kind of motion, and motion not of the most pleasing sort. There is in 'corporall love, an importunate itching, a furious heate, to wit., the worst of vices'.[19] It is 'irregular agitation and endless motion'. Unchaste love 'kindleth in the mindes of worldly men a firebrand of filthy desires, which defile our souls with a thousand beastly thoughts, and importunate; which of our bodies dedicated to bee temples of God, make an infectious brothel'.[20] The certainty that God and nature made nothing in vain according to the philosophers proves only, Du Moulin said, that our sufferings have a purpose—to make us long for peace in heaven.

Du Moulin's views on woman as the devil's agent were extreme, but his brand of rhetoric was not unique, and its Augustinian credentials were impeccable. Augustine was still supplying a framework for moral reflection in the mid-seventeenth century. Boyle wrote several letters to society women fulminating against 'painting' and *décolletage*, including one that reminded his correspondent that 'Some of the Primitive Fathers have fancy'd Women to have made the first Devills: the Inordinate Love of their Beauty, (ev'n when unassisted & unimproved by Art) being the Fire that seduc't those now Fallen Angells & kindled those Lusts in Heau'n, for which those wretched Spirits now burne in Hell'. Even John Donne (1572–1631) in a sermon posthumously published in 1649 referenced Augustine's definition of sin as *conversio ad creaturam*, proclaiming that 'Every inordinate love of the Creature is a descent from the dignity of our Creation, and a disavowing, a disclaiming of that Charter.... it is a *declination*, a *stooping* in man, to apply himselfe to any Creature, till he meet that Creature in God; for there, it is above him'.[21] Donne warned against Idolatry of Creatures; he allowed, however, that we might 'meet' a creature 'in God', and his sermon continued in a very different vein:

And so, as *Beauty* and *Riches*, and *Honour* are beames that issue from God, and glasses that represent God to us, and idea's that return us into him, in our glorifying of

---

[18]   Pierre Du Moulin, Heraclitus, 27–8.   [19]   Du Moulin, *Theophilus*, p. 19.
[20]   Ibid. 108–9.
[21]   John Donne, sermon XXIII preached at Lincoln's Inn, in *Fifty Sermons Preached by that Learned and Reverend Divine, John Donne* (London: 1649), 193.

him, by these helpes, so we may apply our selves to them; for, in this consideration, as they assist us in our way to God, they are above us.

Linguistic communities create conflicting images of their members, and the declamations of theologians and preachers need to be kept in perspective. Their complaints regarding female display presuppose a flourishing material and emotional culture, at least in the upper tiers of the social order. Painting and poetry had drawn since the fifteenth century on pagan as well as on Christian mythology for imagery and subject matter, and the female body, female generative powers, and luxurious dress were hardly degraded or disvalued. Edmund Spenser's *Faerie Queene* of 1590, a sensous meditation on 'Mutabilitie', the generation, variability, and finitude of forms, notes that 'all that lives is subject to that law; | All things decay in time, and to their end do draw'. Venus, invoked in Lucretian terms in book IV, is, in the system of the poem, 'the nurse of pleasure and delight'; more remarkably, however, she is also the custodian of the Ptolemaic and elemental world. 'By her the heaven is in his course contained, | And all the world in state unmoved stands, | ... Else would the waters overflow the lands, | and fire devour the ayre.'[22] Popular drama in the sixteenth and early seventeenth centuries presented women very differently than did the preachers. Shakespeare's *Antony and Cleopatra* portrayed two magnificent and heroic characters erotically fixated upon one another to the grave, anticipating kisses and 'couching upon flowers' in their pagan heaven. Practical questions surrounding the phenomena of attachment and loss were debated, the inquietude of new acquaintance and the ravages of jealousy described, and models of exemplary conduct—ideals of faithful service and renunciation—proposed in French and English romances. Boyle, who read French fluently, had once intended to write what he called a set of 'amorous controversies', dealing with the social practices of courtship and with the controversy over the value of platonic love, and the young Locke too read romantic novels.

The upheavals of the Civil War following the execution of King Charles I, and the temporary collapse of censorship had brought out radical egalitarian doctrines in the 1640s, and questions of women's status were

[22] Edmund Spenser, *The Faerie Queene*, ed. Kermode (London: Oxford University Press, 1965), bk. IV, canto 35.

much debated in the interregnum. John Milton addressed an eloquent essay to Parliament and the Assembly of Divines in 1643 against 'the bondage of Canon Law' and for freedom of choice in marriage and the right of divorce in the case of marital alienation 'for the good of both sexes'.[23] Radical cults devoted to what J. S. Mill later called 'experiments in living' flourished. One such sect, the Ranters, sang

> Some men another world do prize
> Of which they have no measure,
> Let us make merry, sing, and dance,
> There is no heaven to pleasure.
>
> Which we injoy with sweet content
> A short life, and a merry,
> Is all the heaven we expect,
> Let's drink off our Canary.
>
> The fellow Creature which sits next
> Is more delight to me
> Than any that I else can find
> For that she's alweaies free.[24]

To be sure, this was the libertinism of taverns, Canary wine, and loose behavior, not rose-petalled romance, nor the decorous freedom of the Epicurean garden, which, as Frischer notes, was unique in ancient philosophy in presenting a template for intellectual friendship between men and women.[25] This feature of Epicurus' ethics did not go unremarked. Valla, like Thomas More, took a benign view of relations between the sexes. '[W]ill anyone deny that men and women are born beautiful and especially prone to mutual affection for the one purpose of receiving delight by observing each other, by dwelling together, and by passing their lives together?', Vegio asks.[26] The attraction of women to Epicureanism is a topic that has been little explored and even less explained. Margaret Cavendish, whose alienation from the dominant culture was evident, and Lucy Hutchinson

---

[23] John Milton, *The Doctrine and Discipline of Divorce* (London: 1643).

[24] Quoted in John Reading, *The Ranters Ranting* (London: 1650), 4.

[25] 'The Epicureans do not seek to reform the dominant culture per se', comments Bernard Frischer; 'instead, they attempt to attract as many of its members as possible into the safe harbor of the philosophical community, which for various reasons must aim at co-existence with the dominant culture' (Frischer, *The Sculpted Word: Epicureanism and Philosophical Recruitment in Ancient Greece* (Berkeley/Los Angeles, Calif.: University of California Press, 1982), 40).

[26] Valla, *On Pleasure*, bk. I, § 20; trans. Hieatt and Lorch, p. 99.

seem to have been drawn spontaneously to Lucretius, and the young Aphra Behn welcomed the first English translation of his poem as having unlocked the divine mysteries of love for women.[27]

The corpuscular universe described by Descartes, Gassendi, Boyle, and Spinoza did not incorporate, it might be observed, and indeed deliberately excluded, the Venusian paratheology that haunts Lucretian atomism. The revival of the mechanical philosophy in the seventeenth century has been associated with women's diminished role as agents in human intellectual culture.[28] Nature is portrayed in the most prestigious systems of the moderns as neither intelligent, nor deliberate, nor indeed as an active worker. Color and beauty are illusions, according to the doctrine of primary and secondary qualities, and Francis Bacon famously applied metaphors of vexing and unveiling to a feminine nature, arguing that we need to understand her in order to use her. It is difficult, however, to see such notions as playing a causal role in the worsening fortunes of women. Far more significant were the institutional innovations of the scientific revolution. The rise of secular, apolitical societies devoted to the acquisition of theoretical knowledge from which women were excluded, as they had been earlier from the Church and the official corridors of power, played a greater role than ontology and metaphysics. Beginning with Henry Percy, virtuosi at the center of androphilic societies articulated the greater satisfactions awarded by mistress nature than ordinary mistresses, and such attitudes were hardly conducive to a view of women as cooperative partners in scientific endeavors. Walter Charleton's behavior is one of those small monuments of fundamental decency that the historical record reveals from time to time. He took Margaret Cavendish seriously, taking time to criticize her literary technique and offering the good advice she was unfortunately incapable of responding to, and he even composed a 'Harangue' against the Royal Society for their patronizing and disrespectful attitude towards her, accusing them of subscribing to a 'Salic Law' that was inappropriate

---

[27] Thomas Mayo, *Epicurus in England 1650–1725* (Dallas, Texas: Southwest Press, 1934), 61. Her remark is somewhat unexpected; Ovid would seemingly have been a better unlocker, in view of his extensive treatment of female passion in his *Metamorphoses* (not in his *Ars Amatoria*), the first English translation of which, by George Sandys, appeared in 1632. In any event, the Lucretius translation of Creech omitted certain passages from what modern commentators still refer to delicately as 'the end of book Four'.

[28] Carolyn Merchant has argued that the estimation of women's value and capabilities deteriorated with the rise of the mechanical philosophy and experimentalism (*The Death of Nature* (San Francisco, Calif.: Harper Collins, 1980)).

when 'Ladies are capable of our admiration as well for their *Science* as for their *Beauty*'.[29]

10.2 The Cartesian theodicy

Descartes's *Meditations*, meanwhile, were a distinctive—one might even say aggressive—reversal of the religious *meditatio* of the sort commended by ascetic theologians. 'Let us withdraw some hours to give our souls unto God', says Du Moulin, 'retiring our selves out of the throng and noise of this world, quietly to meditate on those things which pertaine to our salvation.'[30] In the traditional meditation, the meditator turns his attention inward and comes to a view of himself as sinful, abject, and incompetent without God. He broods on the wickedness of his life, and resolves on its amendment, which involves, even when he leaves his study, a turning away from the things of the world. In the upside-down Cartesian version of a meditative exercise, the Meditator withdraws from practical affairs in order to get to know himself better, and assumes a posture of suspicion with respect to his senses. He discovers that he is incompetent without God, in fact God is discovered to sustain him in existence from moment to moment and to guarantee the truth of his clear and distinct perceptions. But that is as far as it goes. The amendment of life does not proceed any further in the expected direction. God turns out to have no personal interest in the Meditator, and the Meditator's errors and frailties are revealed as stemming not from original sin, but from the constitution of his will on the one hand and his bodily machine on the other. Introspection and logic reveal him to himself as an excellent and capable reasoner. Equally important, the Meditator discovers that his body usually works well, and that the experiences it generates are useful. He announces in Meditation VI that there is nothing in our constitutions that does not 'bear witness to the power and goodness of God'.[31] He is all set to embark on further exploration of the corporeal world.

---

[29] Walter Charleton, Bodleian MS Smith 13.   [30] Du Moulin, *Theophilus*, p. 181.
[31] Descartes, Meditation VI, in *Oeuvres*, ed. C. Adam and P. Tannery (Paris: Vrin, 1964–76), vii. 87–8; *Philosophical Writings*, trans. and ed. Cottingham et al. (Cambridge: Cambridge University Press, 1985–9), ii. 60.

Descartes's concerns with physical health dated back at least to the period of the *Discourse*, in which he praised health as the chief good in this life and stated that the improvement of medicine was the most useful potential contribution of philosophy.[32] His last work, the *Passions of the Soul*, transferred his concern with ordinary somatic medicine, which despite his hopes he had not succeeded in improving on philosophical foundations, to psychosomatic medicine.[33] It has been suggested that it was the influence of women—Princess Elizabeth's criticism of dualism, or Queen Christina's libertinism—that encouraged Descartes to take a benign interest in the passions. In any case, it followed from Descartes's earlier conclusions that the passions, like the senses, normally work well and are necessary: '[T]hey dispose our soul to want the things which nature deems useful for us, and to persist in this volition'.[34] In examining the passions, he wrote to Chanut, 'I have found almost all of them to be good, and to be so useful in this life that our soul would have no reason to wish to remain joined to its body for even one minute if it could not feel them'.[35] Cautiously, and with due qualifications, Descartes endorsed Epicurus' identification of ethical goodness with happiness, and happiness with pleasure, noting that Epicurus considered true pleasure to consist in the contentment of the mind, not the indulgence of the senses.[36]

God, in Cartesian physics, is a constrained maximizer of the good. He has imposed certain laws of nature on the basic material entities, and although there are many unfortunate by-products of the laws as far as human interests are concerned, they are inevitable, are part of an overall good system, and are not specially willed by a punitive or instruction-minded God.[37] We are advised to take adversity in stride: If a man meditates on God's greatness and infallibility, and understands them properly, 'he is

[32] Descartes, *Discourse on Method*, pt. VI, in *Oeuvres*, vi. 62; *Writings*, i. 143.

[33] See Gábor Boros, 'Ethics in the Age of Automata: Ambiguities in Descartes's Concept of an Ethics', *History & Philosophy Quarterly*, 18 (2001), 139–54.

[34] Descartes, *Passions of the Soul*, pt. 2 § 52, in *Oeuvres*, xi. 372; *Writings*, i. 349.

[35] Descartes, letter to Chanut, 1 November 1646, in *Oeuvres*, iv. 538; *Writings*, iii. 300. Harold J. Cook, in 'Body and Passions: Materialism and the Early Modern State' (*Osiris*, 17 (2002), 38) suggests that Descartes was taking an Epicurean turn as a result of his attempt to secure the patronage of Queen Christina of Sweden.

[36] Descartes, letter to Elizabeth, 18 August 1645, in *Oeuvres*, iv. 275 ff.; *Writings*, iii. 261–2.

[37] See the concluding chapter of Gábor Boros, *René Descartes's Werdegang: Der allgütige Gott und die wertfreie Natur* (Würzburg: Königshausen and Neumann, 2001).

filled with extreme joy.... He does not shun evils and afflictions, because they come to him from divine providence; still less does he eschew the permissible goods or pleasures he may enjoy in this life, since they too come from God'.[38] This view has little in common with Stoicism, which does not recommend acceptance and enjoyment, so much as anticipation and defensive counteraction. Amorous suffering, for Descartes, was a by-product of the laws of nature, and amorous tears were, in his view, inevitable. They are produced intermittently when persons reflect anew upon the objects of their affection after a period of oblivion,[39] when the pores of the eyes are again constricted by sadness and when blood flow to the heart produces an excess of vapor. Unlike hatred, Descartes insisted, love, 'however immoderate it may be, gives pleasure'. As evidence he adds, '[T]hough the poets often complain of it in their verses, I think that men would naturally give up loving if they did not find it more sweet than bitter'.[40]

Cartesian ethics were introduced into philosophy by Antoine Le Grand in his textbook the *Institutio philosophiae secundum principia D. Renati Descartes* (1672). Le Grand went on to compose a treatise in defense of pleasure, *L'epicure spirituel*, translated into English in 1676 as *The Divine Epicurus, or, The Empire of Pleasure over the Virtues*. Ethics, insofar as it is concerned with the amendment of life, requires an understanding of the physiology of the passions and their serviceability. Pleasure is a sign of the good, to which we are spontaneously drawn, and pain is a sign of evil. Even Augustine admitted this in theory, Le Grand points out. Suffering, by implication, has no theological meaning, and is always undesirable. Our sufferings are not caused by original sin—for where could such a trait reside? Not in the bodily machine, which is only extended matter, but not in the incorporeal human mind either.

Where Descartes had insisted that the human body, when not disordered by illness, was a reliable, trustworthy machine, that emotion and feeling were appropriate guides to the value of the objects encountered in human life, and that the source of our errors was not the hereditary corruption instilled by the Fall, but hasty judgement, Malebranche reintroduced sin

---

[38] Descartes, letter to Chanut, 1 February 1647, in *Oeuvres*, ed. Adam and Tannery, iv. 609; *Writings*, trans. and ed. Cottingham et al., iii. 310.

[39] Descartes, *Passions of the Soul*, pt. 2, art. 131, in *Oeuvres*, xi. 425; *Writings*, i. 374.

[40] Descartes, letter to Chanut, in *Oeuvres*, iv. 614; *Writings*, iii. 312.

into the center of epistemology and moral theory. His position, distinctly marked by Augustinianism, was less straightforward than Descartes's and accordingly unstable. His description of God's deployment of a hedonic system suggested erotic confusion of a familiar and baffling sort:

If we follow Him, he rebuffs us; if we run after Him, He strikes us; if we are obstinate in our pursuit, He continues to maltreat us and makes us suffer severe sensible pain. But when, having been left to tread the hard and painful way of virtue … we do feast on sensible goods, He attaches us to them by the enjoyment of pleasure, seemingly wishing to reward us for turning our back on Him in order to run after false goods.[41]

Malebranche nevertheless enthusiastically accepted the Cartesian doctrine of the animal machine and emphasized that the universe is as perfect as it can possibly be, given the constraints on perfection afforded by the laws of nature. He criticized the Stoics for ascribing pain and pleasure merely to the body, and 'for other false conclusions: e.g., that pain is not an evil, nor pleasure a good; that the pleasures of the senses are not good in themselves; that they are had by both man and beast, and so forth'. The ultimate happiness of the Stoics, he said, was 'only an idea, for there is no felicity without pleasure…. Secret pride and not joy was the source of their bearing; when they were no longer in public view, they lost their wisdom and strength as quickly as kings in theater plays lose their grandeur'.[42] Malebranche criticized the Epicureans for their metaphysics—they believed objects were the cause of their pleasures when God is the only true cause in the universe—and for their abandonment to vice. Yet pleasure, Malebranche admitted, is 'the sensible mark of good',[43] and, provided one realizes, first, that the experience of pleasure is uniquely human, insofar as animals are insensate machines; second, that 'a delicate pleasure' always attends the practice of virtue and the love of God; third, that God, and not material objects, is the cause of all our pleasures; and fourth, that unhappy consequences follow on vice, all should be ethically in order.[44]

Cartesianism and Epicureanism were evident in Walter Charleton's *Epicurus' morals* (1656) and in his *Natural History of the Passions* (1674). The

---

[41] Malebranche, *Search After Truth*, bk.V, ch. 4, trans. Lennon and Olscamp, p. 360.
[42] Ibid. 361.   [43] Ibid. 360.
[44] Ibid., bk. I. ch. 17; trans. Lennon and Olscamp, p. 77.

former sought to rehabilitate Epicurus in the eyes of his critics. Charleton apologized for Epicurus' few condemnation-worthy errors, chiefly the mortality of the soul, and praised him for having exposed the delusions of polytheism and idolatry and for having 'laid a very firm foundation for the true Religion'. Felicity, said Charleton, is 'that Good, to which all other Goods ought to be referred, and cannot it self be referred to any thing'. It is the state than which 'none can be thought more sweet, more desireable, more perfect'.[45] Further, felicity is rooted in pleasure, rather than in virtue, and pleasure is sensory. 'When we have taken away from man all his senses, the Remainder must be nothing.' It is better, he agreed with Descartes, to feel passion and to shed tears than to be exempt from all grief and sorrow.[46] Where sex was concerned, Charleton displayed the usual ambivalence. Friendship is excellent, he thought; the wise man is, however, counseled to avoid both captivation by love and Platonic sublimation. He should also avoid marriage unless he can endure 'a morose and unquiet Wife and untoward and undutifull Children'.[47]

10.3 Angelic and conventional morality

By the mid-seventeenth century pleasure was firmly installed in a positive role in moral philosophy, and the enjoyment of beauty was no longer denounced by the clergy in the strenuous terms of Senault and Du Moulin. Richard Baxter, whose *Christian Directory, or, A Summ of Practical Theologie* devoted all of part VIII to 'Directions against the master sin: Sensuality', was content to warn against excess and 'Grand Idolatry'. 'Excessive scrupulousness', he said, 'may be a greater sin and a greater hindrance in the work of God than excesses of flesh-pleasing, which are committed through ignorance or inadvertency.'[48] It is a help to the work of God to 'have a healthful body, and cheerful spirits', and these can be furthered by 'the sights of prospects, and beauteous buildings, and fields, and country's or the use of gardens'. Music, 'your best apparel', and moderate feasting are permissible, and, by implication, other pleasures

---

[45] Walter Charleton, *Epicurus's morals* (London: 1670), 7–8.   [46] Ibid. 44.   [47] Ibid. 55.
[48] Richard Baxter, *A Christian Directory, or, A Summ of Practical Theologie* (London: Francis Titon, 1673), 267.

too.[49] Poets like Edmund Waller and John Dryden—some of distinctly Epicurean convictions—rang changes on the theme of *carpe diem*.

The softer, less denunciatory sermonizing style of the Cambridge Platonists may have contributed to the formation of the sentimental 'man of feeling' in English letters.[50] In any case, the cult of Platonic love valorized the pursuit of pleasure through elective friendships, reinforcing the Epicurean emphasis on natural affection. Though originally understood to characterize love between men, the concept of Platonic love was stretched to include relations between the sexes.[51] By discriminating between the love of women and the sexual use of women, it defused the anxiety attaching to the nexus *woman-beauty-evil*. Courtly love was service, voluntarily awarded to an object of particular merit, not slavery to an appetite stimulated by some arbitrary individual, and was therefore not demeaning. Hobbes was predictably contemptuous of Platonic love. Love and lust are the same, he maintained, and that emotion is 'as natural as hunger'. In *Human Nature* he wryly remarked that '*Continent* men have the Passion they *contain*, as *much* or more than they that *satiate* the Appetite; which maketh me suspect this *Platonick* Love for meerly sensual; but with an honourable Pretence for the Old to haunt the Company of the young and beautiful'.[52] Nevertheless, the 'angelical amours' described by Boyle in his *Seraphic Love*, the skeptical chemist's best-selling work in his lifetime, were, according to Ruth Perry, realized in many epistolary and paramarital relationships of the time—between John Locke and Lady Masham, Henry More and Anne Conway, John Donne and Mrs Herbert, Simon Patrick and Mrs Gauden, and between John Norris and numerous women.[53]

Platonists and Epicureans thus shared some common ground. The Epicureans, observed Robert Waring, a history professor at Oxford, and the

[49] Ibid.

[50] As argued by Ronald Crane in 'Suggestions Towards a Genealogy of the Man of Feeling' (*English Literary History*, 1 (1934), 205–30), though see the comparison of Norris and Henry More below.

[51] Charles I's Queen, Henrietta Maria, is credited with introducing the cult of Platonic love into England from France, and, while few Platonic dialogues were published in England, Ficinian Platonism had a significant presence in Renaissance moral theory and in literature. (See Jill Kraye, 'Moral Philosophy', in Charles B. Schmidt and Quentin Skinner (eds.), *The Cambridge History of Renaissance Philosophy* (Cambridge: Cambridge University Press, 1988), 353 ff.)

[52] Thomas Hobbes, *Human Nature*, pt. I, ch. 9, in *Human Nature* and *De corpore politico*, ed. J. C. A. Gaskin (Oxford: Oxford University Press, 1999), 57.

[53] On Platonic friendships between married persons see Perry, 'Radical Doubt and the Liberation of Women', *Eighteenth-century Studies*, 18(1985), 485.

author of the hyper-Platonic *Amoris Effigies* (1651), could do without the pretense of God, but not without love 'in whose Religion they might more sweetly entertain themselves'.[54] Our sufferings need not spur us to renounce the world; on the contrary, they are signs of the divinity within us. 'The very defects of love show a disposition greedy of Divinity and the Errors of this one Passion aspire to something Immortal.'[55] The passion of love is, in this respect, very different from the passions of greed or anger. Corporeal beauty, moreover, expresses spiritual beauty: '[S]o graphically does the Body express the lineaments of the soul, that no garment seems more distinctly to decipher those of the Body'.[56] Love can have, literally, a divine origin in accord with the Platonic doctrine of our identity with a natal star, or through prenatal imprinting, '[i]f the stars of any mingle their Lights...in sociable and friendly Conjunctions, if the Species of any be Congenial and Innate to us from our Nativity'.[57]

The second translator of the *Amoris effigies* was none other than the emotional and conflicted John Norris. Though famous as the Malebranchian enthusiast scorned by Locke and Molyneux, Norris followed Epicurus and Hobbes in invoking this-world, utilitarian criteria of moral rightness, by contrast with Henry More's defense of 'eternal and intrinsic' notions of good and evil, and what More termed a '*Moral Perfection* of human nature *antecedent* to all Society'. With *The Theory and Regulation of Love* of 1688, dedicated to Lady Masham, for whom he nursed for a time a hopeless passion, Norris attempted to cover much of the field of ethics by categorizing various sorts of love and then describing the regulations necessary to each and the permissions available.[58] To see a man 'Idolize and dote upon a Masse of *Flesh* and *Blood*, that which the Apostle calls *our Vile Body*... that is at present the *Reversion* of Worms, and may the next minute be a *Carcase*', is, he suggests, astonishing.[59] Yet insofar as man is placed between angel and beast, he maintained,

---

[54] Robert Waring, *Amoris Effigies, The Picture of Love Unveiled*, trans. John Norris (London: 1688; 4th edn., 1744), 25.

[55] Ibid. 32.   [56] Ibid. 47.   [57] Ibid. 56.

[58] 'I must further observe to the Reader, that this way of writing *Ethics* is intirely New and unblown upon. For though the reduction of all Vertue and Vice to the various Modifications of Love be Obvious enough to any one that will consider, yet I do not know of any Moralist that ever drew up a Scheme of Morality upon this *Hypothesis*' (John Norris, preface to the reader, in *The Theory and Regulation of Love* (Oxford, 1688).

[59] Ibid. 48.

he is able to love beauty in a way that mixes intellectual and sensual motives. '*Original Concupiscence* must be far otherwise stated than usually it is. It is commonly understood to be a vicious disposition or Depravation of Nature, whereby we become inclined to *evil*.'[60] This cannot be right, Norris said, turning to the Cartesian theory, for the desire for pleasure is '*Necessary* and *invincible*, implanted in us by the Author of our Nature'. We can 'no more devest ourselves of [it], than we can of any the most essential part of our constitution'.[61] 'Pleasure it self', he maintains, 'is a thing principally regarded and provided for by God; and consequently... is good in itself and *may* be desired by us.'[62] Our animal life 'is a Tree of God's own planting'.[63] As for 'those severe declamations', Norris maintains, 'which the Moralists of all Ages have made against sensual pleasure in general, as a low, base, brutish and dishonourable thing, [they] must either be understood *Comparatively*, with respect to the higher Character of Intellectual Pleasures, or they are *ill grounded* and *unreasonable*'.[64] It is love, not reason, Norris maintained, that makes men images of God.

If Platonic language and concepts helped in the first instance to valorize the passions, the Epicurean emphasis on freedom of association and social welfare tamed its more enthusiastic aspects and gave them a more secure footing in moral theory. As a more objective approach to the study of nature, society, and the social emotions took hold, the regulation of love and the curbing of excesses of passion could be treated in the context of the civic framework and our need to live harmoniously with others. Friendship, while prized by Aristotle and by the Stoics, was especially valued in Epicurus' system. 'Of all the means which are procured by wisdom to ensure happiness throughout the whole of life, by far the most important is the acquisition of friends'.[65] Damaris Masham pointed out that sociability is natural to us. 'Every Man's Experience confutes this Every Day—that no Creature is capable of being a Good to us.'[66] It is nonsense to say that no finite thing has any worth to us. God would not merit our love unless he had given creatures other creatures pleasing to them, since

---

[60] Ibid. 109.   [61] Ibid. 92.   [62] Ibid. 94.

[63] Ibid. 100.   [64] Ibid. 107–8.

[65] Epicurus, saying no. 27, in Diogenes Laertius, *Lives of the Eminent Philosophers*, X. 148; trans. R. D. Hicks (Cambridge, Mass.: Harvard University Press, 1925), ii. 67.

[66] Damaris Masham, *A Discourse Concerning the Love of God* (London: 1696), 125.

we have 'a continual Communication with and necessary Dependence upon these'. She attacked the rhetoric of the author of James 4: 4, who informs his audience of 'Adulterers and Adulteresses ... that the Friendship of the World is Enmity with God'.[67] As for romantic disappointment, it is preventable by the use of sound judgement. Happiness is ours when we proportion our desire to the worth of things, not when we abandon desires. She took aim at the 'Discontented, Devout people' who inhabit monasteries where pride, malevolence, and faction are as widespread as they are outside, along with licentiousness. Those with the most sordid pasts behind them are often the most devout. They write more from disgust than from reason and use metaphysical reasoning to harangue people from the pulpit.[68]

That because all things come from God nothing is evil or sin was a doctrine advanced by the Ranters. This was too hasty a deduction for Norris. Having theorized love as orderly motion towards the good, Norris turned to the important subject of its regulation. He first proposed two general canons for the regulation of pleasure which echoed Epicurus' teaching that 'No pleasure is in itself evil, but the things which produce certain pleasures entail annoyances many times greater than the pleasures themselves'.[69] Pleasure, he declared, 'which has no trouble or pain annex'd, may, nay indeed cannot but be embraced; as on the contrary, that Pain which has Pleasure annex'd is to be avoided.... [P]leasure which either hinders a greater pleasure, or causes a greater pain to be is to be nill'd and avoided, as on the contrary that pain which either takes off a greater Pain, or causes a greater pleasure is to be will'd and embraced'.[70] As we are creatures of God, he says, 'we may desire anything that is not contrary to or Prejudiciall to the *good of Society*'. '[U]sing rich Perfumes, drinking delicious Wines, & c.' are indifferent actions that are not contrary to any particular natural end and so are not forbidden.[71] The duty of mortification requires only 'such a due Repression and Discipline of the Body, that our *natural* desire of sensual pleasure in *Common* may not carry us to the *express* willing of it in *such instances* as are against *Order*, and the *good of Society*'.[72] The life and health of the social world reflect the higher harmonies of the universe, but, as a result, 'no particular pleasure is evil so far as *Pleasure*,

---

[67] Damaris Masham, A Disource Concerning the Love of God 115.   [68] Ibid. 278.
[69] Epicurus, saying no. 8 in Diogenes Laertius, *Lives* X. 141; trans. Hicks, ii. 667.
[70] Norris, *Theory and Regulation*, pp. 94–5.   [71] Ibid. 101.   [72] Ibid. 111.

but only by reason of some accidental Combinations and Circumstances, wherein some higher Interest is opposed by it'.[73]

Hobbes had described virtue under the heading of 'manners', which, he said, relate to 'those qualities of man-kind, that concern their living together in peace and Unity',[74] and Norris drew on the notion of the communal good as he found it expressed in Grotius and Pufendorf.[75] When orthodox writers 'tax the immorality of some instances of Sensual Pleasure (suppose Adultery or Fornication)', Norris said, 'they don't ground their charge wholly upon those Civil inconveniences, which either of them bring upon a Society in their respective Circumstances, but resolve part of their immorality into sensuality as such'.[76] If sensuality were inherently evil, Norris pointed out, marriage could not make it good. The contingency that makes licentious behavior morally wrong is, he claims, the fact that human children need the strength of fathers, not merely mothers, to subdue them. Quoting Aquinas, he agreed that the provision of necessities of life required two parents 'not for a short time as in Birds, but for a considerable space of life'.[77]

Norris's *Theory and Regulation* led to the exchange of a series of vigorously combative letters with Henry More on the question of pleasure. The Malebranchian echoes of his title notwithstanding, Norris presented himself in the correspondence in the role of a dialectically puzzled and pragmatic man. He was well aware, he said, that religion and philosophy have represented sensuality as evil, regardless of its social consequences. He knew that the Platonists and Stoics had declaimed against the body, and that many actions are traditionally described as filthy, brutish, and unclean. He had also noticed that many pleasurable actions are attended with shame. 'From this and more that might be alledg'd', he mused, 'it seems to me that there must be some Moral Turpitude in sensuality as such. But now wherein this immorality should ly, I am still to seek.'[78] In his response, More insisted on a presocial notion of moral purity. The soul of man was 'designed for

---

[73] Ibid. 93.

[74] Thomas Hobbes, *Leviathan*, pt. I, ch. 11; ed. Richard Tuck (Cambridge: Cambridge University Press, 1996), 69.

[75] 'For first, I find that the more Modern Masters of Morality (such as *Grotius*, Dr *Cumberland*, *Puffendorf* with many others) resolve the immorality of Adultery wholly into those pernicious effects it has upon Society, without bringing in the *sensuality as such* into any part of the Account' (Norris, *Theory and Regulation*, p. 166).

[76] Ibid. 96.   [77] Ibid. 104.   [78] Ibid. 166.

an *Angelical life*, where *they neither marry, nor are given in marriage*.[79] There is intrinsically in illicit love 'a foulness and uncleanness... distinct from what it sins against *Political Society*, which by no means is the *adequate measure* of sound Morality, but there is a *Moral Perfection* of human nature *antecedent* to all Society'. The practices of love outstrip their proper function in More's view. The function of appetite or pleasure in eating is simply to 'engage the Animal to eat sufficiently to nourish him and to renew his strength'. If, he argued, some glutton 'had found some Art or Trick, to enjoy the pleasure of the Tast of Meats and Drinks all the day long in a manner, and from day to day, though he eat no more for strength and sustenance than others do, were not this man most wretchedly sensual and gluttonous?'.[80] Shame does not attach to seeing, hearing, smelling, and tasting, because we will employ these senses to our delight in paradise. The shame attaching to the pleasure of irregular loves, which we will not experience there, is a reliable indication of their absolute wrongness. But, More concedes, 'If this Passion of Venereal shame be rightly interpreted, I suppose this is all it signifies, and not that there is any *intrinsick Immorality* or Turpitude in the pleasures of the *sixt sense*'.[81]

The impasse reached by Norris and More, who invoked incommensurable social and angelic criteria respectively, was broken by Shaftesbury, who combined an endorsement of beauty and pleasure with a form of moral idealism. In his *Characteristics of Men, Manners, Opinions, Times*, first published in 1711, passionate attachment was conceptualized as an unselfish and ideally moral relation. Although Shaftesbury overwhelmingly preferred the company of men to the company of women, and did not hold women in great esteem,[82] he took pains to articulate a view of the compossibility and mutual harmony of the two attitudes that were divided in patristic theology: love of the creature and objectively virtuous action. Like Norris, he emphasized at the same time the connections between morality and social welfare:

In creatures who by their particular economy are fitted to the strictest society and rule of common good, the most unnatural of all affections are those which separate

[79] More, letter to Norris, 13 April 1685, in Norris, *Theory and Regulation*, p. 173.
[80] Ibid., 16 January 1683/4, in Norris, *Theory and Regulation*, p. 194.
[81] Ibid., 13 April 1685, in Norris, *Theory and Regulation*, p. 173.
[82] Brian Cowan, 'Reasonable Ecstasies: Evelyn, Shaftesbury and the Languages of Libertinism', *Journal of British Studies*, 37 (1998), 116–18.

from this community and the most truly natural, generous and noble are those which tend towards public service and the interest of the society at large.[83]

He found the love of beauty conducive to virtue. 'The admiration and love of order, harmony and proportion, in whatever kind, is naturally improving to the temper, advantageous to social affection, and highly assistant to virtue, which is itself no other than the love of order and beauty in society.'[84] In the affection between the sexes he perceived a disinterested motive of benevolence adjoined to desire that lent moral worth to their relations. The 'mixture of the kind and friendly' that is found in the passion of love has a dignity to it derived from the element of sacrifice and its lack of expected recompense.[85] Though Shaftesbury expressed a strong preference for the Platonic over the Democritean-Epicurean conception of nature and society, his opposition to the Epicureans did not reflect his rejection of hedonic motives in favour of Stoic apathy, but what he took to be their harshness.[86] Conversely, he appreciated Lucretius' invocation of 'Nurturing Venus, who fills with your presence the ship-bearing sea, beneath the gliding stars of heaven, and the crop-bearing lands' at the start of *On the Nature of Things*. Even the 'cold Lucretius', he says, 'makes use of inspiration when he writes against [divine presence] and is forced to raise an apparition of Nature, in divine form, to animate and conduct him in his very work of degrading nature and despoiling her of all her seeming wisdom and divinity'.[87]

Augustinian harshness did not entirely disappear from the pulpit or from philosophy in course of the seventeenth century. In his writings of the 1690s John Norris revived the view that love of the creature is idolatry. Perhaps as shaken and unraveled by his experiences as Augustine had been, Norris composed his own counterpart to Du Moulin's *Heraclitus*. The effectual remedy against the fear of death, according to the now badly deflated Norris, is to realize that the sweetness of life is a kind of illusion. Every part of life 'is a Cheat, a Delusion, a Lie, and Every Man that Lives walks

---

[83] Lord Shaftesbury, 'Miscellaneous reflections on the preceding treatises and other critical subjects: Miscellany IV', in *Characteristics of Men, Manners, Opinions, Times* (1711), ed. Lawrence Klein (Cambridge: Cambridge University Press, 1999), 432.

[84] Shaftesbury, 'An Inquiry Concerning Virtue or Merit', in *Characteristics*, ed. Klein, p. 191.

[85] Ibid. 203.

[86] Shaftesbury, letter to Pierre Coste, 1 October 1706, quoted in the introduction to *Characteristics*, ed. Klein, p. xxv.

[87] Shaftesbury, 'A Letter Concerning Enthusiasm', in *Characteristics*, ed. Klein, p. 26.

in a Vain Shadow, in the Fog... till his walk is at an end'.[88] Nevertheless, world-renouncing motifs were in retreat as Platonic optimism and amorous worship became fashionable, and as the scientific approach to the study of nature, society, and the social emotions gained in strength and detail. Although references to demons and witches persisted, ordinary women were not viewed as demonic in the mainstream literature.

Epicurus was no longer 'slandered without a cause, and lashed by all posterity', as the sympathetic Robert Burton had described him in the 1620s. In 1694 the passionate, witty, urbane Charles de Marguetel Saint-Évremond, briefly a student of Gassendi, published his own *Reflections on the Doctrine of Epicurus*. After a distinguished military career, Saint-Évremond left France for England in 1661. Associated with the libertine circles of Rochester, Buckingham, the Earl of Ormond, and other notables, Saint-Evremond also knew Wallis, Hobbes, and Cowley. He had notably failed to avoid entrapment in the tight bonds of Venus. The beauty of his expression was not matched by his person, and, relegated to the humiliating position of confidant, an office he nevertheless performed capably and graciously, he nursed a hopeless passion for Hortense de Mazarin, a refugee divorcee, and for a time King Charles II's mistress. An open advocate of pleasure, Saint-Évremond was attuned, like his Epicurean predecessors, to human frailty and to the rigorous entailment of passion and suffering. 'We live in the midst of an infinite number of Goods and Evils, with senses capable of being affected with one and tormented with the other.' Yet, he said, 'It is certain that Nature hath placed in our Hearts something gay and laughing, some secret Principle of Affection, which conceals its own Tenderness from others, but opens and communicates itself to its Friends'.[89] Justice is the work of man, he agreed with Epicurus, established for the good of society, but friendship is the work of nature.[90] His repulsion against the Stoics, especially the 'absurd, frightening, hypocritical Seneca', and their conception of the wise man 'who had his existence only in their brains', was extreme. Epicurus was, in his view, 'a person of Sublime Wit, and profound Judgement; a great Master of Temperance, Sobriety, Continence, Fortitude, and all other other Vertues, no patron of Impiety, Gluttony,

---

[88] John Norris, *An Effectual Remedy Against the Fear of Death* (London: 1733), 77.

[89] Charles de Marguetel Saint-Évremond, *Works*, ed. Pierre des Maizeaux (London: 1714), vol. i, p. xxvi.

[90] Ibid. ii. 120.

Drunkenness, Luxury, nor any other Intemperance ... the greatest of all Philosophers'.[91]

The adoption of an objective perspective on the emotions and secularization of personal ethics was complete in Hume, for whom love of the creature, and not our relation to God, is the foundation of our existence. 'Destroy love and friendship', said Hume, and 'what remains in the world worth accepting?'[92] Hume attacked metaphysics, thrashed the argument from design in his posthumously published *Dialogues Concerning Natural Religion*, and rejected both divine command and the Stoic apathetic ideal. In Hume's formulation, the ground of virtue and vice is social utility and disutility, and moral motivation stems from nothing more than the tendency of the perception of these qualities to please and displease observers.

[91] Saint-Évremond, *An Essay in Vindication of Epicurus's* morals trans. Johnson, repr. in John Digby, *Epicurus's Morals* (London: 1712), 200.

[92] David Hume, 'Of Polygamy and Divorce', in *Essays Moral, Political, and Literary*, ed. Eugene F. Miller (Indianapolis, Ind.: Liberty, 1987), 184.

Bibliography

Primary Sources

AMBROSE, ST, 'Letters to Priests', in *St Ambrose: Theological and Dogmatic Works*, trans. Roy J. Deferrari (Washington, DC: Catholic University Press of America, 1963).

ANON., 'An Account of an Experiment Made by M. Hook, of Preserving Animals Alive by Blowing through their Lungs with a Bellows', *Philosophical Transactions*, 28 (1667), 539.

——— 'An Accompt of Two Books', *Philosophical Transactions*, 9 (1674), 101–13.

AQUINAS, THOMAS, *Summa theologiae*, in *Basic Writings*, ed. A. C. Pegis, 2 vols. (New York: Random House, 1945).

——— *Treatise on Law*, trans. Richard J. Regan (Indianapolis, Ind.: Hackett, 2000).

ARISTOTLE, *Complete Works*, ed. Jonathan Barnes (Princeton, NJ: Princeton University Press, 1984).

AUGUSTINE, ST, *The City of God Against the Pagans*, trans. Henry Bettenson (London: Penguin, 1984).

——— *Confessions*, trans. William Watts (Cambridge, Mass.: Harvard University Press, 1912).

AURELIUS, MARCUS, *Meditations*, trans. G. M. A. Grube (Indianapolis, Ind.: Hackett, 1983).

BACON, FRANCIS, *Works*, ed. J. Spedding, R. Ellis, D. Heath, and W. Rawley, 15 vols. (Boston, Mass.: Brown and Taggard, 1860–4).

BAXTER, RICHARD, *The Certainty of the Worlds of Spirits and, Consequently, of the Immortality of Souls* (London: Salusbury and Parkhurst, 1691).

——— *A Christian Directory, or, A Summ of Practical Theologie* (London: Francis Titon, 1673).

BAYLE, PIERRE, *Penseés diverses ... sur la comete qui parut an mois de decembre 1680* (Rotterdam: 1683).

BEDDOES, THOMAS, *Chemical Experiments and Opinions: Extracted from a Work Published in the Last Century* (Oxford: Clarendon, 1790).

BENTLEY, RICHARD, *The Folly and Unreasonableness of Atheism* (London: Mortlock, 1693).

BERGERAC, CYRANO DE, *Other Worlds*, trans. Geoffrey Strachan (London: Oxford University Press, 1965).

BERKELEY, GEORGE, *Works*, ed. A. A. Luce and T. E. Jessop, 9 vols. (London/New York: Nelson, 1948–57).

BOYLE, ROBERT, *Works*, 5 vols. (London: Millar, 1744).

——— *Works*, ed. Michael Hunter and Edward B. Davis, 14 vols. (London: Pickering and Chatto, 2000).

BRAITHWAITE, RICHARD, *Natures Embassie, or, The Wilde-mans Measures Danced Naked by Twelve Satyres* (London: 1621).

BURNET, GILBERT, *A History of My Own Time*, 4 vols. (London: 1753).

BURTON, ROBERT, *The Anatomy of Melancholy*, ed. Thomas C. Faulkner, Nicholas Kiessling, and Rhonda L. Blair, 2 vols. (Oxford: Clarendon, 1989).

CALVIN, JEAN, *Contre la secte fantastique et furieuse des libertins qui se nomment spirituels* (Geneva: 1545).

CASAUBON, MÉRIC, *A Letter of Meric Casaubon DD. &c. to Peter du Moulin … Concerning Natural Experimental Philosophy* (London: 1669).

CAVENDISH, MARGARET, *Observations upon Experimental Philosophy*, ed. Eileen O'Neill (Cambridge: Cambridge University Press, 2003).

——— *Philosophical Letters* (London: 1664).

——— *Philosophical and Physical Opinions* (London: 1655).

——— *Poems and Fancies* (London: 1664).

CHARLETON, WALTER, Bodeleian MS Smith 13.

——— *The Darknes of Atheism* (London: 1652).

——— *Epicurus's Morals, Collected Partly out of His Own Greek Text, in Diogenes Laertius, and Partly out of the Rhapsodies of Marcus Antoninus, Plutarch, Cicero, & Seneca; And Faithfully Englished* (London: 1670).

——— *The Immortality of the Soul* (London: 1657).

——— *Physiologia Epicuro-Gassendo-Charletoniana* (London: 1654).

——— *A Ternary of Paradoxes* (London: 1650).

CICERO, MARCUS TULLIUS, *On Ends*, trans. H. Rackham, 2nd edn. (Cambridge, Mass.: Harvard University Press, 1931).

——— *On the Nature of the Gods* and *Academica*, trans. H. Rackham (Cambridge, Mass.: Harvard University Press, 1951).

——— *On the Republic* and *On Laws*, trans. Clinton W. Keyes (Cambridge, Mass.: Harvard University Press, 1928).

——— *Tusculan Disputations*, trans. J. E. King (Cambridge, Mass.: Harvard University Press, 1927).

COMENIUS, AMOS, *Pansophia*, in *Opera didactica* (Amsterdam: 1657).

CUDWORTH, RALPH, *A Treatise Concerning Eternal and Immutable Morality* with *A Treatise of Freewill*, ed. Sarah Hutton (Cambridge: Cambridge University Press, 1996).

Cudworth, Ralph, *True Intellectual System of the Universe* (London: Royston, 1678).

Culverwel, Nathaniel, *Discourse of the Light of Nature* (1652; repr. New York/London: Garland, 1978).

Cumberland, Richard, *De legibus naturibus* (London: 1672).

Descartes, René, *Oeuvres*, ed. C. Adam and P. Tannery, 11 vols. (Paris: Vrin, 1964–76).

_____ *Philosophical Essays*, ed. R. Ariew (Indianapolis: Hackett, 2000).

_____ *Philosophical Writings*, trans. and ed. J. Cottingham, R. Stoothoff, D. Murdoch, and A. Kenny, 3 vols. (Cambridge: Cambridge University Press, 1985–9).

Digby, Kenelm, *A Discourse Concerning the Vegetation of Plants* (London: 1661).

_____ *Observations upon Religio Medici* (London: 1643).

Donne, John, *Fifty Sermons Preached by that Learned and Reverend Divine, John Donne* (London: 1649).

Du Moulin, Pierre, *Heraclitus, or Meditations upon the Vanity and Miserie of Humane Life*, trans. R. S. (Oxford: 1609).

_____ *Theophilus, or Loue Diuine*, trans. Richard Goring (London: 1610).

Edwards, John, *A Brief Vindication of the Fundamental Articles of the Christian Faith* (London: 1697).

_____ *The Eternal and Intrinsick Reasons of Good and Evil* (Cambridge: 1699).

Epicurus, *The Epicurus Reader*, trans. and ed. Brad Inwood and L. P. Gerson (Indianapolis, Ind.: Hackett, 1994).

_____ *Epicurus's Morals*, ed. with a commentary by John Digby (London: 1712).

Evelyn, John, *Diary*, ed. E. S. de Beer (London: Oxford University Press, 1959).

_____ *An Essay of the First Book of T. Lucretius Carus 'De rerum natura.' Interpreted and Made Engl. Verse by J. Evelyn* (London: Bedle and Collins, 1656).

Ficino, Marsilio, *Platonic Theology*, trans. Michael J. B. Allen, ed. James Hankins (Cambridge, Mass.: Harvard University Press, 2003).

Galen, Claudius, *On the Use of Parts*, trans. Margaret Tallmadge May, 2 vols. (Ithaca, NY: Cornell University Press, 1968).

Galilei, Galileo, *Discoveries and Opinions of Galileo*, trans. and ed. Stillman Drake (Garden City, NJ: Doubleday, 1957).

_____ *Opere* (Milan: Riccardo Ricciardi, 1953).

Gassendi, Pierre, *De apparente magnitudine solis humilis et sublimis epistolae quatuor* (Paris: 1642).

_____ *Disquisitio metaphysica*, trans. and ed. Bernard Rochot (Paris: Vrin, 1962).

_____ *Exercitationes paradoxicae adversus Aristotelicos* (1624), in *The Selected Works of Pierre Gassendi*, trans. and ed. Craig Brush, (New York/London: Johnson, 1972).

—— *Institutio logica: et philosophiae Epicuri syntagma authore P. Cl. Petro Gassendo*, 2nd edn. (London: 1668).

—— *Opera omnia*, 6 vols. (Lyon: 1658; repr. Hildesheim: Olms, 1968).

—— *Three Discourses of Happiness, Virtue and Liberty*, trans. F. Bernier (London: 1699).

—— *De vita et moribus Epicuri libri octo* (Lyon: 1647).

GLANVILL, JOSEPH, *Scepsis scientifica* (London: 1665; repr. New York/London: Garland, 1978).

—— and MORE, HENRY, *Saducismus triumphatus*, trans. A. Horneck (London: 1681).

GROTIUS, HUGO, *The Rights of War and Peace*, ed. Richard Tuck, 3 vols (Indianapolis, Ind.: Liberty Fund, 2005).

HOBBES, THOMAS, *Dialogus physicus*, trans. Steven Shapin and Simon Schaffer, in *Leviathan and the Air Pump* (Princeton, NJ: Princeton University Press, 1985).

—— *The Elements of Law: Natural and Politic*, ed. Ferdinand Tonnies (New York, Barnes & Noble, 1969).

—— *Elements of Philosophy* (London: 1656).

—— *Human Nature* [1684] and *De corpore politico*, ed. J. C. A. Gaskin (Oxford: Oxford University Press, 1999).

—— *Leviathan*, ed. Richard Tuck (Cambridge: Cambridge University Press, 1996).

—— *On the Citizen*, ed. Richard Tuck and Michael Silverthorne (Cambridge: Cambridge University Press, 1998).

HOOKER, RICHARD, *The Laws of Ecclesiastical Polity*, ed. A. S. McGrade (Cambridge: Cambridge University Press, 1989).

HUME, DAVID, *An Enquiry Concerning the Principles of Morals*, ed. Tom Beauchamp (Oxford: Oxford University Press, 1998).

—— *Essays Moral, Political and Literary*, ed. Eugene F. Miller (Indianapolis, Ind.: Liberty 1987).

—— *Treatise of Human Nature*, ed. L. A. Selby-Bigge (Oxford: Clarendon, 1978).

JAMES I, *A Speach to the Lords and Commons of the Parliament at White-Hall on Wednesday the XXI of March Anno 1609*, repr. in *King James VI and I, Political Writings*, ed. Johann P. Somerville (Cambridge: Cambridge University Press, 2007).

KANT, IMMANUEL, *Universal Natural History and Theory of the Heavens* trans. and ed. Stanley L. Jakias, (Edinburgh: Scottish Academic Press, 1981).

—— *Critique of Judgement*, trans. Werner S. Pluhar (Indianapolis, Ind.: Hackett, 1987).

—— *Gesammelte Schriften*, ed. Akademie der Wissenschaften (Berlin: Reimer/de Gruyter, 1900–).

KIRK, G. S., and RAVEN, J. E., trans. and eds., *The Presocratic Philosophers*, (Cambridge: Cambridge University Press, 1983).

KRAYE, JILL (ed.), *Cambridge Translations of Renaissance Philosophical Texts*, 2 vols. (Cambridge: Cambridge University Press, 1997).

LACTANTIUS, LUCIUS C. F. *The Divine Institutes*, trans. Sister Mary Francis McDonald OP (Washington, DC: Catholic University of America Press, 1965).

——— *The Minor Works*, trans. Sister Mary Francis McDonald OP (Washington, DC: Catholic University of America Press, 1965).

LAERTIUS, DIOGENES, *Lives of the Eminent Philosophers*, trans. R. D. Hicks, 2 vols. (Cambridge, Mass.: Harvard University Press, 1925).

LAYTON, HENRY, *Observations upon a Sermon Intitulated,* A Confutation of Atheism from the Faculties of the Soul, alias, Matter and Motion cannot Think: *Preached April 4, 1692—By way of Refutation* (London: 1692).

LE GRAND, ANTONY, *Institutio philosophiae* (London: 1672).

LEIBNIZ, G. W., *Nouvelles lettres et opuscules inédites de Leibniz*, ed. A. Foucher de Careil (Paris: Durand, 1857).

——— *New Essays on Human Understanding*, trans. and ed. Peter Remnant and Jonathan Bennett (Cambridge: Cambridge University Press, 1981).

——— *Philosophical Essays*, trans. and ed. Roger Ariew and Daniel Garber (Indianapolis, Ind.: Hackett, 1989).

——— *Philosophical Papers and Letters*, trans. and ed. L. E. Loemker 2nd edn., (Dordrecht: Reidel, 1969).

——— *Die philosophische Schriften von Leibniz*, ed. C. I. Gerhardt, 7 vols. (Berlin: 1875–90; repr. Hildesheim: Olms, 1965).

——— *Political Writings*, ed. Patrick Riley (Cambridge: Cambridge University Press, 1972).

——— *Sämtliche Schriften und Briefe*, ed. Akademie der Wissenschaften (Berlin: Akademie-Verlag, 1923–).

——— *De summa rerum*, trans. and ed. G. H. R. Parkinson (New Haven, Conn.: Yale University Press, 1992).

——— *Theodicy: Essays on the Goodness of God, the Freedom of Man, and the Origins of Evil*, ed. August Farrer, trans. E. M. Huggard (La Salle, Ill.: Open Court, 1985).

——— *Vorausedition*, Akademie der Wissenschaften (Münster: University of Münster, 1989–).

LOCKE, JOHN, *The Correspondence of John Locke*, ed. E. S. De Beer, 2 vols. (Oxford: Clarendon, 1976).

——— *An Early Draft of Locke's Essay*, ed. Richard Aaron and Jocelyn Gibb (Oxford: Clarendon, 1936).

——— *An Essay Concerning Human Understanding*, ed. P. H. Nidditch (Oxford: Clarendon, 1975).

_____ *Selected Correspondence*, ed. Mark Goldie (Oxford: Oxford University Press, 2002).

_____ *Two Treatises of Government*, ed. Peter Laslett (Cambridge: Cambridge University Press, 1960).

_____ *Works*, 10 vols. (Aalen: Scientia, 1923).

LONG, A. A., and Sedley, David (eds.) *The Hellenistic Philosophers*, 2 vols. (Cambridge: Cambridge University Press, 1987).

LUCRETIUS, T. C., *De rerum natura*, trans. W. H. Rouse, rev. Martin Ferguson Smith (Cambridge, Mass.: Harvard University Press; 1992).

_____ *Lucy Hutchinson's Translation of Lucretius* De rerum natura, ed. Hugh de Quehen (London: Duckworth, 1996).

_____ *On the Nature of Things*, trans. Martin Ferguson Smith (Indianapolis, Ind.: Hackett, 2001).

MALEBRANCHE, NICOLAS, *Dialogues on Metaphysics*, trans. Willis Doney (New York: Abaris, 1980).

_____ *The Search after Truth*, trans. and ed. Thomas Lennon and Paul Olscamp (Cambridge, Cambridge University Press, 1997).

MASHAM, DAMARIS, *A Discourse Concerning the Love of God* (London: 1696).

MAYOW, JOHN, *Tractatus quinque*, in *Medico-Physico Works* (Oxford: Ashmolean Museum, 1926).

_____ *Untersuchungen über den Salpeter und den salpetrigen Luftgeist, das Brennen und das Athmen*, trans. and ed. F. G. Donnan (Leipzig: Engelmann, 1901).

MILL, J. S., *On Bentham and Coleridge*, ed. F. R. Leavis (Westport, Conn.: Greenwood, 1950).

_____ *Collected Works*, 33 vols. (Toronto: University of Toronto Press, 1963–91).

MILTON, JOHN, *The Doctrine and Discipline of Divorce* (London: 1643).

MORE, HENRY, *An Antidote Against Atheism* (London: 1653).

_____ *Divine Dialogues* (London: 1668).

_____ *Letters on Several Subjects by the Late Dr Henry More* (London: 1694).

MORE, THOMAS, *Utopia: Containing an Impartial History of the Manners, Customs, Polity, Government, &c. of that Island*, trans. Gilbert Burnet (London: 1751).

MORNAY, PHILIPPE DE, *A Woorke Concerning the Trewnesse of the Christian Religion, against Atheists, Epicures, Paynims, Jews, Mahumetists, and Other Infidels*, trans. Sir Philip Sydney and Arthur Golding (London: 1587).

NEWTON, ISAAC, *Correspondence of Isaac Newton*, ed. H. W. Turnbull et al., 7 vols. (Cambridge: Cambridge University Press, 1959–77).

_____ *Mathematical Principles of Natural Philosophy*, trans. I. B. Cohen and Anne Whitman (Berkeley, Calif.: University of California Press, 2001).

_____ *Opticks*, 4th edn., ed. I. B. Cohen (New York: Dover, 1952).

NORRIS, JOHN, *An Effectual Remedy Against the Fear of Death* (London: 1733).

——— *The Theory and Regulation of Love, a Moral Essay* (Oxford: 1688).

OLDENBURG, HENRY, *The Correspondence of Henry Oldenburg*, trans. and ed. A. Rupert Hall and Marie Boas Hall, 13 vols. (Madison, Wisc.: University of Wisconsin Press, 1965–83).

OVERTON, RICHARD, *Man Wholly Mortal*, 2nd edn. (London: 1655).

OVID (Publius Ovidius Naso), *Metamorphoses*, trans. A. D. Melville (Oxford: Oxford University Press, 1986).

PLATO, *Complete Works*, ed. John M. Cooper and D. S. Hutchinson (Princeton, NJ: Princeton University Press, 1997).

PLOTINUS, *Enneads*, trans. Stephen MacKenna, 3rd edn. rev. B. S. Page (London: Faber & Faber, 1956).

POLIGNAC, MELCHIOR, *L'Anti-Lucrece: poëme sur la religion naturelle* (Bruxelles: 1765).

POWER, HENRY, *Experimental Philosophy, in Three Books* (London: 1664).

RAIMONDI, COSMA, 'Letter to Ambrogio Tignosi in defense of Epicurus against the Stoics, Academics, and Peripatetics', trans. Martin Davies, in *Cambridge Translations of Renaissance Texts*, ed. J. Kraye (Cambridge: Cambridge University Press, 1992).

READING, JOHN, *The Ranters Ranting* (London: 1650).

REGIUS, HENRY, *Philosophie naturelle de Henri le Roy* (Utrecht: Rodolphe van Zyll 1687).

SAINT-ÉVREMOND, CHARLES DE MARGUETEL, *An Essay in Vindication of Epicurus's Morals* in *Epicurus' Morals*, ed. John Digby (London: 1712).

——— *Works*, 3 vols., ed. Pierre des Maizeaux (London: 1714).

SENAULT, JEAN-FRANÇOIS, *Man Become Guilty, or, The Corrruption of Nature by Sinne, According to St Augustines Sense* (London: 1650).

SENECA, *Four Dialogues*, ed. C. D. N. Costa (Warminster: Aris and Phillips, 1994).

SENNERT, DANIEL, *Epitome naturalis scientiae* (1600; rev. Wittenberg: 1618), trans. A. Cole and N. Culpeper as *Thirteen Books of Natural Philosophy* (London: 1660).

SHAFTESBURY, ANTHONY ASHLEY COOPER, THIRD EARL OF, *Characteristics of Men, Manners, Opinions, Times* (1711), ed. Lawrence Klein (Cambridge: Cambridge University Press, 1999).

——— *Several Letters Written by a Noble Lord to a Young Man at University* (London: 1716).

SMITH, JOHN, *Select Discourses* (London: 1660).

SPENSER, EDMUND, *The Faerie Queene*, ed. Frank Kermode (London: Oxford University Press, 1965).

SPINOZA, BARUCH, *Collected Works*, ed. and trans. Edwin Curley (Princeton, NJ: Princeton University Press, 1985).

_____ *The Principles of Cartesian Philosophy*, trans. Samuel Shirley (Indianapolis, Ind.: Hackett, 1998).

SPRAT, THOMAS, *A History of the Royal Society* (London: 1667).

STILLINGFLEET, EDWARD, *Origines sacrae: A Rational Account of the Grounds of Christian Faith* (London: 1662).

STUBBE, HENRY, *A Censure upon Certain Passages Contained in the History of the Royal Society as being Destructive to Established Religion and the Church of England* (Oxford: 1670).

_____ *A Reply unto the Letter Written to Mr Henry Stubbe in Defense of the History of the Royal Society* (Oxford: 1671).

TEMPLE, SIR WILLIAM, *Five Miscellaneous Essays*, ed. Samuel H. Monk (Ann Arbor, Mich.: University of Michigan, 1963).

_____ *Miscellanea, in Four Essays* (London: 1690).

TENISON, THOMAS, *The Creed of Mr Hobbes Examined* (London: 1670).

THUCYDIDES, *The Peloponnesian War*, trans. Thomas Hobbes (Chicago, Ill./London: University of Chicago Press, 1989).

VALLA, LORENZO, *On Pleasure*, trans. A. Kent Hieatt and Maristella Lorch (New York: Abaris, 1977).

WARING, ROBERT, *Amoris effigies, The Picture of Love Unveiled* (1664), 4th edn. trans. John Norris (London: 1744).

WEBSTER, JOHN, *The Displaying of Supposed Witchcraft with Other Abstruse Matters* (London: 1677).

_____ *Academiarum Examen* (London, 1654).

WHICHCOTE, BENJAMIN, *Several Discourses*, ed. John Jeffery, 4 vols. (London: 1701–4).

WILLIAM OF CONCHES *Dragmaticon philosophicae*, trans. and ed. Italo Ronca and Matthew Carr (Notre Dame, Ind.: Notre Dame University Press, 1998).

Secondary Sources

ADAM, ANTOINE (ed.), *Les libertins au XVIIe siècle* (Paris: Buchet-Chastel, 1964).

ALBURY, W. R., 'Halley's Ode on the *Principia* of Newton and the Epicurean Revival in England', *Journal of the History of Ideas*, 39 (1978), 24–43.

ALLEN, DON CAMERON, 'The Rehabilitation of Epicurus and his Theory of Pleasure in the Early Renaissance', *Studies in Philology*, 41 (1944), 1–15.

ALTHUSSER, LOUIS, *Philosophie et philosophie spontanée des savants* (Paris: Maspéro, 1974).

AMENT, ERNEST J., 'The Anti-Lucretius of Cardinal Polignac', *Transactions and Proceedings of the American Philological Association*, 101 (1970), 29–49.

ANSTEY, PETER, 'Boyle on Seminal Principles', *Studies in History and Philosophy of Biological and Biomedical Sciences*, 33 (2002), 597–630.

ASMIS, ELIZABETH, *Epicurus's Scientific Method* (Ithaca: Cornell University Press, 1984).

AYERS, MICHAEL J., *Locke*, 2 vols. (London: Routledge, 1991).

BAILLET, ADRIEN, *La vie de Monsieur Descartes*, 2 vols. (1691; repr. Geneva: Sklatine, 1970).

BARBOUR, REID, 'Lucy Hutchinson, Atomism, and the Atheist Dog', in Lynette Hunter and Sarah Hutton (eds.), *Women, Science and Medicine 1500–1700* (Stroud: Sutton, 1997).

BAUMRIN, BERNARD, 'Hobbes's Egalitarianism: The Laws of Natural Equality', in *Thomas Hobbes: de la métaphysique à la politique*, ed. Martin Bertman and Michel Malherbe (Paris: Vrin, 1989).

BLOCH, OLIVIER, *La philosophie de Gassendi* (The Hague: Nijhoff, 1971).

BOBZIEN, SUZANNE, *Determinism and Freedom in Stoic Philosophy* (Oxford: Clarendon, 1998).

BOROS, GÁBOR, 'Ethics in the Age of Automata: Ambiguities in Descartes's Concept of an Ethics', *History of Philosophy Quarterly*, 18 (2001), 139–54.

——— *René Descartes's Werdegang: Der allgütige Gott und die wertfreie Natur* (Würzburg: Königshausen and Neumann, 2001).

——— MOORS, MARTIN, and DE DIJN, HERBERT, *The Concept of Love in Modern Philosophy: Descartes to Kant* (Budapest/Leuven: Eötvös/Leuven University Presses, 2008).

BROWN, ALISON, 'Lucretius and the Epicureans in the Social and Political Context of Renaissance Florence', *I Tatti Studies: Essays in the Renaissance*, 9 (2001), 11–62.

BROWN, STUART C., 'The Proto-monadology of the *De Summa Rerum*', in Stuart C. Brown (ed.), *The Young Leibniz and his Philosophy* (Dordrecht: Kluwer, 1999).

BRUNDELL, BARRY, *Pierre Gassendi: From Aristotelianism to a New Philosophy* (Dordrecht: Reidel, 1987).

BURNS, N. T., *Christian Mortalism from Tyndale to Milton* (Cambridge, Mass.: Harvard University Press, 1972).

CHARLES-DAUBERT, FRANÇOISE, *Les Libertins érudits en France au XVIIe siècle* (Paris: Presses Universitaires, 1998).

CHERNAIK, WARREN, *Sexual Freedom in Restoration Literature* (Cambridge: Cambridge University Press, 1995).

CLAY, JOHN, 'Robert Boyle: A Jungian Perspective', *British Journal for the History of Science*, 32 (1999), 285–98.

CLERICUZIO, ANTONIO, 'Carneades and the Chemists', in Michael Hunter (ed.), *Robert Boyle Reconsidered* (Cambridge: Cambridge University Press, 1994).

——— 'A Redefinition of Boyle's Chemistry and Corpuscular Philosophy', *Annals of Science*, 47 (1990), 561–89.

COOK, HAROLD J., 'Body and Passions: Materialism and the Early Modern State', *Osiris*, 17 (2002), 25–48.

COWAN, BRIAN, 'Reasonable Ecstasies: Shaftesbury and the Languages of Libertinism', *Journal of British Studies*, 37 (1998), 111–38.

CRANE, RONALD S., 'Suggestions Towards a Genealogy of the Man of Feeling', *English Literary History*, 1 (1934) 205–30.

CRANSTON, MAURICE, *John Locke: A Biography* (London: Longmans, 1957).

DAWSON, LESEL, ' "New Sects of Love": Neoplatonism and Constructions of Gender in Davenant's *The Temple of Love* and *The Platonick Lovers*', *Early Modern Literary Studies*, 8 (2002), 1–36.

DEAR, PETER, 'The Church and the New Philosophy', in Stephen Pumfrey, Paolo L. Rossi, and Maurice Slavinski (eds.), *Science, Culture, and Popular Belief in Renaissance Europe* (Manchester: Manchester University Press, 1991), 119–39.

DEASON, GARY, 'Reformation Theology and the Mechanistic Conception of Nature', in David C. Lindberg and Ronald L. Numbers (eds.), *God and Nature: Historical Essays on the Encounter between Christianity and Science* (Berkeley, Calif.: University of California Press, 1986).

DEBUS, ALAN, 'The Paracelsian Aerial Nitre', *Isis*, 55 (1964), 43–61.

DES CHENE, DENNIS, *Physiologia: Natural Philosophy in Late Aristotelian and Cartesian Thought* (Ithaca, NY/London: Cornell University Press, 1996).

DOBBS, B. J. T., *The Foundations of Newton's Alchemy* (Cambridge: Cambridge University Press, 1975).

DUCHESNEAU, FRANÇOIS, *L'empirisme de Locke* (The Hague, Nijhoff, 1973).

ELLIS, OLIVER, *The History of Fire and Flame* (London: Simpkin Marshall, 1932).

FARRINGTON, BENJAMIN, 'The Gods of Epicurus and the Roman State', in *Head and Hand in Ancient Greece* (London: Watts, 1947), 88–113.

FIGLIO, KARL, 'Psychoanalysis and the Scientific Mind: Robert Boyle', *British Journal for the History of Science*, 32 (1999), 299–314.

FINOCCHIARO, MAURICE A., *The Galileo Affair: A Documentary History* (Berkeley/Los Angeles, Calif.: University of California Press, 1989).

FISHER, SAUL, *Pierre Gassendi's Philosophy and Science* (Leiden: Brill, 2005).

FLEITMANN, SABINA, *Walter Charleton (1620–1707), 'Virtuoso': Leben und Werk* (Frankfurt/Berlin, Lang, 1986).

FORSCHNER, MAXIMILIAN, *Über das Handeln im Einklang mit der Natur* (Darmstadt: Wissenschaftliche Buchgesellschaft, 1998).

FOSTER, MICHAEL, 'The Christian Doctrine of Creation and the Rise of Modern Natural Science', *Mind*, 43 (1934), 446–58.

FRANK, ROBERT, *Harvey and the Oxford Physiologists: Scientific Ideas and Social Interaction* (Berkeley/Los Angeles, Calif.: University of California Press, 1980).

FRIEDMANN, G., *Leibniz et Spinoza*, 2nd edn. (Paris: Gallimard, 1962).

FRISCHER, BERNARD, *The Sculpted Word: Epicureanism and Philosophical Recruitment in Ancient Greece* (Berkeley/Los Angeles, Calif.: University of California Press, 1982).

GARBER, DANIEL, *Descartes Embodied* (New York: Cambridge University Press, 2001).

―― 'On the Frontiers of the Scientific Revolution: How Mersenne Learned to Love Galileo', *Perspectives on Science*, 12 (2004), 135–63.

GAUKROGER, STEPHEN, *Descartes: An Intellectual Biography* (Cambridge, Cambridge University Press, 1995).

―― 'The Sources of Descartes's Procedure of Deductive Demonstration in Metaphysics and Natural Philosophy', in J. Cottingham (ed.), *Reason, Will, and Sensation: Studies in Descartes' Metaphysics* (Oxford: Clarendon, 1994).

GRAFTON, ANTHONY, *Commerce with the Classics: Ancient Books and the Renaissance Reader* (Ann Arbor: University of Michigan Press).

GUERLAC, HENRY, 'The Poets' Nitre, Studies in the Chemistry of John Mayow', *Isis*, 45 (1954), 243–55.

HAAS, ALBERT, *Über den Einfluss der epikureischen Staats- und Rechtsphilosophie auf die Philosophie des 16. und 17. Jahrhunderts*, Ph.D. thesis (University of Berlin, 1896).

HALL, T. S., *History of General Physiology*, 2 vols. (Chicago, Ill.: University of Chicago Press, 1969).

HANKINS, JAMES, *Plato in the Italian Renaissance* (Leiden: Brill, 1994).

HARWOOD, JOHN T. (ed.), *The Early Essays and Ethics of Robert Boyle* (Carbondale, Ill.: Southern Illinois University Press, 1991).

HENRY, JOHN, 'Boyle and Cosmical Qualities', in Michael Hunter (ed.), *Robert Boyle Reconsidered* (Cambridge: Cambridge University Press, 1994).

―― 'Occult Qualities and the Experimental Philosophy: Active Principles in Pre-Newtonian Matter Theory', *History of Science*, 24 (1986), 335–81.

HILL, CHRISTOPHER, *Milton and the English Revolution* (London: Faber & Faber, 1977).

―― *The World Turned Upside Down* (London: Temple Smith, 1972).

HIRAI, HIRO, 'Le Concept du semence de Pierre Gassendi entre les theories de la matière et les sciences de la vie au xviiième siècle', *Medicina nei secoli arte e scienza*, 15 (2003), 205–26.

HOLDEN, THOMAS, *The Architecture of Matter* (Cambridge: Cambridge University Press, 2004).

HOOYKAAS, REIJER, *Robert Boyle: A Study in Science and Christian Belief* (Lanham, Md.: University Press of America, 1997).

HOUGHTON, WALTER B., Jr., 'The English Virtuoso in the Seventeenth Century', *Journal of the History of Ideas*, 3 (1942), 51–73, 190–219.

HUNTER, IAN, *Rival Enlightenments* (Cambridge: Cambridge University Press, 2001).

HUNTER, MICHAEL, *Robert Boyle: Scrupulosity and Science* (Woodbridge: Boydell, 2000).

——— (ed.), *Robert Boyle by Himself and by his Friends* (London: Pickering & Chatto, 1994).

——— 'How Boyle Became a Scientist', *History of Science*, 33 (1995), 59–103.

——— 'John Evelyn in the 1650s: A Virtuoso in Search of a Role', in Hunter (ed.), *Science and the Shape of Orthodoxy: Intellectual Change in Late Seventeenth-century Britain* (Woodbridge: Boydell, 1995).

——— 'Robert Boyle: A Suitable Case for Treatment?', *British Journal for the History of Science*, 32 (1999), 261–75.

HUTCHISON, KEITH, 'What Happened to Occult Qualities in the Scientific Revolution?', *Isis*, 73 (1982), 233–53; repr. in Peter Dear (ed.), *The Scientific Enterprise in Early Modern Europe* (Chicago, Ill.: University of Chicago Press, 1996).

HUTTON, SARAH, 'In Dialogue with Thomas Hobbes: Margaret Cavendish's Natural Philosophy', *Women's Writing*, 4 (1997), 421–32.

——— 'Margaret Cavendish and Henry More', in Stephen Clucas (ed.), *A Princely Brave Woman: Essays on Margaret Cavendish, Duchess of Newcastle* (Aldershot: Ashgate, 2003).

ISRAEL, JONATHAN, *Radical Enlightenment* (Oxford: Oxford University Press, 2001).

JACOB, J. R., 'Boyle's Atomism and the Restoration Assault on Pagan Naturalism', *Social Studies of Science*, 8 (1978), 211–33.

JAMES, SUSAN, *Passion and Action: The Emotions in Seventeenth-century Philosophy*, (Oxford: Clarendon, 1997).

——— 'The Philosophical Innovations of Margaret Cavendish', *British Journal for the History of Philosophy*, 7 (1999), 219–44.

JENKINS, R. (ed.), *The Legacy of Rome: A New Appraisal* (Oxford: Oxford University Press, 1990).

JESSEPH, DOUGLAS, 'Hobbes's Atheism', *Midwest Studies in Philosophy*, 26 (2002), 140–66.

JOHNSON, MONTE RANSOME, 'Was Gassendi an Epicurean?', *History of Philosophy Quarterly*, 20 (2003), 339–59.

JONES, HOWARD, *The Epicurean Tradition* (London: Routledge, 1992).

JOY, LYNN, *Gassendi the Atomist: Advocate of History in an Age of Science* (Cambridge: Cambridge University Press, 1987).

——— 'Epicureanism in Renaissance Moral and Natural Philosophy', *Journal of the History of Ideas*, 53 (1992), 573–83.

KAHR, BRETT, 'Robert Boyle: A Freudian Perspective', *British Journal for the History of Science*, 32 (1999), 277–84.

KARGON, R. H., *Atomism in England from Hariot to Newton* (Oxford: Clarendon, 1966).

——— 'Walter Charleton, Robert Boyle, and the Acceptance of Epicurean Atomism in England', *Isis*, 55 (1964), 184–92.

KIM, YUNG SIK, 'Another Look at Robert Boyle's Acceptance of the Mechanical Philosophy', *Ambix*, 38 (1991), 1–10.

KORS, ALAN CHARLES, *Atheism in France, 1650–1720* (Princeton, NJ: Princeton University Press, 1990).

KOYRÉ, ALEXANDRE, *From the Closed World to the Infinite Universe* (Baltimore, Md.: Johns Hopkins University Press, 1953).

KRAYE, JILL, 'Moral Philosophy', in Charles B. Schmidt and Quentin Skinner (eds.), *The Cambridge History of Renaissance Philosophy* (Cambridge: Cambridge University Press, 1988).

KROLL, RICHARD W. F., *The Material Word: Literate Culture in the Restoration and Early Eighteenth Century* (Baltimore, Md.: Johns Hopkins University Press, 1991).

——— 'The Question of Locke's Relation to Gassendi', *Journal of the History of Ideas*, 45 (1984), 339–59.

KUHN, THOMAS, 'Robert Boyle and Structural Chemistry', *Isis*, 43 (1952), 12–35; repr. in Peter Dear (ed.), *The Scientific Enterprise in Early Modern Europe* (Chicago, Ill.: University of Chicago Press, 1997).

LAGRÉE, JACQUELINE, 'Spinoza "Athée et épicurien"', *Archives de Philosophie*, 57 (1994), 541–58.

LASSWITZ, KURD, *Geschichte der Atomistik vom Mittelalter bis Newton*, 2 vols. (Leipzig: Voss, 1926).

LECKY, W. H., *A History of European Morals* (New York: Braziller, 1955).

LEINKAUF, THOMAS, 'Der Natur-Begriff des 17. Jahrhunderts und zwei seiner Interpretationen', *Berichte zu Wissenschaftsgeschichte*, 23 (2000), 399–418.

LENNON, THOMAS M., *The Battle of the Gods and Giants: The Legacies of Descartes and Gassendi, 1655–1715* (Princeton, NJ: Princeton University Press, 1993).

LINDBERG, DAVID C., and NUMBERS, RONALD L., *God and Nature: Historical Essays on the Encounter Between Christianity and Science* (Berkeley, Calif.: University of California Press, 1986).

LOEMKER, L. E., 'Boyle and Leibniz', *Journal of the History of Ideas*, 16 (1955), 22–43.

LoLORDO, ANTONIA, *Pierre Gassendi and the Birth of Modern Philosophy* (Cambridge: Cambridge University Press, 2006).

LONG, A. A., 'Chance and Natural Law in Epicureanism', *Phronesis*, 22 (1977), 63–88.

LOVEJOY, ARTHUR O., *The Great Chain of Being* (Cambridge, Mass.: Harvard University Press, 1964).

LUDWIG, BERND, 'Cicero oder Epikur: Über einen "Paradigmenwechsel" in Hobbes' politischer Philosophie', in Gábor Boros (ed.), *Der Einfluss des Hellenismus auf die Philosophie der fruehen Neuzeit* (Wiesbaden: Harrassowitz, 2005).

LÜTHY, CHRISTOPH, 'Atomism, Lynceus, and the Fate of Seventeenth-century Microscopy', *Early Science and Medicine*, 1 (1996), 1–27.

—— 'Thoughts and Circumstances of Sebastien Basson: Analysis, Micro-history, Questions', *Early Science and Medicine*, 2 (1997), 1–73.

LYNES, JOHN W., 'Descartes' Theory of Elements: From *Le Monde* to the *Principles*', *Journal of the History of Ideas*, 43 (1982), 55–72.

MacCARTHY, B. G., *Women Writers: Their Contribution to the English Novel 1621–1744* (Cork: Cork University Press/Oxford: Blackwell, 1946).

McGUIRE, J. E., 'Force, Active Principles and Newton's Invisible Realm', *Ambix*, 15 (1968), 154–208.

—— and RATTANSI, P., 'Newton and the "Pipes of Pan"', *Notes and Records of the Royal Society*, 21 (1966), 108–43.

MacINTOSH J. J., 'Animals, Morality, and Robert Boyle', *Dialogue*, 35 (1996), 435–72.

—— 'Robert Boyle on Epicurean Atheism and Atomism', in Margaret J. Osler (ed.), *Atoms, Pneuma, and Tranquillity: Epicurean and Stoic Themes in European Thought* (Cambridge: Cambridge University Press, 1991).

McKIE, DOUGLAS, 'Fire and the Flamma Vitalis: Boyle, Hooke, and Mayow', in E. A. Underwood (ed.), *Science, Medicine, and History*, 2 vols. (Oxford: Oxford University Press, 1953), i. 469–87.

McMULLIN, E., *Newton on Matter and Activity* (Notre Dame, Ind.: University of Notre Dame Press, 1978).

MADDISON, R. E. W., 'Studies in the Life of Robert Boyle, 6. The Stalbridge Period, 1645–55, and the Invisible College', *Notes and Records of the Royal Society*, 18 (1963), 104–24.

MAIA NETO, JOSÉ R., 'Boyle's Carneades', *Ambix*, 49/2 (2002), 97–111.

Malcolm, Noel, 'A Summary Biography of Hobbes', in Tom Sorell (ed.), *The Cambridge Companion to Hobbes* (Cambridge: Cambridge University Press, 1996).

Mayo, Thomas, *Epicurus in England 1650–1725* (Dallas, Tex.: Southwest Press, 1934).

Meinel, Christoph, 'Das letzte Blatt im Buch der Natur', *Studia Leibnitiana*, 20/1 (1988), 1–18.

——— 'Early Seventeenth-century Atomism: Theory, Epistemology, and the Insufficiency of Experiment', *Isis*, 79 (1988), 68–103; repr. in Peter Dear, *The Scientific Enterprise in Early Modern Europe* (Chicago, Ill.: University of Chicago Press, 1997), 176–211.

Mercer, Christia, *Leibniz's Metaphysics: Its Origins and Development* (Cambridge, Cambridge University Press, 2001).

Merchant, Carolyn, *The Death of Nature* (San Francisco, Calif.: Harper Collins, 1980).

Michael, Emily, 'Gassendi's Method Illustrated by His Account of the Soul', in *Pierre Gassendi 1592–1992* (Digne-les-Bains: Société Scientifique et Literaire des Alpes de Haute-Provence, 1994), 1: 181–93.

——— 'John Wyclif on Body and Mind', *Journal of the History of Ideas*, 64 (2003), 343–60.

——— 'Renaissance Theories of Body, Soul, and Mind', in P. Potter and J. Wright (eds.), *Psyche and Soma: Physicians and Metaphysicians on the Mind–Body Problem from Antiquity to Enlightenment* (Oxford: Oxford University Press, 2000).

——— and Michael, Fred S., 'Corporeal Ideas in Seventeenth-century Psychology', *Journal of the History of Ideas*, 50 (1989), 31–48.

——— and ——— 'Gassendi on Sensation and Reflection', *History of European Ideas*, 9 (1988), 583–95.

——— and ——— 'Two Early Modern Concepts of Mind: Reflecting Substance vs. Thinking Substance', *Journal of the History of Philosophy*, 27 (1989), 29–47.

Michael, Fred S., and Michael, Emily, 'The Theory of Ideas in Gassendi and Locke', *Journal of the History of Ideas*, 51 (1990), 379–99.

Miller, Michael, 'Epicureanism in Renaissance Thought and Art: Piero di Cosimo's Paintings on the Life of Early Man' (Lecture, Boston: American Philological Association, 2005).

Milton, John, 'The Laws of Nature', in Michael Ayers and Daniel Garber, (eds.), *The Cambridge Companion to Seventeenth-century Philosophy* (Cambridge: Cambridge University Press, 1998).

——— 'Locke and Gassendi: A Reappraisal', in M. A. Stewart (ed.), *English Philosophy in the Age of Locke* (Oxford: Oxford University Press, 2000).

MINTZ, SAMUEL I., *The Hunting of Leviathan: Seventeenth-century Reactions to the Materialism and Moral Philosophy of Thomas Hobbes* (Cambridge: Cambridge University Press, 1962).

MITSIS, PHILIP, *Epicurus' Ethical Theory: The Pleasures of Invulnerability* (Ithaca, NY/London: Cornell University Press, 1988).

NADLER, STEVEN, *Spinoza's Heresy: Immortality and the Jewish Mind* (Oxford: Clarendon, 2001).

NEVES, MARCOS CESAR DANHONI, 'De Imenso [*sic*], *De Minimo* and *De Infinito*: Giordano Bruno's Micro and Infinite Universe and the "A-centric Labyrinth" of Modern Cosmology and its Philosophical Constraints', *Apeiron*, 8 (2001), 1–27.

NEWMAN, W. R., 'The Alchemical Sources of Robert Boyle's Corpuscular Philosophy', *Annals of Science*, 53 (1996), 567–85.

—— 'The Corpuscular Theory of J. B. van Helmont and its Medieval Sources', *Vivarium*, 31 (1993), 161–91.

NORTON, DAVID FATE, 'The Myth of British Empiricism', *History of European Ideas*, 1 (1981), 331–44.

NUSSBAUM, MARTHA, 'Mortal Immortals: Lucretius on Death and the Voice of Nature', *Philosophy and Phenomenological Research*, 1 (1989), 303–51.

OAKLEY, FRANCIS, 'Christian Theology and the Newtonian Science: The Rise of the Concept of the Laws of Nature', *Church History*, 30 (1961), 433–57.

OSLER, MARGARET, *Divine Will and the Mechanical Philosophy* (Cambridge: Cambridge University Press, 1994).

—— 'Baptizing Epicurean Atomism: Pierre Gassendi on the Immortality of the Soul', in Margaret J. Osler and Paul Farber (eds.), *Religion, Science and Worldview* (Cambridge: Cambridge University Press, 1985), 163–83.

—— 'Early Modern Uses of Hellenistic Philosophy: Gassendi's Epicurean Project', in Jon Miller and Brad Inwood (eds.), *Hellenistic and Early Modern Philosophy* (Cambridge: Cambridge University Press, 2003).

OSTER, MALCOLM, 'The Beame of Divinity', *British Journal for the History of Science*, 22 (1990), 151–79.

—— 'Biography, Culture, and Science: The Formative Years of Robert Boyle', *History of Science*, 31 (1993), 177–226.

PARTINGTON, J. R., 'Some Early Appraisals of the Work of John Mayow', *Isis*, 47 (1956), 217–30.

PATTERSON, T. S., 'John Mayow in Contemporary Setting', *Isis*, 15 (1931), 47–96.

PERRY, RUTH, 'Radical Doubt and the Liberation of Women', *Eighteenth-century Studies*, 18 (1985), 472–93.

PINTARD, RENÉ, *Le libertinage érudit dans la première moité du XVII siècle* (Paris: Boivin, 1943).

POPKIN, RICHARD H., *The History of Skepticism from Erasmus to Spinoza* (Berkeley, Calif.: University of California Press, 1979).

PRINCIPE, LAWRENCE, 'Style and Thought of the Early Boyle: The Discovery of the 1648 Manuscript of Seraphic Love', *Isis*, 85 (1994), 247–60.

RAMOND, CHARLES, and DENNEHY, MYRIAM (eds.), *La philosophie naturelle de Robert Boyle* (Paris: Vrin, 2008).

REAL, HERMANN JOSEF, *Untersuchungen zur Lukrez-Uebersetzung von Thomas Creech* (Bad Homburg: Gehlen, 1970).

REDONDI, PIETRO, *Galileo: Heretic* (Princeton, NJ: Princeton University Press, 1987).

REDWOOD, JOHN, *Reason, Ridicule and Religion* (Cambridge, Mass.: Harvard University Press, 1976).

REYNOLDS, L. D. (ed.), *Texts and Transmissions: A Survey of the Latin Classics* (Oxford: Clarendon, 1983).

ROCHOT, BERNARD, 'Pierre Gassendi', in C. Gillespie (ed.), *Dictionary of Scientific Biography* (New York: Scribner, 1971).

ROGERS, G. A. J., 'Boyle, Locke and Reason', *Journal of the History of Ideas*, 27 (1996), 205–16.

ROSEN, F., 'Utility and Justice: Epicurus and the Epicurean Tradition', *Polis*, 19 (2002), 93–107.

RUBY, JANE, 'The Origins of Scientific Law', in Friedel Weinert (ed.), *Laws of Nature: Essays on the Philosophical, Scientific and Historical Dimensions* (Berlin/New York: de Gruyter, 1995).

SALEM, JEAN (ed.), *L'Atomisme aux XVIIe et XVIIIe siècles* (Paris: Sorbonne, 1999).

SARASOHN, LISA, *Gassendi's Ethics* (Cornell: Cornell University Press, 1996).

—— 'Motion and Morality: Pierre Gassendi, Thomas Hobbes and the Mechanical World View', *Journal of the History of Ideas*, 46 (1985), 363–79.

SARGENT, ROSE-MARY, *The Diffident Naturalist: Robert Boyle and the Philosophy of Experiment* (Chicago, Ill.: University of Chicago Press, 1995).

SCHAFFER, SIMON, 'Godly Men and Mechanical Philosophers: Souls and Spirits in Restoration Natural Philosophy', *Science in Context*, 1 (1987), 55–86.

SCHMALZ, TAD, 'What has Cartesianism to do with Jansenism?', *Journal of the History of Ideas*, 60 (1999), 37–56.

SEDLEY, DAVID, *Lucretius and the Transformation of Greek Wisdom* (Cambridge: Cambridge University Press, 1998).

SHAPIN, STEVEN, 'Personal Development and Intellectual Biography: The Case of Robert Boyle', *British Journal for the History of Science*, 26 (1993), 335–45.

＿＿ and SCHAFFER, SIMON, *Leviathan and the Air Pump* (Princeton, NJ: Princeton University Press, 1985).

SHARP, LINDSAY, 'Walter Charleton', *Annals of Science*, 30 (1973), 311–40.

SKINNER, QUENTIN, *Visions of Politics*, ii. *Hobbes and Civil Science* (Cambridge: Cambridge University Press, 2002).

SMALL, ALISTAIR, and SMALL, CAROLA, 'John Evelyn and the Garden of Epicurus', *Journal of the Warburg and Courtauld Institutes*, 60 (1997), 194–214.

SNOBELEN, STEVEN D., 'Isaac Newton, Heretic: The Strategies of a Nicodemite', *British Journal for the History of Science*, 32 (1999), 381–419.

SORELL, TOM, 'Seventeenth-century Materialism: Gassendi and Hobbes', in G. H. R. Parkinson (ed.), *Renaissance and Seventeenth-century Rationalism* (London/New York: Routledge, 2002).

SPINK, J. S., *French Free-Thought from Gassendi to Voltaire* (London: Athalone, 1960).

STEINLE, FRIEDRICH, 'From Principles to Regularities', in Lorraine Daston and Michael Stolleis (eds.), *Natural Laws and the Laws of Nature in Early Modern Europe* (Aldershot: Ashgate, 2007).

SYFRET, R. H., 'Some Early Critics of the Royal Society', *Notes and Records of the Royal Society*, 8 (1950), 20–64.

＿＿ 'Some Early Reactions to the Royal Society', *Notes and Records of the Royal Society*, 7 (1950), 207–58.

THORNDYKE, LYNN, *A History of Magic and Experimental Science*, 8 vols. (New York: Columbia University Press, 1931).

＿＿ 'Censorship by the Sorbonne of Science and Superstition in the First Half of the Seventeenth Century', *Journal of the History of Ideas*, 16 (1955), 119–25.

VIDAL, FERNANDO, 'Brains, Bodies, Selves, and Science: Anthropologies of Identity and the Resurrection of the Body', *Critical Inquiry*, 8 (2002), 930–74.

WARREN, JAMES, *Facing Death: Epicurus and His Critics* (Oxford: Clarendon, 2004).

WESTFALL, RICHARD, *The Construction of Modern Science: Mechanisms and Mechanics* (Cambridge: Cambridge University Press, 1971).

WILSON, CATHERINE, *Leibniz's Metaphysics* (Princeton/Manchester: Princeton University Press/Manchester University Press, 1989).

WILSON, MARGARET, 'Leibniz and Materialism', *Canadian Journal of Philosophy*, 3 (1974), 495–513; repr. in Wilson, *Ideas and Mechanism* (Princeton, NJ: Princeton University Press, 1999).

＿＿ 'Self-Consciousness and Immortality in the *Paris Notes* and After', *Archiv für Geschichte der Philosophie*, 58 (1976), 335–52; repr. in Wilson, *Ideas and Mechanism* (Princeton, NJ: Princeton University Press, 1999).

WOJCIK, JAN, *Robert Boyle and the Limits of Reason* (Cambridge: Cambridge University Press, 1997).

WOOLHOUSE, ROGER, *Locke: A Biography* (Cambridge: Cambridge University Press, 2007).

YOLTON, JOHN, *Locke and French Materialism* (Oxford: Clarendon, 1991).

_____ *Thinking Matter: Materialism in Eighteenth-century Britain* (Minneapolis, Minn.: University of Minnesota Press, 1984).

Index

Descartes, René, Cartesianism 2. 3, 23–4,
26, 27, 31, 52, 62–3, 70, 93, 141, 153,
156–7, 158–9, 160, 161, 162, 166–7,
168, 169–70; *see also* laws of nature,
physical in Descartes
cosmology 98–100
and Democritus and Epicurus 23–4, 29,
113
ethics of 141, 265–8, 271
his explanations 63, 65, 94–5, 156–7,
169–70
on extended substance 54, 60, 62
on immortality 115, 118–20, 135, 241–2
Meditations of 113–21, 123, 264
rejects atoms 57, 113
seeks to prolong and enhance
life 112–3, 265
theory of ideas of 115–6, 222
on thinking substance 113–123, 148
determinism, 87, 128, 134 161–2, 173,
175; *see also* fatalism, laws of nature,
physical; swerve
Epicurean indifference 135
Digby, Kenelm 27, 61–2, 81, 146, 237
on aerial niter 78
on fire atoms 73
on palingenesis 119, 137, 241
Donne, John 260–1, 269
doubt, *see also* knowledge, limits to;
skepticism
theological 19, 20, 148, 208, 228–9,
241–2, 250
Dryden, John 18, 269
Du Moulin, Pierre 258–60, 275

Edwards, John 155, 196, 215
effluvia, corpuscular 71–81
Empedocles 39, 40, 48, 63, 83, 106, 107
Epicurus, Epicureanism, 'Epicurism' 2–38,
86, 250–5, *et passim*; *see also* atom,
cosmos, limits, Epicurean doctrine of;
justice, Epicurean conception of;
friendship, Epicurean conception of,
morality, human interests and.
attitude to science 6–7, 34–5
condemnations of 8–16, *et passim*
praise for 10, 197, 206, 268, 276–7
texts of 13
Evelyn, John, 17, 145, 201, 229, 236
experiment, experimental philosophy 1, 3,
7, 8, 22, 50

as conducive to religion 239–40, 250
and the corpuscularian hypothesis 55,
63–81
frivolous nature of 236–7, 240, 245, 250,
258
as predisposing to atheism 225, 237–8,
240
utility and dignity of 25, 95, 231, 233–4,
239–41

fatalism, 161–2, 169; *see also* determinism
Ficino, Marsilio 15, 255
fire 25, 45, 47, 52, 58, 62, 73, 80–1, 97,
189
friendship 8, 262, 268, 271–2, 276, 277; *see
also* love
Epicurean conception of 10–11

Galilei, Galileo 25
on homogeneity of matter 52–54
on qualities (see qualities, Democritean
theory of)
teaches atomism 23
garden, of Epicurus 10, 262
Gassendi, Gassendism 2–3, 30, 31, 144,
158, 160, 166, 224, 226, 238
anti-Aristotelianism of 24–25
atomism of 24–27, 74, 94–5
Locke and 59, 151, 154, 155, 204–5,
208, 212
on morality and justice 179–80, 254–5
skepticism of 25
on the soul 115, 118, 121–3, 147
theology of 27, 67
generation, *see* animals, generation of
ghosts and/or fairies 52, 73, 111, 188, 191,
247, 260
Glanvill, Joseph 24, 100–101, 226
God, gods, 11, 18, 44, 46, 57, 96, 146, 154,
156, 175, 183, 237, 238, 264, 267, *et
passim*; *see also* atheism; Christianity;
ideas, of God; love, of God;
providence; Venus
as author of moral truth 181, 188,
203–4, 206, 210, 214
as corporeal 126, 186–7, 200
as creator and ruler 26–8, 55, 67, 84–95,
98; *see also* cosmos; creation
as enforcer of morality 119, 159, 174,
210, 212, 219, 253–4, 259
Epicurean account of 6–7, 227

Lightning Source UK Ltd.
Milton Keynes UK
30 October 2010

162127UK00004B/2/P